TIME USE IN ECONOMICS

RESEARCH IN LABOR ECONOMICS

Series Editor: Solomon W. Polachek

Recent Volumes:

Volume 37:	Labor Market Issues in China *Edited by Corrado Giulietti, Konstantinos Tatsiramos and Klaus F. Zimmermann*
Volume 38:	New Analyses in Worker Well-Being *Edited by Solomon W. Polachek and Konstantinos Tatsiramos*
Volume 39:	Safety Nets and Benefit Dependence *Edited by Stéphane Carcillo, Herwig Immervoll, Stephen P. Jenkins, Sebastian Königs and Konstantinos Tatsiramos*
Volume 40:	Factors Affecting Worker Well-Being: The Impact of Change in the Labor Market *Edited by Solomon W. Polachek and Konstantinos Tatsiramos*
Volume 41:	Gender Convergence in the Labor Market *Edited by Solomon W. Polachek, Konstantinos Tatsiramos and Klaus F. Zimmermann*
Volume 42:	Gender and the Labor Market *Edited by Solomon W. Polachek, Konstantinos Tatsiramos and Klaus F. Zimmermann*
Volume 43:	Inequality: Causes and Consequences *Edited by Lorenzo Cappellari, Solomon W. Polachek and Konstantinos Tatsiramos*
Volume 44:	Income Inequality Around the World *Edited by Lorenzo Cappellari, Solomon W. Polachek and Konstantinos Tatsiramos*
Volume 45:	Skill Mismatch in Labor Markets *Edited by Solomon W. Polachek, Konstantinos Pouliakas, Giovanni Russo and Konstantinos Tatsiramos*
Volume 46:	Transitions Through the Labor Market: Work, Occupation, Earnings and Retirement *Edited by Solomon W. Polachek and Konstantinos Tatsiramos*
Volume 47:	Health and Labor Markets *Edited by Solomon W. Polachek and Konstantinos Tatsiramos*

Volume 48: Change at Home, in the Labor Market, and on the Job
Edited by Solomon W. Polachek and Konstantinos Tatsiramos

Volume 49: Workplace Productivity and Management Practices
Edited by Solomon W. Polachek and Konstantinos Tatsiramos

Volume 50: Fiftieth Celebratory Volume
Edited by Solomon W. Polachek and Konstantinos Tatsiramos

EDITORIAL ADVISORY BOARD

RESEARCH IN LABOR ECONOMICS VOLUME 51

TIME USE IN ECONOMICS

EDITED BY

DANIEL S. HAMERMESH
University of Texas at Austin and IZA, USA

AND

SOLOMON W. POLACHEK
State University of New York at Binghamton and IZA, USA

emerald PUBLISHING

United Kingdom – North America – Japan
India – Malaysia – China

Emerald Publishing Limited
Emerald Publishing, Floor 5, Northspring, 21-23 Wellington Street, Leeds LS1 4DL

First edition 2024

British Library Cataloguing in Publication Data
A catalogue record for this book is available from the British Library

ISBN: 978-1-83753-605-4 (Print)
ISBN: 978-1-83753-604-7 (Online)
ISBN: 978-1-83753-606-1 (Epub)

ISSN: 0147-9121 (Series)

Printed and bound by CPI Group (UK) Ltd, Croydon, CR0 4YY

CONTENTS

LIST OF CONTRIBUTORS

Ruben Bostyn	University of Leuven, Belgium
Laurens Cherchye	University of Leuven, Belgium
Bram De Rock	Université libre de Bruxelles, Belgium
Sarah M. Flood	University of Minnesota, USA
Naomi Friedman-Sokuler	Bar-Ilan University, Israel
Katie R. Genadek	University of Colorado Boulder, USA
Seth Gershenson	American University, USA
Victoria Hunter Gibney	American University, USA
Matthew Gibson	Williams College, USA
José Ignacio Giménez-Nadal	University of Zaragoza and IEDIS, Spain
Anja Gruber	University of Colorado Boulder, USA
Maulik Jagnani	University of Colorado Denver, USA
Taehyun Ethan Kim	Ohio State University, USA
Dean R. Lillard	Ohio State University, USA
José Alberto Molina	University of Zaragoza and IEDIS, Spain
Sulagna Mookerjee	Binghamton University, USA
John D. Pedersen	Federal Communications Commission, USA
Hemant K. Pullabhotla	Deakin Business School, Australia
Claudia Senik	Sorbonne University, France; Paris School of Economics, France; IUF, France
Almudena Sevilla	The London School of Economics, UK
David Slichter	Binghamton University, USA; IZA, Germany
Leslie S. Stratton	Virginia Commonwealth University, USA
Frederic Vermeulen	University of Leuven, Belgium
Kristine L. West	St Catherine University, USA

PREFACE

Economics is about scarcity – how to allocate resources in the presence of limits. Time is the scarcest factor at a human's disposal. As Will Rogers said, "Buy land – they ain't making any more of it." He might have said the same thing about time. The statement is not quite correct – the Dutch have proved Rogers wrong over the past millennium; and we have obtained some more time due to increases in life expectancy. Those increases, however, are small compared to the increases in incomes in both rich and middle-income countries. Our time has become increasingly scarce relative the purchasing power that we now have. There remain 24 hours in a day (except when we switch to or from Summer Time).

While economic research has concentrated on our spending on goods and services, it has paid relatively much less attention to how we spend our time. That began to change with the fundamental theoretical ideas of Gary Becker in 1965. Small samples of individuals who agreed to keep diaries of how their spent time at every point in a day, or even a week, had been collected as early as the 1910s; but it is only in the 1960s that large samples of time diaries began to be available. Most wealthy and many less-developed countries now have large random samples of their populations for whom time diaries are available, and these underlie most of the articles included in this volume. Indeed, many base their analyses on the American Time Use Survey (ATUS), the only ongoing such study in the world, which includes around 1,000 diaries each month starting in January 2003. The articles included here cover a variety of aspects of time use, including its effects on our feelings about life; how time is used by children and their parents, and how it is important in familial interactions, and in considering how we measure economic inequality.

In the last 20 years the consideration of happiness has become a major focus of economic research. This makes sense; after all, much of economic theory deals with consumers maximizing their utility; and measures of happiness are a reasonable proxy for the theoretical concept of utility. How happiness relates to income has been a central question of this economic analysis. What has been mostly absent is the relationship between happiness, often measured by answers to questions like, "Rate your satisfaction with your life," and the way people spend their time. In their study *Naomi Friedman-Sokuler* and *Claudia Senik* examine not what people do with their time, but how they allocate it across the day – the variety of things that they engage in during their 24 hours. It is noteworthy and admirable that they study this on two similar sets of data, one from France, and the other the ATUS, thus enabling them to infer whether their findings, about how the variety of uses of time alters feelings of life satisfaction and feelings about well-being during the moments when one is engaging in a particular activity, are more than single country-specific.

In their study of the relation of time use to happiness, also based on the ATUS, *Jose Ignacio Giménez-Nadal*, *José Alberto Molina*, and *Almudena Sevilla* examine people's work time while on the job. This examination is novel, in that a huge literature investigates how much people work, while almost no research has studied what people do while at work and how they feel about it. Does having more breaks in the workplace make workers feel better? Does the timing of breaks – not only their length, but when they occur during the workday – affect workers' well-being? Is the pattern of time use at work related to how stressed workers feel? These are important questions, and the answers are important, not just in terms of our assessment of the role of time use in the economy, but also for enabling employers to structure workdays so as to make workers better off and, in the end, increase efficiency in the workplace.

How children utilize their time throughout the day plays an essential role in shaping their outcomes later in life, including health, human capital accumulation, and earnings. Whereas a number of studies focus on the United States and OECD countries, very few have analyzed children's time allocation in less-developed countries, let alone how time allocation has changed over the last couple of decades. India, with a population of 361 million children aged 14 or under as of 2020, provides an important setting to study children's time use. *Matthew Gibson, Maulik Jagnani*, and *Hemant K. Pullabhotla* utilize two waves of the India Time Use Survey (ITUS) to investigate changes in children's allocation of time between 1998 and 2019. They find that mean learning time increased by 30%, from 310 minutes in 1998 to 420 minutes in 2019, then they decompose the change and explore why and from which activities this increase arose. Did the increase vary across Indian states? Is it related to specific programs like the bicycle program in Bihar? Is it larger for younger children, different for boys than girls? And finally, how did such leisure activities like watching TV, playing games, and simply chatting with friends change? Answers to each of these have to do with social interactions and are important for understanding human development.

A large literature has concentrated on the intergenerational transmission of income/earnings inequality. A less thoroughly researched question is how the community where a child grows up affects her/his economic success later in life. *Sulagna Mookerjee*, *John Pedersen*, and *David Slichter* go one step beyond this literature to consider how parents' time use when there is a young child in the home affects the impact of their community on their children's subsequent incomes. What makes some communities more successful than others in producing young citizens who achieve more later in life? Does the amount of time parents spend with kids in more successful communities contribute to those communities' ability to produce economically successful young adults?

Parents will have more time available to spend with their children if they are compelled to spend less time on other activities. The second-most important activity in the average person's day is time spent working for pay. If a parent loses his/her job, that will give the parent much more time that might potentially be spent with the child. But do they? And if so, how much more time? By utilizing the 2005–2019 American Time Use Survey, *Anja Gruber* not only explores these questions, but in addition analyzes whether the answers depend upon which parent, father or mother, loses their job, as well as on family income. The results shed light on why the negative impact of parental job loss is experienced more severely by children in low-income families.

While Gruber focused on an involuntary reduction in work time through job loss, *Taehyun Ethan Kim* and *Dean R. Lillard* consider another, more felicitous involuntary reduction, namely one created by a legislated mandate and incentives to reduce hours of paid work. Over a period of years, the South Korea government created these mandates, which applied at different times to enterprises of different size. Along with data from the South Korean Labor and Income Panel Study (KLIPS), these phase-ins enabled Kim and Lillard to examine, like Gruber, how time is spent with children. In addition, with this extra time available, an interesting question that they also answer is how expenditures on children – purchasing child care – are altered.

Understanding poverty and assessing individual welfare is crucially important for public policy. However, conventional studies on poverty and inequality tend to focus solely on material consumption, ignoring variations in individuals' time use. Nonetheless, it is worth questioning whether two individuals who have the same level of material consumption can be considered equally well-off if one of them has twice as much leisure time as the other. *Ruben Bostyn, Laurens Cherchye, Bram De Rock*, and *Frederic Vermeulen* utilize the MEqIn survey to evaluate whether incorporating disparities in how individuals allocate their time can affect the outcomes of empirical welfare analyses. They consider how expenditure shares affect the likelihood of women being classified as poor, and whether lesser material consumption can be compensated for by more leisure time? If so, how does this affect poverty and inequality rates? Similarly, in what way does accounting for economies of scale affect the poverty rate of multi-person households differently from singles?

Bostyn et al. show that examining each partner's time allocation in the household is important for welfare analysis. But how is that sharing affected by the nature of the relationships between the people in the household? Using data from the 2001–2019 waves of the Australian HILDA survey, *Leslie S. Stratton* examines how time use changes as men and women transition into and out of relationships and how reported specialization differs by relationship type. She answers such questions as whether cohabitating couples specialize less than married couples. Is specialization different in marriage for previously cohabitating men and women? And in which activities do men rather than women bear the brunt of specialization? Getting the answers to these questions is clearly important to understanding intrahousehold behavior given the roles couples have in family formation and the labor market.

In the past, as is mirrored in most theoretical and empirical studies, a clear boundary existed between time spent at home and time spent at work. However, with advancements in technology, such as email, cellphones, and the internet, this distinction has become increasingly blurred. The COVID-19 pandemic further intensified this delineation, but by how much is not known. *Sarah M. Flood* and *Katie R. Genadek* utilize the 2019–2021 American Time Use Survey to determine where workers performed their jobs during the pandemic, and how this changed from 2019 to 2020. Further, were there any changes in the length of workdays and when workers worked during the pandemic? Did the changes in where workers performed their jobs persist into 2021? Which group of workers experienced the most significant increase in working from home during the pandemic, and which group lost ground?

Independent of COVID-19 and new technology, one job where work–life balance has been particularly blurred is teaching. However, how much so has not been studied. *Victoria Hunter Gibney, Kristine L. West*, and *Seth Gershenson* analyze daily American Time Use Survey time-diary data on 3,168 teachers and 1,886 professionals in comparable prosocial occupations, from 2003 to 2019, to investigate variations in time use between occupations. They determine how much time teachers spend working for pay, volunteering, and working on main job duties outside of the workplace. Further, they analyze the nature of differences in time use between weekdays and weekends.

The contributions to this volume resulted from an open Call for Abstracts that elicited 28 responses, out of which we solicited complete articles from authors of 12 submissions. All were then refereed, each by two scholars whose identity was held anonymous from the contributors. Sadly, two contributions could not be accepted, with the 10 articles included here passing muster by the referees and us. The process was aided by the diligent refereeing provided by: Tina Asgeirsdottir, Cynthia Bansak, Marie Connolly, Dhaval Dave, Osea Giuntella, Nabanita Datta Gupta, Tor Eriksson, Shoshana Grossbard, Tim Halliday, Nathan Jones, Loukas Karabarbounis, Daiji Kawaguchi, Costas Meghir, Richard Murphy, Michał Myck, Monika Oczkowska, Nuria Rodriguez Planas, Jennifer Roff, Anna Sanz de Galdeano, Frank Schilbach, Elena Stancanelli, Jay Stewart, Chao Wei, and Riley Wilson. This volume would not have been possible without their thorough and expeditious help.

Daniel S. Hamermesh
Solomon W. Polachek
Volume Editors

TIME-USE AND SUBJECTIVE WELL-BEING: IS DIVERSITY REALLY THE SPICE OF LIFE?

Naomi Friedman-Sokuler and Claudia Senik

ABSTRACT

Using the American and the French time-use surveys, we examine whether people have a preference for a more diversified mix of activities, in the sense that they experience greater well-being when their time schedule contains many different activities rather than is concentrated on a very small number. This could be due to decreasing marginal utility, as is assumed for goods consumption, if each episode of time is conceived as yielding a certain level of utility per se. With returns to specialization, people would then face a trade-off between efficiency and diversity in choosing how to allocate time. We examine these issues and investigate potential gender differences, considering both instantaneous feelings and life satisfaction.

Keywords: Time allocation; time-use diversity; subjective well-being; life satisfaction; momentary utility; gender

1. INTRODUCTION

Although how to use one's time is certainly the most important decision a person has to make all along their life time, applied economic research has mostly reflected on a limited number of related issues, namely the global quantity of time people devote to labor supply versus leisure, education as an investment in human capital, and the division of tasks within the household. Beyond these specific topics, where time is considered as a pure input, the concrete mix of activities and their temporal arrangement has attracted less attention. In this paper, we are interested in the direct utility derived from the way people use their time, as opposed to the indirect utility allowed by this choice in terms of

Time Use in Economics
Research in Labor Economics, Volume 51, 1–33

ISSN: 0147-9121/doi:10.1108/S0147-912120230000051001

consumption. Hence, we are not considering the value of time as an input into the production of a commodity, as in Becker (1965), but rather as a consumption good that produces "experienced utility" (Kahneman et al., 1997) in itself. In consumer theory, convexity of preferences is generally assumed, implying that consumers have a taste for diversity. Is this assumption also relevant when it comes to the choice of how to allocate one's time over competing activities? If each episode of time is conceived as yielding a certain level of utility per se, people may have a preference for diversity in their mix of activities. They would thus reach a higher level of well-being or "experienced utility" by following a more diversified daily schedule rather than by concentrating their time on a very small number of activities.[1]

Under this hypothesis, we would expect people's schedule to be fragmented into many different activities over the day, week or month span, in the way Karl Marx advocated for a (communist) society where it would be possible "to hunt in the morning, fish in the afternoon, rear cattle in the evening, criticise after dinner [...] without ever becoming hunter, fisherman, herdsman or critic."[2] However, in practice this type of time arrangement remains rare due to the countervailing force of increasing returns to specialized human capital, whereby a person becomes more efficient as she accumulates experience in a given task or type of activity over time. Increasing returns constitute a powerful driver of concentration of one's time and effort on a few activities (not to mention the potential short-run costs of adjusting between one activity and another). Does this create a trade-off between the efficiency of specialization and the taste for diversity, as concerns time allocation?

To enquire, we explore the empirical relationship between the structure of time-use and subjective well-being, using two time-use surveys that contain measures of self-declared life satisfaction and episode-based affect. We test two main hypotheses:

- *H1*. The association between measures of time-use diversity and life satisfaction is positive, potentially concave.
- *H2*. The returns to scale, in terms of subjective well-being, on the time spent on an activity are increasing. Hence, the relationship is convex. This would indicate positive returns to specialization.

An additional motivation for this study comes from the well-known gender differences, both in time-use and life satisfaction. On the one hand, it is common knowledge that women's and men's time-use differ, notably in the greater share of paid-work in men's time (Blau & Kahn, 2017) and the greater variety of women's activities (Gronau & Hamermesh, 2008). On the other hand, a large number of studies, mobilizing many different sources, show that women generally report a higher level of life satisfaction than men, especially in developed countries (Becchetti & Conzo, 2022; Blanchflower & Oswald, 2004; Graham & Chattopadhyay, 2013; Helliwell et al., 2015) although a recent paper qualifies this observation (Blanchflower & Bryson, 2022).

Admittedly, women's higher satisfaction may be due to lower expectations (Plagnol & Easterlin, 2008; Stevenson & Wolfers, 2009). However, it could also be due to the specific pattern of their schedule – an hypothesis that we explore in this paper.

If it turns out that a substantial part of women's life satisfaction can be attributed to the diversity of their time-use, then why do men's schedule tend to focus on paid-work at the expense of diversity? Does this gender gap in time-use reflect different preferences, whereby men do not value diversity of activities as much as women do, or is it the expression of a traditional social norm, along the lines of the so-called "male breadwinner" norm, in which men are judged solely on the basis of professional and financial success, as opposed to women who enjoy a wider range of socially accepted combinations of family care and work commitment?[3]

We thus test three additional hypotheses:

- *H3*. Women's mix of activities is more diversified than that of men.
- *H4*. Women's greater variety of activities accounts for the observed gender gap in life satisfaction.
- *H5*. A greater variety of activities is equally associated with higher subjective well-being for men and women. (This would mean that gender difference in activity-diversity reflects different constraints weighing on women and men, rather than different preferences.)

We test the aforementioned hypotheses using the American (ATUS) and the French (FTUS) time-use surveys, where people report the duration and succession of activities they have undertaken in a given day, together with a general evaluation of their life satisfaction on a Cantril scale. Each of these surveys presents distinct advantages. The ATUS offers a large sample size, where each individual is interviewed once, while that the FTUS sample is much smaller but documents two day-diaries for each individual, one during the week and one on the weekend. Both surveys also collect measures of momentary utility – the emotions felt by respondents during the time episodes of the day.

In both countries we find evidence that higher diversity in a person's activity portfolio is associated with higher life satisfaction (validating hypothesis *H1*). Furthermore, we find no evidence for increasing returns to the duration of activities in terms of "momentary utility" (hypothesis *H2*); rather we more often observe a concave relationship. We also document a significant gender gap in both countries, where women's life satisfaction is higher than men's (*ceteris paribus*) and the activity-mix of women is much more diversified than that of men (*H3*). In both the ATUS and the FTUS samples, women's greater index of activity-variety accounts for a non-negligible share of their higher satisfaction (*H4*), but the association between activity-diversity and life satisfaction is not specific to women, although, in the French sample, the association is stronger for women than for men (*H5*). In sum, the general picture is that activity-diversity contributes to life satisfaction; there are no increasing returns to specialization in terms of subjective well-being; women's daily schedule is more diversified than men's; and this is associated with additional life satisfaction. However, men also enjoy time-use diversity, so that their lower degree of time-use diversity cannot be entirely attributed to different preferences.

To our knowledge, the only existing study that touches upon the question of variety in time-use is Gronau and Hamermesh (2008), who used Australian, Israeli and German time-use data, and observed that more educated people engage into a greater number of activities, which they attribute to the higher efficiency of their time both in the labor market and in household production. They also note the greater variety of women's daily schedules, as compared to men's. We complete this study by looking at how these patterns are associated with subjective well-being. We also extend the exploration of time-use structure by using an indicator of diversity, rather than a simple measure of variety, i.e. by taking into account not only the number of different activities in a person's daily schedule, but also the degree of concentration of their distribution over time.

A large literature based on time-use data has explored the division of tasks within the household, especially the gendered specialization of spouses into paid-work versus housework (Bianchi & Milkie, 2010; Gimenez-Nadal & Molina, 2020; Hamermesh & Lee, 2007). Several studies have documented the upward trend in time spent on parenting, in particular by educated parents (Dotti Sani & Treas, 2016; Ramey & Ramey, 2009). A few papers have devoted attention to the impact of shocks, such as changes in the legal work time, economic fluctuations (Aguiar et al., 2013), child birth (Buddelmeyer et al., 2018), or widowhood (Adena et al., 2023). Others have explored people's preferences over different activities. Biddle and Hamermesh (1990) show that sleep and television-watching are uniformly inferior (and time-consuming) goods, especially TV-watching. Hamermesh (2019) showed that spending time with others increases life satisfaction (especially friends and spouse), and Adena et al. (2023) that, conversely, spending time alone is the reason for the greater unhappiness of widows. Finally, Hamermesh and Biddle (2018) extend the Beckerian commodity production model to study the allocation of time of different segments of the French and American population.

On the other hand, among the abundant literature on subjective well-being, that has been blooming for the last 20 years, not many papers have focused on time-use related issues. A famous paper by Stutzer and Frey (2008) has illustrated the negative impact of long commuting on life satisfaction. The aforementioned papers by Hamermesh (2019) and Adena et al. (2023) stress the importance of social time. Another stream of research has investigated the subjective quality of the experience associated with the different episodes composing people's diary, a.k.a. "momentary utility" (Kahneman et al., 2004; Krueger et al., 2009b, 2009a; Knabe et al., 2010; Robinson & Godbey, 1997; Stone et al., 1999; Stratton, 2012).

This paper thus hopes to contribute a new stylized fact both to the literature dedicated to time-use and to the happiness literature. To do so, it proposes a characterization of activity-diversity, applying the Shannon-Wiener indicator to time-use data for the first time.

The paper continues as follows: Section 2 discusses the measurement of activity-diversity and of subjective well-being. Section 3 presents the estimation strategy; Section 4 the data; Section 5 the results; and Section 6 concludes.

2. MAIN METRICS: ACTIVITY-DIVERSITY AND SUBJECTIVE WELL-BEING

2.1 How to Measure Time-Use Diversity?

Measuring the diversity of time-use raises several challenges. Gronau and Hamermesh (2008) measure time-use variety as the number of *non-work* activities a person engages with throughout a day. However, variety is only one element of diversity, whose full concept also includes balance, i.e. the share of each activity, and disparity, i.e. the nature and degree to which the activity categories themselves are different from each other (Stirling, 1998). Measurement of time-use diversity may also differ according to the time span over which it is measured. In what follows we discuss these characteristics.

Balance. In order to take into account both variety and balance across activities, our measure of diversity must increase in the number of activities as well as in their even distribution of time.

While the simple count of activities puts all the weight on variety, the Gini index, for example, puts all the weight on balance (i.e. it is not sensitive to the number of activities over which it is measured). The most commonly applied diversity measure that encompasses both variety and balance is the Shannon-Wiener (S-W) index of ecological diversity. A similar measure in the economics literature is the Herfindahl-Hirschman Index (HHI), also known as the Simpson Index of market concentration. In the context of time-use, we choose to use the S-W index, given in Eq. (1), rather than the HHI for two main reasons: (1) the S-W index weighs activities precisely by their frequency, without disproportionately weighing common activities, as opposed to the HHI (Jost, 2006); (2) with the S-W, the rank ordering of time use portfolios is not sensitive to changes in the index parameters (either the logarithm base or the exponential power) (Stirling, 1998).[4]

$$D^{SW} = -\sum_{i=1}^{S} p_i ln(p_i) \tag{1}$$

The S-W index weights activities by the time allocated to them relative to the total amount of available time in the following manner: total time during a day is divided into S categories, and p_i denotes the share of time spent on category i. We define total time during a day as the number of minutes a day (1,440) minus the number of minutes dedicated to sleep. To compute the S-W index for each diary day, we sum over activities with positive time shares $p_i > 0$, meaning that the diversity index is constructed over a potentially different subset of activities for each individual. The SW-index increases in the number of activity categories S with a positive share, as well as when these single shares are distributed relatively equally among the performed categories. It thus, takes into account two dimensions of diversity: it penalizes the presence of very dominant activities (with high shares) and increases with the number of activities performed.

Disparity. When determining the set of activities over which people diversify, one faces a trade-off between using a fine classification, separating tasks that may be part of the same category in terms of the individual experience (e.g. laundering and ironing clothes), and coarse classifications that lump together inherently different activities (i.e. sport and watching TV under the category of leisure). Clearly, any classification of activities is limited to the activity definition used in the survey. In this paper we use the two-digit classification of activities defined by the French statistical office (INSEE) for the FTUS, and align the ATUS data accordingly, in order to make the country level analyses comparable.[5] Gronau and Hamermesh (2008) focus on variety in what they define as "non-work" activities. However, in terms of diversity, we expect the work-life balance to play an important role. Therefore, in our measure of diversity, we include all activities except for the share of time dedicated to sleep, as it accounts on average for 35% of a day time, so that variation in sleeping time might dominate the index. We include sleeping time as a control in our regressions. The results of our analysis do not change in a meaningful way when replacing diversity without sleep to diversity with sleep.

Finally, any measure of diversity clearly depends on the time over which individuals diversify. Admittedly, diversity within a single day is likely to be a very noisy indicator for overall diversification, as people may specialize within days and still diversify over weeks or months. However, we are limited by available time-use data, which refer to a single day in the ATUS and two days (a weekday and a weekend) in the FTUS. Therefore, we consider our measure as a lower bound of the degree of diversity for individuals who diversify over larger units of time. However, we also take advantage of the feature of the FTUS that interviews each individual twice. This allows us to construct measures of diversity based on each diary, as well as on the two diaries pooled together. For robustness, we also use a simple measure of variety, i.e. the number of different activities undertaken by respondents.

2.2 Measures of Subjective Well-Being

In the abundant literature dedicated to subjective well-being, self-declared life satisfaction has emerged as the standard metric, one that includes both a cognitive judgmental dimension and a hedonic dimension (Van Praag et al., 2003; Layard, 2011). Self-reported evaluations of time episodes, on the other hand, are now classically seen as measures of momentary utility (Gershuny & Halpin, 1996; Robinson & Godbey, 1999), process benefits (Stratton, 2012), or ecological momentary assessments (Stone et al., 1999). They have been conceptualized as "experienced utility" (Kahneman et al., 2004), i.e. ex-post utility, as opposed to ex-ante decision-utility. Krueger et al. (2009a) have used them to produce so-called National Time Accounts (NTA) that allow comparisons of "evaluated time episodes" across countries, over time, or between groups of people.

The relationship between momentary utility and life satisfaction has also received some attention. Most studies see a disconnect between the two types of measures. Krueger et al. (2009b) for instance, find that American women report higher levels of life satisfaction than French women but that the French spend their days in a more positive mood, on average, and spend more of their time in activities that are more enjoyable. In their eponymous article, Knabe et al. (2010) also note that the unemployed are "dissatisfied with life but having a good time" during weekdays. We use self-declared life satisfaction, as measured by the Cantril scale as our main outcome of interest, and we exploit measures of momentary utility to test the relationship between activity duration and affect.

3. ESTIMATION STRATEGY

3.1 The Relationship Between Life Satisfaction and Time-Use Diversity

Hypothesis [*H1*] addresses the relationship between life satisfaction LS_{iw} of individual i in survey time w, measured on the Cantril scale, and time-use diversity, as measured by the S-W index SW_{iw}. The Cantril scale is an ordinal measure of life satisfaction with no clear interval properties. Therefore, for the estimation of the relationship, we convert responses into a binary variable indicating whether respondents ranked their life satisfaction above the sample mean. Our main estimation equation is presented in Eq. (2):[6]

$$\Pr\left[\mathrm{LS}_{iw} \geq \overline{\mathrm{LS}_{iw}}\right] = \beta_0 + \beta_1 \mathrm{SW}_{iw} + \beta_2 \mathrm{SW}_{iw}^2 + X_i^{'}\gamma + \omega + \epsilon_i \qquad (2)$$

Our coefficients of interest are β_1 and β_2, allowing for a non-linear relationship between diversity and life satisfaction. We expect β_1 to be positive, and β_2 to be negative. This would correspond to a concave relationship between activity diversity and subjective well-being, following the idea that diversifying one's daily schedule is conducive to a higher level of satisfaction, up to a certain optimal point. Given that our measure of diversity increases in the number of activities, one could imagine that after a given threshold, adding activities yields more stress or other negative emotions than hedonic benefits. We estimate Eq. (2) on various sub-samples (by country, weekday, etc.) in order to examine potential heterogeneity in the nature of the relationship.

While our analysis of this relationship is descriptive in nature, we include in our estimation all relevant observable individual characteristics X_i that are likely related to both life satisfaction and time-use diversity. One obvious example is income level, which exhibits a positive relationship with life satisfaction as demonstrated by Easterlin (2001) and enables a diversification of one's leisure portfolio (Gronau & Hamermesh, 2008). On the negative side, people suffering from chronic health conditions that lower their life satisfaction (Steptoe et al., 2015) are also likely to be limited in their ability to engage in a number of activities. Finally, some characteristics may affect life satisfaction and diversity in different directions. For instance, full time employment may boost life satisfaction, as it reflects social worth, but may limit time-use diversity due time crunch. To address such interconnections, our full specification includes controls for observable individual characteristics that are available in the two surveys. Additionally, we include fixed effects w for the timing of the survey, and a quadratic function of time slept, as the latter is not included in our diversity measure.

3.2 Hedonic Returns to Time in Activity

Hypothesis [*H2*] asks whether the returns to the duration of an activity are convex (increasing) or concave (decreasing). If the former is true, concentration on a few activities is conducive to higher subjective well-being; if it is the latter, then time-use diversity is preferable. In order to test hypothesis [*H2*], we estimate the relationship between the duration of an activity episode and the momentary utility (MU) reported for that episode, and we do so both across and within individuals.

We begin with a cross-sectional, minimally parametric estimation strategy, Restricted Cubic Spline (RCS) regression, relating reported momentary utility MU_{ijw} of respondent i during activity j occurring on survey day w as a function of time t spent in activity j on the same day.[7] This allows us to examine the relationship without assuming its shape. The relationship will thus be estimated across individuals.

Ideally, we would like to estimate this relationship "within-individual." However, the short duration of observation in time-use survey limits this ability. We can however exploit the two day structure of the FTUS and estimate the relationship between momentary utility and episode duration with individual fixed effects, as shown in Eq. (3):

$$\Pr[\mathrm{MU}_{iwa} = \max(\mathrm{MU})] = \alpha_0 + \alpha_1 \mathrm{time}_{iwa} + \alpha_2 \mathrm{time}^2_{iwa} + \eta_i + \theta_w + \epsilon_i \quad (3)$$

For each activity type a we estimate α_1 and α_2 to test for increasing returns, conditional on individual fixed effects η_i and a weekend constant θ_w. While this is a more direct way to test for hedonic returns to time, it severely limits the sample as it includes only individuals who took up an activity on both days (for instance, because one day is always a weekend, there will be few observations for time in work), and whose reported momentary utility varies across both days.

Therefore, we use both within and across individual approaches to examine hypothesis [2].

3.3 Diversity, Well-Being, and Gender

In order to test hypothesis *H3*, we simply measure the difference between men and women in terms of the S-W index of activity-diversity. To test hypothesis *H4*, we introduce the S-W diversity index together with the female indicator in the estimates of life satisfaction, as in Eq. (2). If this reduces the magnitude of the coefficient on the female indicator, this will suggest that women's higher life satisfaction is partly due to the greater diversity in their time allocation.

Finally, to test hypothesis *H5*, we ask whether the relationship between diversity and life satisfaction varies between men and women, indicating gender differences in preferences regarding time allocation. If not, we will interpret the lower activity-diversity and greater concentration of men's time on paid-work as a constraint, rather than a revealed preference. To do this, we estimate Eq. (2) separately on the sub-samples of men and women and ask whether the coefficients on the S-W index differ.

4. DATA

We use two sources of data: the 2012 and 2013 waves of the American time-use survey (ATUS) and the 2010 wave of the French time-use survey (FTUS). Each of these waves includes a well-being module, in addition to detailed time-use diaries. In each survey year, only a sub-sample of respondents were asked to fill in the well-being module.[8] Table 1 shows the descriptive statistics for the sample of respondents who were included in the well-being module and completed the survey for at least one full day.[9] The sample size is substantially larger in the ATUS, 19,198 individuals, with each individual reporting activities for one day. The FTUS sample is substantially smaller, 1,222 individuals, but nearly all respondents, 95%, supplied diaries over two days, one during the week and one over the weekend.

The table includes population weighted means and standard deviations for the set of observable characteristics for which the literature has established a strong link with subjective well-being. In both countries, over 60% live with a partner and around 40% live with children, and in both cases the rate is slightly higher in France relative to the USA. In both countries, families with children have on average two children. We define three major age groups that correspond to the different stages of the life cycle: age 18–25 accounts for 12–14% of the population (and of the weighted sample) and includes students and early labor market entrants; age 25–55 includes the main working ages and accounts for more than half of the population; and finally individuals above age 55 is the group transitioning into retirement and accounts for a third of the population. The average age in both surveys is 45.[10]

With respect to work, the two surveys reveal some differences. Two thirds of the ATUS population is employed, compared to 56% in the FTUS. In both countries, a fifth of employed individuals work part-time. The share of retired individuals and students is higher in the FTUS, while unemployment rates are similar. The average monthly income is nearly 6,000 USD in the ATUS and 3,000 EUR in the FTUS.[11]

Both surveys include the same question about health "Would you say your health in general is excellent, very good, good, fair, or poor?", with answers ranging from 1 'excellent' to 5 'poor'. Additionally, they both include a binary question on whether a person had a disability or permanent illness. On average

Table 1. Descriptive Statistics – Individual Characteristics, by Country.

	ATUS (Population weights)	FTUS
N	19,198	1,222
Weekend/Both[a]	0.52	0.95
Female	0.51	0.51
Living with partner	0.61	0.65
Has children	0.38	0.42
N children[b]	1.90	1.89
	(1.03)	(1.1)
Age group		
15–24	0.12	0.14
25–54	0.57	0.54
55+	0.31	0.32
Age	45.08	45.27
	(15.89)	(16.4)
Employment status		
Full-time	0.52	0.44
Part-time	0.15	0.12
Unemployed	0.06	0.08
Retired	0.13	0.20
Student	0.02	0.08
Other	0.13	0.08
Monthly income (USD/EURO)	5,911	3,034
	(4,951)	(1831)
Disability	0.05	0.35
Health (1–5)	2.52	2.06
	(1.04)	(0.84)

Data Source: ATUS, 2012, 2013; FTUS, 2010.

Note: Descriptive statistics calculated using a single observation per respondent and weighted using population weights.

[a]For the ATUS: share of respondents who document time use on a weekend day. For the FTUS: share of respondents filling out time-use journals on two days.

[b]Number of children among individuals with children.

the French respondents score their health as "very good" (2.06) and the Americans as between "very good" and "good" (2.52).[12] In the ATUS, 5% of respondents report having a disability, while the corresponding figure in the FTUS is much larger: 35% of respondents declare that they suffer from a chronic or permanent disease, as illustrated by Table 1. As this is substantially higher than the official rate of invalidity, we consider this measure as less precise than the disability indicator of the ATUS.[13]

4.1 Measures of Subjective Well-Being and Diversity

Both the American and the French surveys include, for each respondent, one measure of self-declared life satisfaction (LS) measured on a (0–10 steps) Cantril scale.[14] In both surveys, this question is asked once, even though in the French survey each person fills a time-diary for two different days. Fig. 1 displays the (weighted) distribution of life satisfaction for each country. We see that in both countries the modal response is eight on a zero-ten scale. The distribution of answers is skewed to the right, and more so among the French. The top panel of Table 2 shows that the average life satisfaction is slightly higher among the FTUS respondents compared to the ATUS. ATUS respondents declare a similar level of life satisfaction whether they are surveyed on weekdays or weekend. Due to the ordinal nature of this measure, we convert the scale into a binary measure indicating whether an individual ranked their life satisfaction above the sample mean which is 7 (closest integer). Here we see a substantive difference between French and American respondents, where 78% of the French rank their satisfaction as 7 or higher, compared to 66% of Americans.

The middle section of Table 2 shows measures of variety and diversity of activities by country and week of the day. These measure are calculated on the two-digit classification that contains 29 activity categories, as detailed in

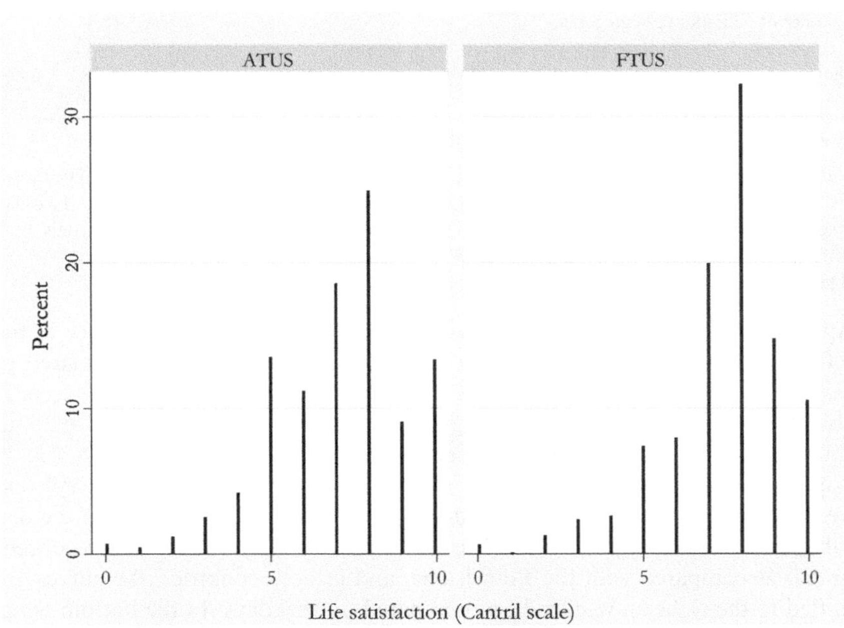

Fig. 1. Distribution of Life Satisfaction.

Note: Sample distributions using population weights, single response per individual. FTUS: "How satisfied are you with your life?" ATUS: "Please imagine a ladder with steps numbered from zero at the bottom to 10 at the top. The top of the ladder represents the best possible life for you and the bottom of the ladder represents the worst possible life for you. If the top step is 10 and the bottom step is 0, on which step of the ladder do you feel you personally stand at the present time?"

Data Source: ATUS, 2012, 2013; FTUS, 2010.

Table 2. Descriptive Statistics – Subjective Well-Being and Time-Use, by Country.

	ATUS		FTUS	
	Weekday	Weekend	Weekday	Weekend
N	9,267	9,931	1,247	1,250
Life satisfaction Cantril scale[a]				
Score	7.10 (2.03)	7.05 (2.01)	7.42 (1.83)	
Score 7 (sample mean) or higher	0.66 (0.47)	0.66 (0.48)	0.78 (0.42)	
Diversity- single day				
Number of activities (29 categories)[b]	8.47 (2.13)	8.03 (2.17)	8.54 (1.88)	8.42 (1.94)
Shannon-Wiener Index – w/o sleep	4.53 (1.67)	4.66 (1.83)	5.34 (1.74)	5.54 (1.74)
Shannon-Wiener Index – all activities	4.98 (1.30)	4.88 (1.40)	5.56 (1.27)	5.62 (1.30)
Diversity- two days (only FTUS)				
Number of activities (29 categories)			10.44 (2.20)	
Shannon-Wiener Index – w/o sleep			5.28 (1.69)	

Data Source: ATUS, 2012, 2013; FTUS, 2010.

Note: Descriptive statistics calculated using population weights. For weekend/weekday means are calculated using a single observation per respondent per weekday/weekend. Two-day diversity measures are calculated only for FTUS respondent who completed two journals.

[a]Life satisfaction measured on a (0–10) scale.

[b]Detailed categories are presented in Table A1 in the appendix.

Appendix Table A1. The declared number of activities is slightly higher in the FTUS compared to the ATUS, and slightly higher on weekdays compared to weekends. Our preferred measure of diversity, the S-W index without sleep, is also higher in the FTUS and is higher on weekends than weekdays in both countries. (This reflects the difference between variety and diversity). Fig. 2 displays the distribution of our measure of diversity by country and weekend-weekday, in the French and American samples. The shapes of the distributions are strikingly similar. The American curve is slightly more concentrated, as compared with the French one, and in both countries, the curves are shifted to the right on weekends, as compared to weekdays. In the bottom panel of Table 2, we see that, as expected, pooling weekends and weekdays (in the FTUS) increases the measured number of activities, but not the S-W index.

Fig. 3 examines the relationship between our S-W measure of diversity (over one day for the ATUS and over 2 days for the FTUS) and the covariates described in Table 1. Because of the much smaller size of the French data, we tend to be more confident in the analysis of heterogeneity that is based on the American data. Panel (a) confirms the expected greater time-use diversity of part-time employed and unemployed people as compared to full-time workers. In

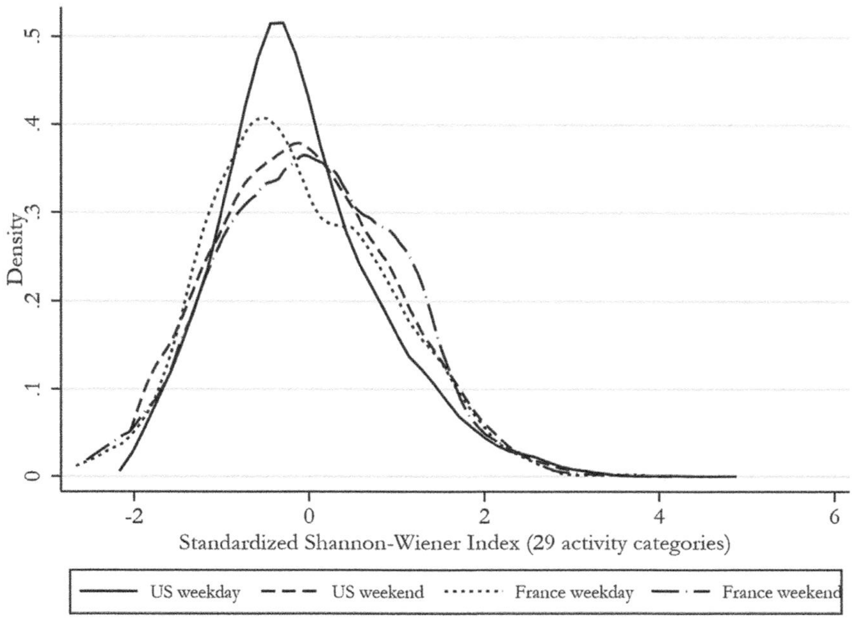

Fig. 2. Distribution of the S-W Index, by Weekday/Weekend.
Note: Sample distributions using population weights. Distribution of Shannon-Wiener Index of diversity by country and weekday using Epanechnikov kernel function with bandwidth 0.266.
Data Source: ATUS, 2012, 2013; FTUS, 2010.

the FTUS, this is also true of retired people. In the other panels, clear patterns appear only in the American data. Panel (b) shows the positive income gradient of activity-diversity. Panel (c) shows no clear pattern in terms of time-use diversity depending on age. Panel (d) shows the positive gradient of S-W in health. Finally, panel (d) illustrates the greater activity-diversity of people who live with children or a partner, and the smaller diversity index of people with a disability.

4.1.1 Activities and Momentary Utility

Table 3 displays the average daily composition of time-use in both countries, for weekdays and for weekends, based on the one-digit level classification. The first two columns present the share of respondents who reported dedicating any positive amount of time to each activity. In both countries, nearly all respondents dedicated at least some amount of time to sleep, meals, and relaxing and hobbies (this category includes watching TV and doing nothing), and over 80% also dedicated time to personal care, domestic work, and commuting. Half of ATUS respondents and only a third of FTUS respondents reported dedicating time to paid work related activities and about a third of each sample dedicated time to care work, roughly corresponding to the share of respondents with children.

The most time consuming activities are sleep, work and education, followed by relaxing and domestic work, which account for about three hours each (on

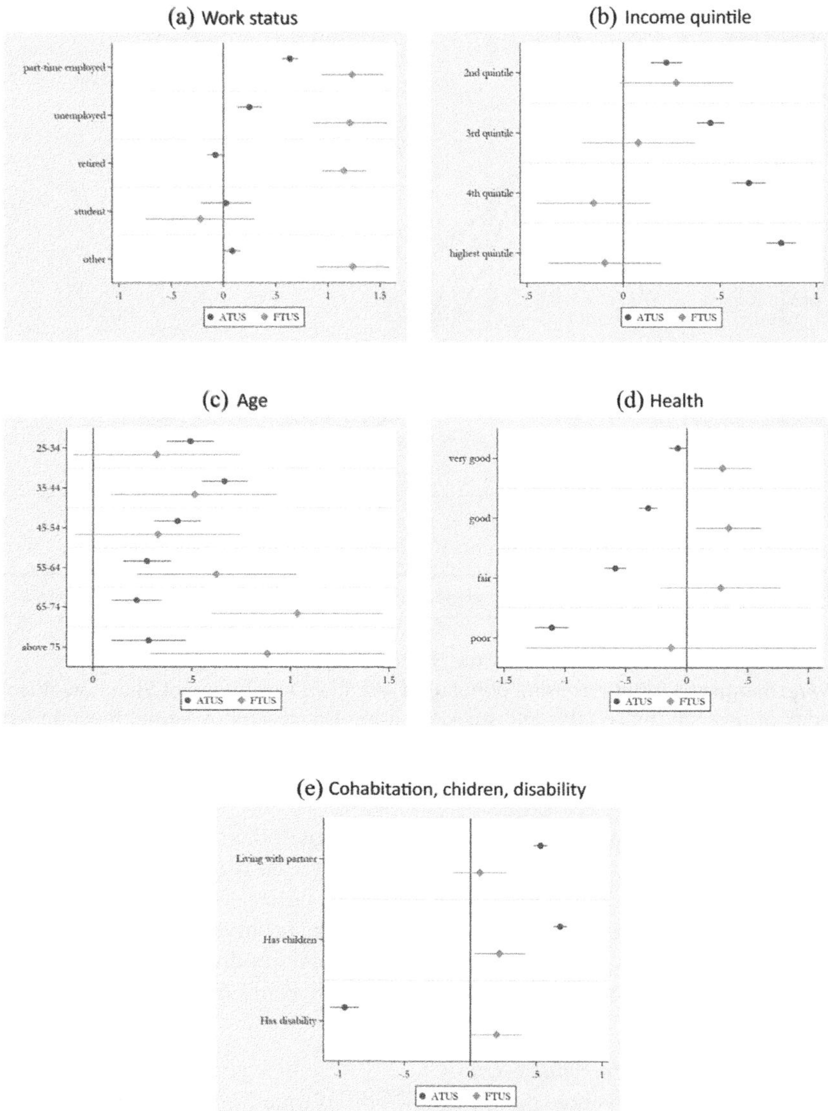

Fig. 3. Heterogeneity in the S-W Index of Diversity.

Notes: Each graph presents point estimates and 95% confidence interval, by country, of the difference in average time-use diversity between demographic categories, with respect to the base category: (a) employed; (b) lowest income quintile; (c) under age 25; (d) excellent health; (e) single; childless; without disability.

Data Source: ATUS, 2012, 2013; FTUS, 2010.

Table 3. Time-Use Categories and Momentary Utility.

	% Reporting		Average Time (hours)[a]				Average MU	
	ATUS	FTUS	ATUS		FTUS		ATUS[b]	FTUS[c]
			Weekday	Weekend	Weekday	Weekend	−6 to 6	−3 to 3
Sleep	1.00	1.00	8.37	9.25	8.32	8.66		
			(2.06)	(2.24)	(1.84)	(1.87)		
Meals	0.96	0.99	1.11	1.28	2.11	2.69	3.43	2.17
			(0.75)	(0.94)	(1.11)	(1.55)	(2.16)	(0.71)
Relaxing and hobbies	0.91	0.91	3.95	4.91	3.36	3.93	3.17	2.05
			(3.06)	(3.41)	(2.33)	(2.66)	(2.23)	(0.85)
Personal care	0.81	0.95	1.01	0.99	0.95	0.99	1.02	1.44
			(1.01)	(1.04)	(0.67)	(0.64)	(3.11)	(1.04)
Domestic work	0.84	0.85	2.46	3.22	3.31	3.50	2.98	1.25
			(2.35)	(2.63)	(2.48)	(2.32)	(2.23)	(1.08)
Commuting	0.86	0.81	1.40	1.45	1.40	1.38	3.17	1.32
			(1.19)	(1.45)	(1.07)	(1.11)	(2.16)	(1.02)
Social activities	0.48	0.52	1.73	2.89	1.62	2.40	3.53	2.26
			(1.75)	(2.39)	(1.59)	(2.06)	(2.34)	(0.91)
Work	0.48	0.33	7.86	5.42	7.08	5.72	2.46	1.07
			(2.84)	(3.88)	(2.94)	(3.55)	(2.18)	(1.27)
Care work	0.37	0.26	1.77	1.87	1.79	1.55	3.57	1.94
			(1.95)	(2.14)	(1.55)	(1.34)	(2.03)	(1.01)

Table 3. *(Continued)*

	% Reporting		Average Time (hours)[a]				Average MU	
	ATUS	FTUS	ATUS		FTUS		ATUS[b]	FTUS[c]
			Weekday	Weekend	Weekday	Weekend	−6 to 6	−3 to 3
Sports and recreation	0.18	0.28	1.39	2.05	1.77	2.25	3.80	2.31
			(1.32)	(2.00)	(1.27)	(1.76)	(1.81)	(0.85)
Education	0.05	0.06	5.08	4.00	5.47	5.12	1.84	0.82
			(3.59)	(2.92)	(3.50)	(3.25)	(2.19)	(1.25)
Events and cultural activities	0.04	0.06	2.48	2.92	2.57	2.44	4.09	2.54
			(1.47)	(1.89)	(1.98)	(1.29)	(1.97)	(0.77)

Data Source: ATUS, 2012, 2013; FTUS, 2010.

Note: Descriptive statistics calculated using population weights. For weekend/weekday, means are calculated using a single observation per respondent. Share reporting and Average MU refer to each respondent's scores over all time-use diaries.

[a]Average time in activity is calculated only over individuals spending at least some time in that activity.

[b]For the ATUS, average MU is the aggregated net-affect score (pain, tiredness, sadness, stress, and happiness) on a scale of −6 to 6 for three randomly chosen episodes throughout the day.

[c]For the FTUS, MU is the average score over all episodes of a given activity within the two days, answering the question: "was it a pleasant or unpleasant time? (from −3 very unpleasant to +3 very pleasant)".

average, per day). As expected, in both countries, the most prominent difference between weekends and weekdays is the share of time allocated to paid work. On average, American respondents dedicate a larger share of their time to work and work-related activities, and the French spend more time on meals. The time dedicated to social activities increases by 50% on weekends, as compared to week days, and the same is true of time dedicated to sports and recreation.

The leftmost columns of Table 3 display the average pleasantness score attributed to each category of activity, as in Kahneman and Krueger (2006). In the ATUS, momentary utility (MU) is, in principle, measured for three randomly drawn activities per respondent. Respondents are asked to indicate the duration of the activity and evaluate it in terms of: level of pain, tiredness, sadness, stress, and happiness, as well as how meaningful the activity is-each on a 0–6 scale. We aggregate these evaluations into an average score of MU, as displayed in Table 2. However, the ATUS documentation acknowledges that, due to a programming error in the data collection software, certain activities were less likely than others to be selected for follow-up questions in the well-being module.[15] For this reason, the MU information based on the ATUS presented in Table 2 should be interpreted with caution. In the French survey, respondents were asked to assess the pleasantness of all of the episodes experienced during an entire weekday and weekend day, each day being divided into slots of 10 minutes. For each episode, they are asked to indicate: "was it a pleasant or unpleasant time? (from −3 very unpleasant to +3 very pleasant)".

As can be seen, in both countries, sports and recreation activities, and attending events are the most appreciated activities. In France, these are followed by eating and drinking, social relations, and relaxing, whereas among ATUS respondents, care work is associated with relatively high momentary utility, ranking third in terms of pleasantness. In both countries, education, work, domestic work, and travel rank last in terms of MU.

4.1.2 Life Satisfaction, Time-Use and Gender

Table 4 shows our measures of life satisfaction by country and gender. In the USA, women report slightly higher life satisfaction than men, while in France there are no gender differences in life satisfaction (but there are, once controls are introduced, as will be shown by Table 5). On the other hand, gender differences in time allocation are well documented. Fig. 4 shows the distribution of time spent over categories of activities by country and gender.[16] Within each country, women dedicate a lower share of their time to market work. The opposite is true for domestic and care work, to which women dedicated more time than men. The gender differences with respect to this unpaid work are larger than those in paid work. The final substantive difference between men in women is with respect to the share of time dedicated to leisure which is substantially larger among men in both countries.

Whether the observed gender differences in time-use imply gender differences in diversity is examined in Table 4. We see that women in both countries take up more activities and exhibit higher diversity in their time-use. In light of the gender

Table 4. Descriptive Statistics – Life Satisfaction and Diversity, by Country and Gender.

	ATUS		FTUS	
	Men	Women	Men	Women
Life Satisfaction- Cantril scale[a]				
Score	6.97 (2.02)	7.18 (2.02)	7.44 (1.75)	7.44 (1.88)
Score 7 (sample mean) or higher	0.65 (0.48)	0.67 (0.47)	0.78 (0.41)	0.78 (0.42)
Diversity- single day				
Number of activities (29 categories)[b]	7.89 (2.05)	8.76 (2.16)	8.02 (1.92)	8.91 (1.79)
Shannon-Wiener Index – w/o sleep	4.14 (1.56)	4.97 (1.77)	4.92 (1.65)	5.94 (1.69)
Shannon-Wiener Index – w/o sleep and work	4.3 (1.62)	5.14 (1.77)	4.87 (1.64)	5.9 (1.57)
Diversity- two days (only FTUS)				
Number of activities (29 categories)			10.03 (2.33)	10.82 (2)
Shannon-Wiener Index – w/o sleep			4.73 (1.55)	5.79 (1.65)

Data Source: ATUS, 2012, 2013; FTUS, 2010.

Note: Descriptive statistics calculated using population weights. For weekend/weekdays, means are calculated using a single observation per respondent. Two-day diversity measures are calculated only for FTUS respondent who completed two diaries.

[a]Life satisfaction measured on a scale of 0–10.

[b]Detailed categories are presented in Table A1 in the Appendix.

differences in time dedicated to paid work, which may limit men's ability to diversify, we calculate diversity over non-work time (and still without sleep) and find that women's S-W index is still substantially higher. Finally, the gender gap remains when we compute our index of diversity over the two days (weekday and weekend) over which respondents are interviewed in the FTUS.

5. ESTIMATION RESULTS

5.1 Time-Use Diversity and Subjective Well-Being

The determinants of life satisfaction in both surveys, following Eq. (2), are presented in Table 5. The columns of the table display the estimates on the entire samples, with and without controls, where, for the French data, the index of activity-diversity is calculated over the weekend and weekday pooled. The top panel of Table 5 presents the average marginal effect of an increase in the diversity index (by a standard deviation) on the probability of declaring a level of life satisfaction above the average. All the results confirm [*H1*], as the estimated

Table 5. Probit Estimates Relating Life Satisfaction and Time-Use Diversity, by Country.

	ATUS		FTUS	
	(1)	(2)	(3)	(4)
	Average Marginal Effects			
Diversity	0.053 (0.000)	0.018 (0.000)	0.001 (0.000)	0.019 (0.000)
	Probit Coefficients			
SW_i	0.139 (0.000)	0.054 (0.000)	0.008 (0.000)	0.077 (0.000)
SW_{i2}	−0.028 (0.000)	−0.005 (0.000)	0.036 (0.000)	0.032 (0.000)
Female		0.085 (0.000)		0.017 (0.001)
Living with partner		0.314 (0.000)		0.485 (0.001)
Has children		0.067 (0.000)		−0.050 (0.001)
Part-time employment		−0.075 (0.000)		0.047 (0.001)
Unemployed		−0.402 (0.000)		−0.812 (0.001)
Retired		0.116 (0.000)		0.139 (0.001)
Income		0.078 (0.000)		0.139 (0.000)
Health status "very good"		−0.234 (0.000)		−0.232 (0.001)
Has disability		−0.206 (0.000)		−0.034 (0.001)
Constant	0.434 (0.000)	−0.155 (0.000)	0.703 (0.000)	−0.333 (0.004)
Observations	19,198	19,198	1,222	1,218

Data Source: ATUS, 2012, 2013; FTUS, 2010.

Note: The dependent variable is whether and individual scored their life satisfaction at 7 or above (7 is the closest integer value to sample mean). All estimates are obtained using a probit regression weighted by population weights for each survey. The S-W index is calculated for a single day in the ATUS and over two days in the FTUS. The top panel presents calculated average marginal effects for a standard deviation change in the S-W index, standard errors calculated using the delta method. The lower panel presents probit coefficients for the main variables of interest. All regressions include controls for survey waves (12 in the ATUS and 3 in the FTUS) as well as year and weekend dummies (ATUS only). Columns (2) and (4) include controls for seven age categories, where the omitted category is 45–54, and a second degree polynomial of sleeping time. For employment status, the omitted category is "full-time," and coefficients for "student" and "other" are suppressed. The omitted category for health status is "Excellent (1)," and coefficients for "good (3)," "fair (4)" and "poor (5)" are suppressed.

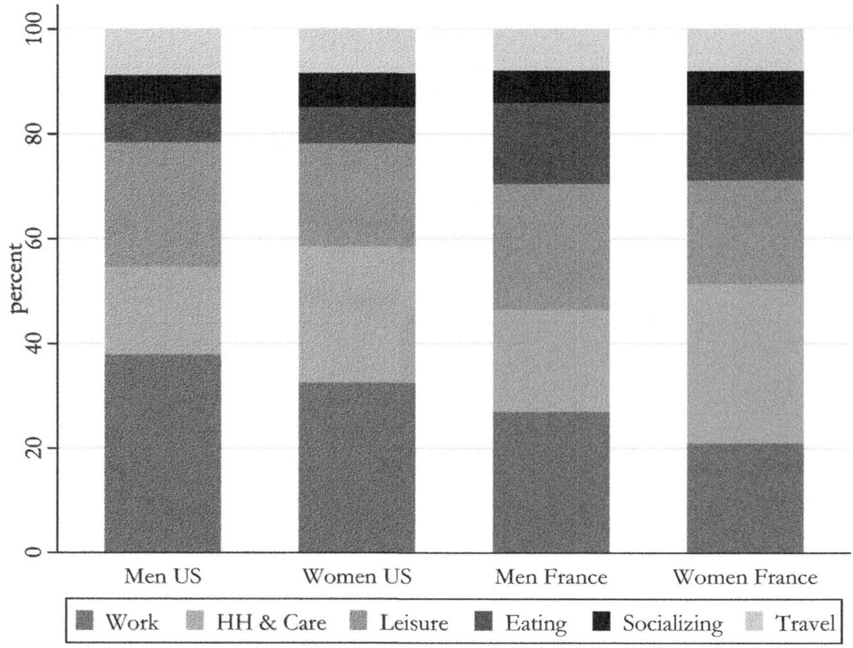

Fig. 4. Composition of Activities by Country and Gender.

Note: Shares of time use are calculated using population weights. For ease of presentation, sleep is omitted as it is the largest category and is similar across groups and several activity categories are combined as follows: Work includes all work and training related activities, including education; HH & Care includes personal care, care work and domestic work; Leisure includes relaxing & hobbies, recreation & sports and events & cultural activities. Shares are calculated over the entire time reported by each individual (single day in ATUS and two days in FTUS).

Data Source: ATUS, 2012, 2013; FTUS, 2010.

coefficients are always positive. While the unconditional estimates differ between the ATUS and the FTUS, controlling for individual characteristics yields nearly identical marginal effects – a standard deviation increase in the S-W index is associated with a 2 percentage points higher probability of ranking at or above 7 on the life satisfaction scale. Regarding the form of the relationship, results differ between the ATUS where the relationship is concave and the FTUS where it is convex. The magnitude of the association between a standard deviation increase in time-use diversity and life satisfaction is similar to the gender difference in life satisfaction, the association with having children, or the difference between full-time and part-time employment.

Controlling for observable characteristics has a substantial effect on the estimated relationships for both samples – the coefficient of interest is reduced in the ATUS and enhanced in the FTUS. This is a result of different relationships between individual characteristics and diversity, as discussed in the previous section. Table 5 also illustrates the different correlates of life satisfaction in the two countries. For instance, in the ATUS, having children is positively related to life satisfaction, while for the French the opposite is true, echoing the finding in Table 3, where care work is associated with high MU in the ATUS. Part-time employment is beneficial to life satisfaction in France but detrimental in the US. The rest of the coefficients are "well-behaved," in the sense that the usual correlations are found in both samples: life satisfaction is positively correlated with income, being employed, and living with a partner, and negatively associated with unemployment.

The upper panel of Table 6 displays the estimates on the sub-samples of weekdays and weekends, with individual and survey controls. The results are essentially the same, but of larger magnitude over weekends. As we have seen (Fig. 2), weekdays are clearly less diverse in terms of time-use compared to weekends. The lower part of Table 6 displays the same estimates separately on the sub-samples of working-age people (25–55) and of respondents aged 55 and above. The results are similar, and of similar magnitude in both age ranges.

For robustness, we also estimate these relationships using the number of different activities undertaken by respondents, i.e. an indicator of variety, instead of the S-W index of diversity. The results are displayed in Appendix Table A2.

5.2 Returns to Time Spent on Activities

Are there increasing hedonic returns to scale with respect to the time spent on a given activity? We test this hypothesis (*H2*) using scores of momentary utility as measured in the FTUS. For this section, we only use the French data (FTUS) where the pleasantness of an episode is scored from −3 'very unpleasant' to +3 'very pleasant' (see Section 4.1.1).

Fig. 5 illustrates the relationship between momentary utility associated with a given type of activity and the amount of time spent on that activity over the span of two days (conditional on the usual controls). As can be seen, no relation is convex. Some have a concave shape, e.g. meals, personal care, relaxing and hobbies (which includes a large chunk of TV watching), or work. Others have a more irregular shape, e.g. recreation and sports.

Fig. 5 shows the cross-sectional relationship between the duration of an activity and MU by comparing different individuals. However, ideally, we would like to estimate this relationship "within individual." As explained in Section 3.2, we dichotomize the pleasantness score and estimate a logit model of MU over the duration of an activity, with two observations per person, i.e. weekend and weekday. This allows us to introduce individual fixed-effects.

Table 7 displays these estimates. Each column refers to an activity category. The size of the regression sample is reduced because the estimates can only be performed on individuals who scored the same activity on both reporting days, and whose reported momentary utility varied across these two days. It turns out that most estimated relations are concave, i.e. the coefficient on the duration of the activity is positive and the coefficient on the squared duration term is negative

Table 6. Probit Estimates Relating Life Satisfaction and Time-Use Diversity, by Weekday and Age Group.

	ATUS		FTUS	
	Weekday	Weekend	Weekday	Weekend
	Average Marginal Effects			
Diversity	0.016 (0.000)	0.022 (0.000)	0.019 (0.000)	0.030 (0.000)
	Probit Coefficients			
SW_i	0.046 (0.000)	0.066 (0.000)	0.080 (0.000)	0.115 (0.000)
SW_{i2}	−0.008 (0.000)	0.001 (0.000)	0.027 (0.000)	−0.010 (0.000)
Observations	9,267	9,931	1,243	1,246
	Age 25–55	Age 55+	Age 25–55	Age 55+
	Average Marginal Effects			
Diversity	0.017 (0.000)	0.016 (0.000)	0.019 (0.000)	0.015 (0.000)
	Probit Coefficients			
SW_i	0.052 (0.000)	0.051 (0.000)	0.076 (0.000)	0.057 (0.001)
SW_{i2}	−0.005 (0.000)	−0.014 (0.000)	0.021 (0.000)	0.051 (0.000)
Observations	11,484	6,562	637	495

Data Source: ATUS, 2012, 2013; FTUS, 2010.

Note: The dependent variable is whether an individual scored their life satisfaction at or above the score of 7 (the closest integer value to sample mean). All estimates are obtained using a probit regression weighted by population weights for each survey. The S-W index is calculated for a single day in the ATUS and over two days in the FTUS. Average marginal effects are presented for a standard deviation change in the S-W index, standard errors calculated using the delta method. The top panel splits the sample by whether time-use was reported for a weekday or weekend. The bottom panel splits the sample by the two largest age groups. All regressions include controls for survey waves (12 in ATUS and 3 in FTUS) as well as year and weekend dummies (ATUS only), a continuous measure of household income, a second degree polynomial of sleeping time and indicators for: gender, cohabitation, presence of children, employment status, age categories (each category over 10 years), health status and disability.

(both statistically significant). The exception is care work, where the coefficient on duration is negative. Table A3 in the Appendix displays OLS estimates on the continuous life satisfaction scale, with similar results, although less statistical power. (Note that people enjoy pleasant activities more during weekends than during weekdays). Hence, hypothesis *H2* is not validated by the data; rather, it

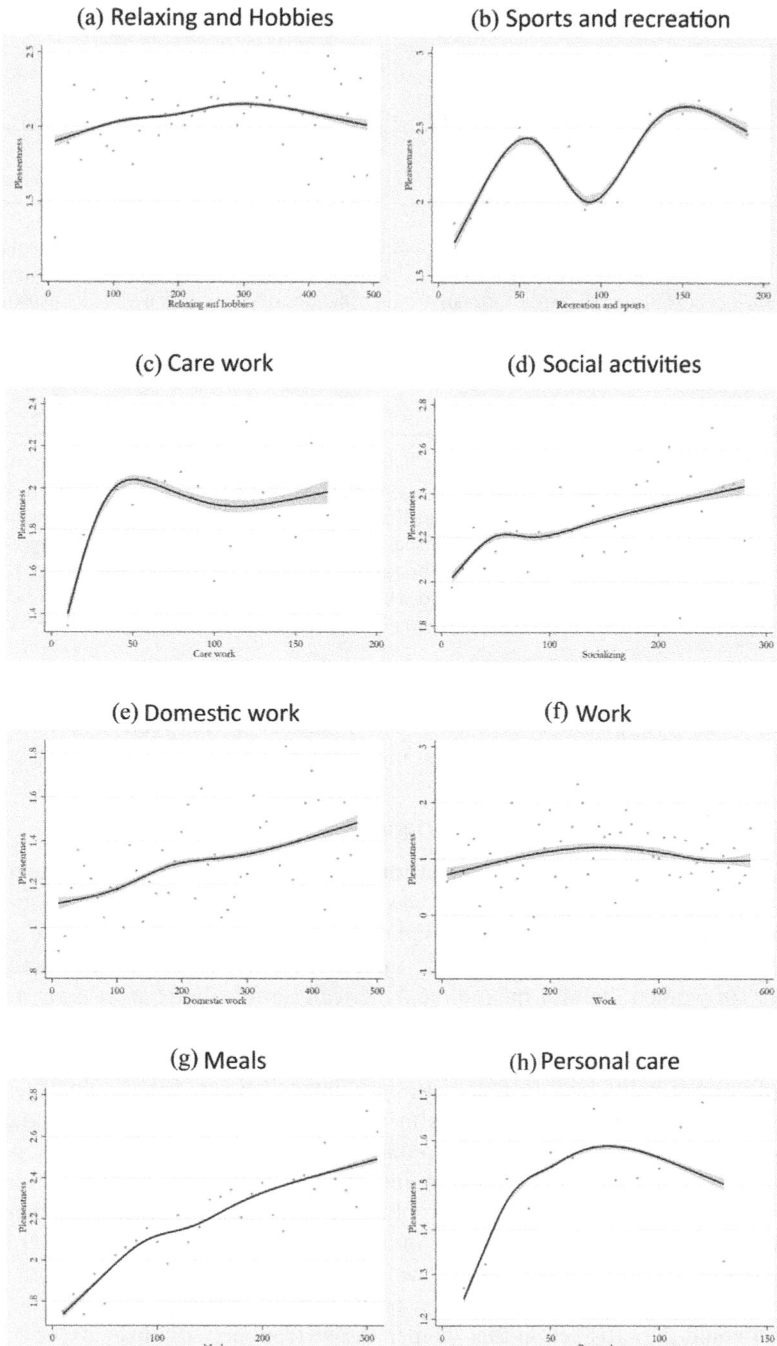

Fig. 5. Pleasantness and Time Spent on an Activity.
Notes: Each figure represents restricted cubic spline estimates of the relationship between the pleasantness score of an activity (which ranges from −3 to 3) on the *y*-axis and the time spent on an activity, in minutes.
Data Source: FTUS, 2010.

Table 7. Momentary Utility and Activity Duration With Individual Fixed Effects.

	Personal Care	Meals	Domestic Work	Care Work	Socializing	Relaxing and hobbies	Commuting
Time in activity	0.679 (0.003)	0.955 (0.001)	0.056 (0.001)	−0.776 (0.076)	1.001 (0.001)	0.290 (0.001)	0.151 (0.001)
Time in activity^2	−0.110 (0.001)	−0.079 (0.000)	−0.002 (0.000)	1.702 (0.026)	−0.022 (0.000)	−0.022 (0.000)	−0.001 (0.000)
Weekend	0.184 (0.001)	0.474 (0.001)	0.046 (0.001)	−0.044 (0.002)	0.389 (0.001)	−0.012 (0.001)	0.365 (0.001)
Observations	454	534	362	76	162	376	348
Individuals	227	267	181	38	81	188	174

Data Source: FTUS, 2010.

Note: Each column refers to an activity category. The dependent variable is whether and individual scored their momentary utility in that activity as 3 (the highest score). Coefficients from a logit regression with individual fixed effects, weighted by population weights. All regressions include a weekend dummies. The sample includes respondents who engaged in an activity category in both reporting days and whose reported momentary utility varied between both days.

seems that, for pleasant activities, the relationship between duration and momentary utility exhibits decreasing marginal returns.

5.3 Activity-Diversity and Gender

We now turn to the gender dimension of the association between activity-diversity and life satisfaction. As was shown by Table 4, our measure of time-use diversity is systematically higher for women than for men. The upper panel of that Table showed that the unconditional level of life satisfaction is higher for women than for men in the American sample, but, surprisingly, not in the French ones. However, the first column in Table 8 shows that the average marginal effect of the female indicator on life satisfaction is positive in both samples, once individual characteristics are controlled for. Introducing the S-W index of diversity into the estimates in the second column reduces the average satisfaction level of women relative to that of men, by about 10 percentage points in the ATUS and by 18 percentage points in the FTUS, as can be seen from the comparison of the second and third columns. The same patterns hold when the estimates are over the sub-samples of weekends and weekdays. These results suggest that the greater diversity of women's time-use contributes to their subjective well-being, and that it explains part of the gender gap.

But could the satisfaction that women derive from activity-diversity be due to the specific composition of their schedule, namely the fact that they devote a large amount of time to care and household work? The fourth column in Table 8 addresses this question and shows that it is not the case, in either country. It displays the estimates of Eq. (2) including a measure of the time spent on care

Table 8. Gender, Activity-Diversity, and Life Satisfaction.

	All	All	All	Men	Women
Female	0.035	0.028	0.030		
	(0.000)	(0.000)	(0.000)		
SW_i		0.018	0.023	0.020	0.021
		(0.000)	(0.000)	(0.000)	(0.000)
Controls					
Time FE	Yes	Yes	Yes	Yes	Yes
Individual characteristics	Yes	Yes	Yes	Yes	Yes
Time in HH & Care			Yes	Yes	Yes
Observations	19,198	19,198	19,198	8,598	10,600
	All	All	All	Men	Women
Female	0.014	0.004	0.008		
	(0.000)	(0.000)	(0.000)		
SW_i		0.019	0.025	0.026	0.041
		(0.000)	(0.000)	(0.000)	(0.000)
Controls	Yes	Yes	Yes	Yes	Yes
Time FE					
Individual characteristics	Yes	Yes	Yes	Yes	Yes
Time in HH & Care			Yes		
Observations	1,218	1,218	1,218	569	647

Data Source: ATUS, 2012, 2013; FTUS, 2010.

Note: The dependent variable is whether an individual scored their life satisfaction at or above the score of 7 (the closest integer value to sample mean). Coefficients are average marginal effects for a standard deviation change in the S-W index, and are derived from a probit regression weighted by population weights for each survey. The S-W index is calculated for a single day in the ATUS and over two days in the FTUS. Average marginal effects are presented, with standard errors calculated using the delta method. The top panel reports results for the ATUS sample, and the bottom panel for the FTUS. The last two columns are estimated on the sample of men and women separately. All regressions include controls for survey waves (12 in the ATUS and 3 in the FTUS), as well as year and weekend dummies (ATUS only), a continuous measure of household income, a second degree polynomial of sleeping time, and indicators for: gender, cohabitation, presence of children, employment status, age categories (each category over 10 years), health status and disability.

(including child care) and household work. Including this measure in the regression does not explain away the positive gender gap in life satisfaction. On the contrary, this even increases the coefficient on the female indicator, suggesting that the higher level of women's satisfaction is not due to this part of their schedule. Similarly, the coefficient on diversity is larger when this measure of the time spent on care work is controlled for, which suggests that the hedonic benefit of activity-diversity is not only due to a preference for such tasks.

If activity-diversity is a factor in life satisfaction, why is it less developed among men than among women? Is it the result of different preferences or different constraints? The last two columns of Table 8 show that the association between the S-W index and life satisfaction is the same among men and women in the ATUS (0.020 and 0.021). This suggests that this relationship is general, and not due to gendered preferences. In the French sample however, the coefficient on S-W is about 50% greater in the estimates on the sub-sample of women, as opposed to men. The same patterns hold on the sub-samples of weekends and weekdays (not shown). We also checked that the coefficient on diversity is higher for both men and women, when we include the measure of time spent on care and housework, than when this measure is not included (not shown for space reasons).

Hence, the taste for diversity is not specific to women, although it seems higher for women in the French sample. It is true that women have a more diverse schedule, and that schedule-diversity is associated with higher life satisfaction. But this relationship holds for both men and women. It also does not reflect a specific taste for care and housework.

Overall, the results of this section indicate that the greater diversity of women's time use contributes to their subjective well-being, and that it explains a significant part of the gender gap. The greater diversity of women's daily schedule cannot be attributed to a difference in preferences; rather, it points to the different constraints weighing on men's and women's time-use.

6. CONCLUSIONS

This study presents a first descriptive approach to the relationship between time-use diversity and subjective well-being. We use the Shannon-Wiener Index that captures both the variety of activities as well as the balance in the distribution activities over time. We find that allocating one's time to a more diverse set of activities is associated with a higher level of life satisfaction. In the same line, we find no evidence that the relationship between momentary utility and the duration of an activity is convex, on the contrary, for most pleasant activities, the relationship is concave.

We are only able to observe the ex-post relationship between time-use diversity and subjective well-being, i.e. ex-post *experienced utility*, rather than ex-ante *decision-utility*. We document a de facto higher utility associated, on average, with more diversified schedules, rather than a conscious preference guiding people's time-use choices. It may be the case that some people are unaware of this relationship, and therefore under-diversify their time-use, in the same way as it has been shown that most people underestimate the negative hedonic toll of long commutes (as measured ex-post). For example, men may be less aware of this relationship than women, which would explain why their schedule is less diversified.

Indeed, women's time-use is more diversified than men's, and this partly explains their higher level of happiness, conditional on observable individual characteristics – time-use diversity explains a fifth of the gender gap in happiness among Americans and two thirds of the (smaller) gap among the French. This does not reflect gender differences in preferences, as the positive association between diversity and subjective well-being is not specific to women. One interpretation is that the less diversified schedules of men, and their lower life satisfaction, are at least partly the outcomes of the specific constraints that weigh on their allocation of time, rather than being a reflection of their preferences.

These results have implications for gender equality policies. They call for caution about measures that would lead to the generalization of men's typical time use, which is less diversified and more focused on paid work. On the contrary, it should be borne in mind that the structure of women's time use seems to be more conducive to happiness.

These conclusions are based on correlations rather than causal relations, and are thus open to alternative interpretations, such as reverse causality. For example, happier people, or those in a better mood, may have a higher demand for a more diversified mix of activities. In the same vein, the happiness literature has often discussed whether marriage makes people happy or whether happier people are more likely to get married, and found that causality flows both ways. Similarly, the relationship between income and happiness has been shown to go in both directions. It is likely that the same is true of the association between time-use diversity and happiness, but this remains to be established by future work. For the moment, this paper shows that a more diversified time-use is, on average, the sign of a happier life style.

This finding opens an avenue for thinking about time, not only as an input for producing some outcome, but as a commodity in itself. Our choices in terms of time allocation turn the total amount of abstract time that is available to each of us into a certain set of experiences. This paper shows that in order to maximize one's total "utility" or happiness, it is not enough to spend more time on pleasant activities. The sequencing of these episodes also matters, and so does the general structure of one's schedule.

ACKNOWLEDGMENTS

This work has been funded by a French government subsidy managed by the Agence Nationale de la Recherche under the framework of the Investissements d'avenir program reference ANR-17-EURE-001, as well as CEPREMAP. It has benefited from the excellent research assistance of David Pfeffer (PSE). We are indebted to the cautious reading of the editor and two anonymous referees for their useful suggestions.

NOTES

1. An additional reason why people who have a more diversified mix of activities are happier could be that this complexity goes together with a greater degree of autonomy and control over one's organization, hence a greater sense of agency – known to be an important driver of happiness.
2. Karl Marx, The German Ideology/Theses on Feuerbach/Introduction to the Critique of Political Economy, 1845.
3. See the surveys of cultural gender norms by Fernández (2013), Goldin (2014), or Giuliano (2020).

4. See also Jost (2006).

5. While quite close, the American and French classifications of activities differ, as the former was elaborated by the US Bureau of Labor Statistics, and the latter by INSEE. Our common classification at the 1 and 2-digit levels, largely following the INSEE classification, can be found in Table A1 in the Appendix.

6. For robustness, we also use ordered probit estimates of life satisfaction, keeping the entire scale.

7. The Equation of the RCS is given below. For maximum flexibility we use $k = 5$ knots s for the spline at Harrell's recommended percentiles – at the 5th, 27.5th, 50th, 72.5th and 95th percentiles of time in the activity (Frank E. Harrell Jr, 2015).

$$\text{MU} = \alpha_0 + \alpha_1 t_1 + \ldots \alpha_{k-1} t_{k-1} \text{ where } t_1 = t$$

$$t_c = (t - s_{c-1})^3_+ - \frac{(t - s_{k-1})^3_+ (s_k - s_{c-1})}{s_k - s_{k-1}} + \frac{(t - s_k)^3_+ (s_{k-1} - s_{c-1})}{s_k - s_{k-1}} \text{ for}$$

$$c = 2, \ldots, k - 1$$

8. These sub-samples are then weighted using the official survey weights to make them representative of the general population. All descriptive statistics and estimation results in the paper use these sampling weights.

9. We drop respondents who did not report time-use for more than 10% of the day as well as respondents for whom key variables were missing, such as household income.

10. In the unweighted sample, this group is smaller than in the actual population, especially in the FTUS. Therefore, when analyzing age groups separately, we do not use this group.

11. In the ATUS, income is initially reported in intervals. We recode this measure into a continuous variable, namely the midpoint of each interval, and 1.5 × the lower bound of the upper open interval. The distribution of the income measure for each country is shown in Appendix Fig. A1.

12. The right panel in appendix Fig. A1 shows the distribution of answers in both surveys. The FTUS distribution is more condensed, nearly 50% of respondents reported their health as 2 "very good," while the majority of ATUS respondent divide nearly equally across categories 2 and 3.

13. Other surveys of the French population lead to the same observation. For example, in the annual survey of the French population run by Credoc (Centre de Recherche pour l'Etude et l'Observation des Conditions de Vie), 26% of individuals typically declare that they suffer from a handicap or a chronic or long run illness. However, only 6% of French people aged 15 to 64, have a certificate of invalidity that opens the right to a subsidy, and the official proportion of workers whose activity is limited by a handicap or an illness is 18% (See https://drees.solidarites-sante.gouv.fr/sources-outils-et-enquetes/02-les-enquetes-handicap-sante).

14. The ATUS question reads: "Please imagine a ladder with steps numbered from zero at the bottom to 10 at the top. The top of the ladder represents the best possible life for you and the bottom of the ladder represents the worst possible life for you. If the top step is 10 and the bottom step is 0, on which step of the ladder do you feel you personally stand at the present time?"

15. https://www.bls.gov/tus/wbmintcodebk.pdf.

16. Sleep is the largest category and is similar across groups, so it is omitted for presentation.

REFERENCES

Adena, M., Hamermesh, D., Myck, M., & Oczkowska, M. (2023). Home alone: Widows' well-being and time. *Journal of Happiness Studies*, *24*(2), 813–838.

Aguiar, M., Hurst, E., & Karabarbounis, L. (2013). Time use during the great recession. *The American Economic Review*, *103*(5), 1664–1696.

Becchetti, L., & Conzo, G. (2022). The gender life satisfaction/depression paradox. *Social Indicators Research*, *160*(1), 35–113.

Becker, G. S. (1965). A theory of the allocation of time. *The Economic Journal*, *75*(299), 493–517.

Bianchi, S. M., & Milkie, M. A. (2010). Work and family research in the first decade of the 21st century. *Journal of Marriage and Family*, *72*(3), 705–725.

Biddle, J. E., & Hamermesh, D. S. (1990). Sleep and the allocation of time. *Journal of Political Economy*, *98*(5, Part 1), 922–943.

Blanchflower, D. G., & Bryson, A. (2022). *The female happiness paradox*. Working paper. National Bureau of Economic Research.

Blanchflower, D. G., & Oswald, A. J. (2004). Well-being over time in Britain and the USA. *Journal of Public Economics*, *88*(7–8), 1359–1386.

Blau, F. D., & Kahn, L. M. (2017). The gender wage gap: Extent, trends, and explanations. *Journal of Economic Literature*, *55*(3), 789–865.

Buddelmeyer, H., Hamermesh, D. S., & Wooden, M. (2018). The stress cost of children on moms and dads. *European Economic Review*, *109*, 148–161.

Dotti Sani, G. M., & Treas, J. (2016). Educational gradients in parents' child-care time across countries, 1965–2012. *Journal of Marriage and Family*, *78*(4), 1083–1096.

Easterlin, R. A. (2001). Income and happiness: Towards a unified theory. *The Economic Journal*, *111*(473), 465–484.

Fernández, R. (2013). Cultural change as learning: The evolution of female labor force participation over a century. *The American Economic Review*, *103*(1), 472–500.

Gershuny, J., & Halpin, B. (1996). Time use, quality of life and process benefits. In *Pursuit of the quality of life* (pp. 188–210). Clarendon Press.

Gimenez-Nadal, J. I., & Molina, J. A. (2020). *The gender gap in time allocation in Europe*. IZA discussion papers. Institute of Labor Economics (IZA). Number: 13461 Publisher.

Goldin, C. (2014). A grand gender convergence: Its last chapter. *The American Economic Review*, *104*(4), 1091–1119.

Graham, C., & Chattopadhyay, S. (2013). Gender and well-being around the world. *International Journal on Hydropower and Dams*, *1*(2), 212.

Gronau, R., & Hamermesh, D. S. (2008). The demand for variety: A household production perspective. *The Review of Economics and Statistics*, *90*(3), 562–572.

Giuliano, P. (2020). Gender and culture. *Oxford Review of Economic Policy*, *36*(4), 944–961.

Hamermesh, D. S. (2019). *Spending time: The most valuable resource*. Oxford University Press.

Hamermesh, D. S., & Biddle, J. (2018). *Taking time use seriously: Income, wages and price discrimination*. Working paper. National Bureau of Economic Research.

Hamermesh, D. S., & Lee, J. (2007). Stressed out on four continents: Time crunch or Yuppie Kvetch? *The Review of Economics and Statistics*, *89*(2), 374–383.

Harrell, F. E., Jr. (2015). *Regression modeling strategies: With applications to linear models, logistic and ordinal regression, and survival analysis*. Springer International Publishing.

Helliwell, J. F., Layard, R., & Sachs, J. D. (2015). *World happiness report 2015*.

Jost, L. (2006). Entropy and diversity. *Oikos*, *113*(2), 363–375.

Kahneman, D., & Krueger, A. B. (2006). Developments in the measurement of subjective well-being. *The Journal of Economic Perspectives*, *20*(1), 3–24.

Kahneman, D., Krueger, A. B., Schkade, D. A., Schwarz, N., & Stone, A. A. (2004). A survey method for characterizing daily life experience: The day reconstruction method. *Science*, *306*(5702), 1776–1780.

Kahneman, D., Wakker, P. P., & Sarin, R. (1997). Back to Bentham? Explorations of experienced utility. *Quarterly Journal of Economics*, *112*(2), 375–406.

Knabe, A., Rätzel, S., Schöb, R., & Weimann, J. (2010). Dissatisfied with life but having a good day: Time-use and well-being of the unemployed. *The Economic Journal*, *120*(547), 867–889.

Krueger, A. B., Kahneman, D., Fischler, C., Schkade, D., Schwarz, N., & Stone, A. A. (2009). Time use and subjective well-being in France and the US. *Social Indicators Research*, *93*(1), 7–18.

Krueger, A. B., Kahneman, D., Schkade, D., Schwarz, N., & Stone, A. A. (2009). 1. National time accounting: The currency of life. In *1. National time accounting: The currency of life* (pp. 9–86). University of Chicago Press.

Layard, R. (2011). *Happiness: Lessons from a new science*. Penguin UK.

Marx, K., & Engels, F. (1845). *The German Ideology: Including theses on Feuerbach and introduction to the Critique of political Economy*. Prometheus Books.

Plagnol, A. C., & Easterlin, R. A. (2008). Aspirations, attainments, and satisfaction: Life cycle differences between American women and men. *Journal of Happiness Studies*, *9*(4), 601–619.

Ramey, G., & Ramey, V. A. (2009). *The rug rat race*. Working Paper 15284. National Bureau of Economic Research.

Robinson, J. P., & Godbey, G. (1997). *Time for life: The surprising ways Americans use their time*. Penn State Press.

Robinson, J., & Godbey, G. (1999). *Time for life: The surprising ways Americans use their time* (2nd ed.). Pennsylvania State University Press.

Steptoe, A., Deaton, A., & Stone, A. A. (2015). Subjective wellbeing, health, and ageing. *The Lancet*, *385*(9968).

Stevenson, B., & Wolfers, J. (2009). The paradox of declining female happiness. *American Economic Journal: Economic Policy*, *1*(2), 190–225.

Stirling, A. (1998). *On the economics and analysis of diversity*. Working paper 28.

Stone, A. A., Shiffman, S. S., & DeVries, M. W. (1999). Ecological momentary assessment. In *Well-being: The foundations of hedonic psychology* (pp. 26–39). Russell Sage Foundation.

Stratton, L. S. (2012). The role of preferences and opportunity costs in determining the time allocated to housework. *The American Economic Review*, *102*(3), 606–611.

Stutzer, A., & Frey, B. S. (2008). Stress that doesn't pay: The commuting paradox. *The Scandinavian Journal of Economics*, *110*(2), 339–366.

Van Praag, B. M., Frijters, P., & Ferrer-i Carbonell, A. (2003). The anatomy of subjective well-being. *Journal of Economic Behavior & Organization*, *51*(1), 29–49.

APPENDIX

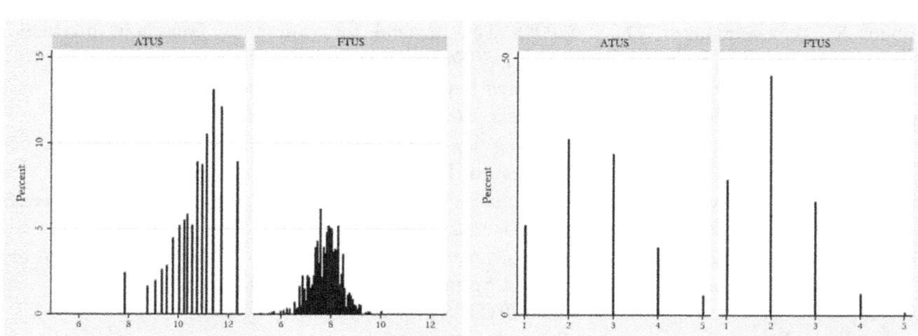

Fig. A1. Distribution of Log Income and Health for ATUS and FTUS Samples.

Notes: Sample distribution using population weights. Income: in the ATUS, household annual income is measured in categories; we assigned to each individual the mid-point income of each interval, and 1.5 × the lower bound of the upper open interval. In FTUS, household income (per head) is measured as a continuous variable//Health: *n* both the FTUS and ATUS, health status is measured by respondents' answer to the question "Would you say your health in general is excellent (1), very good (2), good (3), fair (4), or poor (5)?"

Table A1. Tier 1 and 2 Activity Category Definitions.

Tier 1	Tier 2	FTUS- Tier 2 Description	ATUS Categories
Sleep	11	Sleep	0101
Personal care	12	Personal care	0102, 0104,0105,0805
Personal care	13	Medical care	0103,0804
Personal care	15	Other personal activities	0199
Eating and drinking	14	Meals	1101,1102,1199
Work	21	Normal work	0501
Work	22	Other work	0503,0599
Work	23	Non-work at the workplace	0502
Work	24	Job search	0504
Education and training	26	Professional training	
Education and training	26	Study and studying internships	0601,0602,0603,0604,0699
Education and training	26	Non-vocational training and courses	
HH work	31	Meal preparation	0202
HH work	32	Cleaning and laundry	0201,0901
HH work	32	Washing, ironing, clothes cleaning	
HH work	34	Housekeeping activities	0209
HH work	35	Groceries and shopping	0701,0702,0703,0799
HH work	36	Use of administrative services	0801,0802,0803,0806,0807,0808,0899,1501
HH work	37	Construction, repair and maintenance work	0203,0204,0207,0208,0902,0905,1503
HH work	38	Gardening, artistic creations, pet care	0205,0206,0904,0903
HH work	39	Other domestic activities	0299,0999
Care work	41	Care of child of own and/or other household	0301,0303,0401,0403
Care work	42	Play and instruction activities for children	0302,0402
Care work	43	Care of adults	0304,0305,0404,0405,0399,0499,1502
Socializing	51	Social events and outings	1202,1505,1506,1599
Socializing	52	Different forms of conversations	1201,1601,1,699
Socializing	53	Religious practices, civil ceremonies	1401,1499
Socializing	54	Civic, and political activities and meetings	1001,1002,1003,1004,1099
Recreation and sports	61	Different sports	1301, 1303,1304,1399
Recreation and sports	61	Recreation Walks, fishing, camping, motorized rides	
Relaxing and hobbies	63	Reading, watching TV, listening to music	
Relaxing and hobbies	63	Doing nothing	1203,1205,1299,1504
Relaxing and hobbies	63	Hobbies: Playing	

Table A1. *(Continued)*

Tier 1	Tier 2	FTUS- Tier 2 Description	ATUS Categories
Relaxing and hobbies	63	Computer activities	
Cultural activities	65	Visits & events	1204,1302
Commuting	81	Commuting for associative purposes	18XX

Table A2. Estimated Average Marginal Effects of Variety (N Activities) on Life Satisfaction.

	Life Satisfaction Above Sample Average ATUS				
	Main	Weekday	Weekend	Men	Women
N activities	0.003 (0.000)	0.001 (0.000)	0.007 (0.000)	0.005 (0.000)	0.001 (0.000)
Observations	19,198	9,267	9,931	8,598	10,600
	FTUS				
	Main	Weekday	Weekend	Men	Women
N activities	0.012 (0.000)	0.010 (0.000)	0.015 (0.000)	0.007 (0.000)	0.024 (0.000)
Observations	1,218	1,243	1,246	569	647

Data Source: ATUS, 2012, 2013; FTUS, 2010.

Note: Dependent variable is whether and individual scored their life satisfaction at or above the score of 7 (the closest integer value to sample mean). Coefficients are average marginal effects for a standard deviation change in S-W index are derived from a probit regression weighted by population weights for each survey. Number of activities are counted for a single day in ATUS and over two days in FTUS. Average marginal effects are presented, standard error calculated using the delta method. All regressions include control for survey wave (12 in ATUS and 3 in FTUS) as well as year and weekend dummies (ATUS only), a continuous measure of household income, a second degree polynomial of sleeping time and indicators for: gender, cohabitation, presence of children, employment status, age categories (each category over 10 years), health status and disability.

Table A3. Continuous Fixed Effects Estimates of the Relationship Between Momentary Utility and Activity Duration.

	Personal Care	Meals	Domestic Work	Care Work	Socializing	Relaxing and hobbies	Commuting	
Time in activity	0.221 (0.193)	0.235 (0.059)	0.036 (0.045)	0.264 (0.615)	0.095 (0.045)	−0.051 (0.045)	−0.242 (0.145)	0.088 (0.123)
Time in activity^2	−0.112 (0.079)	−0.024 (0.010)	−0.004 (0.005)	0.048 (0.173)	0.005 (0.005)	0.005 (0.005)	0.067 (0.042)	−0.002 (0.011)
Weekend	0.138 (0.033)	0.110 (0.022)	0.044 (0.035)	0.078 (0.067)	0.136 (0.058)	0.022 (0.029)	0.176 (0.041)	0.242 (0.117)
Observations	2,082	2,242	1826	404	616	1,570	1,568	284
Individuals	1,041	1,121	913	202	308	785	784	142

Data Source: FTUS, 2010.

Note: Each column refers to an activity category. The dependent variable is an individual's average momentary utility score during that activity. Coefficients from a fixed-effects linear regression with individual fixed effects, weighted by population weights. All regressions include a weekend dummy. Sample includes respondents who engaged in an activity category in both reporting days and whose reported momentary utility varied between both days.

EFFORT AT WORK AND WORKER WELL-BEING

José Ignacio Giménez-Nadal, José Alberto Molina and Almudena Sevilla

ABSTRACT

This chapter analyzes detailed 24-hour diary data from the United States to provide evidence on the relationship between workers' effort and well-being while at work. In doing so, we first measure workers' effort in terms of the amount of on-the-job leisure, number of on-the-job leisure episodes, and the time working until consuming on-the-job leisure. Second, we link these three measures of worker effort to data on instantaneous well-being while at work. We find that the less time devoted to on-the-job leisure and the number of on-the-job leisure episodes, and the more time workers spend working until on-the-job-leisure, the higher the levels of stress during their work tasks. In analyzing workers' effort and stress during market work activities, we contribute to the scant literature on the determinants of worker happiness while at work, positing the consumption and the frequency of on-the-job leisure as affective factors.

Keywords: Time-use; effort at work; stress; on-the-job leisure; well-being; timing of time use

1. INTRODUCTION

In this paper, we analyze effort at work and well-being while at work. The analysis of worker well-being/happiness is important, as they are positively related to worker and firm productivity. Bryson et al. (2017) and Böckerman and Ilmakunnas (2012) show positive effects from retrospective job satisfaction on workplace performance. Recent findings from the lab show that a worker's instantaneous well-being while at work is also positively correlated with productivity (Oswald et al., 2015). But despite prior analyses of worker happiness,

Time Use in Economics
Research in Labor Economics, Volume 51, 35–53

ISSN: 0147-9121/doi:10.1108/S0147-912120230000051002

the mechanisms underlying well-being while at work in real-world settings remain an open question in the literature. Here we identify one such mechanism, analyzing the relationship between the structure of work tasks, aimed at measuring worker effort, on the one hand, and worker instantaneous well-being, on the other.

We analyze the structure of work in the US in three dimensions: amount of on-the-job leisure, number of on-the-job leisure episodes, and the length of uninterrupted time working until leisure. We link these three indicators to the well-being of workers, measured through instantaneous well-being data during their work episodes. To that end, we use data from the 2010, 2012, and 2013 Well-Being Module (WBM) of the American Time Use Survey (ATUS) and compute the three measures of worker effort, together with instantaneous well-being during market work episodes. The nature of the data allows us to identify workers on their working days and focus on their work episodes and the well-being experienced during those episodes. This makes this dataset especially useful for the analysis of well-being while at work. Furthermore, the fact that there is information at the episode level allows us to create the indicators of work effort and link them to worker well-being.

We find that the amount of on-the-job leisure and its frequency – that is, the number of on-the-job leisure episodes and the uninterrupted time working before consuming on-the-job leisure – appear to be key determinants of instantaneous well-being during market work activities. Increases in on-the-job leisure hours and episodes, and decreases in the uninterrupted time spent working, are associated with decreases in the stress workers report during their market work activities. In particular, a decrease of one hour in the amount of on-the-job leisure is associated with an increase of 0.01 standard deviations in stress during work episodes, and a decrease of one on-the-job leisure episode is associated with an increase of 0.025 standard deviations in stress during work episodes. Furthermore, a one-hour increase in the time spent working before consuming on-the-job leisure is associated with an increase of 0.013 standard deviations in stress during work episodes. These are not large effects, but they are not tiny either.

We contribute to the analysis of worker well-being while at work. Prior evidence has looked at work/job satisfaction, and the happiness of workers, although no previous analysis has directly analyzed well-being while at work. The only exception is Oswald et al. (2015), who show (in an experimental setting) that increased happiness makes people more productive while at work. This evidence is based on a classic piece-rate context, with randomly selected individuals, but no external validity has been provided and the findings are applicable only to the lab setting. How firm-level interventions that increase well-being while at work play out in real-business settings remains an open question in the literature. We focus on the structure of work tasks as a factor affecting workers' instantaneous utility. Our results come from a national-scale survey, and thus are based on representative data that covers all industries and occupations, which makes them of general interest. Furthermore, Clark et al. (2018) show that the quality of work is the second-most important factor accounting for inequality of well-being in a population.

The remainder of the manuscript is organized as follows. Section 2 presents a review of the literature on effort at work and worker well-being. Section 3 describes the data, and Section 4 presents the main results. Section 5 sets out our main conclusions.

2. BACKGROUND

Effort at work is routinely measured as the number of hours worked, which are normally gathered from nationally representative labor surveys asking respondents about annual/monthly/weekly hours worked. However, this measure can be only an approximation of hours actually worked and may miss important information on what workers do while on the job. For instance, Hamermesh (1990) analyses the use of time on the job, considering scheduled and unscheduled breaks, finding positive correlations of this non-productive time with earnings. The labor supply literature has extended the traditional labor supply model of work-leisure choice to account explicitly for on-the-job leisure to get a better picture of actual hours of work. Dickinson (1999) augments the neoclassical labor supply model with consumption of on-the-job leisure to show that substitution between on- and off-the-job leisure can reconcile the negative compensated wage elasticity estimates often observed in empirical studies with the positive compensated wage elasticity predicted by classical labor supply theory.

More recently, studies have established "non-work while at work" as a measure of work effort. Burda et al. (2020) define work effort using non-work time at the workplace in the American Time Use Survey (ATUS) where non-work might be interpreted as "loafing," "shirking" or "goofing off on the job." Their measure is a measure of not working while at work and is what the respondent believes it to be. In the same way, Gimenez-Nadal and Sevilla (2022) define three measures of on-the-job leisure (i.e., non-work while at work) to measure the work effort of UK workers, between the 1980s and the 2010s, linking its evolution to trends in automation and the routinization of jobs (routine-biased technological change). That these authors use time-use data allows them to analyze what workers do while they are at work, which may represent a good proxy for work effort and complement work effort measures based on weekly, monthly, or annual hours of work.[1]

Regarding the literature on worker well-being, a long tradition in economics has analyzed its correlates. Analyses of life satisfaction or happiness of workers, or job satisfaction, are used to measure workers' well-being, although job satisfaction is preferred in the current context.[2] Economists mostly rely on Clark's (1996) utility theory to assess job satisfaction, which defines it as the utility derived from the combination of wages and working hours, and a range of other job characteristics. Several factors have been found to be correlated with job satisfaction. The wage is observed to be positively correlated with job satisfaction

(Clark et al., 2008; Easterlin, 1995), and the number of working hours a job requires has a non-linear relation to job satisfaction (Clark, 1996).

Other job characteristics found to be associated with job satisfaction include company provision of additional services or fringe benefits (Erro-Garcés & Ferreira, 2019; Krumbiegel et al., 2018), intrinsic rewards, such as promotion opportunities, job content, and autonomy (García-Mainar & Montuenga-Gómez, 2020; Herzberg, 1987; Wen et al., 2019), and contextual characteristics, such as the size of the firm and the working environment, including temperature and noise at the workplace (Bóo et al., 2010; Razafindrakoto & Roubaud, 2013; Erro-Garcés & Ferreira, 2019). Furthermore, job satisfaction typically follows a U-shaped relationship with age, decreases with the number of children and the education level of workers, and is positively related to being coupled/married and good health conditions. Also, women are more likely to be satisfied with their job (Clark, 1996, 1997; Clark et al., 1996; Izvercian et al., 2016; Sousa-Poza & Sousa-Poza, 2000; van Praag et al., 2003).

The analysis of the well-being of workers is important, as it is related to worker productivity, although the literature is scant in this respect, and economists still know relatively little about the causal linkages between these two variables. Edmands (2012) finds that levels of employee job satisfaction predict a company's future stock market performance. Böckerman and Ilmakunnas (2012) show in longitudinal European data that an increase in the measure of job satisfaction by one within-plant standard deviation increases value-added per hours worked in manufacturing by 6.6%.

3. DATA AND VARIABLES

For the analysis of how workers feel during their market work activities, we use information on instantaneous well-being from the 2010, 2012, and 2013 American Time Use Survey (ATUS) Well-Being Modules (WBM).[3] The ATUS data provide us with socioeconomic variables about respondents, but also with information on individual time use, based on diaries, in which respondents report their activities from 4 a.m. through 3:59 a.m. of the next day. Time-use diaries have become the gold standard in the analysis of workers' daily behavior (Aguiar & Hurst, 2007; Gimenez-Nadal & Sevilla, 2012; Guryan et al., 2008).[4]

The ATUS Well-being modules were fielded from January through December in each year. Diaries are divided into episodes where the respondent records a main activity and certain additional information, such as whether the activity was done in the company of another individual, and where the activity took place.[5] The ATUS WBM provides a unique opportunity to analyze worker well-being during market work activities, as it uses the Day Reconstruction Method, in which respondents are asked to fill out a diary summarizing episodes of activities for the selected day, and then are asked about their feelings while doing the activities (Kahneman et al., 2004).[6] In the ATUS WBM, one diary is completed by a given respondent on selected days of the week, and then respondents are asked to rank three randomly selected episodes lasting at least five minutes, describing the extent to which felt happy, stressed, sad, tired, or felt pain during the activity, the five feelings that we analyze.[7] Values are recorded on a seven-point scale, with "0" indicating that the respondent "did not experience the feeling at all," and "6" indicating that a "feeling was extremely strong."

We follow the literature and restrict the sample to non-retired/non-student individuals between the ages of 21 and 65, inclusive (Aguiar & Hurst, 2007; Gimenez-Nadal & Sevilla, 2012, 2022), who devote at least one hour to market work activities during the diary day, excluding commuting (i.e., workers on their working days), and report to work full-time.[8] Then, we select episodes in the diary during which the respondent is at work, i.e., episodes between the times in which the respondent first starts to work and the time in which the respondent records stopping work. For the analysis of well-being at work, we restrict the analysis to workers' market work episodes – working while at work – containing well-being information. There are 4,065 work episodes with information on the five feelings of interest, corresponding to 3,051 workers.[9]

Regarding the indicators of effort at work, *time at work* is defined as the time from the moment the respondent first begins work until the moment of the last recorded work episode during the diary day. From this time period, we compute the variables *time working*, which measures the total time devoted to market work activities, and the *consumption of on-the-job leisure*, which measures the total time spent in a different activity (i.e., time spent not working while on the job).[10] We follow Hamermesh (1990) and divide the consumption of on-the-job leisure into leisure-related activities and other non-work activities. Leisure-related activities include social leisure, active leisure, such as going to the gym, and passive leisure such as reading and watching TV. Meals at work are included as part of on-the-job leisure. Other non-work activities include housework-related activities, and personal care activities. We also consider the commuting that is done between the main work episodes (Table A1 in the Appendix provides a detailed description of all activities included in each of the categories of on-the-job leisure).

The frequency of on-the-job leisure has only been analyzed by Gimenez-Nadal and Sevilla (2022). We construct two other indicators of work effort: *number of on-the-job leisure episodes* and *working time until consuming on-the-job leisure*. A higher number of on-the-job leisure episodes indicates a higher frequency of on-the-job leisure, whereas a longer uninterrupted working time indicates a lower frequency of on-the-job leisure. This latter indicator is computed by dividing the total amount of time spent working by the number of work spells in the diary.

Table 1 shows an example of a working day from a randomly chosen worker in the ATUS. The diarist spent 8 hours and 40 minutes at work, starting work at 8:00 a.m., when the first episode of market work was recorded in the diary, and finishing at 4:40 p.m. when the last episode of market work was recorded in the diary. Of the 8 hours and 40 spent at work, 7 hours and 30 minutes were spent working. There were 3 work spells of 3 hours, 2 hours and 10 minutes, and 2 hours and 20 minutes. The first work spell started at 8:00 a.m. and lasted until 11:00 a.m. From 11:00 a.m. to 11:20 a.m. the respondent had a snack, followed by relax/do nothing from 11:20 a.m. to 12:00 p.m. The respondent returned to

Table 1. Example of the Consumption and Frequency of On-The-Job Leisure. ATUS 2012.

(1) Start Time	(2) Finish Time	(3) Activity Type	(4) Duration
8:00 a.m.	11:00 a.m.	Market work	3.00
11:00 a.m.	11:20 a.m.	Meals or snacks in other places	0.33
11:20 a.m.	12:00 p.m.	Relax/do nothing	0.66
12:00 p.m.	2:10 p.m.	Market work	2.16
2:10 p.m.	2:20 p.m.	Work breaks	0.16
2:20 p.m.	4:40 p.m.	Market work	2.33
Time at work (hours)			8.66
Time working (hours)			7.50
Consumption of on-the-job leisure (hours)			1.16
Number of on-the-job leisure episodes			2.00
Working time until consuming on-the-job leisure (hours)			2.50

work at 12:00 p.m., finishing this second work spell at 2:10 to have a lunch break. The third work spell started at 2:20 p.m. and lasted until 4:40 p.m.

The consumption of on-the-job leisure was 1 hour and 10 minutes. Of this time, the respondent spent 40 minutes in leisure activities (relax/do nothing), while the remaining 30 minutes were spent in meals at work. There are two on-the-job leisure episodes during the 1 hour and 10 minutes of on-the-job leisure. A first episode of on-the-job leisure between 11:00 and 12:00, with one passive leisure activity and a meal at work, and a second on-the-job leisure episode between 2:10 p.m. and 2:20 p.m. with a meal at work. Similarly, the respondent worked for an average of two and a half hours until consuming on-the-job leisure, which is calculated by dividing the 7 hours and 30 minutes that the respondent is working over the 3 work spells recorded in the diary.

Table 2 shows the average amount of market work time, and the average consumption of on-the-job leisure for our main sample of full-time workers. Workers devote an average of 8 hours and 51 minutes (8.85 hours) to market work activities, and 1 hour and 19 minutes (1.32 hours) to on-the-job leisure activities. From these two activities – market work time and on-the-job leisure – it follows that the time from when a worker starts his working day until he ends it is about 10 hours and 10 minutes at work (10.17 hours). From the total consumption of on-the-job leisure, 39% are meal-related activities, 25% is taken up by other non-work activities (mostly housework activities), and 5 and 16% are taken up by social and passive leisure activities, respectively. When we focus on the average number of on-the-job leisure episodes and the average time working until consuming on-the-job leisure, workers have 1.62 on-the-job leisure episodes and spend 4 hours uninterrupted time working until leisure. These figures are consistent with Gimenez-Nadal and Sevilla (2022).

Table 2. Consumption of On-The-Job Leisure, WBM ATUS 2010, 2012 and 2013, Workers Aged 21–65 on Working Days, With 60+ Minutes of Market Work and Well-Being Information for at Least One Market Work Episode.[a]

	Hours per Day	Standard Deviation	% of On-the-Job Consumption of Leisure
Time at work	10.173	(2.771)	
Time working	8.851	(2.298)	
On-the-job consumption of leisure	1.322	(1.737)	
Working time until consuming on-the-job leisure	4.017	(2.282)	
Number of on-the-job leisure episodes	1.629	(1.101)	
Composition of on-the-job leisure			
Leisure	0.356	(0.829)	26.92%
Social leisure	0.072	(0.326)	5.45%
Active leisure and exercise	0.071	(0.293)	5.38%
Passive leisure	0.213	(0.607)	16.10%
Meals at work and related	0.518	(0.479)	39.16%
Other non-work	0.324	(0.958)	24.50%
Housework	0.244	(0.707)	18.42%
Personal care	0.080	(0.502)	6.08%
Commuting	0.125	(0.419)	9.42%
Number of workers	3,501		

[a]Table A1 in the Appendix A describes the activities included in the variables measuring on-the-job leisure.

Note: Time at work, time working, consumption of on-the-job leisure and working time until on-the-job leisure are measured in hours per day.

Fig. 1 shows the percentage of workers in our sample who are either working or at on-the-job leisure, for every hour of the diary day. (See Appendix Table A2 for all the values, measured as the percentage of the total number of workers.). For example, at 10 a.m. around 87% of American full-time workers at work, 80% working and 7% at leisure. The proportion of workers who are working begins to increase from about 6 a.m., reaching a maximum of 75–80% around 11 a.m., with a decrease around 12 p.m. – perhaps a break for lunch – and an increase around 2 p.m., gradually decreasing again from about 2 p.m. The consumption of on-the-job leisure begins to increase after 8 a.m., reaching about 10% of workers right before 12 p.m. and peaking between 11:30 a.m. and 1 p.m. After 1 p.m. the proportion of workers at leisure gradually decreases.

Regarding the analysis of well-being, Table 3 shows that the average happiness level during work activities is 3.90, 2.77 for stress, 2.38 for tiredness, and less than 1 for both pain and sadness. Krueger (2007) documents similar levels of happiness, pain, sadness, stress, and tiredness during market work activities.

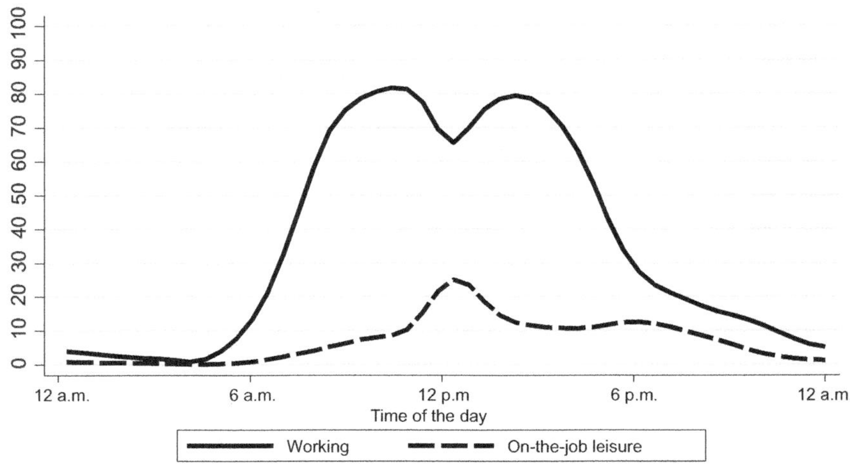

Fig. 1. Frequency of Work and On-The-Job Leisure as the Proportion of Workers Doing the Activity, WBM ATUS 2010, 2012 and 2013. The Time Window Considered for This Graph is 15 Minutes.

We also define a set of socio-demographic characteristics to account for the heterogeneity of individuals. These variables include gender, age, indicators for 12 years of education, 13–15 years of education, 16 years of education, and 16+ years of education, an indicator for living in a couple/married, the number of children under 18 in the household, and indicators for whether the youngest child in the household is less than 3 years or between 3 and 5 years old. Additionally, we control for the total number of activities reported and hours worked.[11]

Table 3 shows the summary statistics of the socio-demographic characteristics for the sample of 3,501 workers. Regarding education, 30% of workers have 12 years of education, while the rest of the education groups (13–15 years, 16 years, and 16+ years of education) represent 20% of workers each. The average age of workers is 42.39 years, and 62% of workers are male, 60% of workers are coupled/married, the number of children under 18 in worker's households is 0.75, while 10% and 7% of workers have their youngest child aged between 0 and 2, and 3 and 5, respectively. The number of different activities done by workers during their working days is 9.69.

4. WORKERS' EFFORT AND WELL-BEING AT WORK

To see the relationship between the consumption and frequency of on-the-job leisure, on the one hand, and workers' instantaneous well-being, on the other, we estimate three different models where we separately control for each indicator of the consumption and frequency of leisure.[12] We rely on Random Effects (RE) panel data estimators to account for the multilevel nature of our data in which

Table 3. Summary of Variables, WBM ATUS 2010, 2012 and 2013[a].

	Mean	Std. Dev.
Wellbeing (4,065 episodes)		
Happiness	3.903	(1.540)
Pain	0.836	(1.453)
Sadness	0.745	(2.934)
Stress	2.772	(5.401)
Tiredness	2.383	(2.149)
Socio-demographics (3,501 workers)		
Male	0.616	(0.486)
Age	42.394	(11.912)
12 years of education	0.307	(0.461)
13–15 years	0.206	(0.405)
16 years	0.205	(0.403)
16+ years	0.205	(0.404)
Coupled/Married	0.600	(0.490)
Number children <18	0.747	(1.131)
Age youngest child 0–2	0.098	(0.297)
Age youngest child 3–5	0.070	(0.254)
Has more than one job	0.089	(0.285)
Self-employed	0.102	(0.303)
Union worker	0.114	(0.318)
State unemployment rate	8.341	(1.848)
Number of activities in diary	9.696	(2.772)
Metabolic value of activity	2.329	(0.717)

[a]Standard deviations in parentheses. Well-being variables are measured on a 6-0 scale.

episodes are nested within individuals (Allison, 2009). Ferrer-i-Carbonell and Frijters (2004) show the importance of controlling for the unobserved heterogeneity of individuals when analyzing well-being/happiness. This methodology is similar to results obtained with OLS models, when clustering the error term $\varepsilon_{j,i}$ at the individual level (Kahneman & Krueger, 2006). We estimate the following Equation:

$$W_{ij} = \alpha_0 + \alpha_1 E_i + \alpha_2 X_i + \alpha_3 Z_i + \varepsilon_{ij} \qquad (1)$$

where "i" is the respondent, and j refers to the market work episode. (The analysis is restricted to market work episodes; we do not analyze activities classified as on-the-job leisure.) Our dependent variable, W_{ij}, refers to the standardized instantaneous well-being score for respondent i in episode j. We standardize these scores by subtracting the mean and dividing by the standard deviation. E_i represents one of our three measures of work effort, measured at the diary level. The coefficient of interest is α_1, capturing the average number of standard deviation changes in instantaneous well-being associated with a one-unit change in the work effort indicator.

The remaining controls included in X_i refer to person-specific socio-demographic characteristics: gender (ref.: male), age, the level of education (ref.: less than 12 years of education), living in a couple (ref.: not in a couple), the number of children under 18 in the household, whether the youngest child in the household is 0–2 or 3–5, and the total number of activities reported by the individual in the diary day. It is important to control for the number of hours worked, so that the relationship between the work effort indicators and feelings reported by workers during market work episodes is net of between-worker differences in market work hours; we thus control for work time (hours) on the diary day. We also account for differences in scaling across individuals (individuals' inherent optimism or pessimism, for example) by including an individual effect in Eq. (1), computed as the average in the feelings reported for individual "*i*" during non-market work activities (*Personal heterogeneity measure*). In this sense, from the three randomly-chosen episodes with well-being information for each worker, we compute the average of the feeling under analysis for all the episodes that are not market-work episodes. (This control does not include feelings during the market work episode under analysis).

Z_i represents a vector of job characteristics, which are important to consider, as the variation in on-the-job leisure across respondents could be reflecting other factors and not necessarily the composition of the workday between work tasks and non-work. This vector includes variables to control for whether the worker is unionized, the type of worker (e.g., self-employed vs. employed), and whether the worker has more than one job. We also include year indicators (ref.: 2010), and vectors of industry and occupational indicators.[13] It may also be relevant to control for the area unemployment rate, given that the ATUS Well-being module spanned 2010 (when unemployment was still close to its peak after the Great Recession) and 2012–2013 when it was sharply declining, given the results in Burda et al. (2020) suggesting a link between labor market slack and worker effort.

Panels A to C of Table 4 show the results of estimating Eq. (1) for each of the three indicators (The results for the rest of the controls are available upon request from the first author). We observe that the consumption of on-the-job leisure (the time workers spend in on-the-job leisure), the frequency of on-the-job leisure (the number of leisure episodes), and the uninterrupted time spent working before leisure, all are key determinants of instantaneous well-being during work activities. A decrease of one hour in the amount of on-the-job leisure is associated with an increase of 0.01 standard deviations in stress during work episodes, and a decrease of one on-the-job leisure episode is associated with an increase of 0.025 standard deviations in stress. Furthermore, a one-hour increase in the time spent working before consuming on-the-job leisure is associated with an increase of 0.013 standard deviations in stress during work episodes. Thus, less consumption of on-the-job leisure, fewer on-the job leisure episodes, and more uninterrupted time working are all related to higher levels of stress of workers during their work episodes. The effects are admittedly not large, although statistically significant; but they do provide some indicator of how a restructuring of work could improve workers' well-being.

We develop a set of alternative estimates to test for the robustness of our results. First, we use the Metabolic Equivalent (MET) value for market work activities, computed as the average value for each industry, rather than including industry fixed effects in the regressions.[14] Second, we control for total leisure of the individuals, as it could be that those with lower amounts of on-the-job leisure have more leisure outside work hours, and thus the relationship between stress and on-the-job leisure is driven by differences in leisure time outside work hours. Third, we exclude commuting as part of on-the-job leisure activities, since commuting time may be defensible as a measured job/person characteristic (location of the job vs. residential choice) to potentially include as a control. We estimate Eq. (1) excluding commuting time as part of on-the-job leisure activities, and include the total amount of commuting time as a control. The three sets of results – available upon request – are robust to our main results.

5. CONCLUSIONS

We analyze effort at work and well-being while at work. We analyze the structure of work tasks in the US, as a measure of worker effort, in three dimensions: the amount of on-the-job leisure, the number of on-the-job leisure episodes, and the uninterrupted time working until on-the-job leisure is enjoyed. We find that the amount and frequency of on-the-job leisure are important determinants of the stress felt during work activities.

How firm-level interventions that increase well-being while at work play out in real-world settings remains an open question in the literature, and here we focus on the relationship between the structure of work tasks and workers' instantaneous well-being. The structure of work tasks should be considered by employers in designing the flow of work, in the sense that they should try to avoid having employees working for too long a time before a break for some kind of leisure. This could be achieved through scheduled breaks, where workers would be asked to stop at regular times. This would enhance the well-being of workers, and thus the productivity of firms, consistent with the notion of Hamermesh (1990) that more closely monitoring workers would yield returns to firms.

Our research presents several limitations. First, the data are a cross-section of individuals, and thus we cannot talk about a causal link between our indicators and the level of well-being at work. Second, the ATUS includes information on well-being from three episodes per diary only, which prevents us from doing a more in-depth analysis. For instance, if we had information on all the episodes in the workers' time diaries, we could directly compare the duration of market work activities for the same individuals, analyzing whether more uninterrupted time working before a break is related to more stress, net of individual personal heterogeneity. In this last instance, the use of the 2014 United Kingdom Time Use

Table 4. On-The-Job Leisure and Instantaneous Well-Being While at Work, WBM ATUS 2010, 2012 and 2013.

Number of Episodes 4,065 Number of Workers 3,501	Happiness	Pain	Sadness	Stress	Tiredness
Panel A: Consumption of on-the-job leisure					
Consumption of on-the-job leisure	0.011	0.013	−0.010	−0.007**	0.011
	(0.008)	(0.011)	(0.007)	(0.003)	(0.008)
Personal heterogeneity measure	0.383***	0.126*	0.216***	0.106**	0.163***
	(0.013)	(0.070)	(0.056)	(0.042)	(0.033)
Constant	−1.598***	−0.385	−0.307	−0.408*	−0.389**
	(0.196)	(0.289)	(0.190)	(0.226)	(0.173)
R^2	0.314	0.161	0.292	0.184	0.115
Panel B: Number of on-the-job leisure episodes					
Number of on-the-job leisure episodes	0.007	0.013	−0.009	−0.025***	−0.017
	(0.012)	(0.010)	(0.013)	(0.007)	(0.014)
Personal heterogeneity measure	0.382***	0.126*	0.216***	0.106**	0.162***
	(0.013)	(0.070)	(0.056)	(0.042)	(0.033)
Constant	−1.593***	−0.378	−0.312	−0.423*	−0.399**
	(0.197)	(0.286)	(0.190)	(0.224)	(0.175)
R^2	0.314	0.161	0.292	0.186	0.115
Panel C: Working time until consuming on-the-job leisure					
Working time until consuming on-the-job leisure	−0.004	−0.007	0.004	0.013***	0.004
	(0.008)	(0.009)	(0.008)	(0.003)	(0.007)
Personal heterogeneity measure	0.382***	0.126*	0.216***	0.106**	0.162***
	(0.013)	(0.070)	(0.056)	(0.042)	(0.033)

Constant	−1.585***	−0.365	−0.317*	−0.445**	−0.400**
	(0.197)	(0.278)	(0.191)	(0.224)	(0.177)
R^2	0.314	0.161	0.292	0.185	0.115

[a]Additional covariates include gender (ref.: male), age, dummy for secondary and university education (ref.: primary education), dummy for living in couple (ref.: not in couple), the number of children under 18 in the household, the presence of one child under 6 in the household, work time (hours) on the diary day, the total number of activities reported by the individual on the diary day, and the individual effect (personal heterogeneity measure). We also control for whether the worker is a union worker, whether the worker is self-employed or employed, and whether the worker has more than one job. We include year dummies (ref.: 2010), and industry and occupational dummies. *Significant at the 10% level; **significant at the 5% level; ***significant at the 1% level.

Survey, which contains information on the enjoyment of individuals for all episodes in diaries, could be used to perform a more complete analysis of the structure of work.

ACKNOWLEDGMENTS

Giménez-Nadal and Molina acknowledge funding from the Spanish Ministry of Science and Innovation (Project PID 2019:108348RA-I00), and from the Government of Aragón (Grant S32_20R). Sevilla acknowledges funding from the European Research Council (CoG PARENTIME-770839).

NOTES

1. Our definition of on-the-job leisure differs from regulated or scheduled rest breaks at work. The concept of on-the-job leisure measured here is broader than regulated or scheduled rest breaks, as our measure include these breaks and other activities. Furthermore, while the former may to a certain extent be voluntary for workers and may be a reflection of their choice, the latter are regulated and may not reflect their choice. We follow Hamermesh (1990) who differentiated between periods that may be regulated and scheduled (lunch and coffee breaks) and other breaks.
2. Life satisfaction and happiness are studied to complement monetary indicators, such as income per capita, while job satisfaction is measured to complement the hourly wage as a purely monetary and objective measure of work (Clark et al., 2018).
3. The ATUS in the year 2021 also includes a well-being module, but the COVID-19 outbreak makes this data non-comparable.
4. The ATUS is considered the official time use survey of the US. It is sponsored by the Bureau of Labor Statistics, and conducted as part of the Current Population Survey (CPS) by the US Census Bureau. The ATUS data are maintained in the Integrated Public Use Microdata Series (IPUMS) of the Institute for Social Research and Data Innovation of the University of Minnesota (Hofferth et al., 2015).
5. For a methodological review of time use surveys, see Gimenez-Nadal and Molina (2022).
6. The type of well-being that is measured with these questions refers to experienced utility (Kahneman, 2000; Kahneman et al., 2004; Kahneman & Krueger, 2006; Kahneman et al., 1997), defined as the continuous hedonic flow of pleasure or pain. It represents a measure of subjective well-being that assesses the emotional, affective components of happiness. We refer to these measures as "instantaneous well-being."
7. See Stone et al. (2018) for an in-depth description of the ATUS Well-Being Module, including how the selection of the three randomly selected episodes is done.
8. Around 1% of workers who report positive market work spend less than 60 minutes in work during the diary day.
9. The fact that only those workers with at least one market work episode with well-being information are selected may induce sample selection, as those with more or longer market work episodes are more likely to be selected for the analysis of well-being. Comparing the sample of analyzed workers and a group of similar workers without well-being information for market work episodes, we observe that our sample of workers has comparatively more market work time, more on-the-job leisure, and more on-the-job leisure episodes, and spends less time working until consuming on-the-job leisure. Furthermore, there is a larger proportion of males with a lower level of education, and a greater likelihood of having more than one job, in comparison to workers without well-being information in market work activities.

10. As argued by Burda et al. (2020), "an important question is what reported non-work actually represents. This is a measure of not working while at work and is what the respondent believes it to be, just as reported hours of work in the household surveys underlying the immense literature on labor supply represent what respondents believe their work time to be. Unlike recall about past weekly hours in those surveys, non-work time in the ATUS is specifically limited to and anchored by the time an individual spends at the workplace on the randomly selected diary day. These data are based on one-day recall, and errors should thus be fewer than those in the one-week recall of hours of work that are used in most labor force surveys."

11. To compute the number of different activities in the diary, we recode the original activity codes to the 69-activity classification used by the Multinational Time Use Study, and from that classification we count the number of different activities done by the diarist. For instance, if the respondent performed personal care, e.g., bathing, we count this activity once, independently of whether there are two or more episodes of personal care in the diary.

12. We estimate separate regressions for each on-the-job leisure indicator to avoid problems of multi-collinearity between them. The correlations between the consumption of on-the-job leisure and the number of leisure episodes is 0.48, is −0.43 for consumption of on-the-job leisure and the uninterrupted working time until leisure, and is −0.70 between the number of leisure episodes and the uninterrupted working time until leisure.

13. The industry and occupation classifications used are the two-digit levels offered by the ATUS, which contains 22 occupations and 51 industries.

14. The METVALUE reports the metabolic equivalent (MET) associated with ATUS primary activity codes. This is an activity-level variable and each METVALUE is computed by aggregating and averaging MET values associated with lexicon example activities for each 6-digit activity level. METVALUE associated with Work (050001 and 050002) is derived from an extensive and iterative process of averaging MET values for all 22 occupational categories. (See https://www.atusdata.org/atus-action/variables/METVALUE#description_section for additional information.)

REFERENCES

Aguiar, M., & Hurst, E. (2007). Measuring trends in leisure: The allocation of time over five decades. *Quarterly Journal of Economics*, *115*, 969–1006.

Allison, P. D. (2009). *Fixed effects regression models*. Series: Quantitative applications in the social sciences. Sage.

Böckerman, P., & Ilmakunnas, P. (2012). The job satisfaction-productivity nexus: A study using matched survey and register data. *Industrial and Labor Relations Review*, *65*, 244–262.

Bóo, F. L., Lucia, M., & Pagés, C. (2010). Part-time work, gender and job satisfaction: Evidence from a developing country. *Journal of Development Studies*, *46*, 1543–1571.

Bryson, A., Forth, J., & Stokes, L. (2017). Does employees' subjective well-being affect workplace performance? *Human Relations*, *70*, 1017–1037.

Burda, M., Genadek, K. R., & Hamermesh, D. S. (2020). Unemployment and effort at work. *Economica*, *347*, 662–681.

Clark, A. E. (1996). Job satisfaction in Britain. *British Journal of Industrial Relations*, *34*, 189–217.

Clark, A. E. (1997). Job satisfaction and gender: Why are women so happy at work? *Labour Economics*, *4*, 341–372.

Clark, A. E., Flèche, S., Layard, R., Powdthavee, N., & Ward, G. (2018). *The origins of happiness. The science of well-being over the life course*. Princeton University Press.

Clark, A. E., Frijters, P., & Shields, M. A. (2008). Relative income, happiness, and utility: An explanation for the Easterlin paradox and other puzzles. *Journal of Economic Literature*, *46*, 95–144.

Clark, A., Oswald, A., & Warr, P. (1996). Is job satisfaction U-shaped in age? *Journal of Occupational and Organizational Psychology*, *69*, 57–81.

Dickinson, D. L. (1999). An experimental examination of labor supply and work intensities. *Journal of Labor Economics*, *17*, 638–670.

Easterlin, R. A. (1995). Will raising the incomes of all increase the happiness of all? *Journal of Economic Behavior & Organization*, *27*, 35–47.

Edmans, A. (2012). The link between job satisfaction and firm value, with implications for corporate social responsibility. *Academy of Management Perspectives*, *26*, 4.

Erro-Garcés, A., & Ferreira, S. (2019). Do better workplace environmental conditions improve job satisfaction? *Journal of Cleaner Production*, *219*, 936–948.

Ferrer-i-Carbonell, A., & Frijters, P. (2004). How important is methodology for the estimates of the determinants of happiness? *Economic Journal*, *114*, 641–659.

García-Mainar, I., & Montuenga-Gómez, V. M. (2020). Over-qualification and the dimensions of job satisfaction. *Social Indicators Research*, *147*, 591–620.

Gimenez-Nadal, J. I., & Molina, J. A. (2022). Time use surveys. In K. F. Zimmermann (Ed.), *Handbook of labor, human resources and population economics*. Springer.

Gimenez-Nadal, J. I., & Sevilla, A. (2012). Trends in time allocation: A cross-country analysis. *European Economic Review*, *56*, 1338–1359.

Gimenez-Nadal, J. I., & Sevilla, A. (2022). *Work effort in the UK: Trends and explanations*. IZA DP No. 15329.

Guryan, J., Hurst, E., & Kearney, M. (2008). Parental education and parental time with children. *The Journal of Economic Perspectives*, *22*, 23–46.

Hamermesh, D. S. (1990). Shirking or productive schmoozing: Wages and the allocation of time at work. *Industrial and Labor Relations Review*, *43*, 121s–133s.

Herzberg, F. (1987). *One more time: How do you motivate your employees*. Harvard Business Review Press.

Hofferth, S. L., Flood, S. M., & Sobek, M. (2015). *American time use survey data extract builder: Version 2.5 [dataset]*. University of Maryland and University of Minnesota.

Izvercian, M., Potra, S., & Ivascu, L. (2016). Job satisfaction variables: A grounded theory approach. *Procedia- Social and Behavioral Sciences*, *221*, 86–94.

Kahneman, D. (2000). Evaluation by moments: Past and future. In D. Kahneman & A. Tversky (Eds.), *Choices, values and frames* Chapter 38. Cambridge University Press and the Russell Sage Foundation.

Kahneman, D., & Krueger, A. B. (2006). Developments in the measurement of subjective well-being. *The Journal of Economic Perspectives*, *20*, 3–24.

Kahneman, D., Krueger, A. B., Schkade, D., Schwarz, N., & Stone, A. (2004). A survey method for characterizing daily life experience: The day reconstruction method. *Science*, *3*, 1776–1780.

Kahneman, D., Wakker, P. P., & Sarin, R. (1997). Back to Bentham? Explorations of experienced utility. *Quarterly Journal of Economics*, *112*, 375–405.

Krueger, A. B. (2007). Are we having more fun yet? Categorizing and evaluating changes in time allocation. *Brookings Papers on Economic Activity*, *2*, 193–217.

Krumbiegel, K., Maertens, M., & Wollni, M. (2018). The role of fairtrade certification for wages and job satisfaction of plantation workers. *World Development*, *102*, 195–212.

Oswald, A., Proto, E., & Sgroi, D. (2015). Happiness and productivity. *Journal of Labor Economics*, *33*, 789–822.

Razafindrakoto, M., & Roubaud, F. (2013). Job satisfaction in eight African cities. *Urban Labor Markets in Sub-Saharan Africa*, 109–133.

Sousa-Poza, A., & Sousa-Poza, A. A. (2000). Well-being at work: A cross-national analysis of the levels and determinants of job satisfaction. *The Journal of Socio-Economics*, *29*, 517–538.

Stone, A. A., Schneider, S., Krueger, A. B., Schwartz, J. E., & Deaton, A. (2018). Experiential well-being data from the American Time Use Survey: Comparisons with other methods and analytic illustrations with age and income. *Social Indicators Research*, *136*, 359–378.

van Praag, B. M. S., Frijters, P., & Ferrer-i-Carbonell, A. (2003). The anatomy of subjective well-being. *Journal of Economic Behavior & Organization*, *51*, 29–49.

Wen, X., Gu, L., & Wen, S. (2019). Job satisfaction and job engagement: Empirical evidence from food safety regulators in Guangdong, China. *Journal of Cleaner Production*, *208*, 999–1008.

APPENDIX

Table A1. Definition of On-the-Job Leisure Activities.

Meals at Work	Meals at work, meals or snacks in other places
Leisure-related activities	
Social leisure	Voluntary, civic, organizational act; worship and religion; other public event, venue; restaurant, café, bar, pub; party, social event, gambling; receive or visit friends; voluntary/civic/religious travel
Active leisure	Work breaks, leisure and other education or training; pet care (not walk dog); general out-of-home leisure; attend sporting event; cinema, theater, opera, concert; general sport or exercise; walking; cycling; other outside recreation; gardening/pick mushrooms; walk dogs; general indoor leisure; art or music; knit, crafts or hobbies; no activity, imputed or recorded transport; other travel; no recorded activity
Passive leisure	Conversation (in person, phone); games (social and solitary)/other in-home social; correspondence (not e-mail); relax, think, do nothing; read; listen to music or other audio content; listen to radio; watch TV, video, DVD; computer games; e-mail, surf internet, computing; travel to and from work
Other non-work activities	
Personal Care	Imputed personal or household care; sleep and naps; imputed sleep; wash, dress, care for self; consume other services
Housework	Regular schooling, education; homework; food preparation, cooking; set table, wash/put away dishes; cleaning; laundry, ironing, clothing repair; maintain home/vehicle, including collect fuel; other domestic work; purchase goods; consume personal care services; physical, medical child care; teach, help with homework; read to, talk or play with child; supervise, accompany, other child care; adult care; education travel; child/adult care travel; shop, person/household care travel
Commuting	Travel to/from work

Notes: Data come from 2010, 2012 and 2013 ATUS WBM.

Table A2. Timing of Work Activities, in Percentage Points.

Time Band	Working	On-The-Job Leisure	At Work	Time Band	Working	On-The-Job Leisure	At Work
				Time band 44	79.26	9.75	89.01
				Time band 45	82.03	9.55	91.58
				Time band 46	75.77	14.37	90.14
				Time band 47	74.64	16.43	91.07
				Time band 48	60.78	31.52	92.30
Time band 1	4.21	0.72	4.93	Time band 49	62.01	31.62	93.63
Time band 2	3.49	0.72	4.21	Time band 50	61.81	32.55	94.35
Time band 3	3.80	0.41	4.21	Time band 51	66.74	28.34	95.07
Time band 4	3.59	0.21	3.80	Time band 52	70.12	24.64	94.76
Time band 5	3.18	0.21	3.39	Time band 53	73.51	20.43	93.94
Time band 6	2.88	0.31	3.18	Time band 54	76.80	15.81	92.61
Time band 7	2.77	0.21	2.98	Time band 55	79.77	13.04	92.81
Time band 8	2.16	0.41	2.57	Time band 56	76.39	13.76	90.14
Time band 9	2.05	0.41	2.46	Time band 57	80.80	12.53	93.33
Time band 10	2.05	0.31	2.36	Time band 58	79.16	10.37	89.53
Time band 11	2.16	0.31	2.46	Time band 59	81.42	9.55	90.97
Time band 12	1.75	0.21	1.95	Time band 60	75.67	11.19	86.86
Time band 13	1.85	0.21	2.05	Time band 61	79.26	10.68	89.94
Time band 14	1.64	0.10	1.75	Time band 62	71.97	10.27	82.24
Time band 15	1.64	0.10	1.75	Time band 63	73.61	9.65	83.27
Time band 16	0.00	0.00	0.00	Time band 64	65.30	10.06	75.36
Time band 17	0.00	0.00	0.00	Time band 65	65.81	9.86	75.67
Time band 18	0.41	0.00	0.41	Time band 66	60.78	9.86	70.64
Time band 19	1.03	0.00	1.03	Time band 67	60.27	9.34	69.61
Time band 20	2.26	0.00	2.26	Time band 68	48.26	11.50	59.75
Time band 21	3.49	0.00	3.49	Time band 69	46.20	11.19	57.39
Time band 22	5.54	0.10	5.65	Time band 70	36.96	12.01	48.97
Time band 23	6.78	0.41	7.19	Time band 71	35.93	11.70	47.64
Time band 24	10.58	0.72	11.29	Time band 72	27.21	13.04	40.25
Time band 25	12.83	0.92	13.76	Time band 73	27.31	13.04	40.35
Time band 26	16.12	1.85	17.97	Time band 74	23.20	13.66	36.86
Time band 27	20.43	1.95	22.38	Time band 75	23.61	13.14	36.76
Time band 28	30.60	2.26	32.85	Time band 76	20.12	12.42	32.55
Time band 29	35.63	2.46	38.09	Time band 77	20.95	12.22	33.16
Time band 30	42.09	3.59	45.69	Time band 78	18.17	10.99	29.16
Time band 31	46.82	3.70	50.51	Time band 79	18.17	10.58	28.75
Time band 32	57.39	5.13	62.53	Time band 80	16.32	10.06	26.39
Time band 33	64.07	5.03	69.10	Time band 81	16.63	9.65	26.28
Time band 34	66.84	5.75	72.59	Time band 82	15.30	8.11	23.41
Time band 35	71.36	5.44	76.80	Time band 83	15.40	7.39	22.79
Time band 36	74.03	8.21	82.24	Time band 84	14.07	5.54	19.61
Time band 37	78.54	7.39	85.93	Time band 85	13.76	4.72	18.48
Time band 38	79.77	6.98	86.76	Time band 86	13.04	3.80	16.84

Table A2. *(Continued)*

Time Band	Working	On-The-Job Leisure	At Work	Time Band	Working	On-The-Job Leisure	At Work
Time band 39	81.31	6.78	88.09	Time band 87	12.63	3.59	16.22
Time band 40	78.44	8.93	87.37	Time band 88	9.65	3.29	12.94
Time band 41	81.52	9.45	90.97	Time band 89	10.27	2.77	13.04
Time band 42	82.03	7.60	89.63	Time band 90	8.62	1.75	10.37
Time band 43	83.06	6.26	89.32	Time band 91	7.91	1.34	9.24
				Time band 92	6.37	1.44	7.80
				Time band 93	6.16	1.23	7.39
				Time band 94	5.96	1.03	6.98
				Time band 95	5.75	0.92	6.67
				Time band 96	4.52	0.82	5.34

Notes: Data from 2010, 2012 and 2013 ATUS WBM.

CHANGES IN CHILDREN'S TIME USE, INDIA 1998–2019

Matthew Gibson, Maulik Jagnani and Hemant K. Pullabhotla

ABSTRACT

Using the two waves of the India Time Use Survey, 1998–1999 and 2019, we document a 110-minute (30%) increase in average daily learning time. The largest offsetting decrease was in work time: 61 minutes. The composition of leisure changed, with television rising by 19 minutes, while talking fell by 10 minutes and games by 17 minutes. We then implement a Gelbach decomposition, showing that 68 minutes of the unconditional learning increase are predicted by demographic covariates. Of these predictors the most important are a child's state of residence and usual principal activity, which captures extensive-margin transitions into schooling.

Keywords: Time use; children; education; child labor; leisure; India

1. INTRODUCTION

Childhood investments have large effects on outcomes later in life, including health (Heckman, 2007), labor earnings (Chetty et al., 2011), and accumulation of human capital (Almond et al., 2018). Such investments plausibly affect macroeconomic growth as well (Mankiw et al., 1992). Nearly all childhood time use is entangled with investment. Some activities, like schooling or job training, are themselves investments, while others, like leisure, may come at the opportunity cost of investments.[1] Therefore, studying children's time use is important, particularly in developing countries.

As a diverse developing country with some 361 million children aged 14 or under as of 2020 (World Bank, 2022a), India comprises a natural setting for such a study. This is doubly so because, in contrast to the intense interest from both

Time Use in Economics
Research in Labor Economics, Volume 51, 55–88

ISSN: 0147-9121/doi:10.1108/S0147-912120230000051003

policymakers and researchers in studying time spent in school, we know extremely little about how children in India spend their time outside of school.[2]

This chapter draws on two waves of the India Time Use Survey (ITUS) to investigate how the allocation of time by children has changed in India between 1998 and 2019, a period of immense economic, social, and political change (Ahluwalia, 2002; Marelli & Signorelli, 2011; Palshikar et al., 2017; World Bank, 2022b). While the chapter pays particular attention to time spent learning, both inside and outside school, it addresses the entire time budget, including work, home production, and leisure (e.g. television). The chapter then uses the method of Gelbach (2016) to (i) estimate the share of the change that can be predicted by observable characteristics; and (ii) decompose the predictable share of the change into the contributions of individual covariates, e.g. sex and age.

We find that mean learning time increased by 110 minutes per day, from 310 minutes in 1998 to 420 minutes in 2019. In proportional terms this is an increase of 30%.[3] Conditional on observable child and household characteristics, the unpredicted learning change across waves is 42 minutes.[4] The largest contributors to the discrepancy are usual-activity fixed effects, particularly the indicator for schooling, suggesting that extensive-margin transitions into schooling account for much of the unconditional learning increase. State fixed effects are also quantitatively important predictors of learning time. This suggests that persistent state-specific factors like the bicycle program in Bihar (Muralidharan & Prakash, 2017) and state-level variation in implementation of national policies, like the NREGA public employment scheme (Imbert & Papp, 2015), may matter.[5] Also important for the gap between conditional and unconditional learning changes are dwelling type fixed effects, which plausibly proxy for wealth.[6] These findings are consistent with the long literature on the income–education relationship (Løken, 2010).

As the time constraint always binds, increased learning time must have been offset by declines in other time uses. Work declined by 61 minutes, home production by 23 minutes, and leisure by 26 minutes. Conditional on observables, the unpredicted declines are 20 (work), 14 (home production), and 9 minutes (leisure), respectively. Because usual-activity fixed effects condition on the extensive margin of work, the conditional 20-minute decline in work represents an intensive-margin change.

We also investigate changes in the composition of leisure time. While total leisure decreased between 1998–1999 and 2019, time spent watching television increased by 19 minutes. Time spent "talking, conversing, chatting" decreased by 10 minutes, and time spent "playing games and other pastime activities" decreased by 17 minutes. Our results *do not* establish a causal link between increases in television time and decreases in more socially connected forms of leisure. They do, however, suggest that Putnam's *Bowling Alone* hypothesis may warrant investigation in India, a setting quite different from the US context in which it was conceived (Putnam, 2001).

This chapter contributes to two literatures. The first is on time allocation in developing countries. Because high-quality time use surveys in developing countries are uncommon, existing literature is relatively sparse. Some papers rely upon public health surveys that were not designed based on survey research in time use. Garg et al. (2020), for example, use the China Health and Nutrition Survey to study the response of work time to extreme temperatures in China. The papers closest to ours are (i) Li (2023), which examines changes in women's work time across the two waves of the ITUS, and (ii) Jagnani (2022), which focuses on the causal effects of child sleep on human capital production using the 1998–1999 ITUS.[7] To the best of our knowledge, ours is the first chapter to study the full allocation of time among children in a developing country.

The second related literature is on education and child labor in India.[8] As a prominent example, Edmonds et al. (2009) investigate the effects of India's 1991 trade liberalization on the probabilities that a child's principal activity is work or schooling. More recently, Bharadwaj et al. (2020) evaluate India's 1986 ban on child labor, finding that the ban increased the probability of child employment. Our chapter makes two contributions to this strand of research. It corroborates previous work on children's usual principal activities and shows how changes in usual activity predict time-use changes. In addition, our study estimates intensive-margin changes in child learning and work over the last two decades.[9]

The rest of the chapter proceeds as follows. Section 2 presents a brief overview of the education sector and policies in India relevant to our analysis period. Section 3 describes the ITUS data. Section 4 explains our use of the Gelbach decomposition to study the changes in time use across ITUS waves. Section 5 presents empirical results and Section 6 concludes.

2. INSTITUTIONAL BACKGROUND

India's education sector is subject to both central (federal) and state-level policies. The central government lays down national policies and guidelines that provide an overall framework for national education policies and programs. However, individual state governments have significant leeway in deciding school policies at the local level and implementing national-level programs. For instance, in 1995, the central government initiated the National Programme of Nutritional Support to Primary Education (popularly known as the Midday Meal Scheme) to provide nutritious, in-school meals to all public schools. However, the implementation and coverage of the scheme varied across states, and the program became operational across all states only by 2004 (Kaur, 2021; Singh et al., 2014). As with the midday meal program, implementation of education and other social sector schemes often varies across states. Our analysis includes state fixed effects to evaluate the role of state-specific factors in predicting the change in children's time use over the 1998–2019 period.

At the start of our sample period, the central guiding policy governing the education sector was the National Policy on Education (NPE) of 1986. The policy made expanding primary education a national priority and committed to increasing resources allocated toward the education sector. The NPE laid the groundwork for a number of centrally sponsored schemes to increase primary enrollment during the 1990s. In addition to the Midday Meal Scheme mentioned earlier, the central government also launched the District Primary Education Program (DPEP) to target underserved districts (World Bank, 2009). Evaluations of DPEP have found that it increased school attendance and educational attainment (Azam & Saing, 2017; Jalan & Glinksya, 2013). These policy efforts resulted in a modest increase in net primary school enrollment from 77% in 1990 to 80% by 2000 (World Bank, 2022c). Building on these programs, the central government initiated the National Program for Universal Elementary Education, also known as the Sarva Shiksha Abhiyan (SSA), in 2001. The SSA aimed for universal enrollment of all 6- to 14-year-olds in schools and retention until grade eight. Broadly these educational policies increased school attendance among low-income rural children, particularly girls (Datta Gupta et al., 2018). The goal of universal education was written into law through the Right to Education (RTE) of 2009. The RTE law made free and compulsory education up to the age of 14 a fundamental, constitutional right.

In conjunction with this increased impetus toward universal education, India also witnessed a strengthening of child labor laws during the course of our sample period. Landmark legislation banning child labor in specific high-risk industries began with the Child Labor (Prohibition and Regulation) Act of 1986. This law made 14 years the uniform age used to define "child" labor and laid down specific penalties for law violations (Bharadwaj et al., 2020). The initial list of industries and sectors included in the 1986 law expanded to cover more industries in the ensuing years. Finally, by 2016, the Child Labor Act was amended to prohibit the use of child labor in all occupations.

The period corresponding to these policy changes saw net primary enrollment grow to 92% by 2013 (World Bank, 2022c), and reach 94.6% by 2020 (UNESCO). While this chapter focuses on intensive-margin changes in learning time, our decomposition analysis also provides estimates of changes in children's time allocation associated with the extensive-margin increase in school enrollment over our sample period (see Section 5 and Fig. A4).

3. DATA

All data used in this chapter are from the India Time Use Survey. Wave one of the ITUS occurred from July 1998 through June 1999 and covered 52 districts in six states: Gujarat, Haryana, Madhya Pradesh, Meghalaya, Odisha, and Tamil Nadu. These states were intended to capture regional variation in time allocations. Households were randomly sampled within each state, and the resulting samples are representative at the state level when used with included sampling weights. Unusually among time-use surveys, the ITUS records time diaries for all household members aged six years or older. In keeping with the recommendations of survey research (Field et al., 2022; Giménez-Nadal & Molina, 2022; Seymour et al., 2017), the ITUS asks respondents for complete 24-hour (1440-minute) time diaries on the day prior to the survey interview. A given respondent was interviewed up to three times, recording a diary for a normal day, an abnormal day (e.g. a festival day), and a "weekly variant" (usually a Sunday).[10] Parents were permitted to assist young children in responding (Jagnani, 2022). Activities were coded using a nested three-digit classification. For example, in the 1998–1999 survey activities 7xx were "learning," and activity 711 was "general education: school/university/other educational institutions attendance." The ITUS survey also included common demographic questions such as sex, monthly expenditure, and religion.

Wave two of the ITUS occurred in 2019 and covered all states in India. Again random sampling was conducted at the household level, and samples are representative at the state level when used with included sampling weights. Again children aged six years or older were included. The format of the 24-hour time diaries was similar to that of the first wave, but an amended activity classification was employed. A given respondent could contribute only one diary, which was classified as covering either a normal or an abnormal day.[11] Respondents could report up to three simultaneous activities for a given period of time, with one identified as primary. To maintain comparability with the 1998–1999 ITUS and ensure respondents faced an adding-up constraint, we use only primary activities in this analysis.

Our sample was constructed as follows. Each ITUS wave was restricted to the six states covered in both 1998–1999 and 2019. Because the state of Chhattisgarh was still part of Madhya Pradesh in 1998–1999, it was included in the 2019 sample.[12] The data were further restricted to children aged six to 16 years (school age) and diaries for normal days (which cover both weekdays and weekends in both waves). Our final sample includes 29,865 diaries from just as many children, with 13,969 from 1998–1999 and 15,896 from 2019.

Following Li (2023), we created a mapping from three-digit 2019 activity codes to one-digit 1998–1999 activity codes. This task was straightforward, requiring no obviously consequential researcher decisions. For example, the 2019 code "620: homework, being tutored, course review, research and activities related to formal education" was mapped to the 1998–1999 code "7: learning." Additionally, for our initial description of children's time allocation, we aggregated one-digit 1998–1999 codes as follows. "Primary production activities," "secondary activities," and "trade, business, and services" were classified as work. "Household maintenance, management, and shopping for own household," "care for children, the sick, elderly, and disabled for own household," and "community services and help to other households" were classified as home production. "Social and cultural activities, mass media, etc." and "personal care and self-maintenance" were classified as leisure. Learning was not aggregated with other one-digit time uses.

Changes in the survey instrument across the ITUS waves make mapping between three-digit 1998–1999 and 2019 codes difficult, particularly for work. Nonetheless, we were able to create a mapping across mutually exclusive and exhaustive time uses within one-digit learning and leisure. For example, the 2019 code "620: homework, being tutored, course review, research and activities related to formal education" was mapped to the 1998–1999 code "721: studies, homework, and course review related to general education." Three-digit codes without an obvious match were placed into an "other learning" or "other leisure" category.

Table 1 presents weighted means for our sample by ITUS wave. The share of children reporting school as their usual principal activity increases from 73% in 1998–1999 to 93% in 2019.[13] The 1998–1999 ITUS share is similar to the 74.6% calculated by Bharadwaj et al. (2020) from the 1987–1998 and 1993–1994 National Sample Surveys (NSS), but lower than the 85% calculated by Edmonds et al. (2009) from the 1999 to 2000 NSS. This difference may arise from the national sampling frame of the NSS. The 2019 ITUS share is similar to the 94.6% share reported by UNESCO for 2020. These comparisons to prior work provide some evidence that the ITUS sample is reasonably representative of broad extensive-margin schooling trends in India. Descriptive statistics for other usual principal activity and state indicators appear in Table A1.

Table 1 also shows that nominal monthly expenditure (in 000 Rupees) increases by a factor greater than three, from 2,650 to 9,400. Because of the difficulty of measuring income in developing countries, and in keeping with standard practice, ITUS uses consumption expenditure to capture household well-being (Meyer & Sullivan, 2003). The World Bank (2000) notes that consumption expenditure is the preferred indicator "for practical reasons of reliability and because consumption is thought to better capture long-run welfare

Table 1. ITUS Descriptive Statistics[a].

	1998	2019
Leisure	1003.0	977.0
Home prod.	49.0	26.1
Work	78.1	16.7
Learning	309.9	420.2
Female	0.46	0.47
Age	11.3	11.5
School	0.73	0.93
Monthly exp.	2.65	9.40
Rural	0.73	0.71
Landless	0.57	0.56
Household size	5.47	4.98
Scheduled tribe	0.14	0.19
Scheduled caste	0.16	0.17
Hinduism	0.90	0.91
Islam	0.063	0.053

[a]Data are from the 1998–1999 and 2019 ITUS. Weighted means are computed using sampling weights from the ITUS. Time-use classification is based on 1-digit 1998 activity codes: 8–9 leisure, 4–6 home production, 1–3 work, and 7 learning. Time-use units are minutes per day. The variable labeled "School" indicates a child's usual principal activity is "Attended educational institution." Descriptive statistics for other usual principal activity and state indicators appear in Table A1. Monthly expenditure is given in thousands of nominal Rupees (000 Rs). Female, rural, landless, scheduled tribe, scheduled caste, Hinduism, and Islam are proportions (shares). Household size is a count of people.

levels than current income" (p. 17). The fraction of rural respondents falls from 73 to 71% in Table 1, consistent with ongoing urbanization. Household size decreases from 5.5 to 5.0.

Note that the fraction of children in Table 1 with "scheduled tribe" status increases from 14 to 19% across ITUS waves. "Scheduled castes" (SC) and "scheduled tribes" (ST) in India consist of groups who have historically been the target of social and economic discrimination stemming from traditional stratifications in Hindu society (Deshpande, 2000). The 1950 Constitution of India designated these caste and tribe groups as protected under various schedules (Tandon, 2018). Despite constitutional safeguards and affirmative action policies, on average SC and ST households have lower incomes (Mehta & Shah, 2003), higher mortality (Subramanian et al., 2006) and less sufficient nutrition (Van de Poel & Speybroeck, 2009) compared to the rest of the population.

4. EMPIRICAL STRATEGY

We begin by considering the following two simple regressions.

$$y_{it} = \beta_{\text{base}}\ Year2019 + \nu_{it} \tag{1}$$

$$y_{it} = \beta_{\text{full}}\ Year2019 + \mathbf{x}'\boldsymbol{\gamma} + \varepsilon_{it} \tag{2}$$

In these equations, y_{it} represents total time spent on a given activity in the 24 hours covered by the diary of individual i in survey year $t \in \{1998, 2019\}$. The indicator *Year2019* equals one for 2019 diaries and it follows that β_{base} is the change in average time spent on the given activity from the 1998–1999 wave to the 2019 wave. In Eq. (1), which we call the base specification, this is the unconditional or unadjusted change over time. Eq. (2), the full specification, includes a vector $\mathbf{x}$ of K observable covariates and corresponding parameters $\boldsymbol{\gamma}$, making β_{full} a conditional or adjusted change over time.[14]

The key insight of Gelbach (2016) is that the formula for omitted variable bias in ordinary least squares regression can be used to decompose the difference between β_{full} and β_{base} into the contributions of particular variables (or sets of variables).

$$\beta_{\text{full}} - \beta_{\text{base}} = \Sigma_k\, \eta_k \gamma_k \tag{3}$$

In Eq. (3), the parameters γ_k correspond to elements of $\boldsymbol{\gamma}$ in Eq. (2). That is, they are the marginal effects from the full regression model. The parameters η_k come from auxiliary regressions of each x_k on the 2019 indicator, controlling for all other variables in $\mathbf{x}$. This decomposition has several desirable properties. First, it is path-independent. One need not make an arbitrary choice of sequence that will influence the estimated contributions of the variables. Second, the Gelbach decomposition adds up: the sum of the variable-specific biases equals the aggregate difference across parameters in the base and full specifications (Fortin et al., 2011). Finally, Gelbach (2016) shows that this decomposition nests the well-known Blinder-Oaxaca decomposition (Blinder, 1973; Oaxaca, 1973).

An estimator for the elements of the sum in Eq. (3) is implemented as the Stata package b1x2 (Gelbach, 2014). Gelbach (2016) provides an analytical solution for the variance-covariance matrix of this estimator, which allows for a variety of heteroskedasticity- and autocorrelation-robust standard errors. We cluster standard errors at the district level throughout the chapter. The provided ITUS sampling weights are employed in both regressions and Gelbach decompositions.

The key assumption required for unbiased aggregate decomposition of β_{base} into a predicted component $\beta_{\text{base}} - \beta_{\text{full}}$ and a residual unpredicted component β_{full} is ignorability, or "selection on observables" (Fortin et al., 2011). Informally, in the setting of this chapter ignorability stipulates that the distribution of unobservables ε_{it} must be the same in both the 1998 and 2019 ITUS waves after conditioning on $\mathbf{x}$. For the detailed decomposition of Eq. (3) to be unbiased one must generally make a stronger assumption, restricting the functional form or imposing independence of ε_{it} with respect to *Year2019* and $\mathbf{x}$. As such an assumption is unlikely to hold in our setting, we interpret our detailed decomposition as primarily descriptive.

5. RESULTS

5.1 Children's Time Allocation

An aggregate view of changes in children's time allocation appears in Fig. 1. Corresponding numerical estimates appear in Table 1. The largest change was in learning time, which rose from 310 minutes in 1998–1999 to 420 minutes in 2019. All other high-level aggregate time uses declined. The largest decline was in work, from 78 minutes in 1998–1999 to 17 minutes in 2019. Home production also fell, from 49 minutes in 1998–1999 to 26 minutes in 2019. Finally, leisure declined from 1,003 minutes in 1998–1999 to 977 minutes in 2019. The largest component of leisure is sleep, which increased slightly from 568 minutes in 1998–1999 to 578 minutes in 2019. Sleep time is of economic interest (Gibson & Shrader, 2018), particularly among children (Jagnani, 2022). Because there is so little change across ITUS waves, however, in the remainder of this chapter we discuss only waking forms of leisure time.

Fig. 2 presents uncontrolled and controlled changes in aggregate time uses between 1998–1999 and 2019. Estimates from regressions following Eqs. (1) and (2) appear as round markers, with 95% confidence intervals represented using whiskers.[15] Corresponding numerical estimates appear in Table 2. Our specification of the full regression (Eq. 2) comprises all child- and household-level covariates that can be feasibly harmonized across ITUS waves.[16] This covariate set includes all observables that appear in Table 1, plus fixed effects for state, dwelling type, and usual activity.[17] In Fig. 2 the change in leisure is small (−26 minutes), and smaller still conditional on covariates (−8.5 minutes, not statistically significant at the 5% level). A similar pattern obtains for home production (−23 minutes unconditional, −14 minutes conditional). The important changes

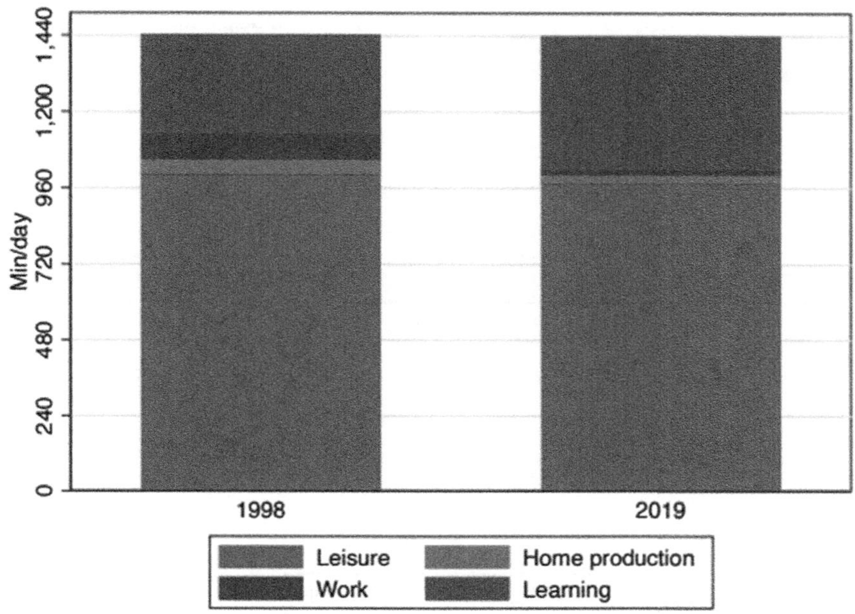

Fig. 1. Children's Time Allocation, 1998–2019.

Notes: Data are from the 1998–1999 and 2019 ITUS. Each diary covers exactly 1,440 minutes (24 hours). Classification is based on 1-digit 1998 activity codes: 8–9 leisure, 4–6 home production, 1–3 work, and 7 learning. Weighted means computed using ITUS sampling weights. Table 1 presents these weighted means in numerical form.

are observed in work and learning. For both of these time uses unconditional changes are large and adding covariates to the regression produces practically meaningful changes in the estimates. The unconditional decline in work is 61 minutes. Conditional on covariates the unpredicted decline is still 20 minutes, with the estimate statistically significant at the 5% level. These work-time changes may influence welfare, as child labor in India is negatively associated with psychosocial measures of well-being like hope and happiness (Feeny et al., 2021). Learning increases by 110 minutes without covariates, 42 minutes with covariates. The last two decades have seen practically a practically large increase in learning time for Indian children, of which 38% cannot be predicted by covariates.

The human capital implications of this increase in learning time are potentially significant. Previous studies using longitudinal time use data find that an additional hour of learning time outside school *per week* has an effect on cognitive skills similar to that of one additional year of parental education (Borga, 2019; Fiorini & Keane, 2014).[18] The conditional increase in learning time we document is much larger than one hour per week and could have contributed to substantial gains in cognitive skills among Indian children over the past two decades.

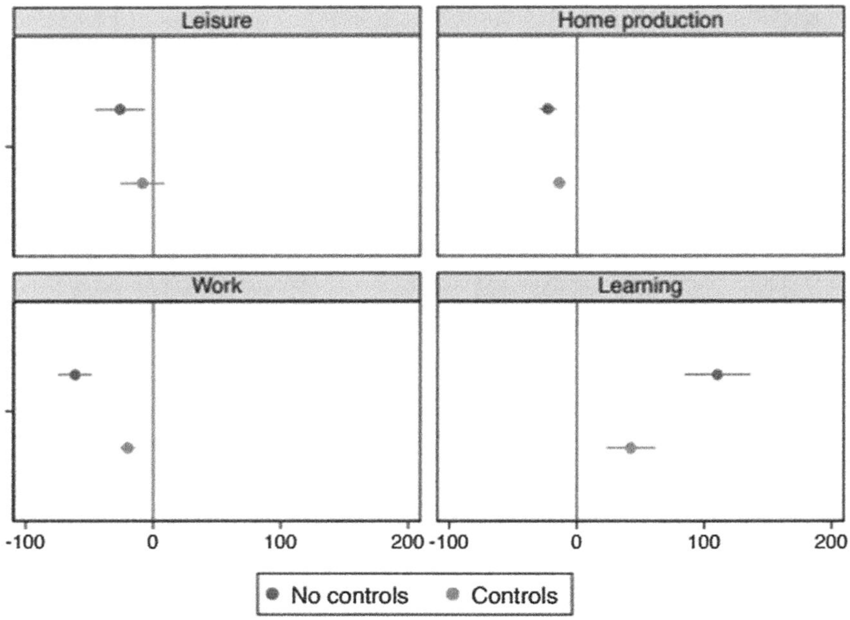

Fig. 2. Children's Time Use Changes, 1998–2019.
Notes: Data are from the 1998–9 and 2019 ITUS. Classification is based on 1-digit 1998 activity codes: 8–9 leisure, 4–6 home production, 1–3 work, and 7 learning. Round markers represent the change in weighted mean duration from 1998–9 to 2019, with and without covariates. Sampling weights are from the ITUS. Markers correspond to regression estimates in Table 2. Whiskers represent 95% confidence intervals based on standard errors clustered at the district level.

Last among our aggregated analyses, Fig. 3 presents Gelbach decompositions of the changes across ITUS waves in leisure, home production, work, and learning. Round markers give the contribution of a variable, or group of variables, to the predicted change in time use. Using the language of Gelbach (2016), these markers give contributions to omitted variable bias in the uncontrolled regression. In keeping with Eq. (3), these contributions add to the "Total predicted change" illustrated at the bottom of each panel. Whiskers represent 95% confidence intervals. Corresponding numerical estimates appear in Table 3. Taking Fig. 3 as whole, most covariates predict little of the changes in time use.[19] For example, the contribution of the female indicator is consistently near zero, and not statistically significant at the 5% level. Two exceptions are apparent. The fixed effects for usual activity predict substantial parts of the changes in all four time uses. In all four cases the sign of usual activity's contribution to total predicted change is the same as the sign of the unconditional change. That is, unexplained time-use changes, net of usual activity, are smaller than raw (unconditional) changes. The largest effects are for work and learning. The

Table 2. Children's Time Use Changes, 1998–2019[a].

	Leisure	Leisure	Home Prod.	Home Prod.	Work	Work	Learning	Learning
2019 survey	−26.0***	−8.50	−22.9***	−13.8***	−61.4***	−19.9***	110.3***	42.3***
	(9.94)	(8.81)	(3.25)	(2.30)	(6.86)	(2.74)	(13.1)	(9.74)
Female		−14.3		5.42*		−9.29		18.2
		(12.7)		(3.19)		(7.86)		(12.5)
Rural		−8.76		10.0***		5.04		−6.28
		(7.89)		(2.27)		(3.18)		(7.28)
Landless		12.2*		4.84*		−4.64***		−12.4**
		(6.40)		(2.46)		(1.74)		(6.16)
Scheduled tribe		−1.77		−0.35		6.58*		−4.46
		(10.7)		(2.89)		(3.56)		(9.53)
Scheduled caste		1.17		2.97		0.42		−4.56
		(6.42)		(2.06)		(2.57)		(6.35)
Hinduism		−22.9		−2.12		12.3**		12.7
		(14.3)		(3.90)		(5.26)		(15.7)
Islam		4.08		1.02		13.7***		−18.8
		(20.7)		(4.25)		(5.15)		(21.0)
Age FE	No	Yes	No	Yes	No	Yes	No	Yes
Female-age FE	No	Yes	No	Yes	No	Yes	No	Yes
Usual activity FE	No	Yes	No	Yes	No	Yes	No	Yes
Exp. Quintiles	No	Yes	No	Yes	No	Yes	No	Yes
HH size quintiles	No	Yes	No	Yes	No	Yes	No	Yes
Dwelling FE	No	Yes	No	Yes	No	Yes	No	Yes
State FE	No	Yes	No	Yes	No	Yes	No	Yes
Observations	29,859	29,859	29,859	29,859	29,859	29,859	29,859	29,859

[a]Data are from the 1998–1999 and 2019 ITUS. Classification is based on 1-digit 1998 activity codes: 8–9 leisure, 4–6 home production, 1–3 work, and 7 learning. Each column presents estimates from a weighted linear regression, with time use in minutes as the dependent variable and an indicator for the 2019 ITUS survey as the regressor of primary interest. Sampling weights are from the ITUS. Odd columns correspond to Eq. (1) and even columns to Eq. (2). Estimates correspond to Fig. 2. Standard errors in parentheses are clustered at the district level. $^{*}p < 0.1$, $^{**}p < 0.05$, $^{***}p < 0.01$.

influence of state fixed effects is more nuanced. They do not matter for work and home production. For leisure and learning, the contributions of the state fixed effects have signs opposite those of the uncontrolled changes, so unpredicted changes are larger. We note that while the estimated predictive contribution of state fixed effects is sometimes large, the associated confidence intervals contain zero.

How and why do usual activity and state matter, particularly for work and learning? Figs. A1–A4 and Table A2 report estimated fixed effects. By far the most important indicator is for the child's usual activity being school. This

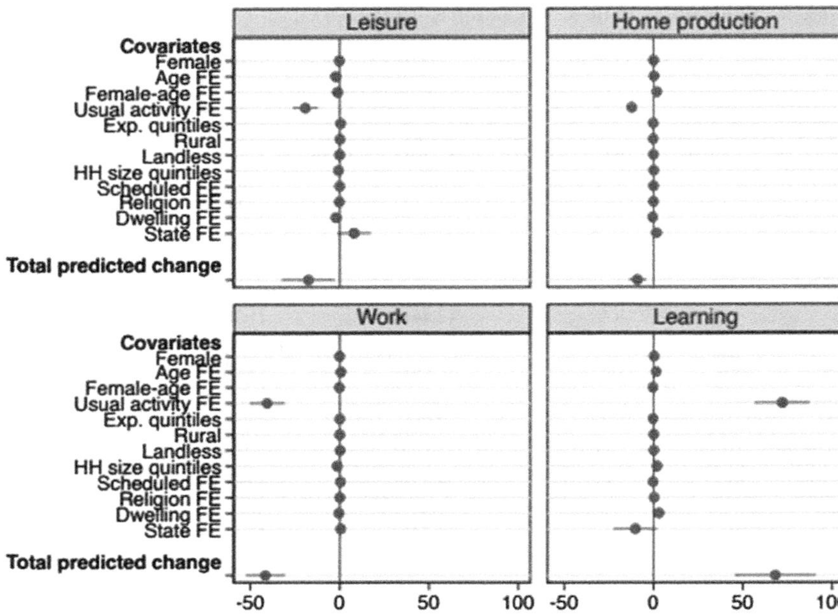

Fig. 3. Gelbach Decompositions of Children's Time Use Changes, 1998–2019.

Notes: Data are from the 1998–1999 and 2019 ITUS. Classification is based on 1-digit 1998 activity codes: 8–9 leisure, 4–6 home production, 1–3 work, and 7 learning. Round markers represent the contributions of covariate groups to the difference between: (i) the uncontrolled change in weighted mean duration from 1998–1999 to 2019; and (ii) the change in weighted mean duration from 1998–1999 to 2019, controlling for covariates. Sampling weights are from the ITUS. The contributions of all covariate groups sum to the Total predicted change. Markers correspond to Gelbach estimates in Table 3. Whiskers represent 95% confidence intervals based on standard errors clustered at the district level. State and usual activity fixed effects are disaggregated in Figs. A1–A4.

covariate predicts a 76-minute reduction in work and an 80-minute increase in learning. The estimated predictive contributions of fixed effects for the usual activity being domestic duties are also practically large and statistically significant. This pattern is consistent with extensive-margin transitions into schooling predicting much–but not all–of the observed changes in work and learning time. Among the state indicators Madhya Pradesh stands out, with the coefficient estimate statistically significant at the 10% level in three of four cases, but magnitudes are small (seven minutes or less).

5.2 Children's Learning Time

To further investigate learning we consider subcategories, learning activities defined at the three-digit level: school attendance, homework, travel for learning,

Table 3. Gelbach Decompositions of Children's Time Use Changes, 1998–2019[a].

	Leisure	Home Prod.	Work	Learning
Female	−0.23	0.086	−0.15	0.29
	(0.25)	(0.087)	(0.16)	(0.26)
Age FE	−2.22**	0.23**	0.63**	1.36**
	(0.92)	(0.12)	(0.29)	(0.63)
Female-age FE	−1.22**	1.86***	−0.29	−0.35
	(0.56)	(0.68)	(0.17)	(0.31)
Usual activity FE	−19.2***	−12.2***	−40.5***	71.9***
	(3.59)	(1.36)	(5.01)	(7.93)
Exp. Quintiles	0.53	−0.14	−0.079	−0.31
	(0.50)	(0.23)	(0.15)	(0.56)
Rural	0.13	−0.15	−0.074	0.092
	(0.39)	(0.47)	(0.23)	(0.34)
Landless	−0.13	−0.051	0.049	0.13
	(0.40)	(0.16)	(0.15)	(0.41)
HH size quintiles	−0.69	0.17	−1.43	1.95
	(1.51)	(0.64)	(1.12)	(1.59)
Scheduled FE	−0.074	0.017	0.33	−0.27
	(0.55)	(0.16)	(0.27)	(0.50)
Religion FE	−0.27	−0.031	−0.014	0.31
	(0.42)	(0.051)	(0.13)	(0.42)
Dwelling FE	−2.10	−0.50	−0.48	3.08**
	(1.37)	(0.72)	(0.47)	(1.55)
State FE	7.95*	1.71	0.53	−10.2
	(4.82)	(1.80)	(0.81)	(6.26)
Total predicted change	−17.5**	−9.03***	−41.5***	68.0***
	(7.58)	(2.45)	(5.64)	(11.6)
Observations	29,859	29,859	29,859	29,859

[a]Data are from the 1998–9 and 2019 ITUS. Classification is based on 1-digit 1998 activity codes: 8–9 leisure, 4–6 home production, 1–3 work, and 7 learning. Estimates represent the contributions of covariate groups to the difference between: (i) the uncontrolled change in weighted mean duration from 1998–1999 to 2019; and (ii) the change in weighted mean duration from 1998–1999 to 2019, controlling for covariates. Sampling weights are from the ITUS. The contributions of all covariate groups sum to the Total predicted change. Estimates correspond to markers in Fig. 3. Standard errors in parentheses are clustered at the district level. $^{*}p < 0.1$, $^{**}p < 0.05$, $^{***}p < 0.01$.

and other learning.[20] Fig. 4 shows that school and homework are the largest constituents of learning time. Fig. 5 estimates changes in learning activities across ITUS waves. Uncontrolled estimates are positive for all four types of learning. Including covariates decreases the estimates; for homework the point estimate becomes negative, but the confidence interval includes zero. The largest unconditional increase is for school time (72 minutes). A 32-minute unexplained increase remains even after accounting for covariates, including the usual activity fixed effects previously discussed in Section 5.1. This is consistent with intensive-margin increases in school time.

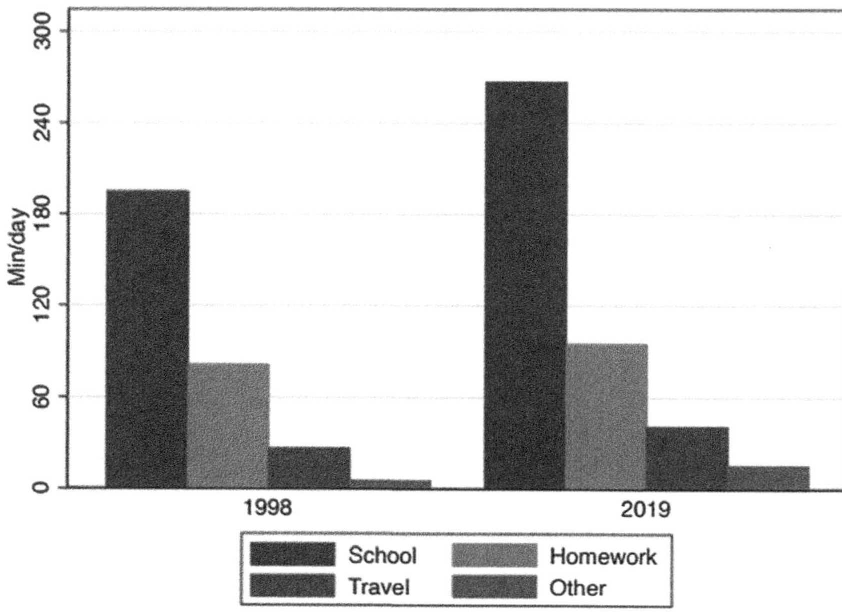

Fig. 4. Children's Learning Time, 1998–2019.

Notes: Data are from the 1998–1999 and 2019 ITUS. Weighted means correspond to "school/university attendance," "homework, being tutored, course review, research and activities related to formal education," "traveling time related to learning," and all others under learning (1998 single-digit code 7). Sampling weights are from the ITUS.

Our Gelbach decomposition does not establish the mechanisms underlying this intensive-margin increase, but some discussion of candidate mechanisms may motivate future research. First, the length of the school day could have increased, holding school type fixed. Second, if private schools have longer days on average, then transitions from public into private schools could have resulted in increased learning time, conditional on usual activity. Third, absenteeism could have decreased, for example because of improved health or better transportation. Fourth, occasional school attendance could have increased among children whose usual principal activity is not school.[21] Fifth, an unobserved variable or an interaction of covariates not included in our regressions could predict the 32-minute unexplained increase. If one is willing to impose the assumptions required for a threefold Blinder-Oaxaca decomposition with 1998–1999 as the reference period, results indicate that both covariate and coefficient changes matter (Table A4). A 41 minute school-time increase is attributed to covariate changes, a 37.5 minute increase to coefficient changes, and a 6.5-minute decrease to the interaction. Examining the indicator for a child's usual activity being school, the Blinder-Oaxaca decomposition attributes a 48.8-minute increase to change in the variable, a 0.7-minute decrease to change in its coefficient, and a 0.2-minute

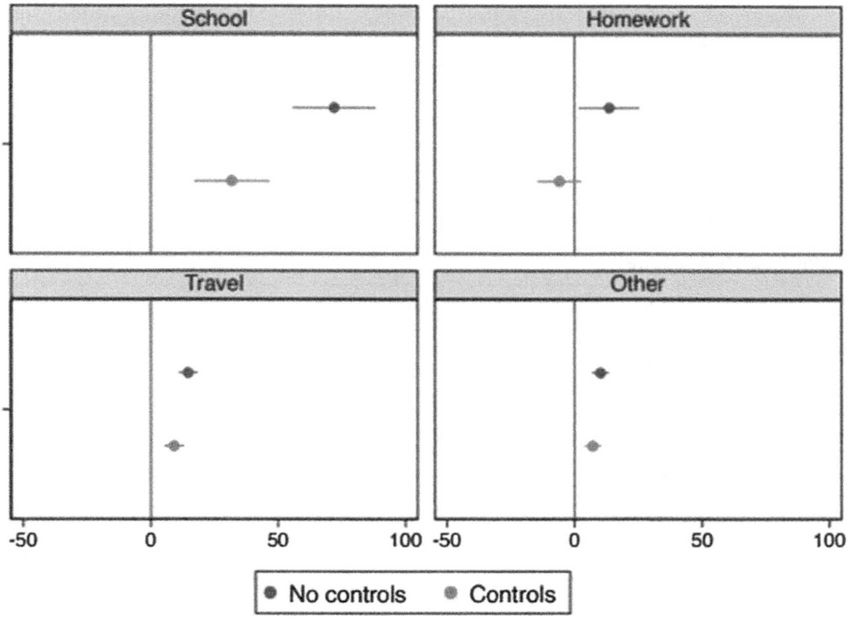

Fig. 5. Children's Learning Changes, 1998–2019.
Notes: Data are from the 1998–1999 and 2019 ITUS. Categories are "school/university attendance," "homework, being tutored, course review, research and activities related to formal education," "traveling time related to learning," and all others under learning (1998 single-digit code 7). Round markers represent the change in weighted mean duration from 1998–1999 to 2019, with and without covariates. Sampling weights are from the ITUS. Markers correspond to regression estimates in Table A3. Whiskers represent 95% confidence intervals based on standard errors clustered at the district level.

decrease to their interaction. That is, Blinder-Oaxaca suggests school time is not increasing among children who identify primarily as students.

Lastly in this subsection, Fig. 6 implements the Gelbach decomposition for learning activities. As in our aggregate decomposition, fixed effects for usual activity and state generally make the largest contributions to the predicted changes across ITUS waves. Dwelling fixed effects also make practically meaningful, statistically significant contributions for homework, travel, and other learning.[22] It is striking that they retain predictive power even in the presence of indicators for quintiles of monthly household expenditure. One possible reason that wealth proxies predict changes in learning time is that household wealth is an important driver of school choice and education inputs. Despite the increase in public sector resources allocated to education, India has seen an expansion of private participation in the education sector. Survey estimates suggest private school enrollment grew from around 19% in 2006 to nearly 26% in 2011, even

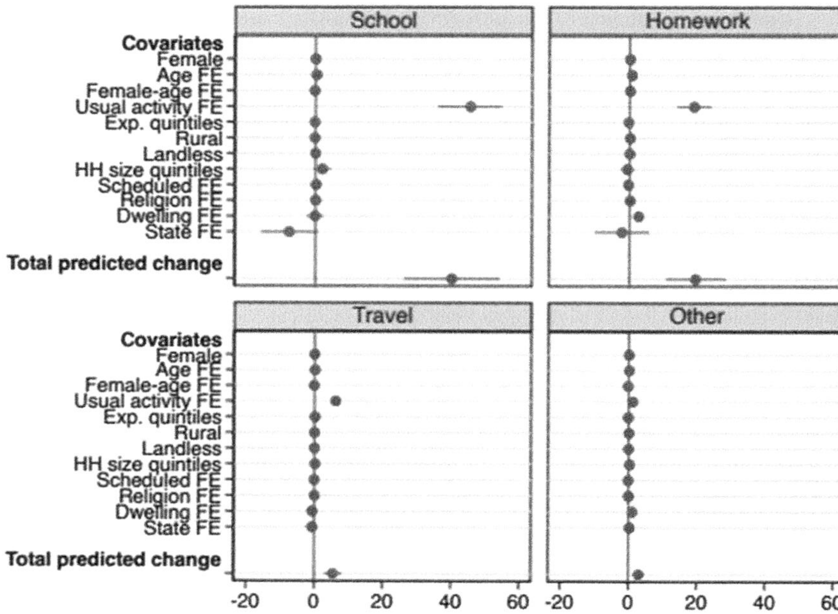

Fig. 6. Gelbach Decompositions of Children's Learning Changes, 1998–2019.

Notes: Data are from the 1998–1999 and 2019 ITUS. Categories are "school/university attendance," "homework, being tutored, course review, research and activities related to formal education," "traveling time related to learning," and all others under learning (1998 single-digit code 7). Round markers represent the contributions of covariate groups to the difference between: (i) the uncontrolled change in weighted mean duration from 1998–1999 to 2019; and (ii) the change in weighted mean duration from 1998–1999 to 2019, controlling for covariates. Sampling weights are from the ITUS. The contributions of all covariate groups sum to the Total predicted change. Markers correspond to Gelbach estimates in Table A5. Whiskers represent 95% confidence intervals based on standard errors clustered at the district level.

though public schools are free and private schools are not (Muralidharan, 2013). The increased demand for private schools plausibly reflects parents' perception of the relative quality of public versus private schools. This perception is supported to some extent by observational studies that find children in private schools have higher reading and arithmetic skills than students in government schools (Dubey et al., 2009). Descriptive evidence also suggests that household wealth predicts private school choice in India (Kumar & Choudhury, 2021).

5.3 Children's Leisure Time

While average leisure time did not exhibit a large change over ITUS waves, it warrants more detailed examination because it is a large share of the time budget for children. Fig. 7 shows that television, talking, games, personal hygiene, and eating are all important constituents of leisure in our sample.[23]

Fig. 8 examines changes in leisure across ITUS waves. The largest unconditional increase–19 minutes–is for television, and covariates predict very little of this change. There are smaller unconditional increases in eating (12 minutes) and hygiene (7 minutes), with covariates again exhibiting little predictive power. Offsetting unconditional declines are observed in talking (10 minutes), games (17 minutes), and other leisure (47 minutes). Again covariates generally predict small shares of these changes, with one exception: the conditional decline in talking is just 5 minutes, and the estimate is not statistically significant.

While this evidence does not establish any causal relationships, the welfare implications of this trend, with more socially connected time uses like games falling while television time increases, are potentially interesting. On the one hand, socially connected time use is associated with increased prosocial behavior and other forms of non-cognitive development (Meroni et al., 2021). On the other hand, evidence from natural experiments in the USA and the UK suggests that an increase in television time can result in an increase in test scores (Gentzkow & Shapiro, 2008; Nieto, 2019).[24]

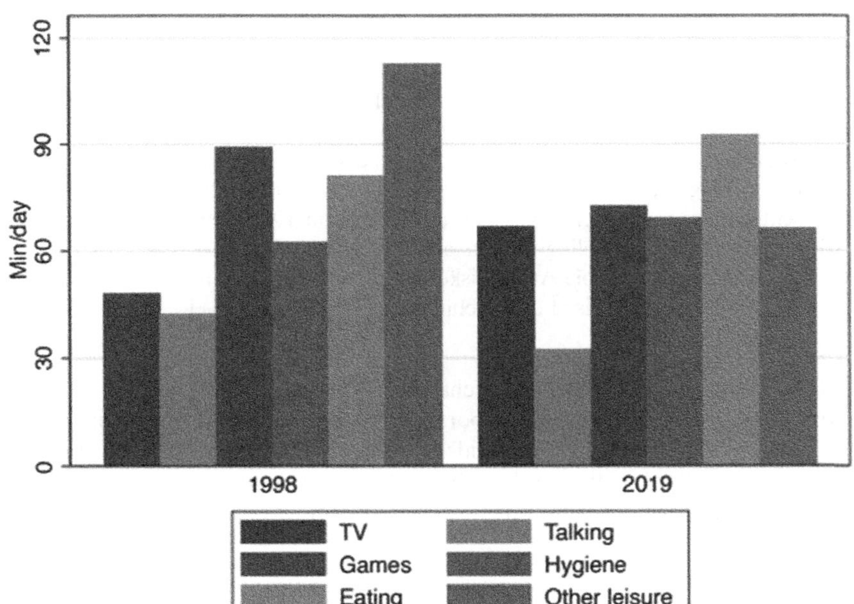

Fig. 7. Children's Leisure Time, 1998–2019.

Notes: Data are from the 1998–1999 and 2019 ITUS. Weighted means correspond to "watching/listening to television and video," "talking, conversing, chatting," "playing games and other pastime activities," "personal hygiene and care," "eating and drinking," and all other waking uses under leisure (1998 single-digit codes 8–9). Sleep is excluded from the figure to preserve legible scale. Sampling weights are from the ITUS.

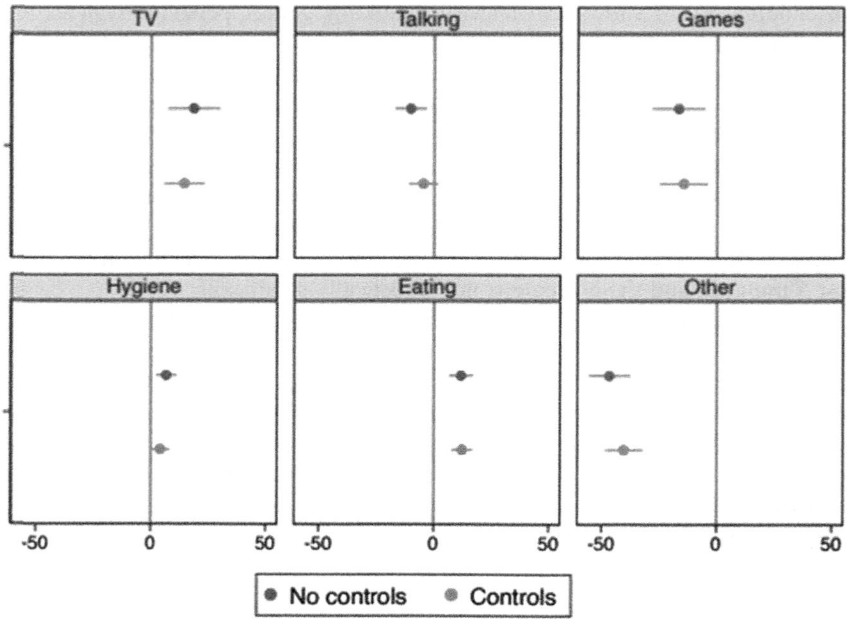

Fig. 8. Children's Leisure Changes, 1998–2019.

Notes: Data are from the 1998–1999 and 2019 ITUS. Categories are "watching/listening to television and video," "talking, conversing, chatting," "playing games and other pastime activities," "personal hygiene and care," "eating and drinking," and all other waking uses under leisure (1998 single-digit codes 8–9). Round markers represent the change in weighted mean duration from 1998–1999 to 2019, with and without covariates. Sampling weights are from the ITUS. Markers correspond to regression estimates in Table A6. Whiskers represent 95% confidence intervals based on standard errors clustered at the district level.

Our Gelbach decomposition of changes in leisure appears in Fig. 9. Usual activity indicators are the most important covariates, and dwelling type indicators again show relatively large and statistically significant estimates in some cases. But broadly, Fig. 9 accords with Fig. 8 in suggesting that covariates predict little of the changes in leisure time uses over ITUS waves.[25]

6. CONCLUSION

We began this chapter with the argument that the investment character of children's time use makes it a vital determinant of long-run welfare at both the individual and macroeconomic scales. Time-use investments are plausibly of particular importance in low-income countries. Our analysis takes two initial steps toward understanding time-use investments by children.

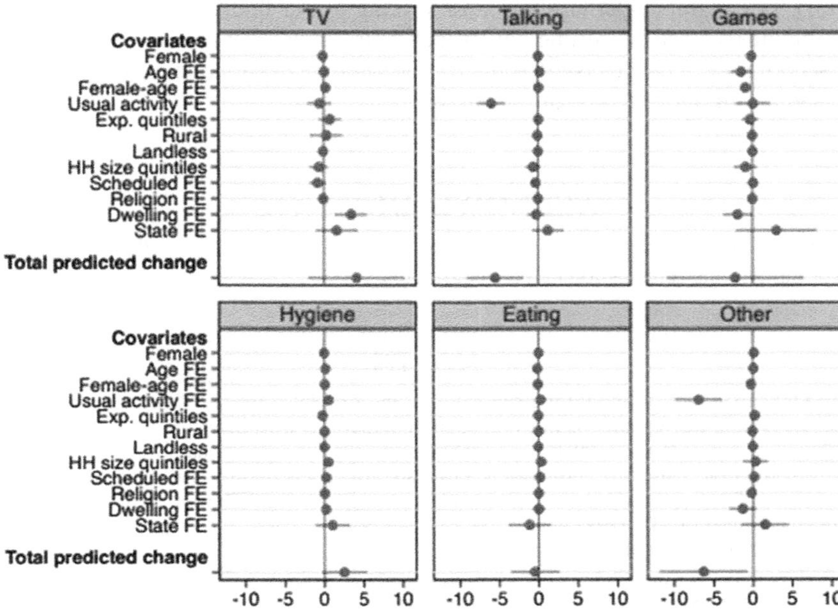

Fig. 9. Gelbach Decompositions of Children's Leisure Changes, 1998–2019.
Notes: Data are from the 1998–1999 and 2019 ITUS. Categories are "watching/listening to television and video," "talking, conversing, chatting," "playing games and other pastime activities," "personal hygiene and care," "eating and drinking," and all other waking uses under leisure (1998 single-digit codes 8–9). Round markers represent the contributions of covariate groups to the difference between: (i) the uncontrolled change in weighted mean duration from 1998–1999 to 2019; and (ii) the change in weighted mean duration from 1998–1999 to 2019, controlling for covariates. Sampling weights are from the ITUS. The contributions of all covariate groups sum to the Total predicted change. Markers correspond to Gelbach estimates in Table A7. Whiskers represent 95% confidence intervals based on standard errors clustered at the district level.

First, we document changes in the time allocation of Indian children from 1998 to 2019. These were two decades of thoroughgoing change in India, including increased foreign trade (Ahluwalia, 2002; Marelli & Signorelli, 2011). Changes in children's time use over this period are intrinsically interesting.

Second, our analysis decomposes the change in children's time use into unpredicted and predicted components and further decomposes the predicted component into the contributions of particular characteristics. State-specific factors, dwelling type, and usual principal activity all prove quantitatively influential. While these results are primarily descriptive, a decomposition like ours points out potentially fruitful areas for future causal research (Fortin et al.,

2011). For example, perhaps the most striking of our findings is an unpredicted 42-minute increase in learning time, which is driven by intensive-margin increases in school time. The effects of such a change on human capital and welfare could be significant and warrant careful study.

ACKNOWLEDGMENTS

We thank Daniel Hamermesh and Solomon Polachek for guidance on this project and two anonymous referees for helpful comments.

NOTES

1. Only an activity without long-run payoffs, and for which the best foregone alternative also lacks long-run payoffs, is not immediately entangled with investment.
2. For instance, the state of Bihar sought to increase the educational attainment of girls by providing bicycles (Muralidharan & Prakash, 2017). Economists have randomized the provision of technology-aided after-school instruction (Muralidharan et al., 2019) and remedial education (Banerjee et al., 2007).
3. 110/(0.5(310 + 420)) = 0.30.
4. This type of unpredicted change is sometimes described as "unexplained." To avoid any inadvertent suggestion of causal results, we do not use this term.
5. Three of the seven "star states" that implemented NREGA particularly effectively are in our ITUS sample (Imbert & Papp, 2015); see Section 3 for details. There is evidence that NREGA affects school enrollment and child labor (Shah & Steinberg, 2021). State fixed effects also potentially reflect state-level variation in higher education (Jagnani & Khanna, 2020) and infrastructure (Adukia et al., 2020) investments.
6. The India Time Use Survey classifies dwellings as "kutcha," "semi pucca," "pucca", or "no dwelling." Pucca houses are built of more durable and expensive materials, e.g. cement or brick.
7. While Li (2023) focuses on women's work time, the paper describes changes in the entire time allocation for adults of both sexes.
8. Basu (1999) and Edmonds and Pavcnik (2005) survey the broader literature on child labor.
9. By "intensive-margin changes" we mean changes within usual activity.
10. As explained below, our analysis does not use abnormal or "weekly variant" diaries.
11. There was no equivalent of the "weekly variant" from the 1998–1999 survey.
12. Formerly part of Madhya Pradesh, Chhattisgarh became a separate state in 2000.
13. In Table 1 this indicator variable is labeled "School" for concision, but in survey documents this usual principal activity is given as "Attended educational institution."
14. Our use of "base" and "full" follows Gelbach (2016).
15. Confidence intervals are based on standard errors clustered at the district level.
16. For all regression and decomposition analyses in Section 5, we have estimated alternative specifications including day-of-week and week-of-year indicators. Naturally these predict time use. However the ITUS sampling procedure makes their covariances with demographics and the 2019 indicator very close to zero, so they make no meaningful difference to the results.
17. See Section 3 for the details of usual principal activity.
18. In Section 5.2 we show the unexplained increase in learning time is driven by school, so the cited results from non-school learning provide only rough benchmarks.
19. This is in contrast with papers like Saffer et al. (2013), which finds that demographic variables predict 30 to 65% of racial and gender differences in time spent on physical activity.

20. See Section 3 for discussion of activity codes.

21. Intensive-margin increases need not be confined to children whose usual principal activity is school. Indeed the unexplained increase in school time can be interpreted as a weighted average of intensive-margin changes in school time among children whose usual principal activity is school, and children whose usual principal activity is something else.

22. This is more apparent in Table A5 than in the corresponding Fig. 6. Dwelling characteristics are an important component of asset-based measures that researchers generally regard as capturing households' longer-run economic wealth (Filmer & Pritchett, 2001; Sahn & Stifel, 2003).

23. As discussed in Section 5.1, sleep increased by 10 minutes across ITUS waves. It is omitted from Fig. 7 to preserve the legibility of differences across other leisure activities.

24. However, evidence from Norway suggests otherwise: Hernæs et al. (2019) finds a negative effect of television exposure on cognitive ability and school graduation rates.

25. A Gelbach decomposition can, in principle, reveal important predicted changes from observables, even when uncontrolled and controlled estimates are close, because the contributions of multiple covariates may offset each other.

REFERENCES

Adukia, A., Asher, S., & Novosad, P. (2020). Educational investment responses to economic opportunity: Evidence from Indian road construction. *American Economic Journal: Applied Economics*, *12*(1), 348–376.

Ahluwalia, M. S. (2002). Economic reforms in India since 1991: Has gradualism worked? *The Journal of Economic Perspectives*, *16*(3), 67–88.

Almond, D., Currie, J., & Duque, V. (2018). Childhood circumstances and adult outcomes: Act II. *Journal of Economic Literature*, *56*(4), 1360–1446.

Azam, M., & Saing, C. H. (2017). Assessing the impact of district primary education program in India. *Review of Development Economics*, *21*(4), 1113–1131.

Banerjee, A. V., Cole, S., Duflo, E., & Linden, L. (2007). Remedying education: Evidence from two randomized experiments in India. *Quarterly Journal of Economics*, *122*(3), 1235–1264.

Basu, K. (1999). Child labor: Cause, consequence, and cure, with remarks on international labor standards. *Journal of Economic Literature*, *37*(3), 1083–1119.

Bharadwaj, P., Lakdawala, L. K., & Li, N. (2020). Perverse consequences of well intentioned regulation: Evidence from India's child labor ban. *Journal of the European Economic Association*, *18*(3), 1158–1195.

Blinder, A. S. (1973). Wage discrimination: Reduced form and structural estimates. *Journal of Human Resources*, *8*(4), 436–455.

Borga, L. G. (2019). Children's own time use and its effect on skill formation. *Journal of Development Studies*, *55*(5), 876–893.

Chetty, R., Friedman, J. N., Hilger, N., Saez, E., Schanzenbach, D. W., & Yagan, D. (2011). How does your kindergarten classroom affect your earnings? Evidence from project STAR. *Quarterly Journal of Economics*, *126*(4), 1593–1660.

Datta Gupta, N., Dubey, A., & Simonsen, M. (2018). Rising school attendance in rural India: An evaluation of the effects of major educational reforms. *Education Economics*, *26*(2), 109–128.

Deshpande, A. (2000). Does caste still define disparity? A look at inequality in Kerala, India. *The American Economic Review*, *90*(2), 322–325.

Dubey, A., Vanneman, R., & Banerji, R. (2009). Private schooling in India: A new educational landscape. In *India policy forum 2008–09* (Vol. 5, pp. 1). SAGE Publications India.

Edmonds, E. V., & Pavcnik, N. (2005). Child labor in the global economy. *The Journal of Economic Perspectives*, *19*(1), 199–220.

Edmonds, E. V., Topalova, P., & Pavcnik, N. (2009). Child labor and schooling in a globalizing world: Some evidence from urban India. *Journal of the European Economic Association*, *7*(2–3), 498–507.

Feeny, S., Posso, A., Skali, A., Jyotishi, A., Nath, S., & Viswanathan, P. (2021). Child labor and psychosocial wellbeing: Findings from India. *Health Economics*, *30*(4), 876–902.

Field, E. M., Pande, R., Rigol, N., Schaner, S. G., Stacy, E. M., & Moore, C. M. T. (2022). *Understanding rural households' time use in a developing setting: Validating a low-cost time use module*. National Bureau of Economic Research. Technical report.

Filmer, D., & Pritchett, L. H. (2001). Estimating wealth effects without expenditure data or tears: An application to educational enrollments in states of India. *Demography*, *38*(1), 115–132.

Fiorini, M., & Keane, M. P. (2014). How the allocation of children's time affects cognitive and noncognitive development. *Journal of Labor Economics*, *32*(4), 787–836.

Fortin, N., Lemieux, T., & Firpo, S. (2011). Decomposition methods in economics. In *Handbook of Labor Economics* (Vol. 4, pp. 1–102). Elsevier.

Garg, T., Gibson, M., & Sun, F. (2020). Extreme temperatures and time use in China. *Journal of Economic Behavior & Organization*, *180*, 309–324.

Gelbach, J. (2014). *B1x2: Stata module to account for changes when x2 is added to a base model with x1*.

Gelbach, J. B. (2016). When do covariates matter? And which ones, and how much? *Journal of Labor Economics*, *34*(2), 509–543.

Gentzkow, M., & Shapiro, J. M. (2008). Preschool television viewing and adolescent test scores: Historical evidence from the Coleman study. *Quarterly Journal of Economics*, *123*(1), 279–323.

Gibson, M., & Shrader, J. (2018). Time use and labor productivity: The returns to sleep. *The Review of Economics and Statistics*, *100*(5):783–798.

Giménez-Nadal, J. I., & Molina, J. A. (2022). Time use surveys. In *Handbook of Labor, Human Resources and Population Economics* (pp. 1–18). Springer International Publishing.

Heckman, J. J. (2007). The economics, technology, and neuroscience of human capability formation. *Proceedings of the National Academy of Sciences*, *104*(33), 13250–13255.

Hernæs, Ø., Markussen, S., & Røed, K. (2019). Television, cognitive ability, and high school completion. *Journal of Human Resources*, *54*(2), 371–400.

Imbert, C., & Papp, J. (2015). Labor market effects of social programs: Evidence from India's employment guarantee. *American Economic Journal: Applied Economics*, *7*(2), 233–263.

Jagnani, M. (2022). Children's sleep and human capital production. *The Review of Economics and Statistics* (pp. 1–45).

Jagnani, M., & Khanna, G. (2020). The effects of elite public colleges on primary and secondary schooling markets in India. *Journal of Development Economics*, *146*, 102512.

Jalan, J., & Glinksya, E. (2013). *Improving primary school education in India: An impact assessment of DPEP-phase one*. Indian Statistical Institute (New Delhi) and The World Bank.

Kaur, R. (2021). Estimating the impact of school feeding programs: Evidence from mid day meal scheme of India. *Economics of Education Review*, *84*, 102171.

Kumar, D., & Choudhury, P. K. (2021). Determinants of private school choice in India: All about the family backgrounds? *Journal of School Choice*, *15*(4), 576–602.

Li, N. (2023). Women's work in India: Evidence from changes in time use between 1998 and 2019. *World Development*, *161*, 106107.

Løken, K. V. (2010). Family income and children's education: Using the Norwegian oil boom as a natural experiment. *Labour Economics*, *17*(1), 118–129.

Mankiw, N. G., Romer, D., & Weil, D. N. (1992). A contribution to the empirics of economic growth. *Quarterly Journal of Economics*, *107*(2), 407–437.

Marelli, E., & Signorelli, M. (2011). China and India: Openness, trade and effects on economic growth. *The European Journal of Comparative Economics*, *8*(1), 129.

Mehta, A. K., & Shah, A. (2003). Chronic poverty in India: Incidence, causes and policies. *World Development*, *31*(3):491–511.

Meroni, E. C., Piazzalunga, D., & Pronzato, C. (2021). Allocation of time and child socio-emotional skills. *Review of the Economics of the Household*, 1–38.

Meyer, B. D., & Sullivan, J. X. (2003). Measuring the well-being of the poor using income and consumption. *Journal of Human Resources*, 1180–1220.

Muralidharan, K. (2013). Priorities for primary education policy in India's 12th five-year plan In *India Policy Forum* (Vol. 9, pp. 1–61). National Council of Applied Economic Research.

Muralidharan, K., & Prakash, N. (2017). Cycling to school: Increasing secondary school enrollment for girls in India. *American Economic Journal: Applied Economics*, *9*(3), 321–350.

Muralidharan, K., Singh, A., & Ganimian, A. J. (2019). Disrupting education? Experimental evidence on technology-aided instruction in India. *The American Economic Review*, *109*(4), 1426–1460.

Nieto, A. (2019). *Television, time use and academic achievement: Evidence from a natural experiment*. Technical report.

Oaxaca, R. (1973). Male-female wage differentials in urban labor markets. *International Economic Review*, 693–709.

Palshikar, S., Kumar, S., & Lodha, S. (2017). *Electoral politics in India: The resurgence of the Bharatiya Janata Party*. Taylor & Francis.

Putnam, R. D. (2001). *Bowling alone: The collapse and revival of American community*. Simon & Schuster.

Saffer, H., Dave, D., Grossman, M., & Ann Leung, L. (2013). Racial, ethnic, and gender differences in physical activity. *Journal of Human Capital*, *7*(4), 378–410.

Sahn, D. E., & Stifel, D. (2003). Exploring alternative measures of welfare in the absence of expenditure data. *Review of Income and Wealth*, *49*(4), 463–489.

Seymour, G., Malapit, H. J., & Quisumbing, A. R. (2017). *Measuring time use in development settings*. World Bank Policy Research Working Paper, (8147).

Shah, M., & Steinberg, B. M. (2021). Workfare and human capital investment: Evidence from India. *Journal of Human Resources*, *56*(2), 380–405.

Singh, A., Park, A., & Dercon, S. (2014). School meals as a safety net: An evaluation of the midday meal scheme in India. *Economic Development and Cultural Change*, *62*(2), 275–306.

Subramanian, S. V., Nandy, S., Irving, M., Gordon, D., Lambert, H., & Davey Smith, G. (2006). The mortality divide in India: The differential contributions of gender, caste, and standard of living across the life course. *American Journal of Public Health*, *96*(5), 818–825.

Tandon, S. (2018). Election outcomes and the poor: Evidence from the consumption of scheduled castes and tribes in India. *Economic Development and Cultural Change*, *66*(2), 331–382.

UNESCO. (2020). *UIS statistics: Total net enrollment rate by level of education*. Technical report.

Van de Poel, E., & Speybroeck, N. (2009). Decomposing malnutrition inequalities between scheduled castes and tribes and the remaining Indian population. *Ethnicity and Health*, *14*(3), 271–287.

World Bank. (2000). *World development report 2000/2001: Attacking poverty*. The World Bank.

World Bank. (2009). *Secondary education in India: Universalizing opportunity*. The World Bank.

World Bank. (2022a). *World development indicators: GDP growth (annual %) – India*. Technical report.

World Bank. (2022b). *World development indicators: Population ages 0–14, total – India*. Technical report.

World Bank. (2022c). *World development indicators: School enrollment, primary (% net) – India*. Technical report.

APPENDIX A. ADDITIONAL FIGURES

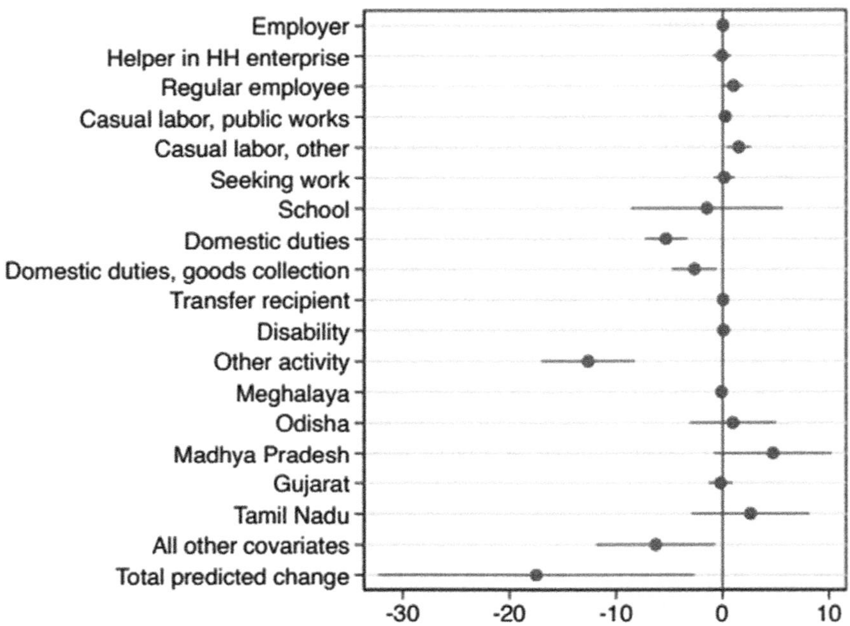

Fig. A1. Gelbach Decomposition Showing FE, Leisure, 1998–2019.
Note: This is an alternative presentation of the leisure results in Fig. 3. Round markers represent the contributions of covariate groups to the difference between: (i) the uncontrolled change in weighted mean duration from 1998–1999 to 2019; and (ii) the change in weighted mean duration from 1998–1999 to 2019, controlling for covariates. Sampling weights are from the ITUS. The contributions of all covariate groups sum to the Total predicted change. Whiskers represent 95% confidence intervals based on standard errors clustered at the district level. Corresponding numerical estimates are in Table A2.

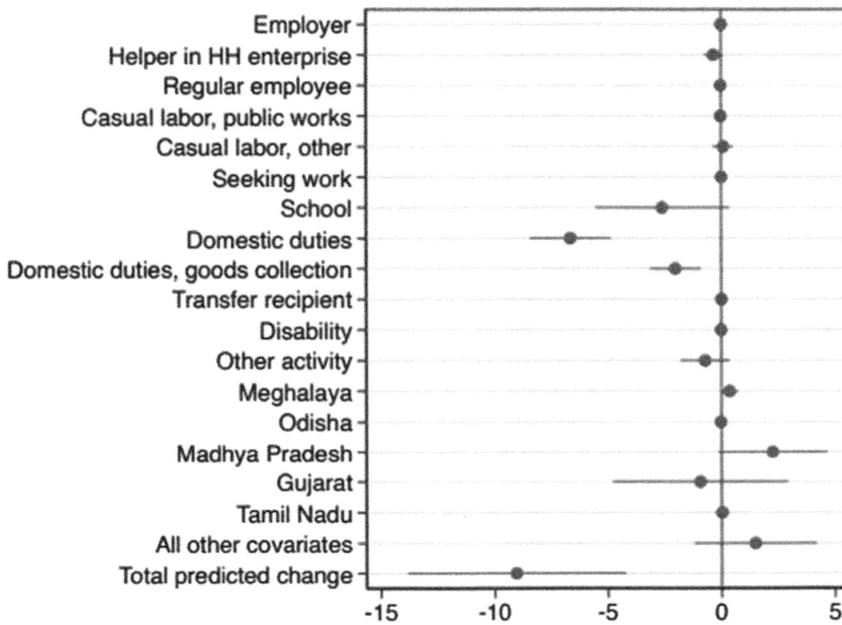

Fig. A2. Gelbach Decomposition Showing FE, Home Production, 1998–2019.

Note: This is an alternative presentation of the home production results in Fig. 3. Round markers represent the contributions of covariate groups to the difference between: (i) the uncontrolled change in weighted mean duration from 1998–1999 to 2019; and (ii) the change in weighted mean duration from 1998–1999 to 2019, controlling for covariates. Sampling weights are from the ITUS. The contributions of all covariate groups sum to the Total predicted change. Whiskers represent 95% confidence intervals based on standard errors clustered at the district level. Corresponding numerical estimates are in Table A2.

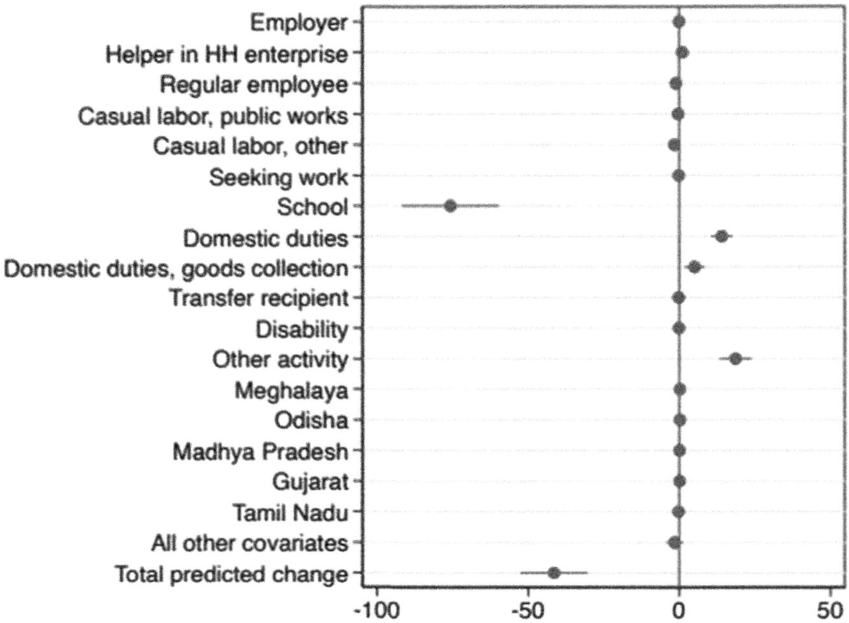

Fig. A3. Gelbach Decomposition Showing FE, Work, 1998–2019.
Note: This is an alternative presentation of the work results in Fig. 3. Round markers represent the contributions of covariate groups to the difference between: (i) the uncontrolled change in weighted mean duration from 1998–1999 to 2019; and (ii) the change in weighted mean duration from 1998–1999 to 2019, controlling for covariates. Sampling weights are from the ITUS. The contributions of all covariate groups sum to the Total predicted change. Whiskers represent 95% confidence intervals based on standard errors clustered at the district level. Corresponding numerical estimates are in Table A2.

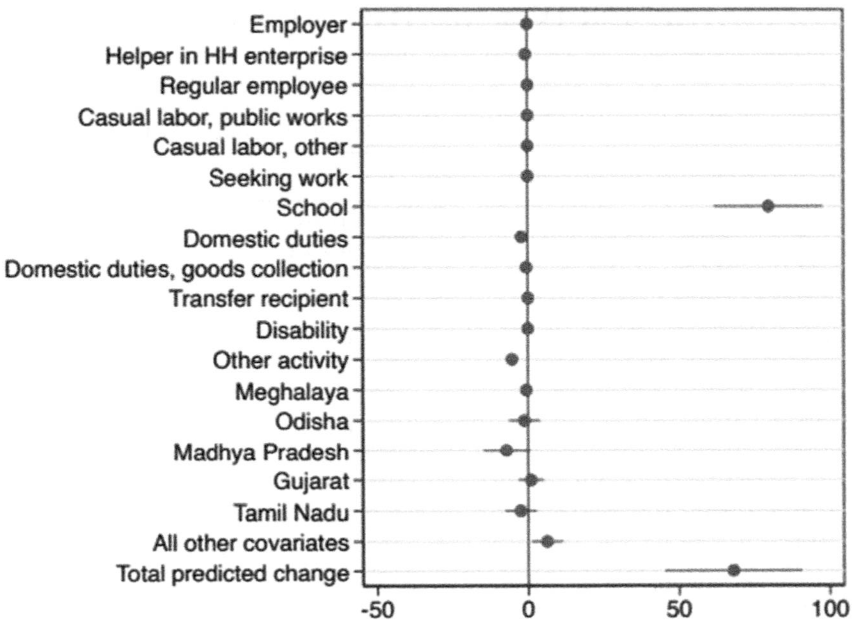

Fig. A4. Gelbach Decomposition Showing FE, Learning, 1998–2019.
Note: This is an alternative presentation of the learning results in Fig. 3. Round markers represent the contributions of covariate groups to the difference between: (i) the uncontrolled change in weighted mean duration from 1998–1999 to 2019; and (ii) the change in weighted mean duration from 1998–1999 to 2019, controlling for covariates. Sampling weights are from the ITUS. The contributions of all covariate groups sum to the Total predicted change. Whiskers represent 95% confidence intervals based on standard errors clustered at the district level. Corresponding numerical estimates are in Table A2.

APPENDIX B. ADDITIONAL TABLES

Table A1. ITUS Descriptive Statistics, Usual Activity and State Indicators.

	1998	2019
Self-employed	0.0094	0.0021
Employer	0.00021	0.000052
Helper in HH enterprise	0.029	0.0083
Regular employee	0.012	0.0029
Casual labor, public works	0.0050	0.0010
Casual labor, other	0.035	0.0078
Seeking work	0.0053	0.0057
School	0.73	0.93
Domestic duties	0.068	0.024
Domestic duties, goods collection	0.033	0.0069
Transfer recipient	0.00016	0.00056
Disability	0.0022	0.0024
Other activity	0.066	0.0097
Haryana	0.090	0.068
Meghalaya	0.0068	0.017
Odisha	0.17	0.15
Madhya Pradesh	0.26	0.38
Gujarat	0.25	0.21
Tamil Nadu	0.22	0.17

Note: Data are from the 1998–1999 and 2019 ITUS. Weighted means are computed using sampling weights from the ITUS.

Table A2. Gelbach Decompositions Showing FE, 1998–2019.

	Leisure	Home Prod.	Work	Learning
Employer	0.033	−0.0043	−0.022	−0.0067
Helper in HH enterprise	−0.072	−0.33	1.03**	−0.62*
Regular employee	0.99**	−0.024	−1.08*	0.11
Casual labor, public works	0.25	−0.022	−0.33	0.10
Casual labor, other	1.49**	0.093	−1.62***	0.029
Seeking work	0.14	0.0045	−0.15	0.00094
School	−1.50	−2.59*	−75.8***	79.8***
Domestic duties	−5.32***	−6.64***	14.0***	−2.06***
Domestic duties, goods collection	−2.66**	−2.01***	5.07***	−0.41
Transfer recipient	0.043	0.0071	−0.16	0.11
Disability	0.089	−0.0091	−0.096	0.016
Other	−12.6***	−0.71	18.6***	−5.21***
Meghalaya	−0.10	0.36*	0.21*	−0.47
Odisha	0.95	−0.023	0.26	−1.19
Madhya Pradesh	4.70*	2.26*	0.13	−7.09*
Gujarat	−0.20	−0.92	0.13	0.99
Tamil Nadu	2.60	0.030	−0.21	−2.43
All other covariates	−6.28**	1.50	−1.50	6.28**
Total predicted change	−17.5**	−9.03***	−41.5***	68.0***
Observations	29,859	29,859	29,859	29,859

Note: This is an alternative presentation of the results in Table 3. Graphical analogs appear in Figs. A1–A4. Data are from the 1998–1999 and 2019 ITUS. Classification is based on 1-digit 1998 activity codes: 8–9 leisure, 4–6 home production, 1–3 work, and 7 learning. Estimates represent the contributions of covariate groups to the difference between: (i) the uncontrolled change in weighted mean duration from 1998–1999 to 2019; and (ii) the change in weighted mean duration from 1998–1999 to 2019, controlling for covariates. Sampling weights are from the ITUS. The contributions of all covariate groups sum to the Total predicted change. Standard errors in parentheses are clustered at the district level. $^{*}p < 0.1$, $^{**}p < 0.05$, $^{***}p < 0.01$.

Table A3. Children's Learning Changes, 1998–2019.

	School	School	Homework	Homework	Travel	Travel	Other	Other
2019 survey	71.9***	31.9***	13.6**	−5.88	14.7***	9.20***	10.1***	7.09***
	(8.23)	(7.50)	(6.10)	(4.34)	(1.92)	(1.95)	(1.77)	(1.60)
Female		5.35		6.61		1.77		4.44
		(9.86)		(4.38)		(2.44)		(2.69)
Rural		12.1**		−10.6***		−2.24		−5.53***
		(6.02)		(3.96)		(1.93)		(1.98)
Landless		−6.26		−1.69		−4.91***		0.44
		(4.15)		(2.71)		(1.09)		(1.00)
Scheduled tribe		4.16		−6.19		−0.84		−1.59
		(6.55)		(4.68)		(1.94)		(2.11)
Scheduled caste		−0.10		−4.36		0.28		−0.37
		(4.52)		(2.85)		(1.12)		(1.51)
Hinduism		−2.05		11.8		1.59		1.40
		(7.96)		(7.87)		(2.52)		(2.04)
Islam		−14.7		−3.70		−3.04		2.56
		(13.1)		(7.86)		(2.93)		(2.87)
Age FE	No	Yes	No	Yes	No	Yes	No	Yes
Female-age FE	No	Yes	No	Yes	No	Yes	No	Yes
Usual activity FE	No	Yes	No	Yes	No	Yes	No	Yes
Exp. Quintiles	No	Yes	No	Yes	No	Yes	No	Yes
HH size quintiles	No	Yes	No	Yes	No	Yes	No	Yes
Dwelling FE	No	Yes	No	Yes	No	Yes	No	Yes
State FE	No	Yes	No	Yes	No	Yes	No	Yes
Observations	29,859	29,859	29,859	29,859	29,859	29,859	29,859	29,859

Note: Data are from the 1998–1999 and 2019 ITUS. Categories are "school/university attendance," "homework, being tutored, course review, research and activities related to formal education," "traveling time related to learning," and all others under learning (1998 single-digit code 7). Each column presents estimates from a weighted linear regression, with time use in minutes as the dependent variable and an indicator for the 2019 ITUS survey as the regressor of primary interest. Sampling weights are from the ITUS. Odd columns correspond to Eq. (1) and even columns to Eq. (2). Estimates correspond to Fig. 5. Standard errors in parentheses are clustered at the district level. *$p < 0.1$, **$p < 0.05$, ***$p < 0.01$.

Table A4. Blinder-Oaxaca Decomposition of Children's School Time Change, 1998–2019.

	School Time
Overall	
2019 survey	267.4***
	(5.85)
1998 survey	195.5***
	(7.31)
Difference	71.9***
	(8.49)
Endowments	41.0***
	(6.87)
Coefficients	37.5***
	(6.89)
Interaction	−6.54
	(5.78)
Endowments	
Usual activity is school	48.8***
	(5.19)
Coefficients	
Usual activity is school	−0.71
	(9.91)
Interaction	
Usual activity is school	−0.19
	(2.62)
Observations	29,859

Note: Data are from the 1998–1999 and 2019 ITUS. Dependent variable is time in "school/university attendance." Sampling weights are from the ITUS. Standard errors in parentheses are clustered at the district level. $^{*}p < 0.1$, $^{**}p < 0.05$, $^{***}p < 0.01$.

Table A5. Gelbach Decompositions of Children's Learning Changes, 1998–2019.

	School	Homework	Travel	Other
Female	0.085	0.10	0.028	0.070
	(0.16)	(0.094)	(0.041)	(0.063)
Age FE	0.33*	0.71*	0.18*	0.14
	(0.18)	(0.38)	(0.11)	(0.11)
Female-age FE	−0.20	0.13	−0.11	−0.17*
	(0.20)	(0.14)	(0.079)	(0.096)
Usual activity FE	45.4***	19.0***	6.22***	1.30***
	(4.83)	(2.55)	(0.67)	(0.26)
Exp. Quintiles	−0.16	−0.24	0.19	−0.093
	(0.32)	(0.23)	(0.21)	(0.15)
Rural	−0.18	0.15	0.033	0.081
	(0.56)	(0.50)	(0.12)	(0.27)
Landless	0.066	0.018	0.051	−0.0046
	(0.21)	(0.062)	(0.16)	(0.018)
HH size quintiles	2.06*	−0.64	0.19	0.34
	(1.24)	(1.00)	(0.22)	(0.29)
Scheduled FE	0.20	−0.36	−0.038	−0.082
	(0.36)	(0.26)	(0.11)	(0.12)
Religion FE	0.13	0.15	0.046	−0.012
	(0.18)	(0.24)	(0.059)	(0.033)
Dwelling FE	−0.11	2.69***	−0.65**	1.15**
	(1.22)	(0.87)	(0.29)	(0.47)
State FE	−7.62*	−2.19	−0.67	0.28
	(4.25)	(4.09)	(0.79)	(0.46)
Total predicted change	40.1***	19.5***	5.46***	3.00***
	(7.19)	(4.47)	(1.31)	(0.82)
Observations	29,859	29,859	29,859	29,859

Note: Data are from the 1998–1999 and 2019 ITUS. Categories are "school/university attendance," "homework, being tutored, course review, research and activities related to formal education," "traveling time related to learning," and all others under learning (1998 single-digit code 7). Estimates represent the contributions of covariate groups to the difference between: (i) the uncontrolled change in weighted mean duration from 1998–1999 to 2019; and (ii) the change in weighted mean duration from 1998–1999 to 2019, controlling for covariates. Sampling weights are from the ITUS. The contributions of all covariate groups sum to the Total predicted change. Estimates correspond to markers in Fig. 6. Standard errors in parentheses are clustered at the district level. $^*p < 0.1$, $^{**}p < 0.05$, $^{***}p < 0.01$.

Table A6. Children's Leisure Changes, 1998–2019.

	TV	TV	Talking	Talking	Games	Games	Hygiene	Hygiene	Eating	Eating	Other	Other
2019 survey	18.6***	14.5***	−10.1***	−4.61	−16.7***	−14.5***	6.79***	4.31**	11.8***	12.2***	−46.7***	−40.4***
	(5.73)	(4.43)	(3.49)	(3.22)	(5.84)	(5.30)	(2.26)	(2.08)	(2.64)	(2.35)	(4.59)	(4.09)
Female		−6.96		2.42		−7.01		−1.10		1.99		7.53
		(5.84)		(3.40)		(6.84)		(2.06)		(3.66)		(7.32)
Rural		−22.3***		4.57**		1.22		−1.50		−1.02		4.10
		(3.53)		(2.17)		(3.98)		(1.27)		(1.67)		(3.78)
Landless		8.44***		−1.21		−1.11		0.27		1.83		2.16
		(2.29)		(1.63)		(2.49)		(0.99)		(1.15)		(2.95)
Sched. Tribe		−15.0***		−6.15*		2.36		4.91***		3.30		1.73
		(4.33)		(3.33)		(5.30)		(1.72)		(2.41)		(4.65)
Sched. Caste		−5.60		0.077		−1.69		−1.76		2.54*		5.47*
		(3.60)		(1.91)		(3.47)		(1.06)		(1.39)		(2.86)
Hinduism		−3.22		−7.23**		4.61		−0.97		−5.71		−8.48
		(4.90)		(2.82)		(5.06)		(2.65)		(4.11)		(9.65)
Islam		5.82		−8.39**		6.42		−5.43*		−7.25		8.91
		(6.81)		(4.14)		(8.87)		(3.04)		(4.52)		(10.9)
Age FE	No	Yes	No	Yes	No	Yes	No	Yes	No	Yes	No	Yes
Female-age FE	No	Yes	No	Yes	No	Yes	No	Yes	No	Yes	No	Yes
Usual activity FE	No	Yes	No	Yes	No	Yes	No	Yes	No	Yes	No	Yes
Exp. Quintiles	No	Yes	No	Yes	No	Yes	No	Yes	No	Yes	No	Yes
HH size quintiles	No	Yes	No	Yes	No	Yes	No	Yes	No	Yes	No	Yes
Dwelling FE	No	Yes	No	Yes	No	Yes	No	Yes	No	Yes	No	Yes
State FE	No	Yes	No	Yes	No	Yes	No	Yes	No	Yes	No	Yes
Observations	29,859	29,859	29,859	29,859	29,859	29,859	29,859	29,859	29,859	29,859	29,859	29,859

Note: Data are from the 1998–1999 and 2019 ITUS. Categories are "watching/listening to television and video," "talking, conversing, chatting," "playing games and other pastime activities," "personal hygiene and care," "eating and drinking," and all other waking uses under leisure (1998 single-digit codes 8–9). Each column presents estimates from a weighted linear regression, with time use in minutes as the dependent variable and an indicator for the 2019 ITUS survey as the regressor of primary interest. Sampling weights are from the ITUS. Odd columns correspond to Eq. (1) and even columns to Eq. (2). Estimates correspond to Fig. 8. Standard errors in parentheses are clustered at the district level. $*p < 0.1$, $**p < 0.05$, $***p < 0.01$.

Table A7. Gelbach Decompositions of Children's Leisure Changes, 1998–2019.

	TV	Talking	Games	Hygiene	Eating	Other
Female	−0.11	0.038	−0.11	−0.018	0.031	0.12
	(0.12)	(0.064)	(0.13)	(0.034)	(0.060)	(0.15)
Age FE	0.062	0.24	−1.41**	0.15**	−0.13	0.068
	(0.14)	(0.17)	(0.70)	(0.076)	(0.086)	(0.31)
Female-age FE	0.23*	0.087	−0.85***	0.063	−0.059	−0.27
	(0.13)	(0.075)	(0.32)	(0.056)	(0.070)	(0.28)
Usual activity FE	−0.56	−5.97***	0.092	0.54**	0.27	−6.90***
	(0.78)	(0.92)	(1.11)	(0.25)	(0.31)	(1.50)
Exp. Quintiles	0.76	0.065	−0.29	−0.24**	−0.0042	0.22
	(0.73)	(0.28)	(0.52)	(0.10)	(0.13)	(0.20)
Rural	0.33	−0.067	−0.018	0.022	0.015	−0.060
	(1.05)	(0.22)	(0.096)	(0.078)	(0.053)	(0.20)
Landless	−0.088	0.013	0.012	−0.0029	−0.019	−0.023
	(0.27)	(0.045)	(0.047)	(0.014)	(0.061)	(0.082)
HH size quintiles	−0.63	−0.61	−0.87	0.50	0.34	0.33
	(0.60)	(0.49)	(0.74)	(0.32)	(0.38)	(0.81)
Scheduled FE	−0.80	−0.30	0.097	0.22	0.19	0.15
	(0.52)	(0.29)	(0.30)	(0.21)	(0.17)	(0.25)
Religion FE	−0.090	0.011	−0.018	0.044	0.015	−0.17
	(0.11)	(0.084)	(0.089)	(0.060)	(0.069)	(0.24)
Dwelling FE	3.42***	−0.24	−1.86*	0.18	0.018	−1.30
	(1.05)	(0.55)	(0.95)	(0.29)	(0.41)	(0.89)
State FE	1.61	1.24	3.04	1.02	−1.14	1.53
	(1.35)	(1.02)	(2.62)	(1.11)	(1.39)	(1.57)
Total predicted change	4.12	−5.49***	−2.19	2.49*	−0.48	−6.31**
	(3.13)	(1.85)	(4.43)	(1.46)	(1.58)	(2.85)
Observations	29,859	29,859	29,859	29,859	29,859	29,859

Note: Data are from the 1998–1999 and 2019 ITUS. Categories are "watching/listening to television and video," "talking, conversing, chatting," "playing games and other pastime activities," "personal hygiene and care," "eating and drinking," and all other waking uses under leisure (1998 single-digit codes 8–9). Estimates represent the contributions of covariate groups to the difference between: (i) the uncontrolled change in weighted mean duration from 1998–1999 to 2019; and (ii) the change in weighted mean duration from 1998–1999 to 2019, controlling for covariates. Sampling weights are from the ITUS. The contributions of all covariate groups sum to the Total predicted change. Estimates correspond to markers in Fig. 9. Standard errors in parentheses are clustered at the district level. $^{*}p < 0.1$, $^{**}p < 0.05$, $^{***}p < 0.01$.

TIME USE AND THE GEOGRAPHY OF ECONOMIC OPPORTUNITY

Sulagna Mookerjee, John D. Pedersen and David Slichter

ABSTRACT

The community in which a child is raised has a substantial effect on their income in adulthood. To help understand what is different about communities which produce higher incomes, we document how time use differs between communities which increase their members' future incomes more. The main differences are that, in areas which produce higher incomes, people spend more time at work, and adults spend more time with children. The data do not support some theories of what makes communities effective at producing human capital: People do not spend more time on educational activities, or on community events and institutions, in areas which increase incomes by more.

Keywords: Time use; intergenerational mobility; human capital; urban economics; work time; caring time

1. INTRODUCTION

It has long been believed that the community where a child is raised has a substantial impact on a child's life course (e.g., Benabou, 1993; Katz et al., 2001). Recently, Chetty and Hendren (2018a) quantified one dimension of this effect by measuring the effect of childhood community on income in adulthood (relative to living in a randomly chosen other community), finding large differences across communities.[1]

However, it is not known exactly *why* communities differ in their effects on the adult incomes of children raised there. A natural first step toward this is to characterize what is different between these communities. Chetty and Hendren (2018b) document that communities which increase the incomes of children who

Time Use in Economics
Research in Labor Economics, Volume 51, 89–104

ISSN: 0147-9121/doi:10.1108/S0147-912120230000051004

were raised there have higher standardized test scores, lower levels of segregation, and greater social capital – potentially pointing to explanations relating to the school system and social interactions. Subsequent research along these lines suggests that places which generate growth in test score performances are not better at producing incomes (Mookerjee & Slichter, 2023; Rothstein, 2019), and that effects on income are more correlated with historical than contemporary segregation (Andrews et al., 2017).

We contribute to the question of what makes some places increase incomes in adulthood more than others by characterizing how time use differs among these places. Differences in time use are potentially informative in this regard for two reasons. First, time use is a marker for community characteristics such as cultural values about the importance of children, work, and education. Second, the allocation of time is per se an important input into child development (e.g., Caetano et al., 2019; Kofman & Bianchi, 2012; Sayer et al., 2004a).[2]

We use the American Time Use Survey, which provides information on how much time is spent by individuals on different activities. We observe the *quantity* of time spent but not the *quality*, as is common in the literature; however, we present a simple theoretical model in the Appendix demonstrating why one would expect differences in the quality of time inputs to be reflected in the amount of time spent on each activity. For example, in communities with a comparative advantage in producing human capital through time use on social activities, we would expect to see more time spent on social activities.

We examine time use separately for three subgroups within our sample. These subgroups are (i) adults who have at least one child in the household, and are therefore likely to be caregivers to children; (ii) adults with no children in the household, who are therefore unlikely to be primary caregivers to children; and (iii) teens (ages 15–18), to capture how the people being raised in a community spend their time.

Our first empirical finding is that adults spend more time with children in communities which increase incomes in adulthood. (For the rest of the chapter, we refer to communities which increase incomes in adulthood as "high-effect" communities.) This is consistent with both the views that such communities are more child-centric in the sense of placing a greater utility weight on children's outcomes, and that time spent with family is a key input for children's cognitive development (Caetano et al., 2019).[3]

Second, we find that individuals spend more time at work in high-effect communities. This finding is consistent with the theory that communities vary in their cultural emphasis on work, and that children learn how much to emphasize their careers from observing adults (Huang et al., 2001). It is also potentially consistent with the possibility that high-effect communities are increasing children's incomes in adulthood by placing them into healthier labor markets, rather than by increasing their human capital.

Also notable are some correlations that we fail to find. First, we examine time spent on adult care as a placebo category, and do not find that respondents in high-effect communities are any more likely to allocate time toward taking care of adult household members. This suggests that additional time on caregiving is specific to children, and not necessarily indicative of generalized values about the importance of helping others. Second, Chetty and Hendren (2018b) find evidence that high-effect communities might have greater social capital and stronger social networks. We, however, find no correlation between a community's effect on incomes and time spent on social or community-building activities such as attending social gatherings, participating in community or religious organizations or events, or attending sports or entertainment events. Third, despite the higher average test scores in such communities (Chetty & Hendren, 2018b), we do not find evidence that more time is spent by teens on educational activities in high-effect communities.

The rest of the chapter proceeds as follows. Section 2 describes the data. Section 3 gives the results. Section 4 concludes.

2. DATA AND METHODS

We obtain our measures of time use from the American Time Use Survey (ATUS). The ATUS is a Bureau of Labor Statistics Survey, conducted by the US Census Bureau, on a nationally representative sample of people aged 15 and older from households that recently completed the Current Population Survey (CPS). One person from each household is randomly chosen to complete a diary detailing their time use for one day: what activities they engaged in and for how long, the location, who they were accompanied by, etc. We use survey years from 2003 to 2018.

We categorize respondents into three mutually exclusive subgroups. The first is "teens," composed of all respondents ages 15–18, and intended to capture the time use of people who are being raised in the community. For this sample, we focus on categories of time use which might influence the respondent's own human capital accumulation, as follows: (i) *education*, which includes time spent on classes, homework, and education-related travel, (ii) *work*, encompassing time spent actually on the job as well as searching, traveling, and other work-related actions (note that results are unchanged if we define work to exclusively mean time spent on the job), (iii) *watching television* as part of leisure time, such as watching sports on TV, (iv) *sports*, including participating in sports, exercising, or recreational outdoor activities, (v) *social activities* which are organized and formal, consisting of religious, social and civic actions, social services, related travel, and volunteering, and (vi) *socializing* informally, which includes time spent visiting or communicating with family, friends, and neighbors.

Our other two subgroups are adults with children in the household, and adults without children in the household. We define an adult to be a respondent aged 19 or older, and adults with children are adults who report at least one person under the age of 18 residing in their household.

Among adults, our key categories of time use are (i) *child care*, which is any time spent with household children (getting them ready, helping them with schoolwork, playing with them, entertaining them, planning activities for them, time spent on grooming or healthcare, etc.) as well as any time spent with non-household children; (ii) *adult care*, which captures time spent caring for household and non-household adults and helping non-household adults with a range of activities such as running errands for them, giving them rides, helping them with technology, attending to their medical needs, etc.; (iii) *work*, encompassing time spent actually working as well as searching, traveling, and other work-related actions; and (iv) *social activities*, consisting of religious, social, and civic actions, social services, related travel, and volunteering. The goal of these measures is (1) to capture inputs directly given from caregivers to children, and (2) to proxy for attitudes, values, and behaviors common among the people children interact with.

The survey also provides standard socioeconomic and demographic information for all members of each household. Table 1 provides an overview of our sample from the ATUS. Two variables are of particular importance for our analysis: (i) family income, which allows us to create an indicator for whether households are high or low income, and (ii) the number of children in the household, which lets us separately explore time allocation for adults with and without children in the household (which we treat as a proxy for whether they could be potential caregivers). Our definition of high and low income roughly corresponds to the median of income in the data for each year: On average, households are denoted as high income if they have income above $60,000 and above, which corresponds to about 52% of our sample.[4]

We combine these data with Chetty and Hendren's (2018b) estimates of counties' effects on the adult incomes of children raised there. Chetty and Hendren construct estimated effects on income separately for children from families at the 25th (low) and the 75th (high) percentiles of income. They use cohorts born between 1980 and 1988, which partially overlaps with our data; the results are robust to restricting the sample to the overlapping cohorts. Since the CPS suppresses geographic identifiers for areas with population less than 100,000, we can only match counties with a population greater than 100,000, which accounts for around 20% of counties but around 80% of the population. The average county exposure effects for both the 25th and the 75th percentile are lower for the matched (more populated) counties than the non-matched (less populated) counties.[5]

For simplicity, we convert their estimates of county exposure effects into units of standard deviations above or below the average. To perform this conversion, we use their estimate of the true standard deviation of county effects, which is 0.517 for the 25th and 0.321 for the 75th percentile, in units of percent effect on income per year of exposure.[6] Their estimates are designed to be forecast-unbiased in the presence of estimation error, which necessitates shrinkage;[7] therefore, the standard deviation of their estimates is smaller than these estimates of the standard deviation of county quality. Specifically, Chetty and Hendren's estimates are constructed using a convex combination of two estimates: (i) estimates using children who move between counties at different ages, and (ii) average outcomes for children who spend their entire childhood in one county ("permanent residents"). Chetty and Hendren argue that (i) is approximately unbiased but has high variance due to sampling error, while (ii) has low variance but is biased. In practice, most of the variation in their combined estimates comes from (ii) rather than (i).

For each income category, high and low, we assign the individuals in that category the corresponding standard deviation measure of the effect on adult incomes for children in that income group (derived from Chetty and Hendren's (2018b) estimates).[8] We then measure the difference in average time spent on each activity category between more and less effective communities by regressing time use on the measure of place effects, as follows:

Table 1. Descriptive Statistics.

	Adults		
	Hhd Child	No hhd Child	Teens
Age	39.77 (10.48)	55.21 (17.10)	16.47 (1.04)
Male	0.41 (0.49)	0.45 (0.50)	0.51 (0.50)
White	0.80 (0.40)	0.77 (0.42)	0.77 (0.42)
College grad	0.40 (0.49)	0.35 (0.48)	0.00 (0.03)
Employed	0.71 (0.45)	0.53 (0.50)	0.16 (0.37)
Observations	33,610	44,624	4,334

Notes: The table provides means and standard deviations of the demographic variables in the sample.

$$t_{ic} = \beta_0 + \beta_1 Q_{ic} + u_{ic},$$

where t_{ic} is the time in minutes spent on an activity by individual i residing in county c, and Q_{ic} is the place effect, i.e. standard deviation measure of the effect of being raised in county c on adult income for children belonging to individual i's income category (high or low). We weight the regression using ATUS sampling weights. A positive estimated $\widehat{\beta_1}$ indicates that high-effect communities invest more time in that particular activity, and the magnitude is the number of additional minutes that people in a community with a 1 standard deviation above-average effect on income spend on that activity relative to people in the average community.

Because Q is estimated by Chetty and Hendren, it is important to consider how measurement error in their estimates might affect our results. Our ideal regression is

$$t_{ic} = \beta_0 + \beta_1 Q^*_{ic} + v_{ic},$$

where Q^*_{ic} is the true exposure effect as opposed to Chetty and Hendren's estimate, and $E(v_{ic}|Q^*_{ic}) = 0$. Let $\epsilon_{ic} := Q_{ic} - Q^*_{ic}$ be the measurement error in the estimate of Q^*.

We have

$$E(t_{ic}|Q_{ic}) = E\left(\alpha_0 + \alpha_1 Q^*_{ic} + v_{ic}|Q_{ic}\right)$$

$$= \alpha_0 + \alpha_1 E\left(Q^*_{ic}|Q_{ic}\right) + E(v_{ic}|Q_{ic})$$

$$= \alpha_0 + \alpha_1 Q_{ic} + E(v_{ic}|Q_{ic})$$

where the last equality holds because Chetty and Hendren's measure is designed to be forecast-unbiased. It follows that our regression estimand β_1 is equal to the ideal estimand α_1 if $E(v_{ic}|Q_{ic}) = 0$. While $E(v_{ic}|Q^*_{ic}) = 0$, it can still be the case that $E(v_{ic}|Q_{ic}) \neq 0$ *if* $E(v_{ic}|\epsilon_{ic}) \neq 0$. That is, our estimates might be biased due to measurement error if the errors in Chetty and Hendren's estimates are correlated with time usage in the same community. As discussed above, the main source of potential error in Chetty and Hendren's estimates is that permanent residents of different communities are systematically different. Therefore, to assess whether our estimates are likely to be sensitive to measurement error, we estimate specifications using individual-level controls.

In particular, in order to rule out that these differences are simply driven by differences in socioeconomic and demographic characteristics, we estimate a specification controlling for individuals' age, gender, race, education, and income bracket. Comparing individuals across communities who are identical in these respects eliminates the possibility that the differential time use patterns are accounted for purely by selection along these dimensions (e.g., richer or college educated people being both more likely to live in high-effect communities as well as more likely to spend time on work). With limited exceptions, our results turn out not to be sensitive to these controls.

3. RESULTS

Table 2 reports the results for adults with children in the household, and Table 3 for adults without. For each sample, we report both the results from an uncontrolled specification (Panel A) and a specification including the controls described above (Panel B).

The first set of results is for time allocated toward childcare activities. For each category, the coefficient denotes the additional number of minutes spent by individuals in one standard deviation higher-effect communities on that category per day, averaged over all 7 days in a week.

Households in high-effect communities spend significantly more time with children overall. Each standard deviation increase in community effect on incomes is associated with an additional 2 minutes per day of childcare by

Table 2. Relationship Between a One Standard Deviation Increase in Place Effect and Minutes per Day Spent on Activities by Adults With Children in the Household.

	Childcare				
	Hhd	Non-hhd	Adult Care	Work	Soc.Act.
		Panel (A): No controls			
Place effect (Q)	2.11	−0.08	0.06	10.75	0.76
	(1.02)	(0.19)	(0.15)	(2.80)	(0.54)
Baseline	78.60	1.57	1.40	204.64	23.08
Observations	33,610	33,610	33,610	33,610	33,610
		Panel (B): With controls			
Place effect (Q)	1.61	0.00	0.08	4.89	0.81
	(0.99)	(0.17)	(0.16)	(2.69)	(0.54)
Baseline	78.60	1.57	1.40	204.64	23.08
Observations	33,610	33,610	33,610	33,610	33,610

Notes: The table provides results from regressions of time spent on different activity categories by individuals aged 19 and above who have at least one child under the age of 18 residing in their household, on the income-specific effect of their community at increasing incomes in adulthood (Q). Robust standard errors in parentheses. All regressions include ATUS sampling weights.

Table 3. Relationship Between a One Standard Deviation Increase in Place Effect and Minutes per Day Spent on Activities by Adults Without Children in the Household.

	Childcare				
	Hhd	Non-hhd	Adult Care	Work	Soc.Act.
		Panel (A): No controls			
Place effect (Q)	–	0.48	−0.22	2.89	−0.65
		(0.29)	(0.18)	(2.63)	(0.50)
Baseline		5.83	1.98	162.24	25.71
Observations		44,624	44,624	44,624	44,624
		Panel (B): With controls			
Place effect (Q)	–	0.36	−0.26	6.49	−0.58
		(0.29)	(0.18)	(2.45)	(0.50)
Baseline		5.83	1.98	162.24	25.71
Observations		44,624	44,624	44,624	44,624

Notes: The table provides results from regressions of time spent on different activity categories by individuals aged 19 and above who have no children residing in their household, on the income-specific effect of their community at increasing incomes in adulthood (Q). Robust standard errors in parentheses. All regressions include ATUS sampling weights.

respondents in households with children, off a baseline of 80 minutes per day. This is driven by additional time specifically with children from the same household, who absorb the overwhelming majority of childcare time (78 minutes per day) among such households. The coefficient becomes insignificant with the inclusion of controls. However, as discussed below, the additional childcare time continues to be significant for the controlled specification when we restrict the sample to adults with full-time employment (coefficient 2.39 and S.E. 1.04), as well as when we restrict the sample to adults aged above 23 to match the age cutoffs in Chetty and Hendren (2018b) (coefficient 1.66 and S.E. 1.00). Households without children also spend more time caring for children, though the amounts of time involved are small – half a minute per day per standard deviation, off a baseline of 6 minutes per day.

We also examine time spent on taking care of adults, in the spirit of a placebo test, to see whether the larger amount of time on child care reflects a general tendency to spend time caring for others as opposed to a specific orientation to children. We find no pattern of higher time spent on adult care in high-effect communities.

The third time use category we study is work. Our results suggest that adult respondents spend more time on work in high-effect communities. The results within each household type are sensitive to the inclusion of controls, but the overall pattern suggests that adults generally spend about 5 additional minutes on work per day in counties which have one standard deviation higher effects on income. If we run the work regressions by pooling all respondents over the age of 19, regardless of whether or not there are children present, we obtain a coefficient of 5.81 (standard error of 1.95) without controls and 5.70 (standard error of 1.86) with controls. We also examine the sub-categories of time expenditure on work, and find that the additional time spent is on actually working, rather than on other work-related activities such as searching for work or traveling for work.[9]

The last category which we explore for adults is social, civic, and religious activities. We find zero differences between high-effect and low-effect communities in these time expenditures.[10]

Next, because we find evidence that people in high-effect communities spend more time with children, we also look in greater detail at how time with children is spent. In Table 4, we report results dividing time with children into three subcategories: time on educational activities (e.g., helping children with school projects, checking their homework, attending meetings at school), time on health-related activities (e.g., taking children to the doctor, bandaging cuts and scrapes, sitting with sick children, taking their temperature), and all other time expenditures (feeding children, bathing them, helping them get dressed, playing with them, reading to them, doing crafts or playing sports with them, having conversations, and generally looking after them). The latter subcategory appears to be the main difference in time use. This may also be indicative of more quality time spent with children, on traditionally enriching activities such as reading.[11]

Table 4 shows that families in high-effect communities are not spending more time on educational activities with their children, suggesting that high-effect communities might not be distinguished by a greater family emphasis on education. Because family time spent on educational activities is often intended to be remedial, it is also possible that this simply reflects greater satisfaction with

Table 4. Relationship Between a One Standard Deviation Increase in Place Effect and Minutes per Day Spent on Each Childcare Category by Adults With Children in the Household.

	Education	Health	Other
	Panel (A): No controls		
Place effect (Q)	−0.39	0.07	2.42
	(0.24)	(0.16)	(0.96)
Baseline	6.54	1.81	70.25
Observations	33,610	33,610	33,610
	Panel (B): With controls		
Place Effect (Q)	−0.27	0.09	1.79
	(0.24)	(0.15)	(0.93)
Baseline	6.54	1.81	70.25
Observations	33,610	33,610	33,610

Notes: The table provides results from regressions of time spent on different childcare categories by individuals aged 19 and above who have at least one child under the age of 18 residing in their household, on the income-specific effect of their community at increasing incomes in adulthood (Q). Robust standard errors in parentheses. All regressions include ATUS sampling weights.

children's progress in school. However, the remedial motive is probably less important for children's educational time expenditures, and we will see momentarily that the children themselves are also not spending more time on educational activities in high-effect communities.

Table 5. Relationship Between a One Standard Deviation Increase in Place Effect and Minutes per Day Spent on Activities by Teens.

	Educ	Work	Watch TV	Sports	Soc. Act.	Socialize
			Panel (A): No controls			
Place effect (Q)	−2.68	5.16	0.83	−2.22	0.41	1.11
	(6.58)	(3.64)	(3.54)	(2.13)	(2.43)	(1.28)
Baseline	173.01	49.67	141.72	45.54	57.10	24.14
Observations	4,334	4,334	4,334	4,334	4,334	4,334
			Panel (B): With controls			
Place effect (Q)	−4.19	4.65	2.22	−2.40	−0.39	1.24
	(6.43)	(3.54)	(3.55)	(2.01)	(2.49)	(1.33)
Baseline	173.01	49.67	141.72	45.54	57.10	24.14
Observations	4,334	4,334	4,334	4,334	4,334	4,334

Notes: The table provides results from regressions of time spent on different activity categories by individuals aged between 15 and 18, on the income-specific effect of their community at increasing incomes in adulthood (Q). Robust standard errors in parentheses. All regressions include ATUS sampling weights.

Finally, we examine time spent by teens, i.e. individuals aged between 15 and 18. The results are reported in Table 5, and are broadly consistent with the results among older adults.

The coefficient with the largest magnitude is for time spent on work, with teens from a one standard deviation higher-effect community spending on average 4 to 5 additional minutes per day working, from a baseline of 50 minutes. This difference is not statistically significant but becomes significant at the 10% level if we restrict our sample to only those teens who are still in school, i.e., enrolled full-time at school or college (coefficient 6.46 and S.E. 3.66).

We find no difference in time spent on education between high- and low-effect communities. (In fact, our point estimate is negative, i.e., time spent on education is lower in high-effect communities.)

There also seems to be little difference in time expenditure on key leisure activities. Similar to older adults, we do not find any differences in time spent on social and community activities. This is true for both structured social events and informal socializing. We also do not find differences in time spent watching TV.

For additional robustness, we also attempt to match the age brackets used by Chetty and Hendren (2018b), who define where a child is raised by where they lived between ages 9 through 23. For the teen cohort, we re-estimate our specification for respondents aged between 15 and 23. We are limited to start at age 15 because ATUS does not collect information on the time use of children under 15. The results are in Appendix Table A1, and are qualitatively similar to those presented in the body of this article, with the coefficient for time spent on work being significant both with and without controls. Consistent with Chetty and Hendren's definition, we also re-estimate the results for adults aged 24 and above, with and without children in the household; Appendix Tables A2 and A3 report these results. The findings are qualitatively the same, the only exception being that the coefficient for the time spent on childcare by adult caregivers is significant at the 10% level for the controlled specification.

4. CONCLUSION

We find that communities' effects on incomes in adulthood are correlated with how people there use their time. In particular, individuals living in areas which increase incomes tend to spend more time at work, and adults in those communities spend more time on childcare activities. This is consistent with the views that high-effect communities are distinguished by a greater cultural emphasis on work, or on children's welfare. It is also consistent with the views that high-effect communities induce higher earnings in adulthood directly as a result of additional time spent with children, or as a result of stronger labor market conditions.

However, we fail to find some correlations which would have been expected under other theories of why some communities have greater effects on income in adulthood. In particular, we do not find a positive correlation with time spent on educational activities (in general, the point estimates are negative), inconsistent with differences in cultural values about education, and inconsistent with differences in the production of human capital directly caused by time expenditure on education. Additionally, we do not find that people of any age spend additional time on social or community activities in high-effect communities, which is not consistent with the view that high-effect communities are primarily distinguished by stronger social ties and greater social capital.

While the evidence is suggestive, our results are correlational, and so we cannot make strong causal claims. Future research should apply causal inference methods to disentangle the roles that parental interactions and employment opportunities and norms play, and make appropriate policy recommendations.

NOTES

1. Other recent work such as Chetty et al. (2016) and Fletcher and Han (2019) also provide quantitative support for the importance of the community where a child is raised.
2. Prior literature has considered that parental time spent on children might play a role in the intergenerational transmission of income inequalities, at the individual (rather than community) level (e.g., Hill & Stafford, 1980; Kalil et al., 2012).
3. Prior papers also find that more educated parents spend more time with children (Guryan et al., 2008; Sayer et al., 2004b).
4. We are not able to divide at exactly the median because income is binned in the data.
5. For the 25th percentile effects, the mean and the standard deviation are −0.01 and 0.37 for matched counties and 0.26 and 0.54 for non-matched counties respectively. For the 75th percentile effects, the mean and the standard deviation are −0.02 and 0.19 for matched counties and 0.16 and 0.21 for non-matched counties respectively.
6. The mean of their measure is 0 by construction.
7. See their paper for more details.
8. For consistency with Chetty and Hendren, who give estimated effects at the 25th and 75th percentiles of the income distribution, we match our below-median income individuals to their 25th percentile estimates and our above-median income individuals to their 75th percentile estimates. For additional robustness, we also re-estimate our model using the average county effect corresponding to the 50th percentile of income distribution, instead of the matched income-specific effect. The results, reported in Appendix Table A5, are qualitatively the same.
9. Our results are similar if we restrict the sample to adults who have full-time employment, reported in Appendix Table A4. That parents with full-time employment spend more time with children in higher-effect communities is consistent with the finding in Ramey and Ramey (2010) that more educated parents also spend more time on childcare.
10. We also explore potential heterogeneity in time use by income at places which are more effective for raising incomes at the 25th percentile and the 50th percentile, but fail to find any differences between time use patterns of low and high income individuals.
11. The additional time spent with children in high-effect communities is primarily by mothers, and statistically insignificant for fathers. Interestingly, the differences by category are consistent with those among women of different marital statuses in Hamermesh (2022).

REFERENCES

Andrews, R., Casey, M., Hardy, B. L., & Logan, T. D. (2017). Location matters: Historical racial segregation and intergenerational mobility. *Economics Letters*, *158*, 67–72.

Benabou, R. (1993). Workings of a city: Location, education, and production. *Quarterly Journal of Economics*, *108*, 619–652.

Caetano, G., Kinsler, J., & Teng, H. (2019). Towards causal estimates of children's time allocation on skill development. *Journal of Applied Econometrics*, *19*(34), 588–605.

Chetty, R., & Hendren, N. (2018a). The impacts of neighborhoods on intergenerational mobility I: Childhood exposure effects. *Quarterly Journal of Economics, 133*(3), 1107–1162.

Chetty, R., & Hendren, N. (2018b). The impacts of neighborhoods on intergenerational mobility II: County level estimates. *Quarterly Journal of Economics, 133*(3), 1163–1228.

Chetty, R., Hendren, N., & Katz, L. (2016). The effects of exposure to better neighborhoods on children: New evidence from the moving to opportunity experiment. *The American Economic Review, 106*(4), 855–902.

Fletcher, J., & Han, J. (2019). Intergenerational mobility in education: Variation in Geography and time. *Journal of Human Capital, 13*(4), 585–634.

Guryan, J., Hurst, E., & Kearney, M. (2008). Parental education and parental time with children. *The Journal of Economic Perspectives, 22*(3), 23–46.

Hamermesh, D. S. (2022). Moms' time – Married or not. In *Mothers in the labor market* (Vols. 1–27). Springer International Publishing.

Hill, C. R., & Stafford, F. P. (1980). Parental care of children: Time diary estimates of quantity, predictability, and variety. *Journal of Human Resources, 15*(2), 219–239.

Huang, L., Pergamit, M., & Shkolnik, J. (2001). Youth initiation into the labor market. *Monthly Labor Review, 124*, 18.

Kalil, A., Ryan, R., & Corey, M. (2012). Diverging destinies: Maternal education and the developmental gradient in time with children. *Demography, 49*(4), 1361–1383.

Katz, L., Kling, J., & Liebman, J. (2001). Moving to opportunity in Boston: Early results of a randomized mobility experiment. *Quarterly Journal of Economics, 116*(2), 607–654.

Kofman, Y., & Bianchi, S. (2012). *Time use of youths by immigrant and native-born parents: ATUS results* (Vol. 135, pp. 3–24). Monthly labor review/U.S. Department of Labor, Bureau of Labor Statistics.

Mookerjee, S., & Slichter, D. (2023). Test scores, schools, and the geography of economic opportunity. *Journal of Urban Economics* (forthcoming).

Ramey, G., & Ramey, V. A. (2010). *The Rug Rat race*. Brookings Papers on economic activity.

Rothstein, J. (2019). Inequality of educational opportunity? Schools as mediators of the intergenerational transmission of income. *Journal of Labor Economics, 37*(S1), 85–123.

Rupasingha, A., & Goetz, S. J. (2008). *US county-level social capital data, 1990–2005*. The Northeast Regional Center for Rural Development.

Sayer, L. C., Bianchi, S. M., & Robinson, J. P. (2004a). Are parents investing less in children? Trends in mothers' and fathers' time with children. *American Journal of Sociology, 110*, 1–43.

Sayer, L. C., Gauthier, A. H., & Furstenberg, F. F., Jr. (2004b). Educational differences in parents' time with children: Cross-national variations. *Journal of Marriage and Family, 66*(5), 1152–1169.

APPENDIX

THEORETICAL MODEL

To guide our interpretation of the empirical results, we develop the following simple model of time allocation.

Suppose that families have m ways to spend their time, and choose a vector of time allocations to activities $(t_1, \ldots, t_m)$ to maximize human capital production y subject to a time constraint $t_1 + \ldots + t_m = 1$ and the constraint imposed by the human capital production function $y \leq f(t_1, \ldots, t_m)$. Assume that f is differentiable and the technology set is convex.

Let $t^* = (t_1^*, \ldots, t_m^*)$ be the human capital-maximizing time use. By the Envelope Theorem, the marginal product $MP_k := \frac{\partial f}{\partial t_k}$ evaluated at t^* is equal for all activities t_k.

Suppose that, for some activity k, we altered the technology of human capital production to increase MP_k at all time allocation bundles. Because the technology set is convex, every activity has a diminishing marginal product. Therefore, the new optimal input bundle t' would have a greater time use on activity k than t^* does.

This suggests that improvements in the quality of an activity are likely to result in an increase in the quantity of time spent on that activity. However, there are three caveats to this claim.

First, if one were to change the production function in a way that increases the marginal product of activity k only at levels of $t_k < t_k^*$, then this change to the production function would make activity k more productive without increasing time expenditure on activity k. Therefore, not all differences in activity quality will show up in quantities.

Second, time use reflects *comparative* advantages in quality, not *absolute* advantages. If one were to change the production function by multiplying all marginal products by the same scalar (e.g. by changing f to $f' = .9 * f$), then one would not alter the optimal time allocation.

Third, this model assumes that families are maximizing children's human capital production. In practice, time use is also motivated by competing interests such as consumption value, institutional constraints, and social norms. To the extent that these competing motivations vary across communities, we would expect to see time use vary across communities in a way that reflects underlying values.

We can incorporate this final consideration into our framework, as follows. Suppose that, instead of maximizing human capital production, families choose a time allocation to maximize a utility function $U = \alpha\, f(t_1, \ldots, t_m) + (1-\alpha)\, c(t_1, \ldots, t_m)$, where the function c reflects the value that families derive from other considerations such as consumption. Let $\tilde{t}$ be the time allocation that a family would select with $\alpha = 0$, i.e. considering only this consumption value.

In communities where α is greater, time use will be more closely aligned with t^*; and, where α is smaller, time use will be more closely aligned with $\tilde{t}$. That is, time use reflects the extent of prioritizing children's human capital accumulation. Furthermore, time use differences across places might reflect differences in c: e.g., in particularly religious communities, we would expect to see people spend more time in church, regardless of its value to human capital accumulation.

Summing up, time use likely reflects a combination of (i) comparative advantages in human capital production, (ii) differences in the priority placed on child development, and (iii) differences in values related to the consumption value of activities.

LIST OF MOBILITY CORRELATES

The following place characteristics are documented as important correlates of upward mobility by Chetty and Hendren (2018b).

Group-Level Characteristics

- Segregation (measured using a Theil index)
- Measures of sprawl (fraction of people within a commute time less than 15 minutes)
- Income inequality (measured using the Gini coefficient)
- Education (output-based proxies for K-12 school quality, such as test scores and high school dropout rates controlling for parental income)
- Social capital (measures by the social capital index of Rupasingha & Goetz, 2008)

Individual-Level Demographic Characteristics

- Family structure (fraction of single mothers)
- Immigrant share (fraction of immigrants in an area measured during Census Data)
- Racial shares (share of black residents)

APPENDIX TABLES

Table A1. Relationship Between a One Standard Deviation Increase in Place Effect and Minutes per Day Spent on Activities by Young Adults (Ages 15–23).

	Educ	Work	Watch TV	Sports	Soc. Act.	Socialize
			Panel (A): No controls			
Place effect (*Q*)	−5.35	13.27	2.26	−0.34	1.23	−0.19
	(4.54)	(5.00)	(2.73)	(1.57)	(2.04)	(0.95)
Baseline	123.50	106.44	144.03	36.70	60.17	19.90
Observations	7,847	7,847	7,847	7,847	7,847	7,847
			Panel (B): With controls			
Place effect (*Q*)	−3.35	8.44	3.17	−0.83	0.38	0.23
	(4.24)	(4.45)	(2.72)	(1.50)	(1.99)	(0.96)
Baseline	123.50	106.44	144.03	36.70	60.17	19.90
Observations	7,847	7,847	7,847	7,847	7,847	7,847

Notes: The table provides results from regressions of time spent on different activity categories by individuals aged between 15 and 23, on the income-specific effect of their community at increasing incomes in adulthood (*Q*). Robust standard errors in parentheses. All regressions include ATUS sampling weights.

Table A2. Relationship Between a One Standard Deviation Increase in Place Effect and Minutes per Day Spent on Activities by Adults (Ages 24 and Above) With Children in Household.

	Childcare				
	Hhd	Non-hhd	Adult Care	Work	Soc.Act.
		Panel (A): No controls			
Place effect (Q)	2.58	−0.04	−0.04	9.49	0.46
	(1.04)	(0.18)	(0.15)	(2.86)	(0.54)
Baseline	79.99	1.53	1.41	207.29	23.45
Observations	31,889	31,889	31,889	31,889	31,889
		Panel (B): With controls			
Place effect (Q)	1.66	0.06	−0.00	3.64	0.56
	(1.00)	(0.18)	(0.16)	(2.72)	(0.54)
Baseline	79.99	1.53	1.41	207.29	23.45
Observations	31,889	31,889	31,889	31,889	31,889

Notes: The table provides results from regressions of time spent on different activity categories by individuals aged 24 and above who have at least one child under the age of 18 residing in their household, on the income-specific effect of their community at increasing incomes in adulthood (Q). Robust standard errors in parentheses. All regressions include ATUS sampling weights.

Table A3. Relationship Between a One Standard Deviation Increase in Place Effect and Minutes per Day Spent on Activities by Adults (Ages 24 and Above) Without Children in Household.

	Childcare				
	Hhd	Non-hhd	Adult Care	Work	Soc.Act.
		Panel (A): No controls			
Place effect (Q)	–	0.52	−0.26	1.98	−0.35
		(0.31)	(0.19)	(2.67)	(0.52)
Baseline		5.94	2.02	160.80	26.24
Observations		42,832	42,832	42,832	42,832
		Panel (B): With controls			
Place effect (Q)	–	0.38	−0.31	7.52	−0.38
		(0.31)	(0.19)	(2.42)	(0.52)
Baseline		5.94	2.02	160.80	26.24
Observations		42,832	42,832	42,832	42,832

Notes: The table provides results from regressions of time spent on different activity categories by individuals aged 24 and above who have no children residing in their household, on the income-specific effect of their community at increasing incomes in adulthood (Q). Robust standard errors in parentheses. All regressions include ATUS sampling weights.

Table A4. Relationship Between a One Standard Deviation Increase in Place Effect and Minutes per Day Spent on Activities by Adults With Full-Time Employment.

	Childcare				
	Hhd	Non-hhd	Adult Care	Work	Soc.Act.
		Panel (A): No controls			
Place effect (Q)	2.56	−0.21	−0.25	9.82	0.53^{**}
	(1.07)	(0.18)	(0.17)	(3.36)	(0.61)
Baseline	65.88	1.37	1.26	270.87	20.63
Observations	21,997	21,997	21,997	21,997	21,997
		Panel (B): With controls			
Place effect (Q)	2.39	−0.12	−0.24	6.44	0.52
	(1.04)	(0.17)	(0.17)	(3.33)	(0.62)
Baseline	65.88	1.37	1.26	270.87	20.63
Observations	21,997	21,997	21,997	21,997	21,997

Notes: The table provides results from regressions of time spent on different activity categories by individuals with full-time employment aged 19 and above who have at least one child under the age of 18 residing in their household, on the income-specific effect of their community at increasing incomes in adulthood (Q). Robust standard errors in parentheses. All regressions include ATUS sampling weights.

Table A5. Results for Adult Time Use Using 50th Percentile Measure for Place Effect.

	Childcare				
	Hhd	Non-hhd	Adult Care	Work	Soc.Act.
		Panel (A): No controls			
Place effect (50th percentile)	4.52	−0.01	−0.02	17.65	1.13
Baseline	(1.08)	(0.16)	(0.17)	(3.06)	(0.57)
	78.60	1.57	1.40	204.64	23.08
Observations	35,713	35,713	35,713	35,713	35,713
		Panel (B): With controls			
Place effect (50th percentile)	3.68	0.15	0.06	4.99	0.93
	(1.07)	(0.17)	(0.18)	(2.95)	(0.58)
Baseline	78.60	1.57	1.40	204.64	23.08
Observations	35,713	35,713	35,713	35,713	35,713

Notes: The table provides results from regressions of time spent on different activity categories by individuals aged 19 and above who have at least one child under the age of 18 residing in their household, on the effectiveness of their community at increasing incomes in adulthood at the 50th percentile. Robust standard errors in parentheses. All regressions include ATUS sampling weights.

THE IMPACT OF JOB LOSS ON PARENTAL TIME INVESTMENT

Anja Gruber

ABSTRACT

Parental job loss has been shown to have a negative impact on a large number of children's outcomes, in particular for low-income children. Given the amount of time freed up by loss of employment and the fact that active time with one's children appears to be a productive input in their human capital production function, increases in the time parents spend with their children have the potential to positively impact a child or to counteract other negative consequences of parental job loss. This chapter studies how low- and higher-income parents change their time investment in their children when faced with job loss. Using national time-diary data from the American Time Use Survey (ATUS) linked to longitudinal labor market data from the Current Population Survey (CPS), I find that parents spend almost 15% of the time freed up by job loss – roughly 3.5 additional hours per week – actively with their children. Low-income parents invest their freed-up time no differently from higher-income parents. While mothers who lose their job respond by spending more time actively with their children, this adjustment is much smaller for fathers. This suggests that differential adjustments in time investment may play a role in the impact maternal versus paternal job loss has on children's outcomes.

Keywords: Time use; job loss; childcare; parental time investment; parental job loss; child outcomes

1. INTRODUCTION

The economic well-being of one's parents is a large predictor of future income and wealth. One way in which this has been extensively studied in the literature is through the impact of parental job loss on children's outcomes. Work in this area

Time Use in Economics
Research in Labor Economics, Volume 51, 105–134

ISSN: 0147-9121/doi:10.1108/S0147-912120230000051005

has documented a negative impact of parental job loss on a wide range of short- and long-term children's outcomes.[1] The negative impact appears to be particularly large for children at the bottom of the income distribution and is mostly limited to paternal job loss.[2,3]

Given the substantial amount of time employed parents spend at work each day, loss of employment is likely associated with an increase in the amount of time available to be invested in one's children. At the same time, the existing literature has identified time spent actively with one's children as a productive input in their human capital production function.[4] This raises the question of whether parents who lose their job do in fact increase their time investment in their children. Further, if mothers or higher-income parents disproportionately increase their time and consequently their human capital investment when faced with job loss, this could help explain why the literature has documented significant heterogeneity in the negative impact of job loss on children's outcomes.

In this chapter, I use detailed national time-diary data from the American Time Use Survey (ATUS) from 2005 to 2019 and the ability to link this data set to individuals' longitudinal labor market records from the Current Population Survey (CPS) to examine the impact of parental job loss on parents' use of time with respect to their children. I also specifically examine whether these responses are different by gender or by the family's income level. To overcome the issue that parents who experience unemployment are likely systematically different from those who do not, and that these systematic differences likely impact the way parents invest their time in their children, I employ two different empirical strategies. First, I rely on a sample of individuals with similar labor market histories and utilize a multivariate OLS regression design to control for observable differences. Second, I exploit the differential timing of unemployment within a sample of parents who all experience unemployment in the same year to conduct a regression analysis that allows me to additionally control for unobservable differences between the treated and comparison group. This analysis allows me to correct for omitted variable bias and uncover a plausibly causal effect of job loss on parental time investment.

My analysis provides robust evidence that parents increase the time they spend with their children when they experience loss of employment. Specifically, I find that parents spend about 60% of the time freed up by job loss with their children. While most of this increase appears to be in the form of time spent passively with one's children, I find that loss of employment leads to a meaningful additional active time investment of 3.5 hours per week – roughly 15% of the time freed-up by job loss. I do not find any evidence that low-income parents differently adjust how they spend time with their children. Further, I find no evidence that parents whose spouse is present in the household differently adjust the time they spend with their children. I also find no evidence of an added worker effect in my analysis: spouses of parents who have lost employment do not appear to increase their labor market hours on the extensive or intensive margin. Instead, the increase in quality time investment appears to be concentrated among mothers who lose their job.

This chapter contributes to our understanding of how parents adjust their time investment in their children in response to a job loss. In addition to loss of income, a number of negative consequences of parental job loss that may also affect one's children have been identified in the literature. These include worsened parental physical and mental health (Eliason & Storrie, 2009b; Gathmann et al., 2021; Kuhn et al., 2009), more risky and unhealthy behaviors by affected parents (De Cao et al., 2022), and a cascade of negative family events caused by job loss (Eliason & Storrie, 2009a; Eliason, 2012). However, no paper has explicitly addressed potential adjustments in parents' time investment as a channel through which a parent's job loss affects a child. Considering the impact of increased income on parental time investment, Morrissey (2022) finds little impact of Earned Income Tax Credit (EITC) receipt on the short-term patterns of parental time investment in their children. Perhaps most closely related to my chapter, Arnup et al. (2021) consider the changes to the ways parents and children spend their time when a family experiences a financial hardship. They find that children are more likely to spend excessive amounts of time on screens and see less rule enforcement by parents. My chapter shows that parents who experience job loss do in fact increase the time they passively and actively spend with their children, likely amounting to a significant increase in the investment in their children's human capital.

This chapter is particularly relevant to the literature that has identified that negative impacts of parental job loss on children are experienced more severely by low-income children. For example, Gregg et al. (2012), Oreopoulos et al. (2008), and Pan and Ost (2014) all show that the results of their analyses are driven by the negative impact on children with parents at the bottom of the income distribution. My chapter provides a first piece of evidence to the question of why this is the case. I show that the differential impact of parental job loss on low-income children cannot be explained by different adjustments in parents' time investment in their children.

Finally, my chapter contributes to the literature that finds a much less clear negative impact of maternal job loss on children's outcomes, relative to paternal job loss. For example, Schaller and Zerpa (2019), Rege et al. (2011) and Lindemann and Gangl (2019) all find that the adverse impact is confined to paternal job loss. Hsin and Felfe (2014) study the impact of maternal employment on parents' time with their children and find that it does not appear to reduce quality time investments. My study finds that increases in active time investments following parental job loss are driven by mothers who experience job loss. Consequently, I further add to the evidence that mothers adjust their time use differently from fathers. It seems plausible that increased maternal time investment may play a role in limiting the negative impact of maternal job loss on children.

The remainder of this chapter is organized as follows. Section 2 discusses the economics underlying this research. Section 3 presents the data used in this project and Section 4 discusses the empirical strategy. The results of this chapter are presented in Section 5. Section 6 addresses the robustness of the results, and Section 7 concludes.

2. CONCEPTUAL FRAMEWORK

When a parent loses their job, it appears likely that a significant amount of time becomes freed up each day. In my sample, work- and work-related activities take up on average 280 minutes per day for employed parents. While Aguiar et al. (2013) find that forgone market hours during the Great Recession were mainly spent on leisure and home production, parents may invest at least some of this time in their children.

Increases in time investment in one's children may occur in two ways: First, parents may use their extra available time to substitute for (often costly) market-provided childcare, such as babysitting or daycare. Alternatively, additional free time may allow a parent to spend more time actively with their children, engaging in activities such as playing with them or reading to them. Based on the literature on early childhood environment and children's human capital accumulation, we would expect that an increase in the time a child spends actively with a parent is a productive input in their human capital production function and therefore should have a positively impact on the child's cognitive development (Bono et al., 2016; Caetano et al., 2019; Fiorini & Keane, 2014; Rokicki & McGovern, 2020).[5]

Given the well-documented negative impacts of parental job loss on children's outcomes, it is apparent that any effective investments in children's human capital in the form of increased active time investments do not make up for the other negative impacts of parental job loss, such as loss of income or increased parental stress. Of course, it may also be true that parents simply do not increase the time they spend actively with their children. For example, this may be the case if a parent expects to return to work quickly and thus doesn't adjust their routine, or if parents feel stress and overwhelm following job loss, inhibiting them from productively engaging with their children. Alternatively, any additional active time investment made by the parent who has lost their job may be canceled out by a decrease in the active time the other parent spends with their children. My chapter sheds light on these questions.

Using data from the ATUS, Guryan et al. (2008) show that a significant difference exists in how parents with different levels of education allocate their time: Parents with higher levels of education on average spend more time at work. Yet, they also spend more time actively caring (i.e., in primary, educational, or recreational childcare) for their children. This education gradient translates into an income gradient. Table 1 illustrates this using time-use data from my sample of the ATUS and annual household income categories from ATUS respondents' last CPS survey. In addition to documenting the differences in time use between parents with different levels of income, this table also documents the stark differences in the way mothers and fathers invest time in their children.

Table 1. Parental Time Investment by Family Income and Sex of Respondent.[a]

	Male			Female		
	<25K	25 to 50K	>50K	<25K	25 to 50K	>50K
Labor market						
Work and related	266	309	296	185	205	214
(Min/day)	(282)	(296)	(296)	(240)	(246)	(254)
Employed	0.91	0.95	0.98	0.82	0.93	0.97
(Fraction)	(0.28)	(0.21)	(0.14)	(0.39)	(0.26)	(0.17)
Work and related if employed	305	314	307	242	235	225
(Min/day)	(285)	(298)	(300)	(257)	(257)	(259)
Spouse employed if present	0.37	0.55	0.73	0.70	0.85	0.95
(Fraction)	(0.48)	(0.50)	(0.44)	(0.46)	(0.35)	(0.22)
Work spouse if present	31.6	33.9	36.1	41.8	42.2	45.1
(Hrs/week)	(14.0)	(13.4)	(12.7)	(15.4)	(10.8)	(10.2)
Child care						
Primary childcare	25	24	28	50	48	52
(Min/day)	(54)	(60)	(54)	(74)	(68)	(71)
Educational childcare	9	7	10	16	14	16
(Min/day)	(24)	(21)	(26)	(40)	(33)	(34)
Recreational childcare	31	23	31	25	26	33
(Min/day)	(74)	(62)	(70)	(67)	(66)	(68)
Secondary childcare	338	337	337	442	442	408
(Min/day)	(269)	(274)	(273)	(269)	(264)	(2589)
Demographic characteristics						
Spouse present	0.85	0.90	0.96	0.32	0.60	0.91
(Fraction)	(0.36)	(0.31)	(0.19)	(0.47)	(0.49)	(0.30)
Number of kids	2.2	2.0	2.0	2.1	2.1	2.0
	(1.1)	(1.0)	(0.8)	(0.9)	(1.0)	(0.8)
Age of youngest child	5.0	5.2	5.5	4.9	5.2	5.5
	(3.7)	(3.8)	(3.8)	(3.6)	(3.7)	(3.8)
Observations	1,013	2,508	9,771	1,964	2,860	9,170

[a]Means are calculated from 2005 to 2019 ATUS. Standard errors are in parentheses. Sample includes parents with at least one child aged 0–12 in the household. Income categories refer to annual family income for the previous 12 months as reported at the last CPS interview.

While parents with higher family incomes spend more time at work, most of this gradient is explained by a higher fraction of higher-income parents being employed. At the same time, parents with higher incomes are much more likely to be supported by a spouse who is present in the household. Further, when a spouse is present, this person is much more likely to be employed in higher-income households. Spouses in families with higher incomes also tend to work more hours. Relative to fathers, mothers are less likely to be working and work fewer hours within each income category. Across all income categories, mothers spend roughly twice as much time on primary childcare and educational childcare relative to fathers. The difference is smaller for recreational childcare and secondary childcare. Parents with higher incomes spend slightly more time in primary childcare activities and in activities specific to children's education and recreation. They do spend less time on secondary childcare activities (such as watching TV while a child is present in the home). Note that the differences in how much active time parents spend with their children time cannot be explained by differences in the age or the number of children across income categories. In fact, low-income households on average have slightly more children. If we expect that total time investment is positively correlated with the number of children, we would then see a decrease in time spent with children with an increase in income. The opposite is the case in my data, at least for active time investments.

Differential adjustments in the time parents actively spend with their children following job loss may help explain some of the heterogeneous impact of job loss on children's outcomes depending on parents' demographic characteristics. Specifically, if mothers or higher-income parents increase the time they spend actively with their children significantly more than low-income parents or fathers, this may counteract other negative consequences of job loss and therefore limit the negative impact on children's outcomes. My analysis tests this hypothesis.

3. DATA

To assess how parents in the US allocate their time to their children's human capital accumulation, I utilize national data from the American Time Use Survey (ATUS) obtained through IPUMS (Hofferth et al., 2020). The ATUS is an annual time-diary survey that provides detailed and comprehensive information on how a representative sample of Americans spend their time. The survey has been administered since 2003 to a monthly sample of about 2,190 households. Respondents are asked to provide exact information on their use of time for one single 24-hour period (from 4 a.m. the day prior to 4 a.m. on the interview day). Hamermesh et al. (2005) provide a detailed overview of the survey and its methodology.

While the ATUS survey itself is purely cross-sectional, the sample is drawn from the outgoing rotation groups of the Current Population Survey (CPS-ORG). These monthly CPS surveys are based on the universe of the civilian, noninstitutional population residing in occupied households in the US. Monthly labor force statistics put forth by the Bureau of Labor Statistics (BLS) are based on estimates from these surveys of roughly 59,000 eligible households each month. Selected households become eligible for the ATUS interview two months after their final CPS interview. The monthly CPS interviews also include a longitudinal component, important for my analysis.

This chapter relies heavily on the ability to link each ATUS respondent to their CPS record and the fact that CPS respondents complete a series of eight monthly interviews over the course of 16 months. Specifically, each CPS respondent will complete four monthly surveys in a row and will do so again for the same months in the following year (eight months later). Given that I also observe the employment status of each ATUS respondent at the time of their ATUS interview, I can therefore reconstruct each respondent's monthly labor market history for the 19 months leading up to the interview with limited gaps.

Aside from a number of additional demographic characteristics that can be obtained from each ATUS respondent's CPS record, my analysis also benefits from the fact that I can obtain a measure of family income from the CPS. While the CPS provides relatively limited information on an individual's earnings or income, this measure was taken prior to the ATUS interview and is consequently not endogenous to a respondent's employment status at the time of their ATUS survey. Specifically, each monthly CPS interview asks for a respondent's estimated total family income in the 12 months prior. I use this information to designate families as "low-income" or "higher-income," based on whether their reported family income was below the 25th percentile of family incomes in a given year. To do so, I first calculate the annual distribution of family incomes from the American Community Survey (ACS).[6] Roughly 25% of my baseline sample are considered to be low-income families.

I restrict my baseline analysis to 2005–2019 and a sample of parents with at least one child aged 12 or younger present in the household. Further, I retain only parents who are either employed or unemployed at the time of their ATUS survey. This leaves me with a sample of 27,286 parents, 4.5% of whom are unemployed at the time of their ATUS survey.

Table 2 shows the main outcome variables of interest in this chapter as well as the specific activities they each consist of. I focus on three measures of time

Table 2. Time-Investment Outcome Variables.

Outcome Variable	Included Activities	Activity Code
Primary childcare	Physical care for household children	030101
	Looking after household children	030109
	Caring for and helping household children, N.E.C.	030199
	Providing medical care to household children	030311
Educational childcare	Activities related to childcare services	080110
	Activities related to household children's education	030200
	Reading to or with household children	030102
	Helping or teaching household children	030107
	Talking with or listening to household children	030106
Recreational childcare	Playing with household children	030103
	Arts and crafts with household children	030104
	Playing sports with household children	030105
	Attending household children's events	030110
Secondary childcare	Total time spent on secondary childcare for household children	030103

parents spend actively with their children and one measure of the time parents spend passively with their children and follow Guryan et al. (2008) in my definition of these variables. I consider primary childcare, educational childcare, and recreational childcare to involve time actively spent with children. Consistent with the literature, I view time actively spent with children as a productive input in their human capital production function (Caetano et al., 2019).

On the other hand, I take secondary childcare to imply that time is passively spent with children. For example, secondary childcare may imply the children are merely present in the same house or room while a parent is working, completing household chores, or watching TV. I do not view time passively spent with one's children as a productive input in their human capital production function. However, I hypothesize that secondary childcare can be viewed a substitute for market-provided care of one's children, such as time spent with a nanny, babysitter, at daycare, preschool, or in an after-school program.

Fig. 1 shows the distribution of how parents in my baseline sample spend their time with their children, depending on whether they have been characterized as a

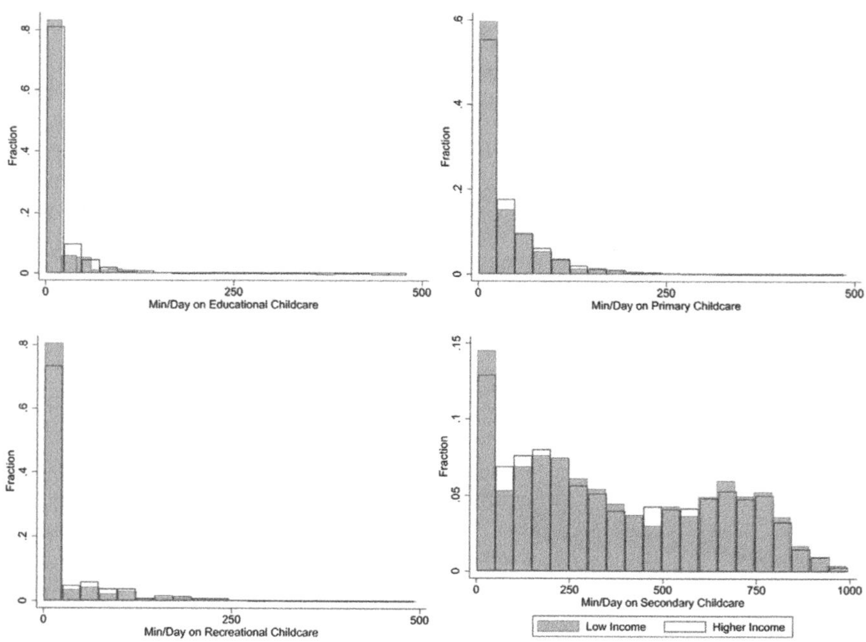

Fig. 1. Distribution of Main Outcome Variables by Income.

Note: Fig. 1 shows the distribution of how low- and higher-income parents in my baseline sample report spending time with their children in the 24 hours leading up to their interview. Since each of the outcome variables depicted in the figure has a long right tail with a number of outliers, time spent on primary childcare, educational childcare, and recreational childcare have been trimmed at 500 minutes and secondary childcare at 1,000 minutes to make the figure more easily comprehensible.

low-income household. Notably, parents report spending much more time on passive childcare than active childcare, and a substantial fraction of parents report not spending any time at all on active childcare. Of the active childcare categories, parents appear to spend most time on primary childcare. Fig. A1 shows the distribution of the same outcome variables by the gender of the parent. As suggested by the summary statistics presented in Table 1, mothers are more likely to spend any time on active childcare and spend more time in each activity if they do so.

Fig. 1 shows the distribution of how low- and higher-income parents in my baseline sample report spending time with their children in the 24 hours leading up to their interview. Since each of the outcome variables depicted in the figure has a long right tail with a number of outliers, time spent on primary childcare, educational childcare, and recreational childcare have been trimmed at 500 minutes and secondary childcare at 1,000 minutes to make the figure more easily comprehensible.

4. EMPIRICAL STRATEGY

The main limitation of a cross-sectional analysis to determine the impact of job loss on parental time investment is that parents who experience unemployment are likely systematically different from parents who do not experience unemployment. Consequently, any analysis that doesn't account for this selection into unemployment is likely to introduce omitted variable bias. While I strongly expect that a naive analysis would suffer from omitted variable bias, it is not obvious if the estimates would be biased toward or away from zero.

Two specific examples illustrate how a cross-sectional analysis might suffer from positive or negative omitted variable bias: First, consider a person's "dedication to their job." If higher dedication is negatively correlated with the probability that a person experiences unemployment, and negatively correlated with the time parents spend with their children, we would likely obtain positively biased estimates. On the other hand, if the omitted variable is a person's conscientiousness or "dedication or motivation more generally," a naive cross-sectional approach would likely lead to negatively biased estimates. This is because such general dedication or motivation is likely negatively correlated with the probability that a person experiences unemployment, and positively correlated with the time parents spend with their children.

By exploiting the rich set of demographic information provided by the ATUS as a set of regression controls, I am able to limit concerns about omitted variable bias in my analysis. However, it is unlikely that my covariates explain all of the differences between parents who experience a job loss and those who do not. Consequently, I rely on the ability to link individuals' ATUS responses to their recent labor market history and longitudinal records from the CPS. This allows me to explore two empirical strategies which ultimately allow me to sign the omitted variable bias and determine the plausibly causal impact of job loss on parental investment in their children.

Note that many studies in this literature rely on individual or family fixed effects to, for example, identify the negative impact of job loss on children's outcomes. While these fixed effects account for unobservable differences between respondents or respondents' families, this strategy relies on the assumption that such differences are time-invariant. Causal interpretation of the parameter of interest then requires that the timing of job loss is independent of other factors that may affect the outcome variable. My empirical strategy allows me to avoid having to make this assumption.

4.1 Multivariate OLS Regression

My first approach assumes that conditional on the inclusion of a rich set of individual-level demographic controls and a similar labor market history, who experiences job loss is essentially random. For this approach, I focus on a subsample of ATUS respondents who did not experience unemployment and were employed at their last CPS interview, on average 3 months prior to the ATUS interview. Treated individuals then experienced a job loss prior to their ATUS survey, whereas the comparison group remained employed. I estimate the following regression equation, where Y_{ist} is the time-use of parent i in state s and year t:

$$Y_{\text{ist}} = \beta_0 + \beta_1 \text{JobLoss}_i + X_i^{'} \phi + \gamma_s + \delta_t + \chi_h + \sigma_m + \pi_d + \epsilon_{\text{ist}} \qquad (1)$$

Eq. (1) includes a vector X_i of individual controls that allow me to account for observable differences between unemployed and employed parents. This vector includes the parent's age, gender, race and ethnicity, highest level of education, the number of children, the age of their youngest child, and whether a spouse is present in the household. I also include an indicator variable for family income below the 25th percentile to identify low-income parents. Additionally, state fixed effects (γ_s) control for time invariant differences between states, such as differences in daycare availability. Year fixed effects (δ_t) account for differences in how parents spend their time across time. For example, these fixed effects control for factors such as daycare enrollment becoming more likely or help from grandparents becoming less likely over the span of my analysis. They also control for changing parental preferences over time. χ_h is an indicator variable equal to one if the interview was conducted on a holiday. Finally, I also include month-of-year (π_m) and day-of-week fixed effects (μ_d) to account for the fact that parents are likely to spend their time differently on different days of the week and different times of the year. For example, the latter control for the fact that parents are likely to spend more time with their children when they are on break from daycare, preschool, or school.

Columns 1 and 2 of Table 3 show the means of the control variables for the treated (Group 2) and comparison group (Group 1) in this analysis. Again, causal interpretation of β_1 as the impact of job loss on parental time investment requires that conditional on the controls included in the model, who lost their job since the last CPS interview is as good as random.[7] Column 3 shows the difference between

Table 3. Characteristics of Treated and Comparison Groups.

	E/E Group 1	E/U Group 2	Δ Group 1&2	U/E Group 3	Δ Group 2&3
Income < 25th pctl	0.215	0.399	−0.184***[a]	0.436	−0.037
Age	38.769	37.659	1.110*	37.38	0.276
Female	0.491	0.563	−0.071**	0.552	0.011
White	0.861	0.810	0.051*	0.822	−0.012
Black	0.065	0.120	−0.054**	0.111	0.009
Native American	0.008	0.020	−0.012	0.014	0.007
Asian	0.054	0.041	0.014	0.042	−0.001
Hispanic origin	0.124	0.207	−0.083***	0.208	−0.001
Other	0.066	0.050	0.016	0.053	−0.004
No HS degree	0.049	0.117	−0.067***	0.118	−0.002
HS degree	0.443	0.586	−0.143***	0.555	0.031
Bachelor's degree	0.306	0.175	0.131***	0.220	−0.045
Higher degree	0.202	0.122	0.079***	0.107	0.016
Number of kids	1.989	1.950	0.038	2.035	−0.084
Child under 6	0.511	0.519	−0.008	0.512	0.007
Child under 3	0.275	0.251	0.025	0.272	−0.021
Spouse present	0.861	0.717	0.144***	0.757	−0.040
Observations	23,762	343		1,462	

[a]*$p < 0.10$, **$p < 0.05$, ***$p < 0.01$

these two groups. A quick glance at this table is sufficient to notice that the two groups do in fact differ a lot from each other. Those that lose their job between their CPS and ATUS interview are almost twice as likely to be in the lowest income quartile, are less likely to be white, and have much lower levels of education (i.e., are almost three times as likely to not hold a high school degree). They are also less likely to have a spouse present in their household.

While the differences between the treated and comparison groups as shown in the table may point to the ability of the observable controls included in the model to account for differences between the two groups, it certainly raises concerns about the internal validity of this estimation strategy. The fact that only 1% of those employed at their ATUS interview experience any unemployment throughout their CPS tenure, but 14% of those unemployed at their ATUS interview (and employed at their last CPS interview) experience any unemployment throughout their CPS tenure illustrates that the probability of job loss is hugely dependent on one's prior labor market experience. I further address this point with my second and preferred estimation strategy.

4.2 Exploiting the Randomness of the Timing of Job Loss

This second estimation strategy avoids the requirement that *who* experiences job loss is as good as random once I condition on observable controls. Instead, it relies on the assumption that the timing of *when* an individual experiences a job loss within their roughly 19-month CPS and ATUS tenure is as good as random.

For this analysis, I rely on a refined subsample of the ATUS for which I retain experienced workers with exactly one spell of unemployment throughout their CPS tenure and are re-employed at the time of their ATUS survey (comparison group) and individuals who had no spell of unemployment throughout their CPS tenure and are employed at their last CPS interview, but experience a job loss prior to their ATUS survey (treated group).[8] Consequently, I am comparing individuals who have recently been unemployed to individuals who are currently unemployed. Note that the treated group therefore is made up of the same exact individuals that make up the treated group of in my first estimation strategy. However, with this approach, the treated and comparison groups differ only in when they experienced a job loss. Column 4 of Table 3 summarizes the demographic characteristics of the comparison group for this analysis and column 5 illustrates that these two groups are statistically identical in all observable variables included in my analysis.

The assumption that for the sample included in this analysis, the timing of job loss is as good as random is further validated by the rotating design of the CPS and ATUS surveys. Individuals who are observed in the same year in the ATUS do not start their CPS tenure in the same month and consequently do not complete their ATUS interview in the same month. This makes it unlikely that there is some omitted external factor that is determining which individuals experience the job loss slightly earlier. Given the as-good-as randomness of the timing of when an individual loses their job within a given year, I interpret the coefficient on job loss in the ATUS as the causal impact of job loss on parental time investment for parents who are likely to experience spells of unemployment. This means that the external validity of my findings is limited to a subset of parents with a high probability of experiencing unemployment at any given time. Of course, this is exactly the subpopulation of parents for whom we would like to estimate this impact.

Finally, to allow the impact of job loss to differ for parents with different demographic characteristics, I modify Eq. (1) and include an interaction term between the treatment, job loss in the ATUS, and an indicator variable for the demographic variable of interest. I first consider the differential impact for low-income parents by estimating the following regression equation:

$$\begin{aligned} Y_{\text{ist}} = {} & \beta_0 + \beta_1 \text{JobLoss}_i + \beta_2 \text{JobLoss}_i * \text{LowInc}_i + X'_i \varphi \\ & + \gamma_s + \delta_t + \chi_h + \sigma_m + \pi_d + \epsilon_{\text{ist}} \end{aligned} \tag{2}$$

In this specification, β_1 identifies the impact of job loss for higher-income parents and $\beta_1 + \beta_2$ yield the impact for low-income parents. I repeat this analysis for mothers, single parents, and parents of young children to test for potential heterogeneity in effects across those demographics.

5. RESULTS

5.1 Labor Market Adjustments

I begin my analysis by considering the impact of job loss on the amount of time a parent spends on market-work on any given day. Table 4 illustrates that parents who lose their job spend considerably less time on work- and work-related activities, regardless of the estimation strategy. On average, job loss frees up about 220 minutes per day of time previously spent on work and related activities. Further, parents with lower family incomes don't experience a statistically significantly different reduction in time spent on work from parents with higher incomes. Similarly, mothers and fathers are impacted roughly the same in terms of time freed up by job loss. Table 4 also illustrates that the estimates with my first empirical strategy, multivariate OLS, are slightly bigger in absolute magnitude than with the second and preferred empirical strategy, which exploits the random timing of job loss in my sample. The same is true for the increase in the time parents spend searching for work when they experience a job loss. On average, I find that parents spend roughly 30 minutes per day on job search. However, my results indicate that compared to fathers, mothers invest less than half as much time on job search. This means that mothers who experience a job loss have about 3 hours and 25 minutes per day freed up because they spend less time at work, net of the time they now invest into search for work, whereas fathers free time increases by less than 3 hours. Job loss appears to lead to a similar increase in time available outside of the labor market for low-income parents relative to higher income parents.

In addition to any increases in time spent on work search following a job loss and time spent on parenting as discussed in the following sections, job loss also leads to an increase in leisure time and household activities. I find that on

Table 4. Impact of Job Loss on Time Spent at Work.[a]

	Work & Work Related	Work & Work Related	Work Search	Work Search
Job loss	−235.82***	−220.37***	30.25***	28.95***
	(11.84)	(13.09)	(0.76)	(2.64)
Job loss	−239.58***	−227.21***	34.36***	32.54***
	(15.21)	(17.03)	(0.97)	(3.44)
Job Loss*Low income	9.51	16.72	−10.40***	−8.77
	(24.17)	(26.62)	(1.55)	(5.37)
Job loss	−252.11***	−239.31***	47.85***	44.54***
	(17.83)	(19.71)	(1.13)	(3.95)
Job Loss*Female	29.06	33.79	−31.40***	−27.82***
	(23.78)	(26.29)	(1.51)	(5.27)
Treated group	Emp/Unemp	Emp/Unemp	Emp/Unemp	Emp/Unemp
Comparison group	Emp/Emp	Unemp/Emp	Emp/Emp	Unemp/Emp
Observations	24,105	1,805	24,105	1,805

[a]Standard errors in parentheses. *$p < 0.10$, **$p < 0.05$, ***$p < 0.01$. All regressions include year, state, holiday, month-of-year and day-of-week FE and a vector of individual control variables.

average, this increase is 51 and 72 minutes per week respectively, but do not find a statistically significant heterogeneous response by family income or parent gender.

5.2 Parental Time Investment

To understand if and how parents utilize this additional available time with respect to their children, I first conduct a naive comparison. Table 5 shows the relationship between job loss and the time parents spend in different activities with their children when relying on a sample of all parents of children aged 12 or younger who are employed or unemployed in the ATUS surveys from 2005 to 2019. While the results shown are obtained from a regression that includes a rich set of individual control variables, year, state, month-of-year, and day-of-week fixed effects, I expect that these results likely suffer from omitted variables bias. Roughly 55% of the parents who report being unemployed at their ATUS survey (2,738 individuals or 5.5% of my naive sample are unemployed in the ATUS) were also unemployed at the time of at least one of their CPS interviews. This suggests that parents who experience job loss are inherently different from those who do not.[9] Still, it is informative to consider the results presented in Table 5 in an effort to sign the bias. Job loss appears to be associated with a roughly 36 minute per day increase in active childcare, and 118 minute per day increase in secondary or passive childcare. Interestingly, low- and higher-income parents do not appear to adjust their time in active childcare any differently, while low-income parents invest roughly 42 additional minutes relative to higher-income parents in secondary childcare. In this naive analysis, the additional time investment of mothers appears no different from that of fathers.

Table 5. Naive Estimation of Relationship Between Job Loss and Time Spent With Children.[a]

	Primary Childcare	Educational Childcare	Recreational Childcare	Secondary Childcare
Job loss	18.63***	5.43***	11.67***	117.62***
	(1.70)	(0.88)	(1.94)	(6.97)
Job loss	17.64***	5.26***	11.62***	97.00***
	(2.39)	(1.23)	(2.72)	(9.77)
Job Loss*Low income	1.99	0.35	0.10	41.57***
	(3.37)	(1.74)	(3.85)	(13.81)
Job loss	15.75***	4.65***	11.68***	121.80***
	(2.96)	(1.53)	(3.38)	(12.13)
Job Loss*Female	4.26	1.15	−0.02	−6.19
	(3.58)	(1.85)	(4.09)	(14.67)
Observations	27,286	27,286	27,286	27,286

[a]Standard errors in parentheses. * $p < 0.10$, ** $p < 0.05$, *** $p < 0.01$. All regressions include year, state, holiday, month-of-year and day-of-week FE and a vector of individual control variables. Sample includes all parents with at least one child aged 0-12 in their household and observed employed or unemployed in the 2005–19 ATUS surveys.

Table 6 shows how job loss impacts a parent's time spent actively spent with their children using the empirical strategies described in Sections 4.1 (columns 1, 3, and 5) and 4.2 (columns 2, 4 and 6). Here, I find that job loss leads to an increase in primary childcare by roughly 15 minutes per day and recreational childcare by roughly 11 minutes per day, but hardly affects educational childcare. Comparing the naive estimates from Table 5 and the results obtained with my two estimation strategies, it becomes clear that a naiver estimation approach induces positive omitted variable bias. In other words, relying on the assumption that job loss is random conditional on an individual's demographics leads to overestimation of the positive impact of job loss on the time parents spend with their children. By relying instead on the assumption that the timing of job loss is random conditional on a rich set of observable control variables, I can overcome this limitation of a purely cross-sectional analysis. Therefore, the results presented in columns 2, 4 and 6 can be interpreted as the causal impact of job loss on the time a parent actively spends with their children. I find that job loss leads to an increase of time spent on active childcare of roughly 30 minutes per day. While low-income parents do not appear to adjust their time any differently from higher-income parents, the increase in primary childcare is entirely due to increases in the time mothers spend on this activity. This means that job loss causes mothers to increase their active time investment in their children by more than double the amount that fathers do.

Note that positive omitted variable bias implies that the impact of the omitted variable on the amount of (quality) time parents spend with their children has the same sign as the correlation between the omitted variable and job loss. A number

Table 6. Impact of Job Loss on Time Spent Actively With Children.[a]

	Primary Childcare		Educational Childcare		Recreational Childcare	
Job loss	16.34***	14.83***	4.02**	3.63*	10.76***	10.73***
	(3.05)	(3.85)	(1.57)	(1.96)	(3.51)	(4.14)
Job loss	18.35***	18.09***	4.57**	4.09	11.80***	12.37**
	(3.91)	(5.02)	(2.02)	(2.55)	(4.51)	(5.38)
Job Loss*Low income	−4.55***	−3.67	0.11	0.22	−2.18	2.48
	(1.16)	(3.98)	(0.60)	(2.03)	(1.33)	(4.27)
Job loss	6.20	4.24	4.65**	4.65	10.90**	15.87**
	(4.59)	(5.80)	(2.36)	(2.96)	(5.29)	(6.23)
Job Loss*Female	18.07***	18.90**	−1.12	−1.82	−0.25	−9.17
	(6.12)	(7.73)	(3.15)	(3.94)	(7.06)	(8.31)
Treated group	E/N	E/N	E/N	E/N	E/N	E/N
Comparison group	E/E	N/E	E/E	N/E	E/E	N/E
Observations	24,105	1,805	24,105	1,805	24,105	1,805

[a]Standard errors in parentheses. * $p < 0.10$, ** $p < 0.05$, *** $p < 0.01$. All regressions include year, state, holiday, month-of-year and day-of-week FE and a vector of individual control variables.

of possible explanations come to mind. For example, it is conceivable that higher dedication to one's job leads to lower time investment in one's children and that at the same time, higher dedication to one's job is associated with a lower probability of unemployment. Alternatively, having a child with special needs is likely to lead to higher time investment in one's children and may also be associated with a higher probability of job loss when a child's needs interfere with the parent's ability to satisfy the requirements of their job. Importantly, the second example illustrates why a parent fixed effects strategy may suffer from similar bias as a naive cross-sectional approach.

Table 7 shows the same set of analyses considering the impact on time spent on secondary childcare. Again, the results confirm that relying on the assumption that job loss is exogenous conditional on individuals' characteristics leads to positive omitted variable bias. Still, considering the results obtained in column 2 with my preferred empirical strategy, I find that job loss increases the time parents spend on secondary childcare by roughly 110 minutes per day. Adjustments are similar for both genders and parents with different family incomes.

5.3 Parental Time Investment at the Extensive Margin

Recall that Fig. 1 illustrates that most parents in the survey respond that they did not spend any active time with their children on any given day, and almost 30% respond that they did not spend any passive time with their children. Consequently, it is worth considering if the results presented above are driven by adjustments at the extensive or intensive margin. In particular, it may be that job loss leads parents who already spend time with their children to increase their time investment (intensive margin). On the other hand, it may also be the case

Table 7. Impact of Job Loss on Time Spent Passively With Children.[a]

	Secondary Childcare	Secondary Childcare
Job loss	112.03***	109.18***
	(12.68)	(15.09)
Job loss	102.47***	104.50***
	(16.29)	(19.64)
Job Loss*Low income	24.21	11.44
	(25.89)	(30.69)
Job loss	108.70***	109.59***
	(19.10)	(22.73)
Job Loss*Female	5.94	−0.72
	(25.47)	(30.33)
Treated group	E/N	E/N
Comparison group	E/E	N/E
Observations	24,105	1,805

[a]Standard errors in parentheses. * $p < 0.10$, ** $p < 0.05$, *** $p < 0.01$. All regressions include year, state, holiday, month-of-year and day-of-week FE and a vector of individual control variables.

that parents who did not previously report spending any time with their children do spend time with their children when experiencing job loss (extensive margin).

Table 8 shows the impact of job loss for all parents and the impact of job loss for low-income parents relative to higher income parents and mothers relative to fathers on whether they spend any time with their children in the three different categories of active childcare and in secondary childcare.

I find some evidence that job loss increases the probability that a parent spends any time on child investments. Job loss appears to particularly increase the likelihood that a parent engages in recreational childcare (8 percentage point increase) and secondary childcare (5 percentage point increase). Interestingly, I do not observe that there are differences in mothers and fathers along this margin, suggesting that this is not driving their differences in active time investment adjustments. In other words, the differential increase in time spent with their children between fathers and mothers is entirely driven by fathers and mothers who already spend time with their children prior to job loss.

5.4 Parental Time Investment by Parent Characteristics

Ceteris paribus, low-income parents increase the time investment in their children no differently from higher-income parents when faced with extra time freed up by loss of job. However, low-income parents differ from higher-income parents along a number of characteristics that could lead to low- and higher-income parents, on average, adjusting their time differently. For example, low-income parents are much more likely to be single parents and therefore are more likely to be female. On average, low-income parents also have younger children. While

Table 8. Impact of Job Loss on Time Spent With Children – Extensive Margin.[a]

	Any Primary Childcare	Any Educational Childcare	Any Recreational Childcare	Any Secondary Childcare
Job loss	0.049*	0.006	0.078***	0.047***
	(0.027)	(0.026)	(0.025)	(0.017)
Job loss	0.091***	0.008	0.087***	0.064***
	(0.035)	(0.034)	(0.033)	(0.023)
Job Loss*Low income	−0.103*	−0.006	−0.023	−0.041
	(0.055)	(0.052)	(0.051)	(0.036)
Job loss	0.026	−0.019	0.059	0.055**
	(0.041)	(0.039)	(0.038)	(0.026)
Job Loss*Female	0.041	0.045	0.034	−0.014
	(0.054)	(0.052)	(0.051)	(0.035)
Observations	1,805	1,805	1,805	1,805

[a]Standard errors in parentheses. * $p < 0.10$, ** $p < 0.05$, *** $p < 0.01$. All regressions include year, state, holiday, month-of-year and day-of-week FE and a vector of individual control variables. Sample is restricted to those parents unemployed either at one point during their CPS tenure or their ATUS interview.

this is a function of parental age more likely recent labor market interruptions by one or both parents of a young child, it may be an important factor.

I consider the heterogeneity of the impact of job loss on parental time investment for single parents and parents with a spouse present in Table 9. Given the evidence of the importance of early investments in one's children, I also consider how the adjustment differs for parents whose youngest child is or is not yet 6 years old.[10] I do not find that single parents respond meaningfully differently to job loss in terms of their investment in their children. Not surprisingly, the increases in active time investment are driven by parents of younger children. While we might expect a similar result for secondary childcare given that younger children are not yet enrolled in school, my analysis does not confirm this. Rather, parents of younger and older children similarly adjust their time spent on secondary childcare. I hypothesize that this result suggests that job loss does not lead to a significant adjustment in the market-childcare that families utilize. If this were the case, I would expect to find a much bigger adjustment in secondary childcare for young children who are more likely to require market childcare when their parents are at work (because they are not in school).

Fig. 2 graphically summarizes the heterogeneity of the impact of job loss by parental characteristics by isolating the impact for different subgroups of parents. As previously discussed, the time adjustment by low- and higher-income parents is remarkably similar, whereas the adjustment in primary childcare is hugely parent-gender dependent. Interestingly, the coefficients and confidence intervals for the adjustment in time spent on secondary childcare are essentially identical for all subsamples of parents.

Table 9. Impact of Job Loss on Time Spent With Children by Parent Characteristics.[a]

	Primary Childcare	Educational Childcare	Recreational Childcare	Secondary Childcare
Job loss	14.20*	−2.17	−0.06	127.12***
	(7.35)	(3.74)	(7.88)	(28.77)
Job Loss*Spouse present	0.88	8.03*	14.94	−24.83
	(8.66)	(4.40)	(9.29)	(33.89)
Job loss	7.41	5.73**	−0.95	114.92***
	(5.56)	(2.83)	(5.96)	(21.78)
Job Loss*Young child	14.40*	−4.07	22.65***	−11.12
	(7.77)	(3.96)	(8.33)	(30.45)
Observations	1,805	1,805	1,805	1,805

[a]Standard errors in parentheses. * $p < 0.10$, ** $p < 0.05$, *** $p < 0.01$. All regressions include year, state, month-of-year and day-of-week FE and a vector of individual control variables. Sample is restricted to those parents unemployed either at one point during their CPS tenure or their ATUS interview.

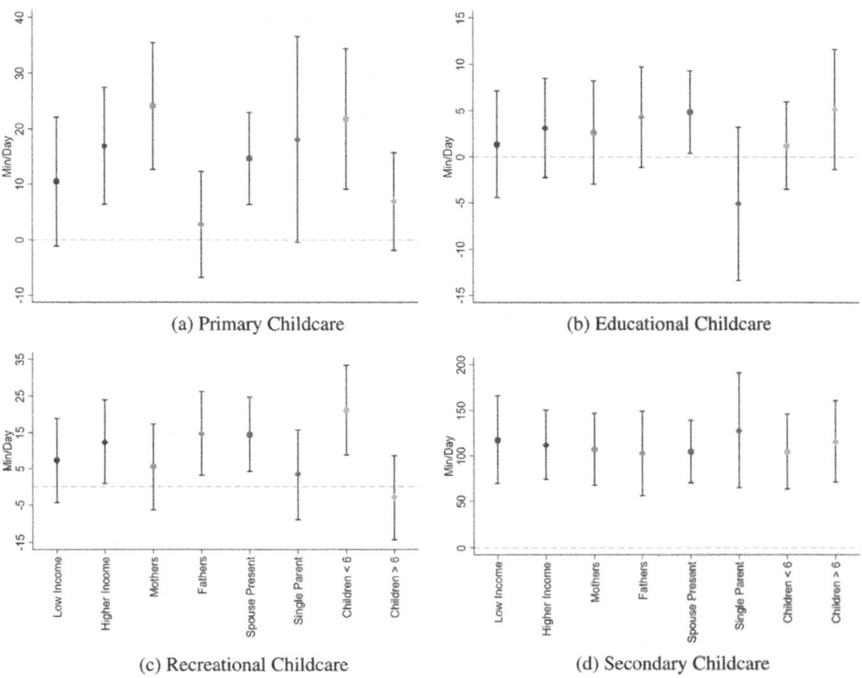

Fig. 2. Impact of Job Loss on Time Spent With Children by Parent Characteristics.

Notes: Fig. 2 shows the coefficients and 95% confidence intervals for the coefficient on job loss for regressions of subsamples of parents according to the characteristics described along the *x*-axis. Each dot presents the coefficient for a separate regression. All regressions include year, state, holiday, month-of-year and day-of-week FE and a vector of individual controls. Sample is restricted to those parents' unemployment either at one point during their CPS tenure or their ATUS interview.

5.5 Added Worker Effect

Finally, I consider the possibility that while a parent who experiences a loss of job increases their (active) time with their children, their spouse may be decreasing their own time investment as a result of increased labor market involvement to make up for lost family earnings. While I cannot test the spouse's adjustment of time spent with their children with my data, I do observe two measures of spousal employment. An indicator variable for spousal employment allows me to test for extensive adjustments in spousal work, while the number of hours a spouse works per week allows me to test for adjustments at the intensive margin. Table 10 shows the impact of job loss on the probability that a parent's spouse is employed at the time of the ATUS survey (column 1) and the number of hours a spouse is reported working on average per week (column 2). I do not find that there is any meaningful added worker effect. The spouse of a parent who experienced job loss

Table 10. Impact of Job Loss on Spousal Employment.[a]

	Spouse Employed	Spouse Weekly Hours
Job loss	−0.048	−1.470
	(0.030)	(0.998)
Job loss	−0.039	−1.571
	(0.036)	(1.128)
Job Loss*Low income	−0.029	0.465
	(0.066)	(2.412)
Job loss	−0.069*	−0.631
	(0.04)	(1.42)
Job Loss*Female	0.047	−1.616
	(0.06)	(1.96)
Job loss	−0.026	−3.142**
	(0.044)	(1.425)
Job Loss*Young child	−0.040	3.247
	(0.060)	(1.978)
Observations	1,353	956

[a]Standard errors in parentheses. * $p < 0.10$, ** $p < 0.05$, *** $p < 0.01$. All regressions include year, state, holiday, month-of-year and day-of-week FE and a vector of individual control variables. Sample is restricted to those parents unemployed either at one point during their CPS tenure or their ATUS interview.

does not appear to increase their labor market involvement on the extensive or intensive margin. This is also true when considering potential heterogeneous effects for low-income parents, women, or parents with young children. Instead, my results suggest that job loss may lead to a slight decrease in time a spouse spends at work. However, given the lack of statistical significance of my results, I interpret this analysis to confirm that job loss of one parent leads to an increase in the total time both parents spend with their children.

6. ROBUSTNES CHECKS

6.1 Duration of Unemployment

A potential limitation of my preferred analysis, which relies on a comparison of those unemployed at some point in their CPS tenure to those unemployed at their ATUS interview, is that I do not observe the length of unemployment for the second group. This may be concerning for two reasons: First, I observe a relatively long stint of continuous employment throughout the CPS for those that are unemployed in the ATUS. Empirically, the length of unemployment declines with a track record of continuous employment. Given that I condition on roughly two years of employment in selecting this group, treated parents may therefore experience shorter unemployment spells than those unemployed in the CPS. Second, my analysis only allows me to estimate the impact of the type of unemployment experienced by those unemployed in the ATUS. This may limit the interpretation of my results if parents who are short-term or longer-term unemployed differently adjust their time investment in their children. For example, it is plausible that someone who has only been unemployed for a short amount of time and expects to return to work quickly will not significantly alter their time use throughout a day. On the other hand, once they have been unemployed for a longer amount of time, they may make adjustments to their daily schedule as they no longer expect to return to work quickly.

Given that the balance Table 3 shows that the two groups of parents are statistically identical, I am not concerned about the potential that a possibly different duration of unemployment of the two groups might be indicative of the two groups being different in the way they utilize their time if they were in fact both employed at the time of the ATUS interview. Still, I verify this with an additional robustness check where I exclude all of those long-term unemployed (more than 26 weeks) in the CPS. Table 11 shows the results and confirms that trimming the comparison group to only those with shorter unemployment spells has no impact on my results.

Again, given the time gap between the last CPS and the ATUS interviews and the fact that I do not observe how long a ATUS respondent has been and will be unemployed for, it is plausible that I am in fact estimating the impact of a specific type of unemployment. The average gap between the two interviews is 13.2 weeks. Based on a cross-section of CPS interviews, I expect the average duration of unemployment for those that are unemployed for at most 13.2 weeks to be 6 weeks. In other words, I estimate that each parent who is unemployed at their ATUS interview has already been unemployed for 6 weeks on average. Fig. 3 shows the survival rate of unemployment for all experienced workers in the CPS with one observed unemployment spell that ends by their last CPS interview. The

Table 11. Main Results Excluding CPS Short-Term Unemployed.[a]

	Primary Childcare	Educational Childcare	Recreational Childcare	Secondary Childcare
Job loss	15.83***	3.63*	11.39***	107.14***
	(4.00)	(2.03)	(4.24)	(15.45)
Job loss	18.93***	3.53	13.42**	100.17***
	(5.19)	(2.64)	(5.50)	(20.06)
Job Loss*Low income	−7.61	0.25	−4.99	17.15
	(8.14)	(4.13)	(8.63)	(31.46)
Job loss	5.75	4.32	15.91**	102.93***
	(6.01)	(3.06)	(6.38)	(23.27)
Job Loss*Female	18.03**	−1.23	−8.09	7.54
	(8.03)	(4.09)	(8.53)	(31.10)
Observations	1,552	1,552	1,552	1,552

[a]Standard errors in parentheses. $*p < 0.10$, $**p < 0.05$, $***p < 0.01$. All regressions include year, state, holiday, month-of-year and day-of-week FE and a vector of individual control variables. Sample is restricted to those parents unemployed either at one point during their CPS tenure or their ATUS interview, where the length of CPS unemployment is less than 26 weeks.

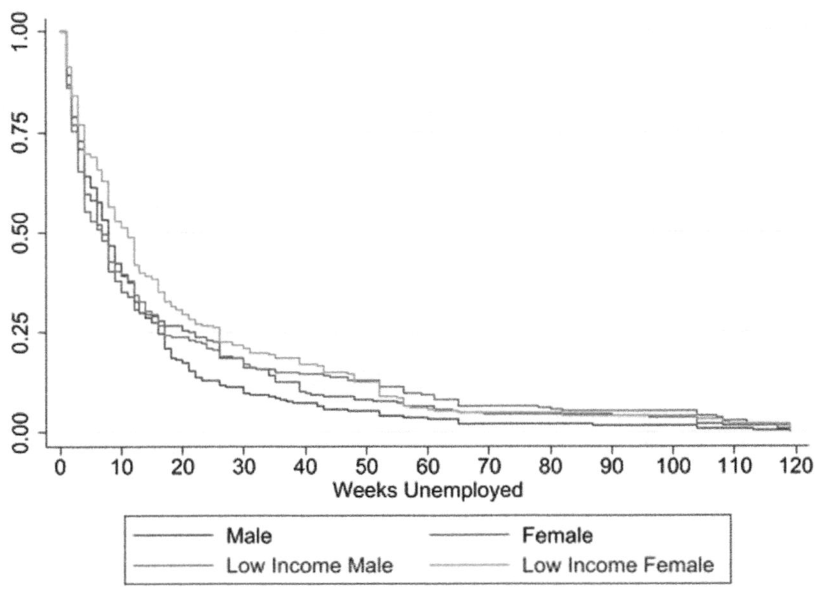

Fig. 3. Probability of Unemployment.
Note: Fig. 3 shows the survival rate of unemployment for all experienced workers in the CPS with one observed unemployment spell that ends by their last CPS interview.

probability of remaining unemployed decreases rapidly in the beginning of an unemployment spell but decreases much more slowly after a person has already been unemployed for some time. Consequently, the median duration of unemployment is 8 weeks, but the median duration of unemployment for those that are unemployed for at least 6 weeks is 16 weeks.

To account for the possibility that the impact of the relatively longer period of unemployment already experienced by those unemployed in the ATUS is different, I conduct a robustness check where I trim the treated group (unemployed in the ATUS) to exclude those that have a gap of more than 3 months between their last CPS interview and their ATUS interview. This will result in a treated group that is, on average, unemployed for a shorter amount of time by their ATUS interview than the treated group in my main analysis. Table 12 shows the results of this robustness check.

The coefficients of interest do not differ qualitatively or quantitatively from those estimated in my main analyses. This suggests that the impact of job loss on parental time investment in their children is not strongly dependent on the amount of time that a parent has already been unemployed for. Consequently, I interpret my results as the impact of job loss on parental time investment more broadly.

Table 12. Main Results Addressing Duration of Unemployment at the ATUS Interview.[a]

	Primary Childcare	Educational Childcare	Recreational Childcare	Secondary Childcare
Job loss	15.32***	2.96	8.35*	110.07***
	(4.28)	(2.17)	(4.51)	(16.67)
Job loss	19.02***	3.62	10.28*	104.84***
	(5.49)	(2.79)	(5.80)	(21.42)
Job Loss*Low income	−9.32	−1.65	−4.86	13.18
	(8.69)	(4.41)	(9.16)	(33.87)
Job loss	3.57	4.94	14.69**	112.17***
	(6.40)	(3.25)	(6.76)	(24.99)
Job Loss*Female	21.03**	−3.55	−11.36	−3.77
	(8.53)	(4.34)	(9.01)	(33.31)
Observations	1,735	1,735	1,735	1,735

[a]Standard errors in parentheses. $^{*}p < 0.10$, $^{**}p < 0.05$, $^{***}p < 0.01$. All regressions include year, state, holiday, month-of-year and day-of-week FE and a vector of individual control variables. Sample is restricted to those parents unemployed either at one point during their CPS tenure or their ATUS interview, where the gap between the CPS and ATUS interviews is no more than 3 months for those unemployed in the ATUS.

6.2 Temporal Spillover Effects of Unemployment Spells

Another specific concern arises with my preferred empirical strategy. Since I rely on a comparison of parents who experienced job loss at a prior point to parents who are experiencing job loss at the time of their ATUS interview, it is possible that there may be temporal spillover effects of unemployment on parental investment. Specifically, if being unemployed systematically alters parents' perception, preference, or ability to spend time with their children, this may bias my estimates. To verify that this is not the case, I construct a sample that mirrors my preferred empirical strategy: I restrict this robustness analysis to all parents that experienced a short-term unemployment spell at one point in their CPS tenure and are either employed or unemployed at the time of their ATUS interview. The sample of this analysis includes 1,247 parents, 17% of whom experience job loss in both the CPS and the ATUS. I then use my empirical specification discussed in Section 4.1 to compare the time-use of parents who remained unemployed, and those who regained employment by the time of the ATUS. In other words, I estimate the impact of job re-gain on the time parents spend with their children.

Table 13 shows the results of this analysis. The symmetry between the estimates presented in this table and the previously discussed results shows that the spillover effects are at most limited. In particular, the absolute magnitude of the impact of job re-gain on the time spent on primary childcare (roughly 16 minutes) is essentially equal to the absolute magnitude of the impact of job loss. Additionally, low- and higher-income parents appear to adjust their time no differently from each other. I do find that job re-gain appears to decrease the time spent on

Table 13. Impact of Job Re-Gain on Time Spent With Children.[a]

	Primary Childcare	Educational Childcare	Recreational Childcare	Secondary Childcare
Job Re-Gain	−16.40***	−5.49***	−15.86***	−132.59***
	(3.58)	(1.88)	(4.24)	(14.30)
Job Re-Gain	−16.02***	−4.96*	−21.25***	−119.43***
	(4.94)	(2.59)	(5.84)	(19.73)
Job Re-Gain*Low income	−0.78	−1.10	11.11	−27.12
	(7.02)	(3.68)	(8.30)	(28.01)
Job Re-Gain	−21.77***	−5.33*	−24.75***	−148.77***
	(5.77)	(3.03)	(6.82)	(23.04)
Job Re-Gain*Female	8.65	−0.26	14.33*	26.07
	(7.29)	(3.83)	(8.62)	(29.10)
Observations	1,859	1,859	1,859	1,859

[a]Standard errors in parentheses. $*p < 0.10$, $**p < 0.05$, $***p < 0.01$. All regressions include year, state, holiday, month-of-year and day-of-week FE and a vector of individual control variables. Sample is restricted to those who had exactly one unemployment spell throughout their CPS tenure and were either employed or unemployed at the time of their ATUS interview.

recreational childcare by slightly more than job loss increases it. However, I do not believe that these results signal that temporal spillover effects pose a major threat to causal identification of job loss on parental time investment.

6.3 Remaining Concerns

My analysis relies on the assumption that job loss leads to unemployment. However, if some individuals who lose their job leave the labor force altogether, and if those individuals adjust their time investments systematically different from the parents included in my sample, this assumption may bias my results. To account for this possibility, I expand my treated group for my preferred analysis to include any parent who is unemployed or out of the labor force at the time of their ATUS interview, following employment at their last CPS interview. My results are robust to this exercise, indicating that such selection bias is not a major concern.

Finally, I re-estimate my main results with the inclusion of metropolitan statistical area (MSA) rather than state fixed effects. This robustness check addresses the potential concern that there are systematic differences between areas within the same state that affect how parents spend their time with their children. For example, this addresses the potential concern that availability of affordable childcare options may vary greatly within a state. Appendix Table A1 shows the full set of results including the relevant heterogeneity analyses with the inclusion of MSA fixed effects. Given the fact that my preferred empirical strategy mimics a randomized control trial (RCT) approach where the treated and comparison groups are identical other than the timing of when they experience job loss, it should come as no surprise that the inclusion of MSA fixed effects, much like the inclusion (or exclusion) of any of the controls in my regression specification, has no impact on the results.

7. CONCLUSION

An extensive body of research shows that parental job loss has a negative impact on children across a wide spectrum of short- and long-term outcomes. The impact is particularly large for young children and low-income children. While much of this impact is likely driven by loss of income, job loss may also lead parents to alter how and how much time they invest in their children's human capital accumulation. Given the amount of time freed up by a loss of employment and the fact that the literature points to large gains in children's long-term cognitive development and outcomes from active (quality) time investments by their parents, we might expect job loss to have a positive impact on children through increased parental time investment.

This chapter studies how parents adjust their time investment in their children's human capital when faced with job loss, and how low- and higher-income families respond differently. I find that parents increase their active time investment in their children by roughly 30 minutes per day and their passive time investment by roughly 100 minutes per day. This means that almost 15% of the time freed up by job loss is actively invested in one's children. This increase is likely to have a meaningful positive impact on the cognitive development of a child. To put it into context, consider that Fiorini and Keane (2014) find that the replacement of one hour of general care and one hour of social care with 2 hours per week of educational activities with a child's parents has the same impact on a child's cognitive skills as measured by the Peabody Picture Vocabulary Test as is associated with 1 additional year of parental education.

My analysis does not find that low-income parents adjust their active time investment differently from higher-income families. Instead, the increase in active time investment appears to be driven by mothers and parents of younger children along the intensive margin. I do not find any evidence that single parents adjust their time investment differently from parents whose spouse is present in the household. Finally, I also do not find any evidence of an added worker effect, likely ruling out the possibility that increased time investment by one spouse is canceled out by the other spouse.

Together, my results suggest that parents from different socioeconomic backgrounds increase their active time investment in their children's human capital very similarly. Consequently, the fact that low-income children suffer more severely from parental job loss cannot be explained by differences in parental time investment. Low-income parents are compensating for other negative consequences of job loss by increasing their time investment in their children as much as higher-income parents do.

On the other hand, fathers increase the time they spend actively with their children much less than mothers. Consequently, this chapter also provides an explanation as to why a number of studies find that the negative impact of job loss is mostly confined to paternal job loss (Lindemann & Gangl, 2019; Rege et al., 2011; Schaller & Zerpa, 2019). Women appear to invest more of their freed-up time in their children's human capital accumulation, likely contributing to the more limited impact of maternal job loss on children's outcomes.

ACKNOWLEDGMENTS

I thank Brian Cadena, Taylor Jaworski and Terra McKinnish for their guidance and feedback on this chapter, as well as participants of the CU Boulder Research Seminar for their feedback.

NOTES

1. For example, see Rege et al. (2011), Schaller and Zerpa (2019), Coelli (2011), Gregg et al. (2012), and Hilger (2016) for the negative impact on children's educational outcomes and attainment, Schaller and Stevens (2015), Lindo (2011), Kristiansen (2020) for the negative impact on children's physical and mental health outcomes, and Oreopoulos et al. (2008), Huttunen and Riukula (2019), and Pan and Ost (2014) the negative impact on children's long-term labor market outcomes.
2. See for example Gregg et al. (2012), Oreopoulos et al. (2008), or Pan and Ost (2014).
3. Schaller and Zerpa (2019), Rege et al. (2011), and Lindemann and Gangl (2019) all find that the adverse impact is confined to paternal job loss.
4. Caetano et al. (2019), Fiorini and Keane (2014), Rokicki and McGovern (2020), Currie and Almond (2011), Bono et al. (2016) all point to time children spend actively with adult family members as a productive input in the human capital production function and children's cognitive development.
5. A comprehensive review of the literature on early childhood environment and children's human capital accumu-lation can be found in Currie and Almond (2011)
6. Note that I cannot exactly identify if a household is just below or just above the 25th percentile of family income given that I only observe income as a categorical measure in the CPS. Instead, I assign a family to be "low-income" if their income lies below the CPS income category that the 25th percentile falls in that year. For reference, CPS income categories are structured as follows: Under \$5,000, \$5,000–\$7,500, \$7,500–\$710,000, \$10,000–\$12,500, \$12,500–\$15,000, \$15,000–\$20,000, \$20,000–\$25,000, \$25,000–\$30,000, \$30,000–\$35,000 etc. From 2005 to 2019, family income at the 25th percentile as calculated from the ACS increases from \$35,000 to \$47,600.
7. Note that some of the parents who experience unemployment at the time of their ATUS interview may have voluntarily left their job. While I can differentiate between the different reasons for unemployment with the CPS data, I do not have this information from the ATUS data. According to the CPS, only 8% of those experiencing unemployment as experienced workers are job leavers. Therefore, I feel comfortable to interpret my estimates as the impact of job loss.
8. Unemployment of experienced workers refers to unemployment of individuals who were previously employed as opposed to not yet having been part of the labor force, which is the type of unemployment that I seek to analysis in this study.
9. I calculate Oster's delta Oster (2019) to get a sense of the magnitude of the omitted variable bias in my naive regressions. This method assesses how the inclusion of control variables affects the predictive power of the regression as well as the coefficient of interest. I follow Oster (2019) and let $R^2 = 1.3 \times R^2$ to calculate the relative importance of unobservables to observables that would be consistent with job loss having no impact on my outcome variables, δ. For the outcome variables shown in Table 5, I calculate δ as 21.8, 36453, -9, and 41 respectively. This suggests that the importance of any omitted variables

would have to be many times larger than the importance of the included variables for the true β1 to be zero. This does not seem plausible.

10. See Francesconi and Heckman (2016) for a review of the relevant literature.

REFERENCES

Aguiar, M., Hurst, E., & Karabarbounis, L. (2013). Time use during the great recession. *The American Economic Review*, *103*(5), 1664–1696.

Arnup, J., Black, N., & Johnston, D. (2021). Changes in children's time use during periods of financial hardship. *Journal of Population Economics*, *35*, 1–30.

Bono, E., Francesconi, M., Kelly, Y., & Sacker, A. (2016). Early maternal time investment and early child outcomes. *The Economic Journal*, *126*, F96–F135.

Caetano, G., Kinsler, J., & Teng, H. (2019). Towards causal estimates of children's time allocation on skill development. *Journal of Applied Econometrics*, *34*(4), 588–605.

Coelli, M. (2011). Parental job loss and the education enrollment of youth. *Labour Economics*, *18*(1), 25–35.

Currie, J., & Almond, D. (2011). Human capital development before age five. In *Handbook of labor economics* (Vol. 4, pp. 1315–1486). Elsevier.

De Cao, E., McCormick, B., & Nicodemo, C. (2022). Does unemployment worsen babies' health? A tale of siblings, maternal behaviour, and selection. *Journal of Health Economics*, *83*, 102601.

Eliason, M. (2012). Lost jobs, broken marriages. *Journal of Population Economics*, *25*(4), 1365–1397.

Eliason, M., & Storrie, D. (2009a). Does job loss shorten life? *Journal of Human Resources*, *44*(2), 277–302.

Eliason, M., & Storrie, D. (2009b). Job loss is bad for your health–Swedish evidence on cause-specific hospitalization following involuntary job loss. *Social Science & Medicine*, *68*(8), 1396–1406.

Fiorini, M., & Keane, M. (2014). How the allocation of children's time affects cognitive and noncognitive development. *Journal of Labor Economics*, *32*(4), 787–836.

Francesconi, M., & Heckman, J. (2016). Child development and parental investment: Introduction. *The Economic Journal*, *126*(596), F1–F27.

Gathmann, C., Huttunen, K., Jernström, L., Sääksvuori, L., & Stitzing, R. (2021). *In sickness and in health: Job displacement and health spillovers in couples*. Unpublished manuscript.

Gregg, P., Macmillan, L., & Nasim, B. (2012). The impact of fathers' job loss during the recession of the 1980s on their children's educational attainment and labour market outcomes. *Fiscal Studies*, *33*(2), 237–264.

Guryan, J., Hurst, E., & Kearney, M. (2008). Parental education and parental time with children. *The Journal of Economic Perspectives*, *22*(3), 23–46.

Hamermesh, D., Frazis, H., & Jay Stewart, J. (2005). Data watch: The American time use survey. *The Journal of Economic Perspectives*, *19*(1), 221–232.

Hilger, N. (2016). Parental job loss and children's long-term outcomes: Evidence from 7 million fathers' layoffs. *American Economic Journal: Applied Economics*, *8*(3), 247–283.

Hofferth, S., Flood, S., Sobek, M., & Backman, D. (2020). *American time use survey data extract builder: Version 2.8*. University of Maryland.

Hsin, A., & Felfe, C. (2014). When does time matter? Maternal employment, children's time with parents, and child development. *Demography*, *51*(5), 1867–1894.

Huttunen, K., & Riukula, K. (2019). *Parental job loss and children's careers*. IZA Discussion Papers.

Kristiansen, I. (2020). *Short-and long-term consequences of serious parental health shocks*. Unpublished Manuscript.

Kuhn, A., Lalive, R., & Zweimüller, J. (2009). The public health costs of job loss. *Journal of Health Economics*, *28*(6), 1099–1115.

Lindemann, K., & Gangl, M. (2019). The intergenerational effects of unemployment: How parental unemployment affects educational transitions in Germany. *Research in Social Stratification and Mobility*, *62*, 100410.

Lindo, J. (2011). Parental job loss and infant health. *Journal of Health Economics*, *30*(5), 869–879.

Morrissey, T. (2022). The earned income Tax Credit and short-term changes in parents' time investments in children. *Journal of Family and Economic Issues*, 1–22.

Oreopoulos, P., Page, M., & Stevens, A. (2008). The intergenerational effects of worker displacement. *Journal of Labor Economics*, *26*(3), 455–483.

Oster, E. (2019). Unobservable selection and coefficient stability: Theory and evidence. *Journal of Business & Economic Statistics*, *37*(2), 187–204.

Pan, W., & Ost, B. (2014). The impact of parental layoff on higher education investment. *Economics of Education Review*, *42*, 53–63.

Rege, M., Telle, K., & Votruba, M. (2011). Parental job loss and children's school performance. *The Review of Economic Studies*, *78*(4), 1462–1489.

Rokicki, S., & McGovern, M. (2020). Heterogeneity in early life investments: A longitudinal analysis of children's time use. *Review of Income and Wealth*, *66*(3), 647–676.

Schaller, J., & Stevens, A. (2015). Short-run effects of job loss on health conditions, health insurance, and health care utilization. *Journal of Health Economics*, *43*, 190–203.

Schaller, J., & Zerpa, M. (2019). Short-run effects of parental job loss on child health. *American Journal of Health Economics*, *5*, 8–41.

APPENDIX

Table A1. Impact of Job Loss on Time Spent With Children by Parent Characteristics.[a]

	Primary Childcare	Educational Childcare	Recreational Childcare	Secondary Childcare
Job loss	11.99**	3.15	6.64	132.93***
	(4.82)	(2.51)	(4.93)	(17.97)
Job loss	16.26***	3.91	5.15	126.06***
	(6.13)	(3.19)	(6.27)	(22.88)
Job Loss*Low income	−11.19	−1.97	3.91	18.02
	(9.95)	(5.18)	(10.17)	(37.13)
Job loss	−1.24	3.85	12.77*	121.38***
	(7.22)	(3.76)	(7.39)	(26.99)
Job Loss*Female	23.86**	−1.25	−11.06	20.84
	(9.72)	(5.07)	(9.95)	(36.33)
Observations	1,456	1,456	1,456	1,456

[a]Standard errors in parentheses. * $p < 0.10$, ** $p < 0.05$, *** $p < 0.01$. All regressions include year, MSA, holiday, month-of-year and day-of-week FE and a vector of individual control variables. Sample is restricted to those parents unemployed either at one point during their CPS tenure or their ATUS interview.

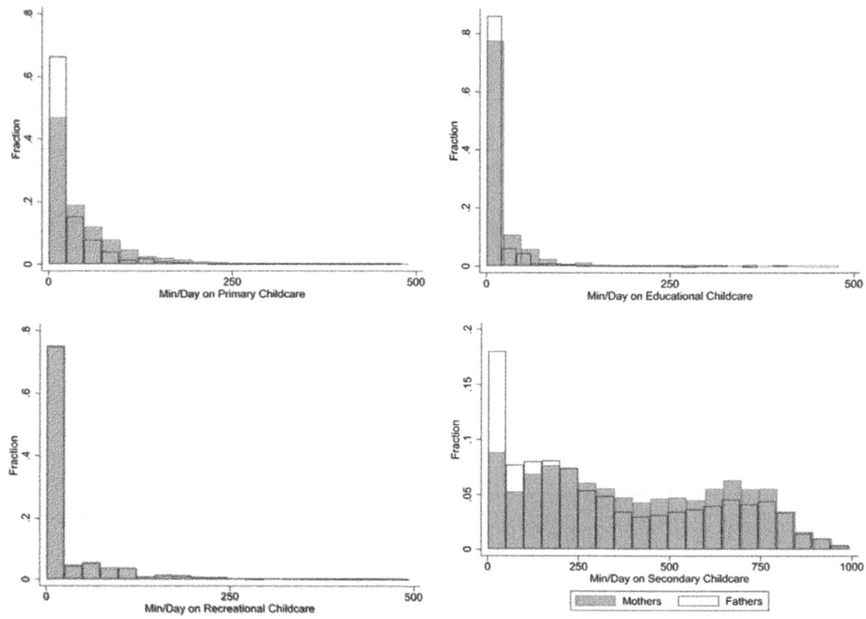

Fig. A1. Distribution of Main Outcome Variables by Parent Gender.
Note: Fig. A1 shows the distribution of how mothers and fathers With at least one child who is 12 years old your younger in my baseline sample report spending time With their children in the 24 hours leading up to their interview. Since each of the outcome variables depicted in the figure has a long right tail With a number of outliers, time spent on primary childcare, educational childcare, and recreational childcare have been trimmed at 500 minutes and secondary childcare at 1,000 minutes to make the figure more easily comprehensible.

PARENTS' WORK HOURS AND CHILDCARE DECISIONS: EXPLOITING A TIME WINDFALL

Taehyun Ethan Kim and Dean R. Lillard

ABSTRACT

We model the conditions under which parents optimally reallocate time to childcare when an outside agent exogenously restricts the number of hours an employer can demand of a working parent. Theoretically, when the restriction binds, a parent's available time increases. We exploit a series of voluntary and mandated labor-market reforms in South Korea that regulated the statutory and maximum work hours of parents. The government implemented the laws in stages by industry and size of firms. This implementation process generates exogenous variation across families where one or both partners worked at jobs that were or were not affected by the reform. We show the reforms affected work hours and use the predicted changes to investigate the total amount they spent on paid childcare and whether or not they changed the relative use of market and parental care. When fathers get more time (work less), parents spend less money on childcare. A change in mother's work time does not affect expenditures. When parents get more time, they are more likely to spend money on paid childcare for school-age children and more likely to use private academies.

Keywords: Work hour reforms; childcare supply; formal and informal childcare; time-goods trade-off; South Korea; home production

1. INTRODUCTION

When scholars discuss household production functions, they frequently invoke a "black box" metaphor. That metaphor glosses over a lacuna that economists have been working to fill over the almost 60 years since Becker introduced the

Time Use in Economics
Research in Labor Economics, Volume 51, 135–159

ISSN: 0147-9121/doi:10.1108/S0147-912120230000051006

idea of "home production" (Becker, 1965). Inside that gap, perceived only dimly, are the nature and details of household production functions. For example, scholars do not easily observe the inputs people use nor how they combine them. Most vexingly, household economists must grapple with how to model the production of goods that are decidedly heterogeneous across a wide range of dimensions.

The latter feature is critically important because it reflects the nature of the factors that complicate the modeling and analysis of home production. People rationally choose to produce a good at home when (a) the good they want consists of a complex set of characteristics specific to their particular (unobserved) preferences, (b) they possess the necessary skills and human capital, and (c) they spend fewer resources (time and money) to produce the (differentiated) product at home than they would to find and buy it in a formal market. They are also more likely to produce a good at home when the production process itself gives them direct utility.

To produce certain types of goods, people may use both home and market production processes. These "hybrid" goods bundle together a more complex set of characteristics than the typical home or market good (Becker, 1965; Lancaster, 1966). Hybrid goods often take a long time to produce. In early production stages, they require relatively basic market inputs and commonly held skills. In later production stages, the process requires more complex and specialized inputs and skills. These features create incentives for people to produce hybrid goods at home in the early stages, use both home and market processes in the middle stages, and use mostly or exclusively market processes in the final stage (Cunha & Heckman, 2007; Heckman, 2007).

We study one example of a hybrid good – a high-quality and educated child. We study whether and how parents use market goods (private tutors, paid childcare) and their own time to produce one. For the empirical analysis, we take advantage of labor market reforms in South Korea in 2003 and 2018. The reforms limited the statutory and maximum number of hours firms could ask employees to work. We exploit the fact that the government implemented the reforms over time by firm size and, to a more limited extent, across industries. That feature allows us to instrument changes in the hours mothers and fathers worked after their firms had to comply with the regulations.

Our main outcomes of interest are the total (logarithm) of childcare expenditures, and whether and how parents change their use of their own time and five different types of childcare when they unexpectedly get more time. We separately investigate these outcomes for parents with preschool- or school-aged children. We compare results from models that ignore substitution and complementarities between types of childcare and models of simultaneous choices across five types of childcare. We estimate each set of models with naïve OLS estimators that treat work hours as endogenous and an IV estimator that exploits the reforms as instruments.

Focusing only on the simultaneous equation IV models, we find that the labor legislation affected work hours, with heterogeneous effects for parents with children in the two samples. Parents of preschool-aged children are less likely to spend their own time on childcare and less likely to use informal care only when mothers' work hours fell. They did not change their use of other types of care. When fathers' work hours changed, they did not change care of any type. Parents of school-age children increased their use of afterschool care when mothers' work hours fell and increased their use of private academies and tutoring when the work hours of fathers fell. For parents of school-age children, the predicted change in work hours of either parent did not alter parents' other childcare choices.

In Section 2, we review the theoretical and empirical literature relevant to household production in general and to the production of child quality in particular. In Section 3, we describe our theoretical framework and its predictions. In Section 4, we describe our sample from the Korea Labor Income Panel Study data and the South Korean work hour reforms. We discuss how we use those data to test the model predictions. In Section 5, we specify models and discuss identification issues and limitations of our data. In Section 6, we present the results and discuss them. Section 7 concludes.

2. BACKGROUND AND PREVIOUS FINDINGS

Our study exploits variation in the available time of parents that results from plausibly exogenous policy changes. A substantial literature exploits the introduction or expansion of parental leave after the birth of a child to study family well-being (Baker et al., 2008), cognitive development, and schooling outcomes in the short- and long-run (Baker & Milligan, 2015; Carneiro et al., 2015; Dahl et al., 2016; Danzer & Lavy, 2018; Dustmann & Schönberg, 2012; Hallberg & Klevmarken, 2003; Liu & Skans, 2010). With one exception, these studies find either no or only weak statistical evidence that parental leave alters parents' labor market activity and mixed evidence that child outcomes vary with parental leave. Using Norwegian data, Carneiro et al. (2015) find that children are less likely to drop out of high school and earn higher wages if their parents got maternity leave when the children were born compared to children whose parents did not take maternity leave. Effects were greater for disadvantaged children. These studies exploit policies that induce parents to withdraw from the labor market temporarily when the child was very young - just after birth or in the very early life of a new child.

Fewer studies exploit changes in the time available to parents when children are older. Several studies analyze the 2003 South Korea reform which we also use. They investigate how that reform affected time allocation decisions devoted to market and nonmarket work and other outcomes at the individual employee level. Using two waves of cross-sectional Korean Time Use Survey data, Lee et al. (2012) and Kawaguchi et al. (2013) compare how respondents allocate time pre-reform (1999) to the allocation of time in 2009 when almost all firms had implemented the legislation (see Table 1). They find no evidence that people substituted market time for household production. They present some evidence, consistent with Hallberg and Klevmarken (2003), suggesting that when one spouse works less, the other spouse works more. In a later study exploiting the same reform and cross-sectional data in pre- and post-reform years (2003 and 2009), Hamermesh et al. find that wives reported higher well-being if the government reforms caused firms to ask their husbands to work less (Hamermesh et al., 2017). Other scholars have exploited the same 2003 reforms to study whether workers affected by the reforms experienced changes in labor productivity (Park & Park, 2019), health behaviors (Ahn, 2016), and industrial injury rates (Lee & Lee, 2016).

Another related literature explores implications from models that predict that parents may invest either their own time, the informal time of others (e.g.,

Table 1. Reform Implementation Schedule.

	Five-day Workweek	
Year	Date	Affected Firms
2002	July 1	Banking industry
2002	November 1	Securities brokerage firms
	2003 Labor Standard Act	
Year	Date	Affected Firms (Number of Employees)
2004	July 1	1000+ workers
2005	July 1	300+ workers
2006	July 1	100+ workers
2007	July 1	50+ workers
2008	July 1	20+ workers
2011	July 1	5+ workers
	2018 Labor Standard Act	
Year	Date	Affected Firms
2018	July 1	Public sector firms (any size); 300+ workers[a]
2019	April 1	Compliance enforcement begins
2019	July 1	300+ workers in 21 industries exempted in 2003 Act[b]
2020	January 1	50+ workers; Compliance enforcement starts at firms in 21 previously exempted industries
2021	July 1	5+ workers

[a]Applies to public sector firms of any size and firms with 300 or more workers in industries not exempted from 2003 Act (see list of 21 industries in footnote 6).

[b]2018 legislation requires compliance of firms in 21 industries that the 2003 reform had exempted (see footnote 6). The 2018 legislation continues to exempt firms (of any size) in the following industries (KSIC 10th codes in parentheses): Land transport (49), Water transport (50), Air transport (51), Support activities for transportation (529), and Human health activities (86).

relatives), or the time of formal market childcare providers (Cunha & Heckman, 2007; Heckman, 2007). Evidence suggests that, when governments subsidize the cost of formal childcare, parents use fewer informal care providers (Baker et al., 2008; Havnes & Mogstad, 2011).

It is to this strand of literature that our study contributes most directly. We explore whether parents change their use of informal and formal childcare providers when labor market reforms change their available time. Relative to existing literature, we model choices over a much larger set of possible childcare providers that may either complement or substitute for parental care. Using panel data, we observe how parents alter the mix of care types they use after the exogenous change in work hours.

We exploit the South Korean work hour legislation which others have used but capture variation in other changes to labor laws. We exploit four additional sources of variation. First, we exploit changes in the maximum weekly hours that firms could ask of workers. Second, we take advantage of changes to the wage penalties the government required firms to pay if employees work more than the statutory limit. Third, in each piece of legislation, the government exempted firms in various industries from the mandated work hours and implemented legislation in a staggered way. We code and use that variation.

3. A SIMPLE FORMAL MODEL

Our main prediction flows from a model of utility maximization. Here we sketch the model and proceed directly to the implied decision rules.[1] Following the literature, we assume that a parent derives utility from her child's quality, Z_i, and a composite good, X_i. To maximize utility, a parent decides the optimal amount of child quality, Z_i, and the composite good, X_i subject to a market wage and prices of each good. Parents produce the optimal amount of child quality by choosing the optimal mix of inputs dictated by the shape and nature of a child quality production function, a market wage, and input prices (Becker, 1965; Cunha & Heckman, 2007; Heckman, 2007). Because parents both produce and consume child quality, the relevant decision reduces to the choice of production inputs. We label Z_i as a child's quality.[2] It is trivial to assume that parents jointly decide how much child quality they will produce.[3] Under that assumption, the model yields testable predictions about heterogeneous effects across partners in a two-parent household.

The model yields the standard decision rules that a parent buys the time of other childcare providers and invests her own time so that the ratio of the respective value of the marginal product of each source's time just equals the ratio of the price of the care by others and parents. Stated differently, across all inputs that produce child quality, a parent chooses the combination of them such that, for the last dollar spent on each, they yield the same value of marginal utility (marginal product).

While straightforward, the model's predictions emphasize that a parent considers whether a given input is a substitute or complement for the time a parent invests herself. It is important to note and realize that time from different types of childcare providers do not need to have the same type of production relationship. For children of each age grouping, we have data on six categories of childcare parents choose (one of which is parental care). We are mostly agnostic about the production relationship between the time of parents and time from each of these types. However, one can, and we do, predict that parental care complements the time of particular childcare providers. For example, we posit that parental care complements time from other childcare providers who not only care for a child but also instill human capital of some type (e.g., music lessons). In such cases, a parent's care is likely to complement the provider's time if the parent ensures the child practices or does homework. More generally, ours is an empirical exercise to explore whether and how parents reallocate the mix of their own time and the time of others when they (exogenously) get some extra time they could spend on childcare.

3.1 Predicted Effect of Market Reform on Equilibrium Allocations

To set up the predicted effects of labor market reforms, we describe the South Korean labor market regulations we exploit, define the implied budget constraint the regulations impose, basic equilibrium choices before and after labor market reforms, and the factors that influence the choices.

The South Korean government enacted the first labor regulations in 1953. The 1953 Labor Standards Act set weekly statutory work hours at 48 per week and banned firms from requiring employees to work more than 12 hours of overtime or holiday work. The 1989 regulations reduced the 1953 weekly statutory work hours from 48 to 44 and increased the maximum hours by four hours from 60 to 64. Table 2 shows the labor regulations in force over our sample period from 1998 to 2019.

The 1989 and later reforms also established overtime pay that firms had to pay when the firm asked employees to work more than the statutory hours. The 1989 legislation set a penalty of 1.50 times the hourly wage for each hour above 44 hours per week. The 2003 reforms stipulate that, in the first 3 years after the

Table 2. History of South Korean Labor Market Reforms.

	Work Hours per Week			Overtime Pay		
Enactment Year	Statutory	Overtime/ Holiday	Maximum	Wage	Hours	Implementation
1989	44	20	64	1.5w	$44 < hrs \leq 64$	1989–1991
2003	40	28	68	1.25w[a]	$40 < hrs \leq 44$	2004–2011[b]
				1.5w	$44 < hrs \leq 68$	
2018	40	12	52	1.5w	$44 < hrs \leq 52$	2018–2021[c]

[a]Overtime pay in 3 years after reform affects a firm. After 3 years, employers must pay 1.5 times of wage for hours above 40.

[b]Implemented in firms of different sizes annually from 2004–2008 and in 2011.

[c]In April 2019, the government began penalizing firms not complying with 2018 reforms.

legislation takes effect at a given firm, the firm will pay 1.25 times the usual wage for the first four hours above 40 and 1.50 times the usual wage for hours above 44 per week. After 3 years, the firm must pay employees 1.50 times the hourly wage for every hour they work above 40 per week.

To give a sense of how these reforms affect choice, in Fig. 1, we plot the budget constraints workers faced before the 2003 reform, in the first three years after their firm had to meet the 2003 limits, and four or more years thereafter. The slope of each budget constraint in Fig. 1 changes at the kink points identified by the black dots. The 3-year phase-in period of the overtime wage penalty is shown in the middle budget constraint. Moving from right to left, the slope of the budget constraint rises and reflects the higher opportunity cost parents pay for each additional hour of time they devoted to childcare when that care requires that they forego working hours above the statutory work limit and temporary thresholds during the phase-in period.

We next plot the equilibrium choice of childcare time by parents and other providers before and after the 2003 reform. To simplify the plot, we only show the post-reform equilibrium for the phase-in period. Below we illustrate how the

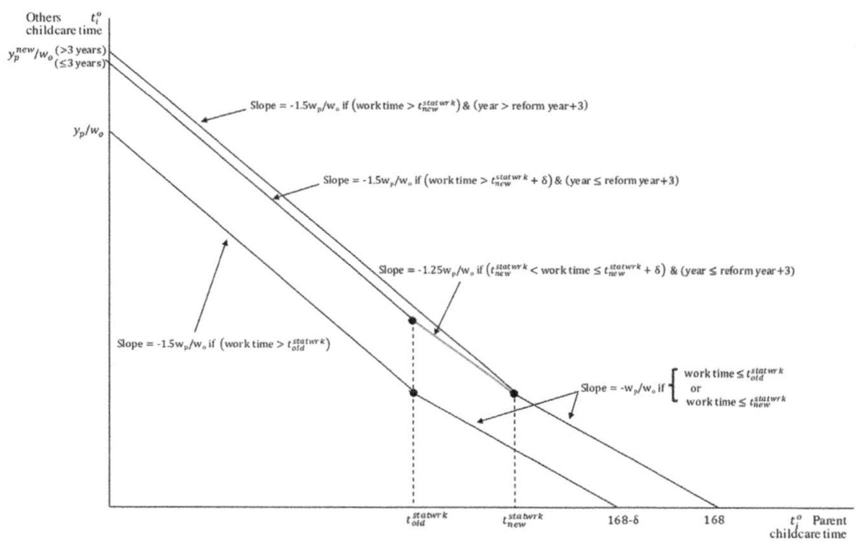

Fig. 1. Budget Constraints Before and After the 2003 Reform.

Notes: y_p and y_p^{new} denote potential full income under the old and new work hour regimes respectively;

$y_p = w * t_{\text{old}}^{\text{statwrk}} + 1.5w * (168 - t_{\text{old}}^{\text{statwrk}})$; $y_p^{\text{new}} = w * t_{\text{new}}^{\text{statwrk}} + 1.25w * (t_{\text{old}}^{\text{statwrk}} - t_{\text{new}}^{\text{statwrk}})$
$+ 1.5w * (168 - t_{\text{old}}^{\text{statwrk}})$ if year ≤ reform year + 3; $y_p^{\text{new}} = w * t_{\text{new}}^{\text{statwrk}}$
$+ 1.5w * (168 - t_{\text{new}}^{\text{statwrk}})$ if year > reform year + 3;
$\delta = t_{\text{old}}^{\text{statwrk}} - t_{\text{new}}^{\text{statwrk}}$; w_p : wage of parents; w_o : wage of others.

relative productivity of time from each source is a key determinant of the equilibrium.

3.2 Illustrating the Dependence on the Relative Marginal Productivity of Childcare Time

As noted above, when wages rise, the substitution effect is always negative (as relative wage of a provider increase, a parent uses less of that provider's time on childcare) but the income effect depends on the relative marginal productivity of the two inputs of time.

Here, we assume parent time and time of other providers are input substitutes (at least over the observed range). In the empirical work, we do not impose this assumption.

Fig. 2 shows that, when the marginal productivity of others' care is greater than that of parents, the parents are more likely to be on a portion of the budget constraint that will have the same relative wage before and after the reform. Because parents get a larger marginal increase in child quality when other providers care for their child, the parents want to work more, devote less of their own time to childcare, and buy more from other providers. For these parents, the legislation does not affect the relative cost of childcare in the range they optimally would choose. Consequently, the substitution effect is zero.

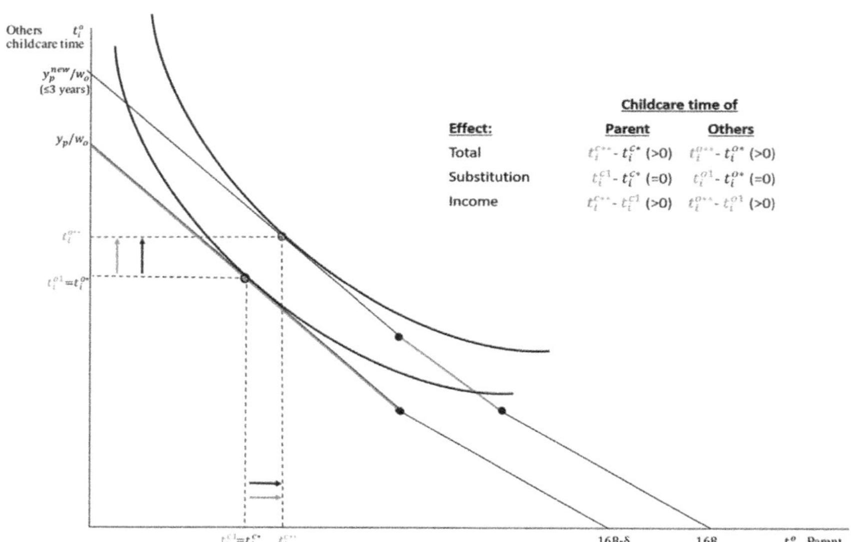

Fig. 2. Income and Substitution Effects: The Case of Marginal Productivity of Others' Time > Marginal Productivity of Parental Time.

However, the reform possibly raises their effective income because, in principle, they get the same income for fewer hours of work. Then, parents use some of their now higher income to "buy" more of their own time that they devote to childcare. They also may buy more or less time from other childcare providers depending on the relationship between inputs in the production function. This prediction highlights the importance of specifying empirical models that allow one to estimate either the total or only the substitution effects.

4. DATA

We use panel data from the Korea Labor and Income Panel Study (KLIPS) and data on work hour limits, maximum permitted work hours, and wage penalties for work above the statutory maximum. Mostly the government adopted these regulations by statute. A few changes occurred because labor unions negotiated with firms in particular industries and agreed to regulate working hours at a subset of firms in those industries.

KLIPS is a household-based panel study whose design resembles that of the US Panel Study of Income Dynamics. KLIPS began in 1998 with a sample of 13,321 individuals aged 15 and older living in 5,000 households. It draws an equal probability sample of households from 7 metropolitan cities and urban areas in 8 provinces in South Korea (excluding Cheju Island). It collects rich demographic data on a wide range of characteristics for all members of the household, including labor force measures (participation, hours of work, occupation, industry of employment, and firm size), earnings of adults, and receipt of income from a variety of sources such as assets, public and private transfers.

4.1 Sample Construction

To select our sample for the analyses, we first choose two-parent families with co-resident children younger than 19 - the age when the modal student completes high school. Within this sample, we retain an observation only if at least one parent works for pay one year before the implementation started. We impose this selection rule to ensure that at least one parent is at risk of being subject to the work-hour reforms. Although they represent a very interesting case, we exclude single-parent households to avoid having to model the couple's decision to separate and/or divorce. Finally, we keep respondents interviewed from 2013 to 2019, because KLIPS began collecting data on parental care only in 2013. Using this sample, we categorize child-parent observations by the age of the child about whom parents report. We separately analyze parental childcare decisions for children younger than seven (preschool-age) and seven to eighteen (school-age). We do so because there are age-specific cutoffs that prevent parents from choosing some childcare types. For example, a parent can enroll a child in afterschool care only when the child is of school age. Similarly, parents use daycare and kindergarten when their child is of preschool age. The set of childcare providers differs between the two groups.

4.2 Dependent Variables

We use KLIPS data on whether parents use each of five different types of childcare (including their own time) and how much money they spend overall for care. On all but three surveys since 1998, KLIPS asks parents to report on the childcare they used for each of up to five children.[4] From 1998 to 2007, parents pick from a list of 21 types of childcare (listed in an online Appendix). Since 2008, KLIPS has allowed parents to list up to eight types of care for each child. Among parents who use childcare, only 2.8% use six or more types of childcare. To reduce the influence of outliers, we use data on up to five types. We group the 21 childcare types into six general categories – parental care, informal care, private academy & tutoring, afterschool, daycare & kindergarten, and a residual category that includes all other types.

For the parental care, informal care, and daycare and kindergarten categories, we created indicator variables. The value of these variables equals zero if parents chose no provider in the category and one if they chose at least one provider in the category. For the afterschool, private academy and tutoring, and "other" categories, we created variables that count the number of providers parents chose to use for each child. Parents could report having used providers in each category up to a maximum of five. Because the survey does not separately identify which parent provides care nor how much time each devotes, each of our observations represents a child-parent pair for each child. We observe up to five children in each household.

To begin, we model the logarithm of the total amount parents spent on care for one child. We then model which, if any, of the five care types parents chose for children in each age group. For the analysis of childcare expenditures, we estimate the effects of changes in parental work hours with OLS and instrumental variable methods. The OLS estimator assumes differences in work hours of mothers and fathers are exogenously assigned across households. The IV estimator accounts for the endogeneity in work hour decisions. In modeling parents' choices among the five types, we use OLS and IV methods under two different additional assumptions: The first assumes that the parent's choice of one type of care is independent of the other types chosen. The second assumes parents simultaneously choose the five types of care. We model choices separately for children of preschool and school age.

4.3 Control Variables

In our multivariate analysis, we control for demographic characteristics that include: the ages of the child, mother, father, and the eldest and youngest co-resident child; the number of children in the household; the logarithm of household income net of taxes and public and private transfers. To control for the education of the mother and father, we include two indicator variables showing whether a parent has less than a high school education or a college (Bachelor's) degree or more. (The reference group is parents who are high school graduates with no further education or high school graduates who had some post-secondary education but have not completed an undergraduate program.) We include indicator variables to flag mothers (fathers) who do not work.

Table 3 describes the samples. We summarize the time-varying data for all child-household-year observations and child-parent-year observations, excluding multiple observations of the same parent. Most (but not all) parents provide care to their preschool-aged child (88.9%). Seventy-five percent of parents enroll their preschool-age child in daycare or kindergarten. Another 12.8% use informal care (which includes not only care by family members but also informal babysitters). Almost none enrolls a preschool child in private academies and tutoring or other types of childcare. Once children are of school age, parents most often enroll their child in multiple types of private academy and tutoring programs (1.59 programs for the average child). About one in four couples enrolls a school-age child in afterschool programs. The samples of parents of preschool and school-age children are broadly the same on other dimensions with two notable exceptions: Mothers and fathers of preschool children are more likely to have completed a university degree, and mothers of preschool children are less likely to be working.

4.4 Independent Variables of Interest

We wish to test whether parents are more likely to report that they provide care for their child or use other types of childcare when the parents' available time changes. The main covariate of interest is the usual hours per week that mothers and fathers work (if they work). Because parents can choose whether they hire

Table 3. Descriptive Statistics for Married Couples With Preschool and School-Aged Children.

	Preschool Children	School-aged Children
Dependent variables		
Total childcare expenditure	33.289 (27.100)	42.180 (32.667)
Childcare Use		
Parental care	0.888 (0.315)	0.000 (0.018)
Informal care	0.128 (0.334)	0.000 (0.011)
Daycare & kindergarten	0.750 (0.433)	
After school (up to 5)		0.226 (0.622)
Private academy (up to 5)	0.001 (0.031)	1.591 (1.290)
Other type (up to 4)	0.000 (0.014)	0.037 (0.219)
Childcare Costs (KRW)		
Informal care	34.688 (6.036)	35.104 (6.264)
Daycare	33.471 (1.460)	
Kindergarten	38.134 (2.198)	

Table 3. *(Continued)*

	Preschool Children		School-aged Children	
After school			4.525 (0.287)	
Private academy	15.153 (1.065)		15.251 (1.084)	
Other type	13.594 (2.309)		13.575 (2.316)	
Number of children	7,060		14,041	
Household variables				
Child age	3.561 (1.840)		12.239 (3.567)	
Age eldest child	5.720 (3.626)		13.972 (4.670)	
Age youngest child	3.153 (1.863)		10.505 (4.449)	
Number of children	1.801 (0.707)		1.693 (0.772)	
Household income (KRW)				
Total post-tax/post-transfers	11,614.007 (6701.408)		12,953.223 (7596.945)	
Capital gains	240.896 (3178.578)		327.553 (2942.166)	
Private transfers	394.657 (1711.131)		278.002 (1,676.543)	
Public transfers	274.723 (484.917)		89.453 (303.501)	
Number of households	5,160		8,887	
Parental variables	Father	Mother	Father	Mother
Age	38.097 (4.602)	35.702 (4.140)	44.852 (5.262)	42.166 (4.827)
Work hours	38.418 (19.813)	12.953 (18.962)	32.991 (22.506)	17.110 (20.829)
Not working (%)	0.019	0.600	0.033	0.441
Education category (%)				
HS dropouts	0.016	0.012	0.039	0.033
HS graduate	0.259	0.279	0.375	0.446
Undergraduate/ graduate	0.726	0.709	0.586	0.520
Annual wage (KRW)	4479.352 (2146.413)	2645.830 (1,508.738)	4969.030 (2804.877)	2566.352 (1,692.483)
Number of parents	5,160	5,160	8,887	8,887

Note: Authors' tabulations of KLIPS for years 2013–2019. The sample includes households with at least one working parent. See text for further sample selection. Standard errors are in parentheses next to or below means. All KRW (Korean Won) amounts are in 10,000 won and adjusted to real term (2020). Wage is defined for the workers only.

others to care for their child and, to a lesser degree, the amount of time they work, we use instruments derived from reforms to work hour regulations.

We employ three instruments: Usual (statutory) weekly work hours, maximum weekly work hours, and overtime pay mandated if an employee worked more than the statutory limit.[5] For each of these, we exploit variation generated by the reforms passed in 2003 and 2018. In both reforms, the government either exempted or delayed the date by which firms had to implement the legislated changes. Sometimes, the government delayed or exempted firms with a given number of workers. Most often, the government exempted firms in certain industries. These exemptions constitute the variation from the 2003 reform that we use.[6] These delays and exemptions generate another source of variation that we exploit. The government had finished implementing the 2003 reform by 2011. The government implemented the 2018 reform over 4 years from 2018 to 2021. Table 1 presents the details.

To set the stage and to show the potential impact of the reforms on work hours, in Fig. 3 we plot the trends in the average weekly work hours of working fathers and mothers from 1998 to 2019. By the last year of our sample period, the average employed father worked fewer than 50 hours per week. The average working mother worked just over 40 hours per week. Over the period of the reforms (after 2004), average weekly work hours decreased steadily.

To delve a bit deeper, in Fig. 4 we plot the fraction of employed fathers and mothers in our sample whose weekly work hours place them in categories of workers whom the reforms were likely to affect.

Starting in 2004, it increasingly less likely that either mothers or fathers work more than the maximum work hours of 68 and 52–64 hours per week. Over that period, the proportion of parents working 40–44 hours per week rose steadily. Conditional on working, the proportion of men who worked 44 to 52 work hours per week remains fairly stable. Over the same period, fewer working mothers were working 44–52 hours per week. Since the mid-2000s, an increasing proportion of working mothers work at or slightly above the statutory work limit.[7]

5. MODEL SPECIFICATIONS

We specify a model of (the logarithm of) total expenditures on childcare and then a system of simultaneous equations that consists of one equation for each type of childcare. For the latter analysis, our dependent variables measure whether (how much) of each of the six childcare types parents choose. The basic estimating equations take the following form:

$$\text{Childcare}_{\text{cit}} = \delta_1 + \widehat{\text{WrkHrs}}_{\text{it}}^{\text{par}} \delta^{\text{par}} + Z_{\text{cit}} \delta^{z} + X_{\text{cit}} \delta^{x} + \varepsilon_{\text{cit}} \tag{1}$$

where the $\text{Childcare}_{\text{cit}}$ refers to the use of each childcare type or the log of total monthly childcare expenditures.

We estimate a "naïve" model that treats the work hours of parents as exogenously assigned and an instrumental variables model that treats the work hours of the mother and father as a function of the work hour reforms. The specification above denotes the vector of predicted work hours of the mother and father by a "hat" ($\widehat{\text{WrkHrs}}_{\text{it}}^{\text{par}}$). The estimating equation for work hours is given by:

$$\text{WrkHrs}_{\text{it}}^{\text{par}} = \theta_1 + \text{Reforms}_{\text{it}}^{\text{par}} \theta^{\text{reform}} + X_{\text{cit}} \theta^{x} + \mu_{\text{cit}} \tag{2}$$

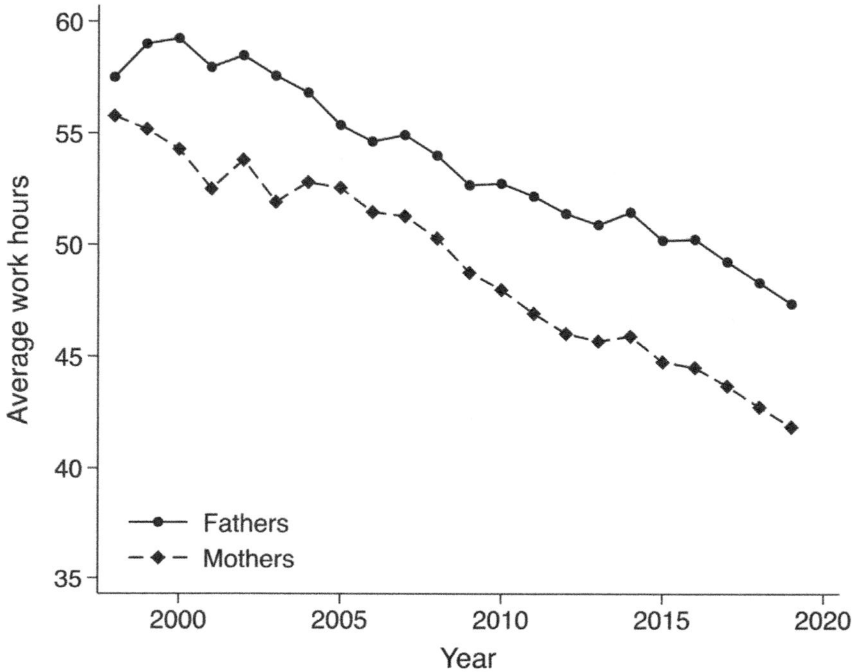

Fig. 3. Changes in Annual Average Weekly Work Hours of Employed Parents, KLIPS 1998–2019.

where the vector $\text{Reforms}_{it}^{par}$ indicates our set of instruments. These instruments are specific to each child's mother and father and take on values set by the legislation. To identify exogenous variation in work hours, we assume the reforms only affect the hours parents work and that they are uncorrelated with the error terms in Eq. (1) models. We include predicted work hours in the second-stage model.

We estimate these models as a form of motivating evidence that the work reforms affected the child production inputs that parents (jointly) chose. They provide evidence that, after the reforms, parents reallocated resources. We describe the determinants of the number of each of the six childcare types using data covering 2013–2019.

To highlight the potential specification errors that arise when one estimates a single equation OLS model versus a simultaneous choice model, we estimate single equation models for each type of care. Those models impose the assumption that parents choose each type of care without regard for any other type of care they might choose. Econometrically this is equivalent to the restriction that the coefficients on the other types of care are all zero. To test the effect of allowing for off-diagonal error terms to have nonzero covariance, we estimate a simultaneous equation model of five childcare equations for each

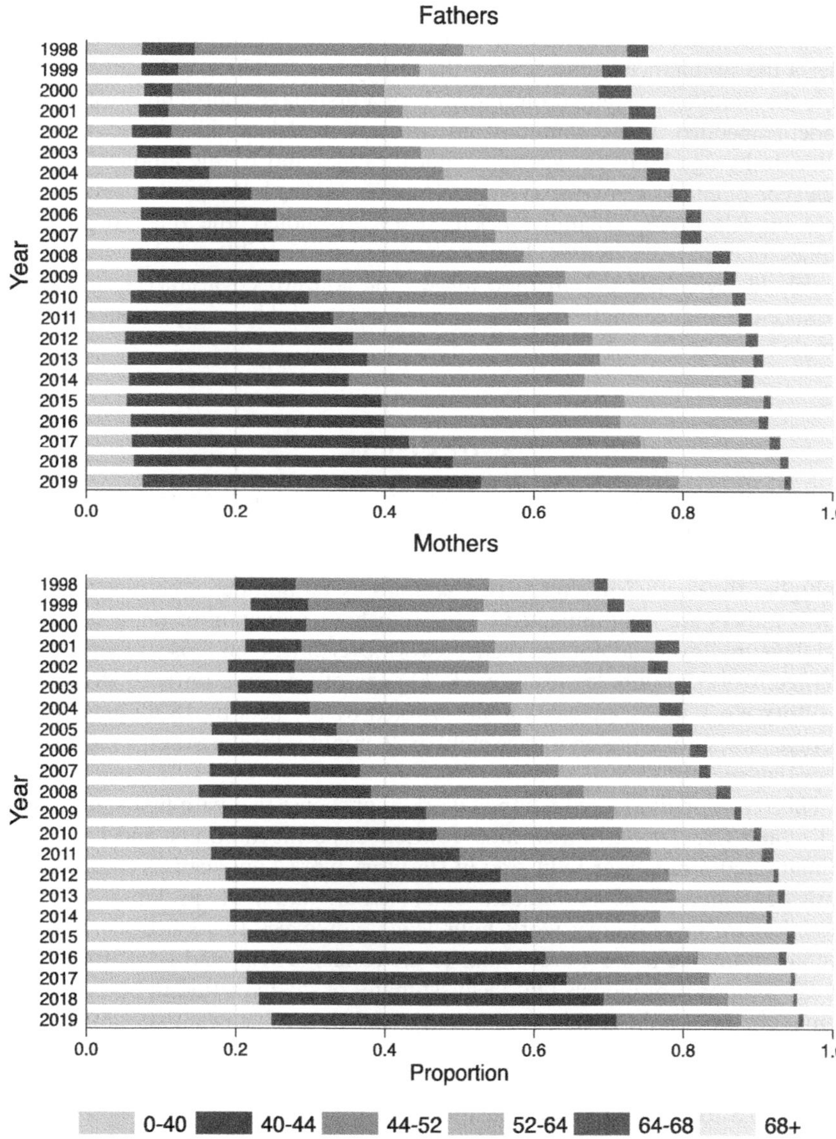

Fig. 4. Proportion of Employed Fathers and Mothers With Average Weekly Work Hours in Each Range, KLIPS 1998–2019.

sample to capture substitution between childcare types. We then use instrumental variable methods to estimate how an exogenous change in parental work hours affects the simultaneous choice over the five types of childcare. Finally, we estimate the simultaneous equations model with a first-stage endogenous work hours model embedded. In the simultaneous equation model, we identify each type of childcare by age limits for specific childcare types and by the amount spent on each type of childcare by the average sample household. We present results from these models in the column labeled SE-IV. As noted, the theoretical model implies that parents jointly decide which types of childcare they use at the household level, and this method allows for nonzero covariance terms in the variance-covariance matrix of the errors for five childcare equations for each sample.

6. RESULTS

We present results of the first-stage regressions of one of the models in Table 4. The first-stage results imply that a one-hour decrease in statutory work hours causes fathers to work between 29 and 33 minutes less each week. That figure multiplies the coefficients in the two samples by 60 minutes. The results predict that if fathers are fully impacted by the four-hour reduction of the 2003 reform and their employers do not ask them to work overtime, then those fathers will, on average, work 2 hours less each week. On the other hand, an hour decrease in statutory work hours increases hours worked by mothers by 18 minutes for the average mother of a preschool age child or 36 minutes for the average mother of a school age child.[8]

This result predicts a reduction in work hours consistent with first-stage results of Lee and Lee (2016). In their most restrictive specification, Lee and Lee (2016) estimate that a one-hour reduction in statutory work hours causes employees to work 15 minutes less. Kawaguchi et al. (2008) find that, in Japan, an hour reduction in the statutory work hour leads employees to reduce work by 8.4 minutes. Our results are more similar to the results of Kim and Lee (2012). They specify a number of models that yield estimates of the reduction in hours worked from a one-hour reduction in the statutory workweek. Their estimates range from 0.14 to 0.68 hours per week. By contrast, Hunt (1999) finds that when Germany reduced statutory work hours, a one-hour reduction caused Germans to work between 0.8 to 1.0 hours fewer each week.[9]

Table 5 presents results from the analysis of expenditures on childcare of preschool and school-aged children. The IV estimates suggest that exogenous changes in the work hours of mothers and fathers affect the amount parents spend on care of school-age children. The estimates imply that, when mothers work one hour less, the average household spends 3.7% more on care of their school-age children. When the weekly work hours of fathers fall by one hour, the average household spends 3.1% less on childcare of school age children. We find that changes in the weekly work hours of neither mothers nor fathers cause households to change their childcare expenditures when they have preschool age children.

Table 4. First-Stage Coefficient Estimates From the IV-Simultaneous Equation Model.

Instruments	Preschool Children		School-Age Children	
	Weekly Hours Mother	Weekly Hours Fathers	Weekly Hours Mothers	Weekly Hours Father
Statutory work hours	−0.296** (0.133)	0.486*** (0.090)	−0.597*** (0.104)	0.550*** (0.055)
Maximum work hours	−0.007 (0.073)	−0.037 (0.048)	−0.247*** (0.074)	0.052 (0.034)
Overtime pay	0.139 (3.785)	−1.317 (2.438)	−0.921 (2.948)	−0.393 (1.857)
N	7,060	7,060	14,041	14,041
F-statistic	1076.80	60.29	1113.56	159.01
Adjusted R-squared	0.895	0.320	0.826	0.403

Notes: Standard errors in parentheses, ***$p < 0.01$, **$p < 0.05$, *$p < 0.10$. All models control for parent and household demographics and a year trend. For full set of coefficient estimates from these and all other IV models, see online Table A1.

The former result is consistent with the following scenario. When mothers work more, the time they need to pick up and drop off their child off at after-school programs is potentially affected. Therefore, they reduce their use of afterschool programs and spend less on formal market care.

In Table 6 we present results from models that examine choice among the five different types of childcare. The first column presents OLS results from models that treat parents' work hours as exogenous and assume households independently choose each type of care without regard to choices among the other types. The second column, labeled IV, uses instrumental variables to predict exogenous changes in work hours but treats choice of each type of care as independent. The third column, labeled SE, again assumes that work hours are exogenous, but models the simultaneous choices across the five childcare types. The fourth column, labeled SE-IV, is our preferred specification. It models the simultaneous choice across the five childcare types and treats work hours as endogenous.

Several results are noteworthy. First, among households with preschool age children, the choice of childcare is only affected by weekly work hours of mothers. Second, for those households, a reduction in weekly work hours of mothers causes households to be 1.6% less likely to use parental care and 2.0% less likely to use informal caregivers. Changes in weekly hours of fathers do not alter choices of any type of childcare for households with preschool age children. We note again that 75% of parents of preschool age children use daycare or kindergarten. Our results suggest that the four-hour reduction in the statutory work week did not induce any change in the use of daycare or kindergarten - perhaps because the typical daycare or kindergarten contract requires parents to pay for a minimum amount of time that is substantially more than four hours per week. If so, the supply of care through daycare

Table 5. Estimates of the Effects of Work Hours on Total Childcare Expenditures, KLIPS 2013–2019.

	Log(Childcare Expenditure)	
	OLS	IV
Preschool Children		
(Predicted) Mother work hours	0.007***	−0.019
	(0.002)	(0.048)
(Predicted) Father work hours	0.001	−0.017
	(0.001)	(0.019)
N	7,024	7,024
Adjusted R-squared	0.466	
F-statistic (First Stage)		
Mother work hours		1815.18
Father work hours		99.90
School-Aged Children		
(Predicted) Mother work hours	−0.000	−0.037***
	(0.001)	(0.009)
(Predicted) Father work hours	0.000	0.031***
	(0.001)	(0.012)
N	11,813	11,813
Adjusted R-squared	0.227	
F-statistic (First Stage)		
Mother work hours		1657.49
Father work hours		179.84

Notes: Standard errors in parentheses, $^{***}p < 0.01$, $^{**}p < 0.05$, $^{*}p < 0.10$. All models control for parent and household demographics and a year trend. For full set of coefficient estimates, see online Table A1.

and kindergarten care is lumpy and therefore not easy to substitute when parental time changes by marginal amounts induced by the reform. For households with school age children, parents are less likely to enroll their child in afterschool programs when weekly work hours of mothers increase.

Accounting for both the joint choice of childcare types and endogeneity of work hours results in point estimates that differ noticeably from the OLS point estimates. For example, among households with preschool age children, the OLS estimate on mothers' weekly work hours in the model of parental care is −0.007 while the SE-IV estimate is 0.016. Among household with school age children, the OLS estimate on mothers' weekly work hours in the model of afterschool programs is −0.001.

Finally, these results correspond to the findings on childcare expenditures reported in Table 5. For households with preschool age children, changes in weekly work hours of mothers alter the probability that households devote

Table 6. Estimates of the Effect of Work Hours on Childcare Use for Preschool and School-Aged Children, KLIPS 2013–2019.

	Preschool Children (N = 7,060)				School-Aged Children (N = 14,041)			
	Parental Care				Parental Care			
	OLS	IV	SE	SE-IV	OLS	IV	SE	SE-IV
Weekly hours mother	−0.007***	−0.045***	−0.001***	0.016***	0.000	−0.000	−0.000	−0.000
	(0.001)	(0.016)	(0.000)	(0.006)	(0.000)	(0.000)	(0.000)	(0.000)
Weekly hours father	0.000	0.002	−0.000	0.002	−0.000	0.000	0.000	−0.000
	(0.000)	(0.006)	(0.000)	(0.003)	(0.000)	(0.000)	(0.000)	(0.000)
R-squared	0.178		0.753		0.003		0.335	
	Informal Care				Informal Care			
	OLS	IV	SE	SE-IV	OLS	IV	SE	SE-IV
Weekly hours mother	0.008***	0.053***	0.002***	0.020***	−0.000	−0.000	−0.000	0.000
	(0.001)	(0.018)	(0.000)	(0.005)	(0.000)	(0.000)	(0.000)	(0.000)
Weekly hours father	−0.000	−0.002	−0.000	0.003	−0.000	0.000	−0.000	0.000
	(0.000)	(0.007)	(0.000)	(0.002)	(0.000)	(0.000)	(0.000)	(0.000)
R-squared	0.211		0.759		0.002		0.334	
	Daycare & Kindergarten				Afterschool			
	OLS	IV	SE	SE-IV	OLS	IV	SE	SE-IV
Weekly hours mother	−0.000	−0.044**	0.001	0.002	−0.001**	−0.015*	−0.002***	−0.021**
	(0.001)	(0.018)	(0.001)	(0.010)	(0.001)	(0.008)	(0.001)	(0.010)
Weekly hours father	0.000	−0.001	0.000	−0.006	0.001	−0.005	0.001	−0.009
	(0.000)	(0.007)	(0.000)	(0.005)	(0.000)	(0.006)	(0.000)	(0.009)
R-squared	0.499		0.511		0.103		0.122	
	Private Academy & Tutoring				Private Academy & Tutoring			
	OLS	IV	SE	SE-IV	OLS	IV	SE	SE-IV
Weekly hours mother	−0.000	−0.000	0.000	−0.001	−0.003***	0.016	−0.003***	−0.007
	(0.000)	(0.001)	(0.000)	(0.001)	(0.001)	(0.015)	(0.001)	(0.028)
Weekly hours father	−0.000	−0.000	−0.000	−0.000	0.002**	−0.022**	0.002***	−0.046*
	(0.000)	(0.001)	(0.000)	(0.000)	(0.001)	(0.011)	(0.001)	(0.024)
R-squared	0.005		0.594		0.196		0.218	
	Preschool Children (N = 7,060)				School-Aged Children (N = 14,041)			
	OLS	IV	SE	SE-IV	OLS	IV	SE	SE-IV
Weekly hours mother	−0.000	−0.000	−0.000	0.000	0.000	−0.002	0.000	−0.000
	(0.000)	(0.001)	(0.000)	(0.000)	(0.000)	(0.003)	(0.000)	(0.002)
Weekly hours father	−0.000	−0.000	0.000	0.000	0.000*	0.000	0.000*	0.002
	(0.000)	(0.000)	(0.000)	(0.000)	(0.000)	(0.002)	(0.000)	(0.002)
R-squared	0.005		0.595		0.008		0.013	
Parents demographics	X	X	X	X	X	X	X	X

Table 6. *(Continued)*

	Preschool Children (N = 7,060)				School-Aged Children (N = 14,041)			
	OLS	IV	SE	SE-IV	OLS	IV	SE	SE-IV
Household demographics	X	X	X	X	X	X	X	X
Year trend	X	X	X	X	X	X	X	X
F-statistic (First Stage)								
Mother work hours		1825.89		1096.53		1905.95		1113.56
Father work hours		100.67		61.38		269.65		159.01

Notes: Standard errors in parentheses, $^{***}p < 0.01$, $^{**}p < 0.05$, $^{*}p < 0.10$. All models control for parent and household demographics and a year trend. For full set of coefficient estimates, see online Table A1.

parental time to childcare or use informal care, but the change in weekly work hours does not affect childcare expenditures. Parents of school age children change their use of after-school programs and private academies when weekly hours of mothers and fathers change. Changes in those hours also affect total childcare expenditures.

7. DISCUSSION AND CONCLUSION

We describe a theoretical model that posits that parents engage in household production of children using both home and market inputs. That model suggests that parents choose the different inputs simultaneously and that any change in relative prices will affect the equilibrium choices of each type. We set out a modest goal to estimate whether the evidence supports the prediction that parents choose types of care jointly. Our contribution is twofold. First, to our knowledge, we are the first to study how parents' childcare decisions respond to exogenous changes in work hours on the intensive labor supply margin. We also investigate childcare choices across a richer set of alternative childcare types than others have studied. We show that modeling simultaneous choices across those types matters - at least in the South Korean context. Our results suggest that attention to a broader set of alternative childcare types is warranted.

Second, using a rich population-wide longitudinal dataset, we investigate how parents change their use of parental and market care when reforms caused mothers and fathers to alter their work hours in different ways. Allowing for this type of heterogeneity is crucial, especially for conventionally gendered societies like South Korea, where the pervasive "bread-winning dad and caregiving mom" norm persists. We find that marginal changes in work hours do not significantly change the traditional gendered childcare pattern. This pattern is distinctive, especially for preschool children, as there are no significant effects of changes in fathers' work hours on any type of childcare use, including parental care. This evidence suggests that labor reforms induce changes in labor demand that affects women differently from men and that alter incentives for household production of children. The reforms might unintentionally burden mothers with extra childcare and exacerbate the already sharply declining fertility rate.

We observe how patterns of use of childcare according to the parents' changing work hours might be affected by multiple factors. First, the substitutability pattern between parental care and market childcare depends on the marginal change in available time. Parents may find it difficult to substitute daycare and kindergarten for their own time if daycare and kindergarten care require a minimum amount of time that makes it a "lumpy" substitute. In the same sense, when parents' work hours change, they may be able to substitute more easily informal care for their own care. Second, the ability of parents to substitute informal care for their own time may differ by the age of the child. It is plausible that for school-age children informal care is an inferior substitute for market care that complements parental care in the production of a high-quality child. The time these children spend in afterschool care and private academies may be more productive (relative to informal care) because parents "buy" the more advanced and age-specific extracurricular education that their informal care providers cannot supply.

These comments are speculative but suggest that a fruitful avenue for future research is to delve more deeply into the model's predictions. The model points to the importance of changes in relative prices, the nature of the production relationships between parental care and other types of informal and market care providers, and requires attention to income and substitution effects.

While our purpose here was to demonstrate that labor reforms did affect choices across different types of childcare, others can refine and extend the research in many fruitful ways. The choice of childcare by parents as related to their work time is a complicated issue, especially because it encompasses two different markets – the labor market and the childcare market. We study the demand side of childcare decisions using exogenously imposed changes in work hours caused by labor market reforms. One caveat is that we assume there is no significant change in the supply side of childcare. We assume that minor potential supply-side changes should be reflected in childcare (market) prices, and these are assumed away in our estimates.

The second caveat is that we do not address the flexibility of the labor market in this chapter. If the labor market is rigid, employees may not be free to decide their work hours and would be dependent on the demand side. In this case, employees would work for the number of hours their employers demand and may not be able to easily substitute parental and market childcare.

The model implies that the total effect of the change in wage rates and statutory work hours will vary with the nature of each input into the production of child quality and whether a given parent experiences a change in his or her wage. We and others should investigate this implication further. Our longitudinal data allow us to know whether a parent at a firm that will be treated next year is working more than what the statutory limit is going to be. These tasks remain for future work. The evidence we present here suggests that researchers might learn much if they jointly model choices of home and market inputs people use to produce a hybrid good (the type of goods that children represent) that results from a combination of home and market production processes.

ACKNOWLEDGMENTS

We have benefitted from the comments of participants at the 2022 Population Association of America and European Society of Population Economics conferences and a seminar at the University of Milan-Bicocca.

NOTES

1. In an online Appendix we develop the model step-by-step. We do so to highlight the importance of the relationships one assumes to hold between different types of childcare. Most of the literature that studies parental versus other types of care do not state what relationship is assumed. Consequently, the empirical controls are only loosely motivated.
2. Empirically, researchers often use education as a proxy measure of child quality.
3. One could also model intra-household child quality production decisions under the assumption of individual utility maximization in the context of a household-bargaining models (Lundberg & Pollak, 1993).
4. KLIPS did not ask the childcare questions in 1999 and 2003 (waves 2 and 6) and only collected data on three types of childcare in 1998 (wave 1).
5. We also control for the introduction of a five-day workweek that resulted at firms in particular industries from voluntary negotiated agreements between employers and labor unions.
6. For example, in the 2003 Act, the government exempted firms in 26 industries from the work hour regulations, regardless of size. In the 2018 legislation, the government required that firms in 21 of the 26 industries to implement the regulations starting July 1, 2019. The exempted industries include (KSIC 10th codes in parentheses): Sewage, wastewater, human, and animal waste treatment services (37); Sale of motor vehicles and parts (45); Wholesale trade on own account or on a fee or contract basis (46); Retail trade except for motor vehicles and motorcycles (47); Land transport (49), Water transport (50) and Air transport (51); Warehousing and storage (521); Support activities for transportation (529); Accommodation (55); Food and beverage service activities (56); Motion picture, video, and television program production, sound recording, and music publishing activities (59); Broadcasting activities (60); Postal activities (611); Telecommunications (612); Financial service activities except insurance and pension funding (64); Insurance and pension funding (65); Activities auxiliary to financial service and insurance activities (66); Research and development (70); Advertising (713); Market research and public opinion polling (714); Cleaning of building and industrial facilities (742); Education (85); Human health activities (86); Social work activities (87); Personal care services (961). The government exempted firms in five industries from work hour regulation in the 2003 and 2018 Acts. The industries were (KSIC 10th codes in parentheses): Land transport (49), Water transport (50), Air transport (51); Support activities for transportation (529); and Human health activities (86). The 2018 legislation continues to exempt firms (of any size) in the following five industries (KSIC 10th codes in parentheses): Land transport (49), Water transport (50), Air transport (51), Support activities for transportation (529), and Human health activities (86).
7. Note that the proportion working in each hour range can change over time in two ways. First, continuously employed workers change the hours they work. Second, people who previously did not work begin jobs or previously employed people quit. The proportions shown in Fig. 4 suggest that, starting with the implementation of the 2003 reforms, a smaller fraction of working women were working 0–40 hours per week.

8. The result for women is consistent with changes in labor demand that the reforms potentially induce which are plausibly heterogenous for men and women. First, when the reforms bite, firms face two choices. They must either pay wage penalties for employees whose work hours exceed the statutory limit or reduce hours of those workers and pay others to replace those hours. The latter strategy might be the lower-cost solution if the firm pays less than the statutory wage penalty for the replacement hours. If the firm employs workers who work less than the statutory limit, they can ask those workers to increase their work time (up to the statutory limit) without paying overtime wages. The firm might also hire new workers if they can pay a wage lower than the overtime wage penalty. As noted above, in the post-2003 years a smaller fraction of working mothers worked in the 0–40 hours while the fraction of working fathers in that lower category remained roughly constant. The results suggest that firms may have asked mothers to work more hours.

9. In a supplementary analysis, we investigate whether the change in weekly work hours causes yearly labor earnings to change. We show, in the sample of parents with school-age children, a one-hour reduction in weekly work hours causes fathers' yearly earnings to decline by 2.8% and mothers' annual earnings to increase by 3.3%. To account for these implied changes to earnings, in our models we control for annual household labor income. We present those results in Table A1.

REFERENCES

Ahn, T. (2016). Reduction of working time: Does it lead to a healthy lifestyle. *Health Economics*, *25*(8), 969–983.

Baker, M., Gruber, J., & Milligan, K. (2008). Universal child care, maternal labor supply, and family well-being. *Journal of Political Economy*, *116*, 709–745.

Baker, M., & Milligan, K. (2015). Maternity leave and children's cognitive and behavioral development. *Journal of Population Economics*, *28*(2), 373–391.

Becker, G. S. (1965). A theory of the allocation of time. *Economic Journal*, *75*(299), 493–517.

Carneiro, P., Løken, K., & Salvances, K. (2015). A flying start? Maternity leave benefits and long-run outcomes of children. *Journal of Political Economy*, *123*(2), 365–412.

Cunha, F., & Heckman, J. (2007). The technology of skill formation. *The American Economic Review*, *97*(2), 31–47.

Dahl, G., Løken, K., Mogstad, M., & Salvanes, K. (2016). What is the case for paid maternity leave? *The Review of Economics and Statistics*, 655–670.

Danzer, N., & Lavy, V. (2018). Paid parental leave and children's schooling outcomes. *The Economic Journal*, *4*(3), 81–117.

Dustmann, C., & Schönberg, U. (2012). Expansions in maternity leave coverage and children's long-term outcomes. *American Economic Journal: Applied Economics*, *4*(3), 190–224.

Hallberg, D., & Klevmarken, A. (2003). Time for children: A study of parent's time allocation. *Journal of Population Economics*, *16*, 205–226.

Hamermesh, D. S., Kawaguchi, D., & Lee, J. (2017). Does labor legislation benefit workers? Well-being after an hours reduction. *Journal of the Japanese and International Economies*, *44*, 1–12. https://doi.org/10.1016/j.jjie.2017.02.003

Havnes, T., & Mogstad, M. (2011). Money for nothing? Universal child care and maternal employment. *Journal of Public Economics*, *95*(11), 1455–1465.

Heckman, J. J. (2007). The economics, technology, and neuroscience of human capability formation. *Proceedings of the National Academy of Sciences*, *104*(33), 13250–13255.

Hunt, J. (1999). Has work-sharing worked in Germany. *Quarterly Journal of Economics*, *114*(1), 117–148.

Kawaguchi, D., Lee, J., & Hamermesh, D. S. (2013). A gift of time. *Labour Economics*, *24*, 205–216.

Kawaguichi, D., Naito, H., & Yokoyama, I. (2008). *Labor market responses to legal work hour reduction: Evidence from Japan*. Economic and Social Research Institute, Cabinet Office.

Kim, H., & Lee, J. (2012). The impacts of the 40 hour work week standard on actual working hours, wages and employment. *Journal of Labour Economics*, *35*(3), 83–100.

Lancaster, K. J. (1966). A new approach to consumer theory. *Journal of Political Economy*, *74*(2), 132–157.

Lee, J., Kawaguichi, D., & Hamermesh, D. S. (2012). Aggregate impacts of a gift of time. *The American Economic Review: Papers & Proceedings*, *102*(3), 612–616.

Lee, J., & Lee, Y. K. (2016). Can working hour reductions save workers? *Labour Economics*, *40*, 25–36.

Liu, Q., & Skans, O. N. (2010). The duration of paid parental leave and children's scholastic performance. *The BE Journal of Economic Analysis & Policy*, *10*(1).

Lundberg, S., & Pollak, R. A. (1993). Separate spheres bargaining and the marriage market. *Journal of Political Economy*, *101*(6), 988–1010.

Park, W., & Park, Y. (2019). The impact of the regulation on standard workweek on labor productivity in South Korea. *Journal of Policy Analysis and Management*, *38*(3), 681–705.

APPENDIX

Table A1. Estimates of the Effects of Work Hours on Parents' Earnings, KLIPS 2013–2019.

	Preschool Age Children	
	OLS	IV
(Predicted) Mother work hours	0.007***	−0.037***
	(0.001)	(0.010)
(Predicted) Father work hours	0.002***	0.052**
	(0.001)	(0.026)
N	6,962	6,962
Adjusted R-squared	0.391	
F-statistic (First Stage)		
Mother work hours		1791.76
Father work hours		52.06
	School-Age Children	
	OLS	IV
(Predicted) Mother work hours	0.001***	−0.033***
	(0.000)	(0.005)
(Predicted) Father work hours	0.004***	0.028***
	(0.000)	(0.007)
N	13,833	13,833
Adjusted R-squared	0.448	
F-statistic (First Stage)		
Mother work hours		1857.50
Father work hours		197.94

Notes: Standard errors in parentheses, $^{***}p < 0.01$, $^{**}p < 0.05$, $^{*}p < 0.10$. All models control for parent and household demographics and a year trend. For full set of coefficient estimates, see online Table A1.

TIME USE, INTRAHOUSEHOLD INEQUALITY, AND INDIVIDUAL WELFARE: REVEALED PREFERENCE ANALYSIS

Ruben Bostyn, Laurens Cherchye, Bram De Rock and Frederic Vermeulen

ABSTRACT

We make use of rich microdata from the Belgian MEqIn survey, which contains detailed information on individual consumption, public consumption inside households, and time use. We explain the observed household behavior by means of a collective model that integrates marriage market restrictions on intrahousehold allocation patterns. We adopt a revealed preference approach that abstains from any functional form assumptions on individual utility functions or intrahousehold decision processes. This allows us to (set) identify the sharing rule, which governs the intrahousehold sharing of time and money, and to quantify economies of scale within households. We use these results to conduct a robust individual welfare and inequality analysis, hereby highlighting the important role of detailed consumption and time use data.

Keywords: Collective model; time use; intrahousehold inequality; individual welfare; revealed preferences; equivalence scales

1. INTRODUCTION

For decades, poverty and inequality have posed major public policy challenges worldwide. Even though extreme poverty has been steadily decreasing, except for a recent spike due to the COVID-19 crisis, the level of inequality has been rising consistently in most rich countries. For example, at the start of the 1980s, the top

Time Use in Economics
Research in Labor Economics, Volume 51, 161–186

ISSN: 0147-9121/doi:10.1108/S0147-912120230000051007

decile of the richest people earned seven times more than the bottom decile. In 2015, the income of the top decile was already ten times higher (Keeley, 2015). To adequately assess the associated impact on the welfare of individuals in households, it is of vital importance to also consider the intrahousehold allocation of resources. If the within-household distribution of resources is highly unbalanced, inequality between individuals in households will be very different from inequality between households. Moreover, individual welfare comparisons should arguably also account for interindividual differences in time use (including leisure and domestic production) and, relatedly, inter-household differences in economies of scale (resulting from public consumption).

The current chapter presents a structural empirical analysis of individual welfare (poverty and inequality) that effectively accounts for these different aspects. We make use of a rich micro dataset that is drawn from the Belgian MEqIn survey, which contains detailed information on individual consumption, public consumption inside households, and time use. Our structural model assumes a collective model of household consumption (à la Chiappori, 1988, 1992) that integrates marriage market restrictions on intrahousehold allocation patterns.[1] Particularly, we adopt the revealed preference methodology of Cherchye et al. (2017).[2] This methodology is intrinsically nonparametric in that it does not impose any prior functional structure on the individual preferences or intrahousehold decision processes, so maximally avoiding functional specification error. Moreover, it allows for an informative empirical analysis, even when (only) using a cross-sectional dataset containing a single observation per household and when accounting for any (unobservable) heterogeneity across households (in terms of individual preferences and within-household decision processes). The methodology allows us to informatively (set) identify the sharing rule that governs the intrahousehold sharing of time and money, and to quantify economies of scale within households.[3] We exploit these features to conduct a robust individual welfare analysis.

Our analysis will particularly highlight the role of time use information. Existing poverty and inequality studies typically consider material consumption only, and abstract from interindividual differences in time use. However, one may well question whether two individuals with the same material consumption levels are equally well off if one has double the leisure time of the other. In this respect, important differences in the use of time (think of time spent on labor, domestic work or leisure) can be found between men and women, between couples with or without children, between highly and lowly educated people or between individuals in different countries (see, for example, Hamermesh, 2019). By providing detailed time use data, the MEqIn survey allows us to assess whether accounting for inter-individual time use differences can substantially impact the conclusions of empirical welfare analyses. Specifically, in our empirical application we will include individuals' leisure time (treated as private consumption by the individual) as well as time spent on domestic production (treated as public consumption by the household given that the majority of time spent on domestic production relates to services with a strong public component inside the household; think of time spent on child care, running the errands, cooking, or cleaning), and we will evaluate how this information affects our empirical findings on individual poverty and inequality.

Next, in welfare comparisons between singles and individuals in multi-person households, a most notable difference relates to public consumption inside households. Indeed, a defining characteristic of multi-person households is that some goods are partly or completely publicly consumed, which gives rise to economies of scale. Motivating examples include housing, transportation, and commodities produced by household work. Obviously, singles do not benefit from such scale economies, so impacting their welfare level in comparison to individuals in multi-person households. Our MEqIn dataset allows us to empirically assess this impact by providing information on both private and public consumption of households.

Our empirical results reveal that accounting for unequal sharing, time use, and economies of scale can significantly affect the empirical welfare analysis. For example, we find that women are substantially more likely to be considered poor due to smaller expenditure shares (particularly on private material consumption). Moreover, poverty and inequality rates generally decrease when accounting for time-use information. This suggests that less material consumption may often be compensated through more leisure time. Finally, accounting for economies of scale substantially reduces the poverty rate of singles relative to individuals in multi-person households. Overall, our analysis strongly indicates the importance of taking these different aspects seriously in individual welfare analysis (and subsequent policy conclusions).

The rest of our chapter is structured as follows. Section 2 introduces our revealed preference methodology. Section 3 presents the setup of our empirical application. Section 4 shows the results of our individual welfare analysis. Section 5 concludes.

2. THEORETICAL FRAMEWORK

Cherchye et al. (2017, hereafter CDDV) introduced a methodology to recover informative bounds on the intrahousehold sharing rule by linking observed consumption behavior with observed marriage allocations. The current section sets the stage for our following empirical analysis by briefly recapturing CDDV's theoretical framework and their identification strategy based on the assumption of marital stability.

2.1 Notation

We assume a marriage market with a set of males M and a set of females W. The marriage market is characterized by a matching function σ that defines the marital matching. Particularly, every man $m \in M$ and woman $w \in M$ is assigned to a partner of the other gender (denoted as $\sigma(m) = w$ and $\sigma(w) = m$) or remains single (denoted as $\sigma(m) = \emptyset$ and $\sigma(w) = \emptyset$). Each single or married couple then decides upon the consumption of private and public goods.[4] We assume n private goods with quantities $q_{m,\sigma(m)} \in \mathbb{R}^n_+$, and k public goods with quantities $Q_{m,\sigma(m)} \in \mathbb{R}^k_+$. When married, private consumption is shared between the household members in a way that defines male quantities $q^m_{m,\sigma(m)} \in \mathbb{R}^n_+$ and female quantities $q^{\sigma(m)}_{m,\sigma(m)} \in \mathbb{R}^n_+$ such that $q^m_{m,\sigma(m)} + q^{\sigma(m)}_{m,\sigma(m)} = q_{m,\sigma(m)}$. In turn, this yields the intrahousehold allocation $(q^m_{m,\sigma(m)}, q^{\sigma(m)}_{m,\sigma(m)}, Q_{m,\sigma(m)})$.

Consumption decisions are made under budget constraints, which are defined by the prices and incomes faced by each (potential) couple (m, w). Prices are denoted by $p_{m,w} \in \mathbb{R}^n_{++}$ for the private goods and $P_{m,w} \in \mathbb{R}^n_{++}$ for the public goods. Similarly, a single man faces the prices $p_{m,\emptyset}$ and $P_{m,\emptyset}$, and a single woman the prices $p_{\emptyset,w}$ and $P_{\emptyset,w}$. Furthermore, $y_{m,w} \in \mathbb{R}_{++}$ represents the income of the couple (m, w), and $y_{m,\emptyset}$ and $y_{\emptyset,w}$ the incomes of a single man and a single woman, respectively.

2.2 Stable Matching Allocation

To keep our exposition simple, we assume that all observed individuals are matched in our theoretical setup. However, in our empirical application we will use a dataset that includes singles, and we account for the possibility that a married individual may consider remarrying a single of the other gender. If all observed individuals are married, we have that $|M| = |W|$. Correspondingly, we can define the *matching allocation*

$$\left(q^m_{m,\sigma(m)}, q^{\sigma(m)}_{m,\sigma(m)}, Q_{m,\sigma(m)}\right)_{m\in M}$$

We say that this matching allocation is stable if it simultaneously meets the following three requirements: (1) *Pareto efficiency*, (2) *individual rationality*, and (3) *no blocking pairs*.

First, *Pareto efficiency* implies that for any married couple $(m, \sigma(m))$, there does not exist a feasible consumption allocation (for the given prices and income) that strictly increases one member's utility while not making the other member worse off. In the collective household literature, we say that the observed consumption behavior is *collectively rational* if it satisfies this Pareto efficiency condition (see, for example, Browning & Chiappori, 1998).

Second, *individual rationality* requires that no individual male or female is better off as single than in the current marriage: (s)he cannot afford a consumption bundle as a single (for the given prices and income faced as a single) that achieves a higher utility level than the one within marriage. Clearly, if this requirement were not met, then the marriage market would be unstable as the individual would prefer to become single.

Third, the *no blocking pairs* condition states that an unmatched couple (m, w) cannot afford (for the given prices and income in the counterfactual situation) a consumption bundle that makes at least one of them strictly better off than in his/her current marriage without making the other individual worse off than in her/his current matching. Indeed, if this condition did not hold, then these individuals would have an incentive to remarry each other and the observed matching allocation would be unstable.

2.3 Revealed Preference Conditions

CDDV define testable implications for observed behavior to be consistent with a stable matching allocation. Observed behavior is summarized in terms of a dataset D that contains the following information: (1) the matching function σ, (2) the consumption bundles $(q_{m,\sigma(m)}, Q_{m,\sigma(m)})$ for each matched couple $(m, \sigma(m))$, with $m \in M$, (3) the budget conditions for any possible marital outcome (i.e. potential couple and single), i.e., the prices $p_{m,w}$, $P_{m,w}$ and incomes $y_{m,w}$ for all $m \in M \cup \emptyset$ and $w \in W \cup \emptyset$.

CDDV's testable conditions are of the revealed preference type and intrinsically nonparametric, meaning that they do not require any functional structure for the utility functions that represent the individual preferences.[5] The conditions allow us to check whether there exists at least one possible specification of these individual utilities that rationalizes the dataset D in terms of a stable matching allocation. An attractive feature of the conditions is that they are linear in the unknowns, which makes them easy to use empirically. The conditions are stated in the next result (Cherchye et al., 2017, *P1*).

P1. If the dataset D *is rationalizable by a stable matching, then there exist.*

(1) Individual quantities $q^{m}_{m,\sigma(m)} q^{\sigma(m)}_{m,\sigma(m)} \in \mathbb{R}^{n}_{+}$, for each matched couple $m \in M$ and $\sigma(m) \in W$ such that

$$q^{m}_{m,\sigma(m)} + q^{\sigma(m)}_{m,\sigma(m)} = q_{m,\sigma(m)},$$

which define a matching allocation $q^{m}_{m,\sigma(m)} + q^{\sigma(m)}_{m,\sigma(m)} = q_{m,\sigma(m)}$, and

(2) Personalized prices $P^{m}_{m,w}, P^{w}_{m,w} \in \mathbb{R}^{k}_{+}$ *for each couple* (m, w) $(m \in M, w \in W)$ such that

$$P^{m}_{m,w} + P^{w}_{m,w} = P_{m,w},$$

that satisfy the following constraints:

i. All males and females are individually rational, i.e., for any $m \in M$ and $w \in W$,

$$y_{m,\emptyset} \leq p_{m,\emptyset} q^{m}_{m,\sigma(m)} + P_{m,\emptyset} Q_{m,\sigma(m)},$$

$$y_{\emptyset,w} \leq p_{\emptyset,w} q^{w}_{\sigma(w),w} + P_{\emptyset,w} Q_{\sigma(w),w}, \text{ and}$$

ii. There is no blocking pair, i.e., for any $m \in M$ and $w \in W$,

$$y_{m,w} \leq \left(p_{m,w} q^{m}_{m,\sigma(m)} + P^{m}_{m,w} Q_{m,\sigma(m)}\right) + \left(p_{m,w} q^{w}_{\sigma(w),w} + P^{w}_{m,w} Q_{\sigma(w),w}\right)$$

In this proposition, condition (1) requires, for every matched couple $(m, \sigma(m))$, that the (unobserved) individual private quantities $q^m_{m,\sigma(m)}$ and $q^{\sigma(m)}_{m,\sigma(m)}$ must add up to the (observed) aggregate private quantities $q_{m,\sigma(m)}$. Next, condition (2) introduces the concept of personalized prices, which represent the individuals' willingness-to-pay for the publicly consumed quantities. For each potential pair consisting of male m and female w, these personalized prices $P^m_{m,w}$ and $P^w_{m,w}$ must add up to the observed actual prices $P_{m,w}$. This adding up condition effectively makes that the personalized prices may also be interpreted as Lindahl prices corresponding to a Pareto efficient provision of public goods.

The rationalizability conditions (i) and (ii) have an intuitive "revealed preference" interpretation in terms of the stable matching requirements that we described before. First, condition (i) imposes individual rationality. It requires that individuals as singles cannot afford a bundle that is more expensive than the bundle they consume within their current marriage. More formally, this means that under the budget conditions as single (i.e., prices $p_{m,\varnothing}$, $P_{m,\varnothing}$ and income $y_{m,\varnothing}$ for male m, and prices $p_{\varnothing,w}$, $P_{\varnothing,w}$ and income $y_{\varnothing,w}$ for female w), the individuals cannot buy a bundle that is more expensive than the bundle $(q^m_{m,\sigma(m)}, Q_{m,\sigma(m)})$ for any male m and the bundle $(q^w_{\sigma(w),w}, Q_{\sigma(w),w})$ for any female w. Indeed, if condition (i) did not hold, then at least one male or female could attain a higher utility by becoming single.

Similarly, condition (ii) imposes the no blocking pair condition. The right hand side of the inequality constraint represents the sum value of the bundles consumed by male m (i.e., $(q^m_{m,\sigma(m)}, Q_{m,\sigma(m)})$ and female m (i.e., $(q^w_{\sigma(w),w}, Q_{\sigma(w),w})$ in their current marriages, evaluated at the prices that would prevail if m and w formed a couple (i.e., $p_{m,w}$ for the private goods and $P^m_{m,w}, P^w_{m,w}$ for the public goods). The inequality constraint then requires that the income $y_{m,w}$ available to the pair (m, w) does not exceed this sum value. If condition (ii) did not hold, then some pair (m, w) could effectively afford a bundle that makes the two individuals better off than in their current marriage, i.e., (m, w) is a blocking pair.

The revealed preference conditions in *P1* are "sharp": they only tell us whether the observed behavior is exactly rationalizable or not. Moreover, they only allow us to check marital stability in terms of observable consumption/economic gains that drive marriage decisions. However, in reality, marriage typically cannot be explained by these economic gains only; immaterial benefits such as love and companionship also play an important role. This makes that observed household consumption behavior need not exactly fit the testable conditions explained above. In addition, marriage markets may be characterized by frictions and search costs, which can equally lead to violations of the rationalizability conditions that we defined above.

To account for these aspects, CCDV introduces the concept of stability indices to relax their sharp individual rationality and no blocking pairs conditions. Formally, they replace the corresponding inequality conditions in *P1* by

$$\left(s^{IR}_{m,\varnothing} \times y_{\varnothing,w}\right) \leq p_{m,\varnothing} q^m_{m,\sigma(m)} + P_{m,\varnothing} Q_{m,\sigma(m)},$$

and

$$\left(s^{IR}_{\varnothing,w} \times y_{\varnothing,w}\right) \leq p_{\varnothing,w} q^{w}_{\sigma(w),w} + P_{\varnothing,w} Q_{\sigma(w),w}$$

$$\left(s^{NBP}_{m,w} \times y_{\varnothing,w}\right) y_{m,w} \leq \left(p_{m,w} q^{m}_{m,\sigma(m)} + P^{m}_{m,w} Q_{m,\sigma(m)}\right) + \left(p_{m,w} q^{w}_{\sigma(w),w} + P^{w}_{m,w} Q_{\sigma(w),w}\right)$$

where the stability indices $s^{IR}_{m,\varnothing}$, $s^{IR}_{\varnothing,w}$ and $s^{NBP}_{m,w}$ take values between zero and one. Clearly, $s^{IR}_{m,\varnothing} = s^{IR}_{\varnothing,w} = s^{NBP}_{m,w} = 1$ reproduces the sharp conditions in *P1*. Generally, lower values for the stability indices imply less stringent rationalizability requirements, so accounting for possible deviations from exact rationalizability. Basically, the outside options (single or remarried) become less attractive, which weakens the incentive to leave the current marriage purely on the basis of (anticipated) material payoffs. Intuitively, we may also interpret these stability indices as divorce costs. More specifically, $(1 - s^{IR}_{m,\varnothing}) \times 100$ and $(1 - s^{IR}_{\varnothing,w}) \times 100$ then indicate the divorce cost associated with becoming single for male m and female w, respectively. In the same way, $(1 - s^{NBP}_{m,w}) \times 100$ gives the divorce cost for m and w if they remarry each other. In our application, we will compute the maximum values of the stability indices that allow us to rationalize the observed matching and consumption behavior. These values correspond to the minimal divorce costs that are needed to represent the observed marital matches as economically stable.

2.4 Estimation Procedure

In the first step of our estimation procedure we compute

$$\max_{s^{IR}_{m,\varnothing}, s^{IR}_{\varnothing,w}, s^{NBP}_{m,w}} \sum_{m} s^{IR}_{m,\varnothing} + \sum_{w} s^{IR}_{\varnothing,w} + \sum_{m}\sum_{w} s^{NBP}_{m,w}, \tag{1}$$

subject to the rationalizability restrictions (with stability indices) that we outlined above. As we explained in the previous section, this obtains the minimal divorce costs that are required to rationalize the observed marital matching as stable.

Subsequently, we multiply the solution values for $s^{IR}_{m,\varnothing}$, $s^{IR}_{\varnothing,w}$ and $s^{NBP}_{m,w}$ with the original income levels, $y_{\varnothing,w}$, $y_{w,\varnothing}$ and $y_{m,w}$. This gives an adjusted dataset that can be rationalized by a stable matching. In turn, this allows us to set identify the intrahousehold resource allocation based on our characterization of stable marriage behavior (so using marital stability as our key identifying assumption).

In their empirical analysis, CDDV focused on identifying a "general" sharing rule, which specifies the individual incomes that are assigned to either the male m or female w, hereby accounting for both private and public expenditures. In contrast to CDDV, our following empirical analysis will make use of the conditional sharing rule, which (only) captures the individual private consumption shares $q^{m}_{m,\sigma(m)}$ and $q^{\sigma(m)}_{m,\sigma(m)}$ conditional upon the public consumption $Q_{m,\sigma(m)}$ (see, for example, Browning et al., 2014, for a detailed discussion). As we detail in Section 4, using this conditional sharing rule will effectively allow us to conduct an informative welfare analysis. Formally, the conditional income shares of males and females are defined as, respectively,

$$z^m_{m,\sigma(m)} = p_{m,\sigma(m)} q^m_{m,\sigma(m)} \text{ and } z^{\sigma(m)}_{m,\sigma(m)} = p_{m,\sigma(m)} q^{\sigma(m)}_{m,\sigma(m)},$$

where $z^m_{m,\sigma(m)}$ and $z^{\sigma(m)}_{m,\sigma(m)}$ must add up to the total private expenditures of the household. This conditional sharing rule can be set identified through. linear programming techniques. In particular, by maximizing (minimizing) $z^m_{m,\sigma(m)}$ and $z^{\sigma(m)}_{m,\sigma(m)}$ subject to our linear rationalizability conditions, upper (lower) bounds on the income shares are obtained. These bounds enable welfare analysis at the level of individuals in households (instead of the aggregate households), which we will use in our empirical application.

2.5 Discussion

At this point, it makes sense to discuss the potential limitations of our approach. As we motivated in the Introduction, a specific feature of our empirical analysis is that we take employ time-use information. More specifically, we consider individual leisure as a privately consumed good and time spent on domestic work as publicly consumed. One could argue that at least part of an individual's leisure involves complementarities or has a public component (see, for example, Cosaert et al., 2023). Think of watching TV together with one's spouse, which is likely more pleasant than watching TV alone. In principle, our methodology is not constrained by the assumption we made. With adequate data (which make a distinction between privately consumed leisure and publicly consumed leisure), we could suitably adapt our empirical application to account for these different components. However, we do not have information on the public component of individuals' leisure in the data we will use in our application. In a similar vein, one may argue that domestic work may generate so-called process benefits (for example, parental time simultaneously produces welfare for the child and leisure-like benefits). We will abstract from modeling such process benefits in our analysis; including these benefits in a revealed preference analysis such as ours may develop along the lines of Cosaert and Hennebel (2022).

The next question that can be asked is which price should be attached to the different time uses. In our application, we opt to set the prices of leisure and domestic work equal to the individuals' wages. Obviously, setting the price of one's domestic work equal to that individual's wage is a strong assumption. In addition, time spent on different activities may be valued differently (see, for example, Hamermesh, 2015). Finding the values of different time uses remains a difficult business, however, and it goes beyond the scope of this chapter. Therefore, we opted for the pragmatic solution that sets the opportunity cost of a unit of time equal to the wage.

Another assumption in our approach is that wages are exogenous. In other words, this implies that one's wage rate does not depend on the number of hours worked (for example, an hour worked full-time or part-time obtains the same hourly wage). There is evidence that this assumption is too strong. Still, one could argue that, when individuals who operate on a marriage market compare alternative individual budget sets (as determined by their shares in the household's resources in alternative situations), they have the wage rate they know best in mind. We note that we could easily adapt our methodology to a setting where wages exogenously change across different situations.[6]

We allow for maximal heterogeneity across individuals (not only over individuals of a different gender, but also over individuals with similar observed characteristics). More specifically, all individuals have their own rational preferences. We assume that these individual preferences remain fixed. This implies that individuals do not have random preferences that may depend on the specific choices made with respect to the allocation of time and money. Specifically important for our method is that an individual's preferences do not change when living with a different partner.

3. EMPIRICAL APPLICATION

We first discuss the setup of our empirical application. Subsequently, we introduce our data and, finally, we present our obtained results for the conditional sharing rule. All this will form the basis for our individual welfare analysis in Section 4.

3.1 Setup

Our empirical application considers a collective labor supply setting in which each household's full income is spent on material consumption and time use (including leisure, domestic work and child care). Material consumption is measured as a Hicksian aggregate good that consists of a private and a public component. Private consumption is partly assignable and partly non-assignable. For some expenditures (for example, clothing) it is observed who consumes what, while other expenditures (for example, holidays or rents) are not directly assignable to individuals. While the assignable expenditures are assumed to be fully privately consumed, part of the non-assignable expenditures of each couple will be treated as public consumption, while the remainder will be treated as non-assignable private consumption (see Section 3.2 for more details). Adding this information to the constraints in Proposition 1 is straightforward; it simply imposes lower bounds on the unknown private quantities $q^{m}_{m,\sigma(m)}$ and $q^{w}_{\sigma(w),w}$.

In the following we will use two different methods (Methods A and B) to calculate leisure. In Method A, we distinguish between leisure time and time spent on domestic work and child care. This avoids that a part-time working mother appears to consume a high amount of leisure, while, in reality, she is spending a significant amount of time on household work and child care. Hours devoted to domestic work and child care are then modeled as an input that is consumed within the household (Becker, 1965). We follow CDDV by assuming that individual spouses produce different household goods through efficient one-input technologies that are characterized by constant returns to scale. As an implication, the value of time spent on domestic production can act as the output value of the household goods. These household goods are then evaluated at personalized Lindahl prices, which have to add up to the wage of the spouse that produced the good. For example, when the male spends an hour on cleaning a room, both spouses have Lindahl prices for this household work (reflecting their willingness to pay for a clean room) that must add up to the male's observed wage.

Next, Method B does not distinguish between leisure time and time spent on domestic work and child care. As such, it treats all time not spent in the labor market as leisure. This effectively mimics practical applications that make use of datasets lacking detailed information on individuals' allocations of time. It allows us to assess whether such a "simplified" model setup creates a bias in the welfare analysis.

3.2 Data

We make use of household data drawn from the Belgian MEqIN survey, which is a random sample of 2098 households that were selected on the basis of the Belgian National Register.[7] The sample is representative of all people living in Belgium. The data set contains a rich set of variables with information on households' labor supply, expenditures, time use, wealth, wages, and socio-demographic variables.

Of special importance for our study are the time use and expenditure information. The time-use questionnaire in the MEqIn survey asks for the average amount of time that individuals spend on a number of broad and exhaustive categories in a typical week. As such these data are retrospective and not diary based. The same applies to the expenditure information. Contrary to standard budget surveys (like the Consumption Expenditure Survey in the US), which focus on households' expenditures on many hundreds goods and services, the MEqIn survey concentrates on an exhaustive set of broad categories of nondurable goods and services (like food, clothing, housing, expenditures on children, etc.). At the same time, the MEqIn data provides information that is richer than that contained in typical budget surveys, in the sense that it also contains information about who is consuming what within the surveyed households. As such, the data set making a distinction between privately and publicly consumed goods and services, while it provides information on the adult household members' shares in the household's total private expenditures.

In what follows, we first present descriptive statistics of the variables that we use. Subsequently, we briefly elaborate on our construction of individual-specific marriage markets.

Sample selection. Our empirical analysis targets households with adult individuals aged between 24 and 65 years old. In order for couples to be included in the sample, both adults have to work at least 10 hours per week.[8] Also, the self-employed are left out of the sample. Their wages are not as straightforwardly obtained as for salaried workers, in part because of the rather vague distinction between private and work-related expenditures. In addition, households with important missing data on age, consumption, wage, time use and marital status were deleted. Finally, our dataset also includes singles, so expanding the remarriage options (i.e., potentially blocking pairs) for the married individuals. These selection criteria result in a sample that consists of 161 couples, 118 single females and 65 single males.

As previously mentioned, consumption can be divided into an assignable part and a non-assignable part. In the MEqIn data, several good categories, such as food, restaurants, cigarettes, clothing, personal care products, education expenses and transportation can be assigned to a particular individual. The remaining part of the observed household consumption is non-assignable, which ranges from rent and mortgages to holiday expenses and medical care. Throughout our analysis, we will assume that 50% of these non-assignable expenditures within households is privately consumed while the other half is publicly consumed. The same assumption was used by Cherchye et al. (2017).[9]

Table 1 presents summary statistics for all married couples in our sample, for both Methods A and B. Wages are expressed as net hourly wages. On average, males earn more than their female counterparts. Full income, expressed in euros per week, is calculated by summing both spouses' maximum labor income and the household's total nonlabor income.

Table 1. Summary Statistics for Married Couples (N = 161).

	Mean	SD	Min.	Max.
Male wage	10.635	3.101	3.22	22.44
Female wage	9.93	2.652	3.401	21.719
Full income	2242.95	540.421	1169.816	4096.556
Total private consumption	532.358	174.773	145.154	1253.769
Assignable male private consumption	122.022	56.65	8.769	311.538
Assignable female private consumption	121.403	61.59	9	369.231
Public consumption	288.932	128.35	74.423	991.846
Male age	41.248	9.128	25	64
Female age	38.658	8.668	25	61
Number of children	1.168	0.976	0	4
Male dummy for college degree	0.429	0.496	0	1
Female dummy for college degree	0.565	0.497	0	1
	Method A			
Male leisure	49.111	14.559	2	84
Female leisure	44.259	15.236	0	80.5
Male household work	16.006	12.171	0	63
Female household work	27.609	15.502	1	98
	Method B			
Male leisure	65.117	10.179	26	90
Female leisure	71.725	9.519	41	98.25

Notes: Leisure and household work are in hours per week. Wages are in euros per hour while full income and consumption are denoted in euros per week.

Total private consumption equals each individual's assignable consumption plus 50% of the non-assignable expenditures, and public consumption corresponds to the other 50% of the non-assignable expenditures. Table 1 also reports on several household characteristics such as age, number of children, and whether the male or female attended college or university.[10] Leisure is denoted in hours per week. We calculate leisure time by making the standard assumption that each individual needs 8 hours per day for personal care and sleep. This means that only 112 hours ((24 − 8) × 7) is maximally spent on the labor market per week.[11] As explained above, Method A further distinguishes between leisure and domestic work plus child care, while Method B treats all time not spent on market labor as leisure. When using Method B, women seem to have more leisure than men. However, this conclusion no longer holds under Method A, because women spend on average substantially more time on domestic work and child care. In the following analysis, we check whether this alternative specification of leisure time yields different welfare conclusions.

Lastly, we compute individual nonlabor incomes associated with the different (re)marriage options. For observed couples, nonlabor income is calculated by subtracting labor income from the reported consumption expenditures (i.e., consumption-based nonlabor income). Following CDDV, individual nonlabor incomes associated with remarriage are treated as unknowns in our linear programming method, which are subject to the condition that they must add up to the total nonlabor income in the observed marriage. Formally, these individual nonlabor incomes are treated similarly as the individual quantities $q^{m}_{m,\sigma(m)}$ and $q^{\sigma(m)}_{m,\sigma(m)}$, and the personalized prices $P^{m}_{m,w}$ and $P^{w}_{m,w}$, which are also unknown and subject to an adding up condition.

Marriage markets. Our Belgian sample consists of males and females aged between 24 and 65 years. Arguably, married males and females do not consider all individuals of the other gender as potential remarriage options. Therefore, in our empirical analysis we construct individual-specific marriage markets on the basis of age (differences). Specifically, each male's individual marriage market contains all females that are at most 12 years younger and at most 6 years older. Similarly, each female's individual marriage market consists of all males that are at most 6 years younger and at most 12 years older. The age brackets that we use for these individual-specific marriage markets are defined on the basis of the age differences between the spouses of observed couples in our Belgian dataset; 95% of the observed marriages respect these age bounds. We refer to Online Appendix A for a more detailed presentation of these individual-specific marriage markets.

3.3 Estimation Results

Proposition 1 states the conditions that a dataset must satisfy in order to be rationalizable by a stable matching. In a first step of our empirical analysis, we examine whether and to what extent the Belgian household data satisfy these sharp rationalizability restrictions. By solving the maximization problem (7.1), we can compute the minimal divorce costs that are required for the dataset to satisfy the individual rationality and no blocking pairs conditions, As

$(1 - s^{IR}_{m,\emptyset}) \times 100$, $(1 - s^{IR}_{\emptyset,w}) \times 100$ and $(1 - s^{NBP}_{m,w}) \times 100$. Overall, we find that small divorce costs are needed to meet the individual rationality constraints, while the (rationalizing) divorce costs for the no blocking pairs constraints are somewhat higher, especially when using Method B. A more detailed discussion of the divorce costs can be found in Online Appendix B.

By using the computed stability indices, we can address identification of the conditional sharing rule. As explained in Section 2, this conditional sharing rule defines the within household allocation of private consumption (conditional on the given level of public consumption). Table 2 reports the bounds on the conditional sharing rule that we obtain when using Method A. We refer to Online Appendix C for more descriptive statistics. For a given spouse, the "Diff" columns in Table 2 describes the difference between the lower and upper bounds in percentage points (as a fraction of total of private expenditures). Our results clearly show that our revealed preference methodology has significant identifying power: the average difference between the lower and upper bounds is very low. In addition, we find that men have on average a larger consumption share than women: the average male share is between 55.9% and 57.7% while the average female share is between 42.3% and 44.1%.

Finally, the average bounds on the conditional sharing rule are even narrower for Method B. This is documented in Table 3, which has a similar interpretation to Table 2. We observe the same general patterns as for Method A. The average difference between male and female consumption shares is somewhat smaller, reflecting Method B's treatment of all nonlabor time as privately consumed leisure time, so particularly increasing the assignable private consumption of females. Thus, erroneously specifying domestic work as leisure seems to create an upward bias on estimated female welfare and a downward bias on male welfare.

4. INDIVIDUAL WELFARE ANALYSIS

We use our identification results for the conditional sharing rule to conduct a welfare analysis at the level of individuals within households. More specifically, our aim is to assess whether and to what extent accounting for unequal

Table 2. Method A - Conditional Sharing Rule Identification.

	Men			Women		
	Lower	Upper	Diff	Lower	Upper	Diff
Mean	0.559	0.577	0.018	0.423	0.441	0.018
Standard Deviation	0.098	0.099	0.018	0.010	0.098	0.018
First Quartile	0.496	0.513	0.005	0.367	0.381	0.005
Median	0.559	0.574	0.014	0.4263	0.441	0.014
Third Quartile	0.617	0.633	0.025	0.485	0.504	0.025

Table 3. Method B - Conditional Sharing Rule Identification.

	Men			Women		
	Lower	Upper	Diff	Lower	Upper	Diff
Mean	0.520	0.533	0.013	0.467	0.480	0.013
Standard Deviation	0.089	0.088	0.014	0.088	0.089	0.014
First Quartile	0.464	0.480	0.003	0.417	0.426	0.003
Median	0.525	0.542	0.011	0.458	0.475	0.011
Third Quartile	0.574	0.583	0.018	0.520	0.536	0.018

intrahousehold sharing, time use and scale economies (through public consumption) impacts the conclusions of poverty and inequality analyses.

4.1 Economies of Scale and Intrahousehold Sharing

To assess the importance of public consumption sharing, we begin by estimating the economies of scale that arise within households. This allows the total value of household consumption to exceed the household expenditures, as the same good may be consumed simultaneously by both spouses. Browning et al. (2013) introduced an economies of scale measure that compares the expenditures needed as singles to obtain the same consumption bundles as when married. More specifically, for each matched pair, this measure of economies of scale is:

$$R_{m,\sigma(m)} = \frac{2 \times P_{m,\sigma(m)} Q_{m,\sigma(m)} + p_{m,\sigma(m)} q_{m,\sigma(m)}}{y_{m,\sigma(m)}}$$

The denominator in this expression equals the expenditures of a couple for the bundle $(q^m_{m,\sigma(m)}, q^{\sigma(m)}_{m,\sigma(m)}, Q_{m,\sigma(m)})$ that is consumed in the marriage, and the numerator gives the expenditures that the two spouses would incur to attain the same individual consumption levels as singles (with public expenditures counted twice). By construction, the value of $R_{m,\sigma(m)}$ is situated between one and two. When all consumption is private, there are no gains to marriage and $R_{m,\sigma(m)} = 1$. By contrast, when all consumption is public, then the married individuals will need twice as much resources as singles to achieve the same level of consumption as in marriage, which yields $R_{m,\sigma(m)} = 2$. Generally, higher $R_{m,\sigma(m)}$-values reveal greater scale economies.

Table 4 lists the $R_{m,\sigma(m)}$-estimates for our Belgian MEqIn sample. We consider three scenarios: (1) consumption includes no time use (i.e., only material consumption), (2) consumption includes time use based on Method A, (3) consumption includes time use based on Method B. Note that these scenarios change both the numerator (i.e., different consumption bundles) and the denominator (i.e., different budgets). As a result, including time use in the analysis does not necessarily need to result in higher or lower estimates of scale economies. By contrast, using Method B instead of Method A yields smaller economies of scale

Table 4. Economies of Scale Measure.

Material Consumption Only	Mean	Std. Dev.
All couples	1.3469	0.0582
Childless couples	1.3111	0.0674
Couples with 1 child	1.3481	0.0464
Couples with more than 1 child	1.3735	0.0399
Method A: Material Consumption + Time Use		
All couples	1.3257	0.1128
Childless couples	1.2230	0.0661
Couples with 1 child	1.3536	0.0958
Couples with more than 1 child	1.3874	0.0947
Method B: Material Consumption + Time Use		
All couples	1.1623	0.0536
Childless couples	1.1247	0.0431
Couples with 1 child	1.1655	0.0405
Couples with more than 1 child	1.1893	0.0510

by construction; Method B wrongly classifies publicly consumed domestic work as privately consumed leisure, thus generating a downward estimation bias.

When only material consumption is included, married individuals need on average approximately 35% more expenditures as singles to achieve the same bundle of goods.[12] Also, we observe that children imply more public expenditures and, through this channel, more gains from being married. Next, in Method A time spent on household tasks and child care are treated as public goods, which leads to additional scale economies. Therefore, we find that individuals as single would need more expenditures to attain the same consumption level as in their current marriage, i.e., about 32% more on average. Again, this increases with the number of children. Finally, Method B does not consider time use as public consumption. As an implication, individuals as single now only need 16% extra expenditures to buy the bundle $\left(q^{m}_{m,\sigma(m)}, q^{\sigma(m)}_{m,\sigma(m)}, Q_{m,\sigma(m)}\right)$. In our opinion, these results clearly highlight how alternative treatments of time use information may significantly impact the empirical analysis of the welfare of individuals (in particular singles). Particularly, wrongly specifying domestic work as leisure (as in Method B) can lead to severe underestimation of the scale economies experienced by multi-person households.

Building further on these $R_{m,\sigma(m)}$-results, we can compute the income that an individual would need as single to buy the same bundle as consumed in the current marriage. To do so, we make use of the concept RICEB (i.e., relative individual cost of equivalent bundle) that was introduced by Cherchye et al. (2020). Basically, individual RICEBs account simultaneously for both the scale economies and the intrahousehold allocation of resources to assess the welfare of individuals in households. They are defined as follows for male m and female $\sigma(m)$ in the couple $(m,\sigma(m))$:

$$R^{m}_{m,\sigma(m)} = \frac{P_{m,\emptyset}Q_{m,\sigma(m)} + p_{m,\emptyset}q^{m}_{m,\sigma(m)}}{y_{m,\sigma(m)}} \text{ and}$$

$$R^{\sigma(m)}_{m,\sigma(m)} = \frac{P_{\emptyset,\sigma(m)}Q_{m,\sigma(m)} + p_{\emptyset,\sigma(m)}q^{\sigma(m)}_{m,\sigma(m)}}{y_{m,\sigma(m)}}.$$

The RICEBs $R^{m}_{m,\sigma(m)}$ and $R^{\sigma(m)}_{m,\sigma(m)}$ give the incomes that the individuals would need as singles (expressed as fraction of the current household income) to attain the same consumption level as in their given marriage. In computing these required income levels, the RICEBs include both the intrahousehold sharing of private consumption (as identified through the conditional sharing rule) and the economies of scale that follow from public consumption.

Table 5 summarizes the estimates. We refer to Online Appendix C for more descriptive statistics. To interpret these results, we recall that our revealed method allows us to identify bounds on the conditional sharing rule. However, as the estimated lower and upper bounds are very close to each other (see Table 2), we restrict ourselves to reporting only the averages of these bounds. Next, we consider the same three scenarios as before regarding the treatment of time-use information (i.e. only material consumption, and including time-use through Method A or Method B). For each of these three scenarios, we report results "with economies of scale" and "without economies of scale". The former indicates that we consider public consumption as simultaneously consumed by both members (as in the RICEBs defined above), while the latter means that we treat all public consumption as private consumption that is split equally between the spouses (i.e., scale economies are assumed away).

Table 5. Relative Individual Cost (RICEB).

	Men		Women	
	Mean	Std. Dev.	Mean	Std. Dev.
Only Material Consumption				
With economies of scale	0.7473	0.0869	0.5996	0.0772
Without economies of scale	0.5737	0.0769	0.4262	0.0769
Material Consumption + Time Use				
Method A: With economies of scale	0.7073	0.0868	0.6184	0.0843
Method B: With economies of scale	0.5866	0.0804	0.5406	0.0762
Method A: Without economies of scale	0.5206	0.0795	0.4794	0.0795
Method B: Without economies of scale	0.5230	0.0761	0.4770	0.0761

Table 5 shows that male RICEBs are substantially above female RICEBs considering only material consumption. With economies of scale, the average RICEB is 0.7473 for men against 0.5996 for women. When excluding economies of scale, the RICEB values are – not surprisingly – substantially lower, but the average difference between males and females remains closely similar (i.e., 0.5737 vs. 0.4262). However, the picture changes quite drastically when including time-use information. While male RICEBs are still systematically above female RICEBs, the gap decreases substantially. Moreover, we find that Methods A and B yield very different results. When using Method B, men appear only slightly better off than women, because women's time invested in domestic work and child care is treated as (privately consumed) leisure. By contrast, when using Method A (treating domestic work and child care as public consumption), the gap between males and females widens again. Overall, when only considering material consumption, women are worse off than men. When including time use, this inequality is reduced, but this reduction largely depends on how leisure is defined. Our results once more demonstrate the importance of adequately modeling domestic work to avoid a bias in the (male vs. female) welfare analysis.

Generally, our estimates of the conditional sharing rule and male and female RICEBs show that intrahousehold resource sharing is often very unequal. In most cases, the share of women is below that of their husbands. Moreover, economies of scale do make individuals living together better off than singles. These analyses call into question the current practice of measuring consumption levels merely in terms of household expenditures while ignoring time use and resource sharing within households.

4.2 Poverty

The poverty rate is commonly calculated as the fraction of households/individuals that is situated under the poverty line. In policy practice, one of the most widely used poverty lines is the US$1.90 per day measure of the World Bank (Jolliffe et al., 2014); individuals are then considered poor when the household per-capita expenditures are below this line. However, this measure assumes that resources are shared equally within households. Also, it abstains from any notion of consumption sharing. For example, individuals in a six-person household that spends US$18 are assumed to be equally well-off as a single individual spending US$3. One way of tackling this issue is to make use of equivalence scales, which make it possible to compare the required expenditures of households with different sizes to achieve the same utility level. For instance, it allows for concluding that a household of two adults and one child will need less than three times the expenditures of a single household to reach the same utility level. A prominent example are the OECD equivalence scales, which are meant to correct for differences in scale economies across household types. However, measuring poverty by using equivalent scales still ignores the possibility of unequal resource sharing within households and the unequal time use of the household members.

The collective model has been used quite extensively to assess individual poverty while accounting for unequal intrahousehold sharing. For example, Cherchye et al. (2015) used estimated sharing rule bounds to investigate the poverty of individual household members. They find that poverty is substantially more prevalent at the individual level than at the household level. Moreover, individual poverty is particularly present among women. Cherchye et al. (2020) extended this analysis by considering economies of scale in addition to unequal sharing in the analysis of individual poverty. By using the RICEB concept introduced in the previous section, these authors find once more that women are worse off than men because of unequal intrahousehold sharing. In addition, they find that the fraction of poor households decreases when intrahousehold scale economies are accounted for.

Dunbar et al. (2013) implemented the collective household model to estimate resource shares of both adult household members and children. Their method makes use of Engel curves of assignable private goods to measure individual poverty in Malawi. Strikingly, child poverty appears to be heavily underestimated when assuming equal sharing: over 90% of children are identified as poor in their analysis. Calvi et al. (2021) extended the method of Dunbar et al. (2013) to allow for different family structures that are more prevalent in developing countries, such as extended families that include multiple children or additional adults. Their results reveal that being part of a larger family leads to a tradeoff between, on the one hand, gains from public consumption (i.e., scale economies) and, on the other hand, smaller individual income shares on average. Calvi et al. (2021) then conducted a poverty analysis that takes into account both unequal resource allocations and consumption sharing. They conclude that this identifies additional poor children in Mexico, and additional poor women and children in Bangladesh.

Whether or not time-use information is included can also have important implications for welfare indices measuring poverty and inequality. Intuitively, two individuals might enjoy the same level of material consumption while having completely different levels of leisure. Are they then truly equally well off? When including time use, defining it as private or public consumption also raises questions. For example, does it make a significant difference if domestic work and child care is treated as public consumption or as privately consumed leisure? Using a general equilibrium model, Boerma and Karabarbounis (2021) found that considering home production increases inequality in US households. By contrast, Attanasio et al. (2015) showed that including time use had a mitigating effect on measured consumption inequality in the US between 1980 and 2010.

More specifically, these authors described how material consumption has grown more rapidly for highly educated households relative to lowly educated families, which has led to more inequality. However, less educated people have been spending more time on leisure than their highly educated counterparts, which muted the initial increase in inequality.[13]

Motivated by these existing studies, in Tables 6 and 7 we report estimated poverty rates (for couples and individuals) for different household types in our selected sample of Belgian households. We again consider three scenarios for the

Table 6. Poverty Rate: Couple Level.

Only Material Consumption	All Couples	Childless Couples	Couples With 1 Child	Couples With More Than 1 Child
Only private consumption, no public cons.	4.35	3.85	7.32	2.94
Private + Public consumption, no economies of scale	9.99	11.54	12.20	7.35
Private + Public consumption, economies of scale	10.56	13.46	12.20	7.35
Material Consumption + Time Use				
Method A: No economies of scale	1.86	0.00	4.88	1.47
Method A: Economies of scale	3.73	3.85	4.88	2.94
Method B: No economies of scale	1.86	0.00	4.88	1.47
Method B: Economies of scale	1.86	0.00	4.88	1.47

treatment of time use, and two scenarios regarding the presence of scale economies.

Table 6 reports computed poverty rates at the household/couple level. We use a standard measure in developed countries to calculate the household poverty line: 60% of the median consumption level in the relevant sample.[14] All households with a consumption level below this poverty line are denoted as poor. It is important to recall that we only include couples in which both spouses worked at least 10 hours per week in our empirical analysis. This results in a different (i.e., higher) poverty line than for other samples that also include unemployed or retired individuals.

When only considering material consumption, the inclusion of public consumption raises the poverty rate in our sample. Intuitively, when public consumption is shared, this gives rise to economies of scale, which makes that particularly childless couples (with little public consumption) are identified as poor. In contrast, including time use (through Methods A or B) generally implies lower poverty rates. For Method B, including scale economies does not alter the result by construction (as all nonlabor time is treated as privately consumed leisure). However, for method A, which considers time spent on household work and child care as public consumption, we again find that more couples are identified as poor, in particular childless couples.

Table 7 documents the prevalence of poverty at the individual level. Individual poverty lines are calculated by halving the couple's poverty lines. Generally, we find that both single and married women are considerably worse off than their male counterparts. In particular, married women seem to have much lower private material consumption than their husbands, with almost 32% of them being identified poor when ignoring time use. This is somewhat mitigated when including public consumption, which reduces the estimated poverty rate of married women to 21.12%; but nonetheless there are still significantly more poor

Table 7. Poverty Rate: Individual Level.

Only Material Consumption	All Individuals	All Males	All Females	All Married Individuals	All Married Males	All Married Females	All Single Individuals	All Single Males	All Single Females
Only private consumption, no public cons.	14.06	5.81	17.73	18.94	6.21	31.68	5.46	3.08	6.78
Total consumption, no economies of scale	11.29	6.69	13.66	13.66	6.21	21.12	7.10	7.69	6.78
Total consumption, economies of scale	15.25	15.70	18.90	10.87	7.45	14.29	22.95	21.54	23.73
Material Consumption + Time Use									
Method A: No economies of scale	2.77	2.03	3.20	3.11	1.86	4.35	2.19	3.08	1.69
Method A: Economies of scale	9.99	11.05	12.79	5.56	3.73	7.45	17.49	15.38	18.64
Method B: No economies of scale	3.37	2.62	3.49	4.04	3.11	4.97	2.19	3.08	1.69
Method B: Economies of scale	4.75	4.94	4.94	4.35	4.35	4.35	5.46	6.15	5.08

women than men. Not surprisingly, by allowing individuals in couples to benefit from sharing (material) public consumption, these individuals are considerably less likely to be seen as poor, while the opposite applies to singles.

The patterns again change when including time-use information. Married women are still worse off than married men using both Methods A and B. However, the difference is not as large as when only material consumption is taken into account. For Method A, the fraction of poor married women rises considerably when allowing for economies of scale. As women spend on average more time on child care and domestic work, this results in higher consumption. However, this public time use is shared by the two spouses, and thus benefits both the male and the female. This vitiates women's advantage, resulting in a higher poverty rate for married women. Because couples can share their consumption, singles are again considerably poorer using either method when accounting for economies of scale. As public consumption is larger by construction in Method A, this method implies higher poverty rates among singles than Method B, so again illustrating that a bias is generated when erroneously classifying domestic work as leisure.

4.3 Inequality

Chiappori and Meghir (2015) highlighted the importance of taking into account the within-household allocation of resources when measuring inequality. For example, Lise and Seitz (2011) analyzed the evolution of inequality in the United Kingdom between 1968 and 2001 by using structural estimates of the sharing rule. One of their main findings is that initial consumption inequality was underestimated by 50% when not considering intrahousehold resource sharing. Strikingly, from 1980 onwards consumption inequality within households has declined. However, this did not result in lower total inequality due to a strong increase of between household inequality. In addition, Lise and Seitz found that including time use (i.e., leisure) in their structural estimates did not change their results dramatically. However, it did lower the between-household inequality as households with unemployed members were compensated for their lower consumption through additional leisure time.

We conclude our empirical analysis by describing inequality in Belgium at the level of households and individuals. Inequality is measured by using the Gini coefficient. Table 8 shows inequality rates at the couple level, i.e., without accounting for intrahousehold inequality. Overall, the distribution of consumption in Belgium is relatively equal, with a Gini coefficient of 0.1749 when only considering private consumption and a slightly higher Gini coefficient when also including public goods. Similar to the results in Lise and Seitz (2011), including time use somewhat lowers our inequality estimates, as households with less material consumption are compensated through additional leisure.

Finally, Table 9 reports measures of inequality among individuals. Overall, the levels of inequality are higher than in Table 8, especially when only including material consumption and ignoring time-use information. When we include time use, albeit that the level of inequality is reduced, it is still higher than when

Table 8. Gini Coefficient: Couple Level.

Only Material Consumption	All Couples	Childless Couples	Couples With 1 Child	Couples With More Than 1 Child
Only private consumption, no public cons.	0.1749	0.1651	0.1729	0.1798
Both, no economies of scale	0.1802	0.1621	0.1607	0.1941
Both, economies of scale	0.1876	0.1669	0.1580	0.2023
Material Consumption + Time Use				
Method A: No economies of scale	0.1325	0.1378	0.1103	0.1352
Method A: Economies of scale	0.1435	0.1422	0.1249	0.1373
Method B: No economies of scale	0.1325	0.1378	0.1103	0.1352
Method B: Economies of scale	0.1365	0.1340	0.1133	0.1440

measured at the level of couples. Finally, using Method A or B does not seem to affect inequality rates significantly, nor does (not) accounting for economies of scale.

5. CONCLUSION

We have used the methodology of Cherchye et al. (2017) to recover within-household patterns of consumption sharing under the identifying assumption of marital stability. The method is intrinsically nonparametric and only requires a single observation per household while allowing for full heterogeneity across households (in terms of individual utilities and intrahousehold decision processes). Attractively, our application to the Belgian MEqIn data obtained informative empirical results on individual welfare (poverty and inequality) under these minimal assumptions.

Our particular focus has been on the impact of time use information on the welfare conclusions that are obtained. Specifically, we compared welfare results under three specifications of individual consumption, which includes respectively (1) only material consumption (ignoring time use information), (2) material consumption and both (private) leisure time and (public) domestic work (called Method A), and (3) material consumption and all nonlabor time treated as (private) leisure (thus ignoring domestic production; called Method B). In addition, we evaluated how economies of scale (resulting from public consumption) affect the individual welfare analysis of singles versus individuals in multi-person households.

Our empirical results indicate that intrahousehold inequality, inter-individual differences in time use and inter-household differences in scale economies may significantly affect individual welfare analyses. First, including time-use

Table 9. Gini Coefficient: Individual Level.

Only Material Consumption	All Individuals	All Males	All Females	All Married Individuals	All Married Males	All Married Females	All Single Individuals	All Single Males	All Single Females
Only private consumption, no public cons.	0.2342	0.2021	0.2364	0.2569	0.2084	0.2454	0.1919	0.1807	0.1956
Total consumption, no economies of scale	0.2165	0.2012	0.2183	0.2161	0.2004	0.1997	0.2121	0.2017	0.2169
Total consumption, economies of scale	0.2158	0.2124	0.2072	0.2072	0.2008	0.1949	0.2121	0.2017	0.2169
Material Consumption + Time Use									
Method A: No economies of scale	0.1568	0.1547	0.1553	0.1562	0.1558	0.1478	0.1561	0.1378	0.1641
Method A: Economies of scale	0.1696	0.1710	0.1624	0.1581	0.1543	0.1515	0.1561	0.1378	0.1641
Method B: No economies of scale	0.1586	0.1557	0.1596	0.1591	0.1621	0.1504	0.1561	0.1378	0.1641
Method B: Economies of scale	0.1579	0.1592	0.1551	0.1570	0.1615	0.1479	0.1561	0.1378	0.1641

information reduces measured poverty and inequality rates, indicating that lower consumption may be compensated through more leisure. Next, as women typically have lower intrahousehold resource shares, welfare analyses that focus on aggregate household consumption typically underestimate female welfare. In this respect, we have also shown that wrongly classifying domestic work as leisure may severely bias the empirical (female vs. male) welfare analysis. Finally, ignoring scale economies in multi-person households means that poverty among singles is underestimated. From a policy perspective, our findings strongly motivate accounting for these different aspects when measuring poverty and inequality, and when evaluating policy decisions aimed at creating a more equal society.

ACKNOWLEDGMENTS

We thank the Editor and two anonymous referees for their insightful comments, which substantially improved our chapter. We are further grateful to the Fund for Scientific Research - Flanders (FWO) and the Research Fund KU Leuven for financial support.

NOTES

1. Throughout, "marriage" stands for legal marriage as well as cohabitation.

2. For the revealed preference approach to analyzing collective consumption behavior and identifying intrahousehold sharing rules, see also Cherchye et al. (2007, 2011, 2015, 2020). Alternative parametric approaches for sharing rule identification have been proposed by Lewbel and Pendakur (2008), Bargain and Donni (2012), Browning et al. (2013) and, more recently, Lechene et al. (2022).

3. In what follows, the household's aggregate resources are equal to the household's full income (after Becker, 1965). This full income contains both the household's budget constraint and the time constraints faced by the individual household members in one constraint. As such, it incorporates the trade-off between time and money. Consequently, the household's sharing rule determines the shares of the individual household members of the household's full income and, therefore, the sharing rule governs both the allocation of money and the allocation of time (and, implicitly, the trade-off between the two). See Chiappori (1988) and Cherchye et al. (2011) for more insights on the theoretical foundation of the sharing rule.

4. Admittedly for a single the distinction between private and public is redundant. For the ease of notation we ignore this.

5. More precisely, individual utility functions are (only) assumed to be nonnegative, increasing, continuous and concave.

6. In this respect, we may actually also impute wages, for example, based on regressions that take account of the so-called marriage premium. See Korenman and Neumark (1991) for a seminal contribution.

7. The MEqIn survey was collected by a team of researchers from the Université Catholique de Louvain, the KU Leuven, the Université libre de Bruxelles and the University of Antwerp. The collection of the MEqIn data was enabled by the financial support of the Belgian Science Policy Office (BELSPO) through grant BR/121/A5/MEQIN (BRAIN MEqIn). See Capéau et al. (2020) for an extensive discussion of the MEqIn survey.

8. This allows us to focus on individuals who can be argued to have a structural attachment to the labor market and whose wage rate we can easily observe.

9. We could relax this assumption by implementing the method introduced in Cherchye et al. (2020). For simplicity of our exposition, we abstract from this extension in the current analysis.

10. Due to privacy reasons, we (only) obtained clusters of 3 years for the age variable. To calculate the average age of a couple, the middle number in each age cluster is used. For example, individuals in the age cluster between 24 and 26 years are listed as 25 years old.

11. Note that this implicitly assumes that the time needed for sleeping and personal care is fixed and the same for each individual. As such, this ignores the fact that, for example, lower-wage individuals sleep more and spend more time on personal care (see Hamermesh, 2019).

12. This figure turns out to be lower than the economies of scale assumed in the (modified) OECD-scale. The latter implies that a married couple needs 50% more expenditures than a single to obtain the same welfare level.

13. Notably, in Attanasio et al. (2015) leisure does not include domestic work such as child care or cleaning.

14. Our 60%-cutoff applied to the individual level implies that if a household's resources are allocated *equally* within the household, then *all* household members fall below the poverty line if the household falls below the poverty line according to the standard definition.

REFERENCES

Attanasio, O., Hurst, E., & Pistaferri, L. (2015). The evolution of income, consumption, and leisure inequality in the United States, 1980–2010. In *Improving the measurement of consumer expenditures* (pp. 100–140). University of Chicago Press.

Bargain, O., & Donni, O. (2012). Expenditure on children: A Rothbarth-type method consistent with scale economies and parents' bargaining. *European Economic Review*, *56*, 792–813.

Becker, G. (1965). A theory of the allocation of time. *The Economic Journal*, *75*, 493–517.

Boerma, J., & Karabarbounis, L. (2021). Inferring inequality with home production. *Econometrica*, *89*, 2517–2556.

Browning, M., & Chiappori, P. A. (1998). Efficient intra-household allocations: A general characterization and empirical tests. *Econometrica*, *66*, 1241–1278.

Browning, M., Chiappori, P., & Lewbel, A. (2013). Estimating consumption economies of scale, adult equivalence scales, and household bargaining power. *The Review of Economic Studies*, *80*, 1267–1303.

Browning, M., Chiappori, P.-A., & Weiss, Y. (2014). *Economics of the family*. Cambridge Surveys of Economic Literature. Cambridge University Press.

Calvi, R., Penglase, J., Tommasi, D., & Wolf, A. (2021). *The more the poorer? Resource sharing and scale economies in large families*. CEPR Discussion Paper No. DP15924.

Capéau, B., Cherchye, L., Decancq, K., Decoster, A., De Rock, B., Maniquet, F., Nys, A., Périlleux, G., Ramaekers, E., Rongé, Z., Schokkaert, E., & Vermeulen, F. (2020). *Well-being in Belgium beyond happiness and income*. Springer International Publishing.

Cherchye, L., De Rock, B., Surana, K., & Vermeulen, F. (2020). Marital matching, economies of scale, and intrahousehold allocations. *The Review of Economics and Statistics*, *102*, 823–837.

Cherchye, L., De Rock, B., & Vermeulen, F. (2007). The collective model of household consumption: A nonparametric characterization. *Econometrica*, *75*, 553–574.

Cherchye, L., De Rock, B., & Vermeulen, F. (2011). The revealed preference approach to collective consumption behaviour: Testing and sharing rule Recovery. *The Review of Economic Studies*, *78*, 176–198.

Cherchye, L., Demuynck, T., De Rock, B., & Vermeulen, F. (2017). Household consumption when the marriage is stable. *The American Economic Review*, *107*, 1507–1534.

Cherchye, L., Lewbel, A., De Rock, B., & Vermeulen, F. (2015). Sharing rule identification for general collective consumption models. *Econometrica*, *83*, 2001–2041.

Chiappori, P.-A. (1988). Rational household labor supply. *Econometrica*, *56*, 63–90.

Chiappori, P.-A. (1992). Collective labor supply and welfare. *Journal of Political Economy*, *100*, 437–467.

Chiappori, P.-A., & Meghir, C. (2015). Chapter 16 – Intrahousehold inequality. In A. B. Atkinson & F. Bourguignon (Eds.), *Handbook of income distribution* (Vol. 2, pp. 1369–1418). Elsevier.

Cosaert, S., & Hennebel, V. (2022). Parental childcare with process benefits. *Economica*. https://doi.org/10.1111/ecca.12448

Cosaert, S., Theloudis, A., & Verheyden, B. (2023). Togetherness in the household. *American Economic Journal: Microeconomics*, *15*, 529–579.

Dunbar, G. R., Lewbel, A., & Pendakur, K. (2013). Children's resources in collective households: Identification, estimation, and an application to child poverty in Malawi. *The American Economic Review*, *103*, 438–471.

Hamermesh, D. (2015). What's to know about time use? *Journal of Economic Surveys*, *30*, 198–203.

Hamermesh, D. (2019). *Spending time. The most valuable resource*. Oxford University Press.

Jolliffe, D., Lanjouw, P., Chen, S., Kraay, A., Meyer, C., Negre, M., Prydz, E., Vakis, R., & Wethli, K. (2014). *A measured approach to ending poverty and boosting shared prosperity: Concepts, data, and the twin goals*. Policy Research Report.

Keeley, B. (2015). *Income inequality*. OECD Publishing.

Korenman, S., & Neumark, D. (1991). Does marriage really make men more productive? *Journal of Human Resources*, *26*, 282–307.

Lechene, V., Pendakur, K., & Wolf, A. (2022). OLS estimation of the intrahousehold distribution of expenditure. *Journal of Political Economy*, *130*, 681–731.

Lewbel, A., & Pendakur, K. (2008). Estimation of collective household models with Engel curves. *Journal of Econometrics*, *147*, 350–358.

Lise, J., & Seitz, S. (2011). Consumption inequality and intra-household allocations. *The Review of Economic Studies*, *78*, 328–355.

MARRIAGE VERSUS COHABITATION: HOW SPECIALIZATION AND TIME USE DIFFER BY RELATIONSHIP TYPE

Leslie S. Stratton

ABSTRACT

Relationships have changed dramatically in the last 50 years. Fewer couples are marrying, more are cohabiting. Reasons for this shift include more attractive labor market opportunities for women and changing social norms, but the shift may have consequences of its own. A number of models predict that those cohabiting will specialize less than those marrying. Panel data on time use – particularly housework time – as well as on the degree of specialization in more narrowly defined household tasks from the 2001–2019 waves of the Household, Income and Labour Dynamics in Australia survey are used to test this prediction.

The time use data for men provides only limited supporting evidence for specialization. The results for women are much stronger. Women who marry without first cohabiting increase their reported housework time more than those who enter cohabitations (by 3.7 hours versus 1.2 hours). The latter generally make up a third of the difference if they do marry. Expanding the analysis to other uses of time yields some further evidence of specialization.

Survey responses on the degree of specialization are more informative. The raw data show substantial intrahousehold specialization and further analysis reveals that on average married couples specialize more than cohabiting couples. Adding couple-specific fixed effects reveals that specialization increases when cohabiting couples marry. Interestingly, there does not appear to be a substantial tradeoff between tasks; partners who report specializing more on one task are more likely to report specializing on other tasks as well.

Time Use in Economics
Research in Labor Economics, Volume 51, 187–218

ISSN: 0147-9121/doi:10.1108/S0147-912120230000051008

Given the important roles couples have in family formation and the labor market, it is important to understand this intrahousehold behavior.

Keywords: Specialization; time use; marriage; cohabitation; housework; social norms

1. INTRODUCTION

Marriage as an institution is in decline around the developed world. More and more couples are choosing to cohabit and not all such couples marry. This shift is likely driven in part by the expanded and more generously compensated employment opportunities now available to women and in part by changing norms that have made cohabitation more socially acceptable, but the shift may in turn have consequences of its own. A key benefit accruing to couple households is the ability to specialize and divide labor, but a number of models predict that there will be more specialization in married as compared to cohabiting households. Panel data from the 2001–2019 waves of the Household, Income and Labour Dynamics in Australia survey (HILDA) are used to examine how individuals' reported time use – particularly housework time but also time on outdoor tasks, errands, and employment – changes as they enter cohabitations and marriages. The degree of self-reported specialization in more narrowly defined household tasks is also examined. Here not only are cohabiting couples compared with married couples, but couples transitioning from cohabitations to marriages are examined. The results support the theoretical predictions. The consequences could be far reaching as time use decisions have the potential to impact not just individuals, but also families and markets.

The chapter is organized as follows. Section 2 documents differences between cohabiting and married couples. Section 3 provides a review of the literature vis-à-vis time use and relationship status. Theories explaining how behavior may differ between cohabiting and married couples are discussed in Section 4. The data are introduced in Section 5. Results regarding time use are presented in Section 6; those regarding task specialization in Section 7. Section 8 concludes.

2. BACKGROUND: MARRIED VERSUS COHABITING COUPLE HOUSEHOLDS

Household composition has changed dramatically over the last 50 years. The fraction of persons in the United States (US) age 18 or older who were married and living with their spouse fell from 70.0% in 1968 to 51.5% in 2019, while the fraction cohabiting rose from 0.4% to 7.4%, indicating that 14% of all couples were cohabiting in 2019 (Table AD-3 from https://www.census.gov/data/tables/time-series/demo/families/adults.html). A Pew research paper (Horowitz et al., 2019) reports that more adults have now "ever cohabited" than have "ever married" in the US. Cohabitation is even more common in Australia where the fraction of couples who were cohabiting was 18% in 2016.

If cohabitations were equivalent to marriages and individuals behaved the same in both types of relationships, then these shifts would have little import. However, there is evidence, both qualitative and quantitative, that these relationships are distinct. Stevenson and Wolfers (2007) report that the majority of cohabiters in the US expect to marry (based on the 2002 National Survey of Family Growth), with 34% already engaged and another 24% almost certain they will. However, these figures suggest that a substantial 42% of cohabiters are uncertain. Data from a 2019 Pew Research survey confirms that most people entering a relationship (marriage or cohabitation) cite love or companionship as a reason (Horowitz et al., 2019). However, married and cohabiting couples surveyed cite other more divergent explanations for their choice. Three times as many cohabiters as married persons mentioned "financial reasons" and/or "convenience" for entering the relationship. Almost 40% of cohabiters say they are not sure their current partner is right for them. Among married persons, 63% said they wanted to make a formal commitment, but 23% of cohabiting persons said they wanted to test the relationship. Certainly, marriages are more expensive to enter and exit as compared to cohabitations, suggesting that the level of commitment in marriages is greater. Overall, these surveys provide qualitative evidence that marriage and cohabitation are not the same.

Quantitative evidence confirms that cohabiting relationships are on average of shorter duration than marriages. In the US, Bumpass and Sweet (1989) found that 40% of cohabitations ended before marriage using the 1988–1989 National Survey of Families and Households (NSFH). Stevenson and Wolfers (2007) report that while 25% of couples cohabiting in 1997 were married in 2002, 50% were no longer together. Lillard et al. (1995) report that marriages following cohabitations are less stable than other marriages, suggesting the need to differentiate between marriages that are and are not preceded by a cohabitation. More recent studies indicate there has been some convergence. Cohabitations are becoming longer and less likely to transition into marriages (Lamidi et al., 2019), and the association between pre-marital cohabitation and shorter duration marriages may be weakening (Reinhold, 2010). There is also a strong socioeconomic gradient in relationship formation, with the less educated significantly more likely to enter cohabitations rather than marriages (Lundberg et al., 2016).

Cohabiting relationships in Australia appear somewhat longer lasting and more likely to transition into marriage as compared to those in the US. Of those in the HILDA survey who were cohabiting in January 2000, about 56% were married five years later and 27% were no longer together.[1] 50 percent of those marrying had been cohabiting for 5 years or less, those splitting up almost 9 years. Of those married in January 2000, 18% of those who had not previously cohabited were separated 5 years later as compared to 29% of those who had previously cohabited, suggesting again that marriages beginning with a cohabitation may be less likely to persist. Whether marriage causes the relationship to be longer lasting or those selecting into marriage are more likely to establish longer lasting relationships is unclear. However, this evidence suggests that married and cohabiting persons may well behave differently in Australia as well as the US. The goal here is to compare how married versus cohabiting couples allocate their time and manage household tasks.

Multiperson households form when each party expects the future benefits of the partnership to exceed the future costs and come to an end either when one party dies or the costs exceed the benefits. Clearly mutual affection and the joy experienced by spending more time together are important benefits. The evolutionary theory of the family highlights the importance of couple formation for reproduction and care of children. But there are also several economic rationales for forming a relationship. Couple households benefit from economies of scale, both monetary and time based. A residence for two typically costs less than two single person residences; it takes less time to prepare a meal for two than to prepare two separate single servings. These benefits likely accrue to both married and cohabiting partners. Partners can also gain from specialization and trade. Those in longer lasting relationships may find it more beneficial and/or easier to invest in skills both at work and in the home. A partner can, for example, provide support while one is making such investments. In addition, some skills, like cooking and home repair, may be perceived as more valuable when caring for a larger household.

It has been hypothesized that changes in couple formation, the declining marriage and rising cohabitation rates, have been driven in part by changes in the associated net benefits. Declining fertility and technological advances in home production (see Greenwood & Guner, 2009) have reduced the time necessary to produce at home. The rise of the service sector, increasing demand for cognitive skills as compared with physical strength (Beaudry & Lewis, 2014), and efforts to reduce discrimination have opened up more opportunities for women in the labor market. These factors have acted to reduce the gender wage gap and thereby the net benefits associated with specialization (Juhn & McCue, 2017). As marriages typically entail a greater commitment (as recognized by survey respondents), are more costly to initiate (the average cost of a marriage was purported to be $24,700 in 2019; Hurst, 2021), and generally more costly to end not just financially (the average cost was reported to be $15,000; Barcus, 2019) but also perhaps emotionally as compared to cohabitations, the lower benefits would make marriages less attractive. A couple that marries must expect to incur larger net benefits from marriage as compared to cohabitation. The goal of this analysis is to see if some of these benefits arise from greater intrahousehold specialization.

3. LITERATURE REVIEW

Differences in reported time use by marital status were documented using the 1987–88 NSFH survey by South and Spitze (1994). They found that married women reported the most time on housework, followed by cohabiting and divorced, followed by widowed and never married women. By contrast, among men, widowers reported the most time on housework, followed by divorced, cohabiting, never married and, finally, married men. These data, however, represent only population averages and are rather dated.

Several researchers examine the degree of specialization within households by constructing specialization indices. Bonke et al. (2008) capture specialization in Danish and US households using seven different measures of home production. They find evidence of greater specialization in relationships that have endured longer. Siminski and Yetsenga (2022) look at specialization between market work and home production, defining the latter broadly to include housework (cooking, cleaning, ...), outdoor tasks (gardening, repair work, ...), errands (bill paying, shopping, ...), and childcare. They find some evidence in a cross-sectional analysis of Australian data that cohabiters specialize less.

The differences in time use and specialization observed for persons in different types of relationships could arise for several reasons. Broadly speaking, one possibility is that the differences are driven by selection – whereby persons who report spending more time on certain tasks are more likely to form partnerships. Another is that the differences may arise as a consequence of partnership formation. To distinguish between these explanations, one needs panel data following individuals as relationships form and dissolve. Panel data analysis does not guarantee a causal relation, but certainly takes a step in that direction. Several researchers have examined such transitions.

Gupta (1999) uses two waves of the NSFH to model, separately by gender, changes in reported time in "female-typed" housework as a function of transitions in relationship status and changes in household composition, paid hours of work, earnings, education, and age. He finds that on average never married men reduce and women significantly increase their time on these tasks when entering into a relationship, whether a marriage or a cohabitation. A number of researchers (Baxter et al., 2008; Gupta, 1999; Wernli & Henchoz, 2011) find that when a marriage ends, on average women reduce their time on housework while men increase their time, though none have been able to see if those changes are the inverse of those observed when a marriage begins.

Work by Borra et al. (2021), henceforth BB&S, is most similar to that proposed here. They use data from the United States, the United Kingdom, and Australia to examine the degree to which raw differences in routine housework time between partnered and never married men and women can be explained by introducing controls then adding individual-specific fixed effects. As in the previously cited literature, cross-sectional results indicate that women who are partnered report more time on routine housework while men report less time as compared to those who are not partnered. Between 25% and 35% of the effect for women and all of the effect for men is explained by individual-specific effects. BB&S (2021) end by examining time spent on both routine and what they call nonroutine housework. Here they find some evidence of specialization by task as women who join a couple spend significantly more time on routine housework and men who join a couple spend significantly more time on nonroutine housework. In their main analysis, BB&S do not distinguish between marriage and cohabitation and focus entirely on changes at the time the first relationship is formed. The goal of this analysis is to use panel data from Australia to examine how time use and specialization differ for those entering cohabitations versus marriages.

4. THEORY

Basic economic principles suggest that partners will specialize up to the point where the expected marginal benefit equals the expected marginal cost. The benefits to specialization in any period derive in part from the increased output possible, in part from the time saved if partners specialize according to comparative advantage, and in part from economies of scale in production. If specialization promotes greater investment in skills or promotes learning by doing, the benefits may rise over time (as observed in Polachek, 1975). In general, the longer the expected duration of the relationship, the greater will be the benefits from specialization and couples will benefit more the earlier they adapt their behavior (Stratton, 2005).

Individuals' perceptions of marginal benefit and marginal cost, their willingness to specialize, will vary depending upon the manner in which household decisions are made. Several models of household decision-making imply that such decisions may differ by relationship type.

The household production model (Becker, 1965, 1981) predicts that couples will divide tasks in such a way as to maximize household utility. Considering the expected net present value of household utility, yields a prediction that households expected to endure longer will have more incentive to specialize. While Becker posited that one partner would specialize completely, Pollak (2013) points out that this result assumes partners' time inputs are perfect substitutes, that there are only two activities, no process benefits, and constant or increasing returns to scale in production. These assumptions are unlikely to hold and highlight the need to look at more narrowly defined activities. Research has, however, generally discredited Becker's unitary household or altruist model (see for example, Lundberg et al., 1997).

The bargaining model of household decision-making posits that individuals retain their individual utility functions when forming joint households and bargain to maximize their utility (Lundberg & Pollak, 1996; Manser & Brown, 1980; McElroy & Horney, 1981). The collective model of household decision-making (Chiappori, 1992) posits that there is a household utility function which consists of a weighted sum of the utility of the individuals within the household, with the weights reflecting each individual's bargaining power. The WIHO or Work in Home model (Grossbard-Shechtman, 1984) posits that men and women barter over the supply of household labor and consumption. Bargaining strength is an important component to each of these models and that strength is often tied to labor market and marriage market opportunities. The better an individual's outside opportunities, the greater that person's bargaining power and the less time the individual is likely to spend on housework, an activity assumed to be undesirable. Empirical work by Stevenson (2007), Nunley and Seals (2011), and Altindag et al. (2017) demonstrates that legislative changes influencing bargaining power have the ability to alter how chores are allocated within married households. Chiappori et al. (2017) demonstrate that changes in bargaining power can also affect outcomes for cohabiting households.

That there may be differences between married and cohabiting households is predicted for several reasons. As the costs of entering and exiting a marriage are substantially higher than those associated with cohabitation, marriage can be perceived as a commitment device that couples use to signal and/or promote longer lasting relationships that consequently encourage greater investment in family specific capital, including task specialization (Lundberg et al., 2016). Lafortune and Low (2017) document that those with larger assets are more likely to marry versus cohabit and theorize that that asset ownership acts as a commitment device that supports greater specialization by married couples. Assuming traditional gender roles, the WIHO model suggests that the greater commitment associated with marriage leaves married women more willing to specialize in household production. In empirical work hypothesizing that Blacks coupling with Whites might have to "pay a price" for such a match, Grossbard et al. (2015) find that White women coupling with Black men do spend less time on housework, but only if they are married, suggesting that White women who marry Black men may have more bargaining power.

Overall, there are numerous reasons to expect married couples to specialize more than cohabiting couples. How couples moving from a cohabitation to a marriage might change their time use is less certain. They might subsequently specialize more and behave similarly to married couples who did not cohabit. Being older and having already formed habits may, however, lead such couples to specialize less following marriage than those who enter directly into marriage. Or, perhaps, these couples were more committed from the start and specialized more upon entering the cohabitation. This effect may be more of an empirical question.

5. DATA

The data employed here come from the 2001–2019 waves of the Household, Income and Labor Dynamics in Australia (HILDA) survey data (see Watson & Wooden, 2012, for a description).[2] These data constitute a nationally representative sample of households in Australia. Individuals interviewed in 2001 are followed through time. Their subsequent partners are primarily interviewed only while partnered. Observations of individuals aged 18–23 who were enrolled full-time in an academic program of study (and their partners) were dropped, as were single persons less than age 30 who were living with their parents. The sample is restricted to persons age 18–64 who reported a full complement of variables. Relationship histories were created for every respondent using the relationship status recorded at each interview date as well as the dates each partner reported entering or exiting a cohabitation/marriage. When these reports were at odds, priority was given to the woman's response.[3] Very few respondents reported same sex relationships, hence the focus here is on heterosexual couples.

The basic sample consists of 83,638 observations of 8,577 men and 8,698 women.[4] About 13% of these individuals are never observed in a relationship and about 60% are always in a relationship with the same partner. In total, 8,816 different relationships are observed within the data. Over 200 individuals are observed entering a marriage without first cohabiting; over 1,300 cohabitations begin; and over 1,200 cohabiting couples marry. Thus, a substantial number of transitions are observed.

A rich set of control variables are included in the analysis that follows. The data include time varying information on age, disability status, urbanicity, residence type, residential ownership and size, as well as such household characteristics as the number of children age 0–4, 5–9, 10–14, the number of other dependents, and indicators for the presence of a disabled child or other household resident. Information on aboriginal status and immigrant status is time invariant but also available. Educational attainment is an important, largely time invariant control factor. Sample statistics for these explanatory variables are reported in Table 1 separately by gender. Controls for year and state of residence are also included in the analyses. Results by gender and relationship status are available upon request. Not surprisingly, unpartnered individuals are younger, less well educated, and less likely to have children in the household as compared to partnered individuals. They are also less likely to live in a house or own their residence. Cohabiting persons are less likely to live in a house or own their residence as compared to married persons. They are younger and, cohabiting men in particular, less educated than married persons.

6. ANALYSIS OF TIME USE

The first analysis to be conducted centers on reported time use measures. Time use is not a definitive measure of specialization but has been studied more extensively than specialization, thus allowing some comparison to previous literature. The focus is primarily upon housework tasks, but information on outdoor activities, errands, and employment is also available. The analysis centers on how time use changes as relationships form and is restricted to each respondent's first observed relationship in order to match previous literature and to obtain a more homogeneous sample.[5] Respondents are also required to have two observations so as to contribute to fixed effects specifications.

6.1 Simple Statistics

Time use for household chores is recorded on a self-completed questionnaire asking "how many hours would you spend on each of the following activities in a typical week?". Time diary data not survey data are the gold standard for empirical work on time use. There is substantial evidence that survey data typically overstate time use (Juster et al., 2003) and there is evidence (Foster & Stratton, 2018) that men overstate and women understate their housework time in HILDA. However, time diary data are typically collected over only a 24 hour

Table 1. Summary Statistics.

	Men		Women	
	Mean	Std. Dev.	Mean	Std. Dev.
Age	42.480	(11.804)	40.690	(11.504)
Disabled	0.131	(0.337)	0.133	(0.339)
Aborigine	0.018	(0.133)	0.025	(0.157)
Immigrant from English Speaking Country	0.099	(0.299)	0.075	(0.264)
Immigrant from Other Country	0.108	(0.311)	0.117	(0.321)
Own Education				
<12th Grade	0.197	(0.398)	0.242	(0.428)
12th Grade	0.125	(0.331)	0.148	(0.356)
Certificate III/IV	0.302	(0.459)	0.166	(0.372)
Diploma	0.096	(0.294)	0.108	(0.310)
BA/Honors	0.161	(0.368)	0.200	(0.400)
Post-Bachelor's	0.119	(0.324)	0.136	(0.343)
Residence in:				
Major Urban Area	0.659	(0.474)	0.664	(0.472)
Other Urban Area	0.204	(0.403)	0.204	(0.403)
Non-Urban	0.137	(0.344)	0.132	(0.339)
Residence Type:				
House	0.834	(0.372)	0.831	(0.375)
Townhouse	0.061	(0.240)	0.065	(0.247)
Flat/NA	0.105	(0.306)	0.104	(0.305)
Owns Residence	0.701	(0.458)	0.700	(0.458)
Number of Bedrooms	3.321	(1.002)	3.327	(0.992)
Household Characteristics				
Number of Other Adults	0.293	(0.686)	0.277	(0.658)
Number of Children				
Age 0–4	0.285	(0.610)	0.298	(0.618)
Age 5–9	0.253	(0.576)	0.269	(0.588)
Age 10–14	0.243	(0.569)	0.253	(0.577)
Number of Other Dependents	0.188	(0.496)	0.194	(0.504)
Disabled Child	0.043	(0.203)	0.042	(0.200)
Other Disabled Resident	0.061	(0.239)	0.041	(0.198)
Number of Observations	67,064		69,257	
Number of Persons	8,577		8,698	

period that may or may not be representative of an individual's "usual" day. Fortunately, these survey figures closely parallel those from time diary data in Australia (Siminski & Yetsenga, 2022) and the HILDA dataset provides the panel information necessary for this analysis. The "activity" classified as housework here is described as: "Housework, such as preparing meals, washing dishes, cleaning house, washing clothes, ironing and sewing." Outdoor activities are described as: "Outdoor tasks, including home maintenance (repairs, improvements, painting etc.), car maintenance or repairs and gardening." Errands are described as: "Household errands, such as shopping, banking, paying bills, and keeping financial records (but do not include driving children to school and to other activities)." Respondents are also asked about their time in paid employment on this questionnaire.[6] Where paid employment time is missing or of uncertain value from this survey, data from the labor force survey component of HILDA are used.[7]

Table 2 presents sample mean hours spent per week for the time use measures. Panel A shows the results for men, Panel B for women. The first column reports data on housework time. Subsequent columns report the data for outdoor tasks, errands, and paid employment. Overall sample averages are presented first, followed by averages by relationship status at the time of the interview. On average, women report more time on housework (15.6 vs. 6.2 hours), less time on outdoor tasks (2.8 vs. 4.7), a little more time on errands (4.9 vs. 3.5), and substantially less time on paid employment (24 vs. 38) as compared to men. There are, however, also significant differences in time use patterns by relationship status by gender.

Men report spending 6 hours per week on housework no matter what their relationship status. Unpartnered men average significantly less time on outdoor tasks, errands, and employment than partnered men. Unpartnered women report spending nine hours per week on housework, a measure that is statistically significantly lower than the average time reported by partnered women. Unpartnered women also report significantly less time spent on outdoor tasks and errands, though more time in employment than unpartnered women. These differences are consistent with a story that upon partnering, women on average specialize in housework while men on average specialize in paid employment.

Table 2. Time Use.

	By Partnered Status			
	Housework	Outdoor Tasks	Errands	Paid Employment
Panel A: Men				
Full Sample	6.20	4.74	3.46	37.98
Not Partnered	6.14	3.03	3.28	31.46
Partnered	6.21	5.05	3.50	39.14
Cohabiting	6.27	4.27	3.47	37.44
Married	6.20	5.25	3.50	39.60
Panel B: Women				
Full Sample	15.56	2.76	4.94	23.84
Not Partnered	9.10	2.19	3.82	27.53
Partnered	16.60	2.85	5.12	23.25
Cohabiting	12.44	2.49	4.39	26.74
Married	17.73	2.95	5.32	22.30

Note: Sample sizes vary.

The means also provide some evidence that cohabiting and married couples allocate time differently. Cohabiting men report significantly less time on errands and in employment than married men. Cohabiting women report significantly less time on housework and errands but significantly more time in employment than married women. These differences are generally in line with the hypothesis proposed here that cohabiting couples specialize less than married couples.

However, Table 2 does not clearly identify how time use differs as relationships form. To compare how time use changes as relationships form, the sample is further restricted to individuals reporting time use both before and after such a change. Fig. 1 illustrates average weekly hours of housework by gender in the three years before and three years after a relationship forms. Separate illustrations are provided for relationships as a whole, marriages not preceded by a cohabitation, cohabitations, and marriages preceded by a cohabitation.[8] On average, men report spending about six hours per week on housework, the same amount of time reported in Table 2. This number is not substantially altered as they enter a relationship, no matter the type of relationship. Women, on the other hand, increase their reported housework time as they enter a relationship, and that increase is greatest for those entering a marriage, providing some evidence of differential specialization.[9] It is also notable that women entering a marriage average almost an hour more time on housework before marriage than those entering a cohabitation average before beginning to cohabit. This differential could be evidence of a selection effect.

A similar analysis was conducted to examine how average time spent on housework changes as relationships end. Fixed effects models that follow individuals both as they enter and exit relationships necessarily assume that changes in time use are symmetric. There is no guarantee, however, that such will be the case. Results (see Fig. A1) indicate that women do indeed report spending less time on housework after marriages end, suggesting the effects of marriage may be symmetric for women. However, while the magnitude of the effect is small, men's reported housework time appears to rise as relationships end. Further analysis indicates that after controlling for a full array of observables and individual-specific fixed effects, women reduce their time on housework upon exiting a relationship, but the magnitude is smaller than the increase observed for women entering relationships, and men do increase their time on housework upon exiting a relationship. Changes in time use upon entry and exit to relationships are not symmetric. For this reason, the analysis that follows focuses only on how time use changes as relationships form. Further analysis is necessary to investigate the asymmetry.

Figures illustrating other time uses are available upon request. Time spent on outdoor tasks clearly increases for men but not women who enter a relationship. Reported time on errands appears to rise over time for both men and women, with no particular change as they enter relationships. Finally, women clearly report less time in employment following marriage. Of course, time use changes as needs change and needs evolve over time. Couples are more likely to have children and to live in (and own) larger homes, causing demand for housework

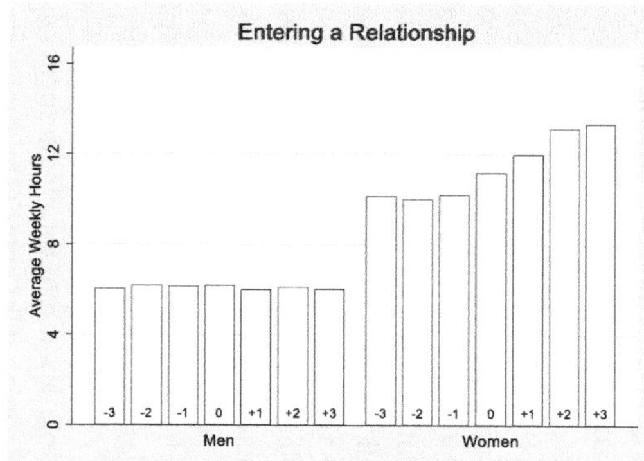

Responses from at least 1,179 men and 1,289 women.

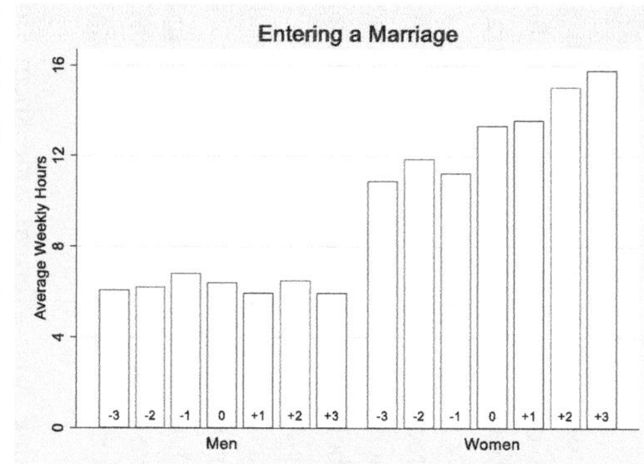

Responses from at least 189 men and 177 women.

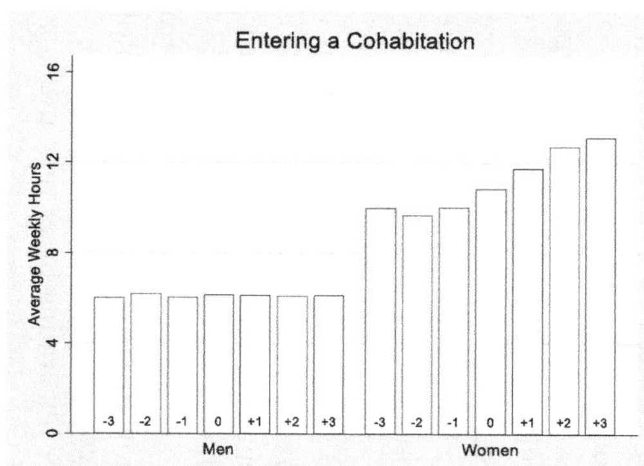

Responses from at least 990 men and 1,117 women.

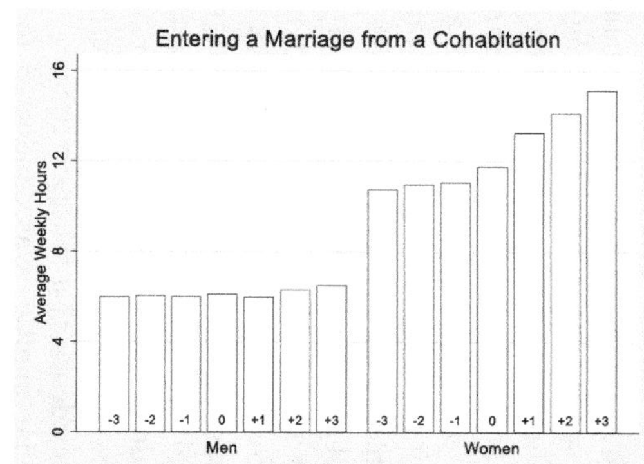

Responses from at least 1,245 men and 1,326 women.

Fig. 1. Time Spent on Housework as Individuals Enter Relationships.

Source: Data from the 2001–2019 waves of HILDA for persons responding at least once before and once after the start of a relationship. "0" reflects the transition year, -# the number of years before, and +# the number of years after.

time and outdoor tasks in particular to increase. It is important to control for these differences when evaluating how time use changes with relationship status.

6.2 Empirical Results Regarding Housework Time

Such controls can be incorporated in regression models. As it is housework time that changes the most dramatically, the initial focus is on housework time. Estimation proceeds with ordinary least squares (OLS) and fixed effects (FE) estimation of housework time for those observed first entering a cohabitation or first marrying, as well as for those transitioning from a cohabitation to a marriage. These samples include persons who are never partnered, always partnered, or transition from unpartnered to partnered status. All models are estimated separately by gender and with robust standard errors. Standard errors are clustered at the individual level.

This approach mimics the work of BB&S. That work is extended here by including many more covariates, in particular more detailed information about household composition (see Table 1), year and state dummies, plus dummy variables identifying relationships that are newly formed in expectation that it may take time to adjust one's time use. Not included are the controls for time spent in paid employment and predicted earnings that BB&S employ. The former is another time use necessarily jointly determined; the latter is controlled for indirectly by the covariates that are included, particularly education, a quadratic in age, and disability status.

The initial results are reported in Table 3 for three different specifications: the first (1) includes only a dummy variable to identify persons in a relationship thus mimicking BB&S's specification, the second (2) includes a dummy variable that distinguishes between those married and those cohabiting, the third (3) includes a dummy variable that further distinguishes between marriages that were and were not preceded by a cohabitation.[10] As discussed earlier, how those transitioning from a cohabitation to a marriage might alter their time use is uncertain. If individuals become accustomed to a particular routine while cohabiting, they may be less likely to change that routine upon transitioning to marriage. Alternatively, those transitioning from a cohabitation to a marriage may do so expecting the relationship to endure and then change their behavior to more nearly match that of married couples. Each specification is estimated first using OLS (columns 1, 3, and 5), then individual-specific fixed effects (FE) (columns 2, 4, 6). Results for men are reported in Panel A, those for women in Panel B. There are 7,943 men of whom 1,758 enter a relationship and 8,099 women of whom 1,838 enter a relationship. In each case about 1,000 of these transitions are from a cohabitation into a marriage. Table 3 presents only the results for the relationship indicators. The full results (excluding year and state dummies) are available upon request.

The OLS results for men indicate that those in a relationship on average report spending 0.7 fewer hours per week as compared to those not in a relationship (specification (1)). This estimate is quite close to that of BB&S (−0.8) despite the different specification. Results from specification (2) indicate that married men on

Table 3. Modeling Reported Time on Housework.

	Upon Entering a First Relationship					
Panel A: Men	OLS (1)	FE (1)	OLS (2)	FE (2)	OLS (3)	FE (3)
In a Relationship	−0.7196 (0.1537)	−0.0508 (0.1779)				
Married			−1.0173 (0.1743)	−0.1367 (0.2125)		
Cohabiting			−0.3097 (0.1599)	−0.0171 (0.1764)	−0.2865 (0.1601)	0.0117 (0.1826)
Married, 1st cohabited					−0.8066 (0.1846)	−0.1204 (0.2299)
Married, w/o 1st cohabiting					−1.4032 (0.2002)	−0.3348 (0.4027)
Number of Observations	63,295	63,295	63,295	63,295	63,295	63,295
Number of Men	7,943	7,943	7,943	7,943	7,943	7,943
Panel B: Women	OLS (1)	FE (1)	OLS (2)	FE (2)	OLS (3)	FE (3)
In a Relationship	3.3059 (0.2212)	1.5702 (0.2806)				
Married			3.9109 (0.2499)	2.1630 (0.3334)		
Cohabiting			2.3940 (0.2367)	1.3391 (0.2771)	2.3327 (0.2364)	1.1576 (0.2793)
Married, 1st cohabited					3.4598 (0.2681)	2.0384 (0.3489)
Married, w/o 1st cohabiting					4.6938 (0.3005)	3.7437 (0.7142)
Number of Observations	65,914	65,914	65,914	65,914	65,914	65,914
Number of Women	8,099	8,099	8,099	8,099	8,099	8,099

Notes: All the specifications include controls for state (7) and year (18). The OLS specifications also include all the controls listed in Table 1 as well as a quadratic in age and dummy variables identifying relationships that began within the last 6 months. FE stands for individual-specific fixed effects. The FE specifications include all these controls except education and other time invariant personal characteristics.
Robust standard errors in parentheses.

average report spending 1.0 fewer hours per week while cohabiting men report spending only 0.3 fewer hours per week as compared to men not currently in a relationship. This difference is statistically significant (p-value 0.00) and could be indicative of less specialization in cohabiting as compared to married households or of differential selection into marriage versus cohabitation. Further distinguishing between marriages that were and were not preceded by a cohabitation (specification (3)) yields estimates suggesting that on average all coupled men report less time on housework, with those married without first cohabiting reporting less than married men who first cohabited, who report less than those cohabiting. One can reject the hypothesis that these effects are the same.

However, none of these differences carry over to the fixed effects specifications. While men in different types of relationships report spending different amounts of time on housework, men observed first transitioning into a relationship do not report spending a significantly different amount of time on housework. As BB&S report, it appears that selection explains all of the observed association between housework time and relationship status for men first transitioning into a relationship. The negative coefficients in the OLS specifications suggest that men who spent less time on housework were more likely to enter relationships. Men who marry without previously cohabiting do, however, report spending a bit more time during the first six months of the relationship than either before or after. This variable was included on the expectation that it might take some time for "usual" activities and expectations to change. The finding of a positive short run impact was not anticipated and could perhaps be a sort of newlywed effect.

The OLS results for women indicate that on average women in a relationship report spending 3.3 hours more per week than women not in a relationship. This result is again, very similar to that reported by BB&S (+3.5). Specification (2) reveals that cohabiting women average 2.4 more hours per week and married women 3.9 more hours per week, a difference of 1.5 hours that is statistically significant (p-value 0.00). Specification (3) indicates that women in marriages not preceded by a cohabitation on average report 4.7 more hours per week on housework; women in marriages preceded by a cohabitation report 3.5 more hours per week (0.9 hours more than cohabiters); and women who are cohabiting report 2.3 more hours per week. In contrast to the results for men, on average all coupled women report more time on housework, with those married without first cohabiting reporting more than married women who first cohabited, who report more than those cohabiting. However, there is a bit of a lag in take up as women in the first 6 months of forming a cohabitation or transitioning into a marriage report spending about an hour less on housework.

The fixed effect results, similar to those reported in BB&S, indicate that about half of these reported time differences, a bit less for those transitioning directly into marriage, are attributable to selection. Women entering relationships for the first time appear to be those who spent more time on housework before. Specification (3) results suggest women transitioning directly into marriage reported increasing their housework time by 3.7 hours (an increase of 40% over the average time reported by unpartnered women), those transitioning into a cohabitation reported increasing their housework time by 1.2 hours (a 13% increase) and those transitioning from a cohabitation to a marriage reported increasing their housework time a total of 2.0 hours (about 0.9 hours more than when cohabiting), though mostly after the first 6 months. One can in this case reject the hypothesis that housework time increased the same for those marrying whether they first cohabited or not at the 5% though not at the 1% level.

These results indicate that all of the differences in reported housework time by relationship status for men entering their first relationships are likely a consequence of selection as men who spend less time on housework are more likely to enter a relationship. By contrast, while women who spend more time on housework are more likely to enter a relationship, no more than half of the difference in time use is explained by selection for women. Assuming that these time use measures capture specialization, the results also support the hypothesis that there is less specialization in housework for women transitioning into cohabitations than there is for women transitioning for the first time into marriages. While these are not paired results, we do not see how time use changes for each partner entering a relationship, these results suggest that time spent on housework, ceteris paribus, may increase with the formation of relationships. Thus, any time savings from economies of scale would seem to be countered by another factor.

6.3 Jointly Modeling Reported Time on Housework, Outdoor Tasks, Errands, and Paid Employment

To examine this hypothesis further, the analysis is extended to look at additional measures of time use: errands, outdoor activities, and paid employment. As selection effects were significant for both men and women, the analysis is restricted to fixed effects specifications. Furthermore, to account for possible cross-equation correlations, the four reported time uses are modeled jointly. The results as they pertain to relationship status are reported in Table 4: Panel A for men and Panel B for women.

Men entering a relationship are not observed significantly altering their time on housework or employment. There is some evidence they increase their time on outdoor chores and errands, but in no case is the change greater than one hour. Only in the case of errands is the change in time use significantly greater for those marrying as compared to those cohabiting, and then only for those who marry without having first cohabited, yielding weak evidence that marriages induce greater specialization than cohabiting relationships.

Women who marry without previously cohabiting report changes in time use that are significantly greater in magnitude than women who enter a cohabitation: increasing housework and errand time more and decreasing time on employment and (weakly) outdoor tasks. The difference in time use between women entering marriage with versus without having first cohabited is significant only for housework and errands. Thus, the fixed effect results for women are consistent with the hypothesis that there is more specialization in married households and with women entering a marriage via a cohabitation in some but not all cases

Table 4. Joint Modeling of Time Use.

	Fixed Effects Specification			
Panel A: Men	Housework	Errands	Outdoor Tasks	Paid Employment
	Entering First Relationship			
Married, w/o 1st cohabiting	−0.3590	0.8125	0.3761	−0.2121
	(0.2936)	(0.1838)	(0.2216)	(0.7907)
Married, 1st cohabited	−0.1246	0.1606	0.4273	0.3756
	(0.1782)	(0.1110)	(0.1394)	(0.4760)
Cohabiting	0.0118	0.2609	0.4723	−0.1144
	(0.1490)	(0.0952)	(0.1174)	(0.4049)
Number of Observations	63,295	62,600	62,735	62,693
Number of Men	7,943	7,913	7,910	8,110
Panel B: Women	Housework	Errands	Outdoor Tasks	Paid Employment
	Entering First Relationship			
Married, w/o 1st cohabiting	3.7683	1.1212	−0.3104	−4.4644
	(0.5064)	(0.2299)	(0.1840)	(0.9948)
Married, 1st cohabited	2.0638	0.4097	−0.1714	−4.5103
	(0.2760)	(0.1223)	(0.1075)	(0.4905)
Cohabiting	1.1638	0.0625	0.1201	−0.6337
	(0.2275)	(0.1029)	(0.0929)	(0.4196)
Number of Observations	65,914	65,135	65,120	64,757
Number of Women	8,099	8,078	8,085	8,216

Notes: All the specifications include controls for state (7) and year (18). They also include all the controls listed in Table 1 except education and other time invariant personal characteristics as well as a quadratic in age and dummy variables identifying relationships that began within the last 6 months.
Robust standard errors in parentheses.

adjusting their time use in much the same way as women entering a marriage more directly.

Correlation terms for both men and women indicate that those who for unobserved reasons reported more time on housework also report more time on outdoor tasks and errands. Similarly, those reporting more time on outdoor tasks report more time on errands. By way of contrast, the correlation between all of these household activities and time in paid employment is negative. All these correlations are highly statistically significant.

In general, the evidence from these joint models regarding the proposed hypothesis is weak. Men do not significantly alter their time on housework or in employment when entering a relationship. They do adjust their time on errands more when entering marriages than cohabitations, but the reverse may be true for time on outdoor tasks. However, the evidence indicates that women adjust their time use across the board more upon entering marriages than they do upon entering cohabitations – a result consistent with predictions.

7. EMPIRICAL EVIDENCE REGARDING TASK SHARES

As noted above, time use is not a definitive measure of specialization. Changes in time use as relationships form and change may reflect specialization but may also reflect economies of scale and changing preferences. The prior analysis also relies on the assumption that specialization occurs at the level of housework, outdoor tasks, errands, and employment broadly defined and is visible in reported time use data. Housework, outdoor chores, and errands each constitute an amalgam of different activities. Housework includes meal preparation, laundry, and cleaning. Outdoor chores include gardening and doing home repairs. Errands include shopping and paying bills. Individuals may specialize in different activities within these broad categories. For example, one partner may specialize in meal preparation and another in laundry. While it may not take twice as much time to do these tasks for a couple as opposed to for an individual, it will take longer. Time spent on each broad time use category then may not decrease much for any individual because no one individual specializes in every component within that category.

To address this possibility, we make use of information collected periodically in the HILDA survey asking couples who in the household is responsible for some more narrowly defined household tasks. More specifically, partnered respondents in HILDA are asked in 2005, 2008, 2011, 2015, and 2019, "Who does the following tasks in your household?", where the tasks include preparing daily meals (Meals), washing the dishes (Dishes), cleaning the house (Cleaning), shopping for food (Shopping), paying bills and keeping financial records (Bills), and doing small repairs in and around the house (Repairs). The first three are subsumed under the broader Housework category, the next two are Errands, the final one is an Outdoor Task. Meals and Repairs are activities that, compared to Dishes and Cleaning, require some skill. Acquiring such skills is costly and so couples are more likely to specialize in these activities. On average, women are more likely to prepare meals, men to complete repairs. Dish washing likely requires the least skill and could at low cost be performed by one partner one day and the other partner another day. Specialization in this activity likely provides little net benefit, but could offset specialization in another activity. Bills comprises activities that on average men are more likely to perform, but couples that are uncertain about their future together might logically choose to keep their financial accounts separate. Differences in bill paying may, however, be less pronounced by relationship status in Australia where for tax reasons individuals generally keep separate accounts. Finally, as noted before, habit formation may limit changes when cohabiting couples marry.

Usual responses include, "Always me", "Usually me", "Shared equally between partner & self", "Usually my partner", and "Always my partner".[11] These questions were administered to both partners and there is a substantial degree of agreement within couples, ranging from 49% for Bills to 58% for Meals, with similar results for married and cohabiting couples. The fraction of individuals giving diametrically opposed answers is less than 0.2%. In the case of activities women report always or usually performing (Meals, Dishes, Cleaning, and Shopping), male partners often assert some credit for the activity. This is especially true of Dishes. In the case of Repairs, typically performed by men, female partners often assert some credit. Disagreements are more evenly distributed in the case of Bills perhaps because individuals are accustomed to doing these activities separately and uncertain how to report responsibility.

Looking first at specialization from a gender-neutral perspective, new measures are created that code complete specialization ("Always" answers) as 1, some specialization ("Usually" answers) as 2, and shared responsibility as 3. Thus, lower numbers are indicative of more specialization. Table 5 reports the sample

Table 5. Specialization by Task and Relationship Status.

	Percent Distribution					
	Meals	Dishes	Cleaning	Shopping	Bills	Repairs
Panel A: Men's Responses						
Married, w/o 1st Cohabiting						
Complete Specialization	19.31	10.72	14.62	16.84	32.22	29.82
Some Specialization	57.90	47.42	54.95	50.77	49.57	60.94
Shared	22.79	41.86	30.42	32.39	18.21	9.24
# of observations	4,532	4,283	4,342	4,607	4,652	4,554
Married, 1st Cohabited						
Complete Specialization	14.26	9.06	10.48	14.90	31.51	28.82
Some Specialization	58.38	48.51	53.54	50.73	48.44	59.77
Shared	27.36	42.43	35.98	34.37	20.05	11.41
# of observations	6,860	6,479	6,587	6,945	6,998	6,843
Cohabiting						
Complete Specialization	12.39	9.43	8.16	10.92	20.98	24.37
Some Specialization	51.96	45.74	47.25	39.12	42.48	57.99
Shared	35.65	44.82	44.59	49.96	36.54	17.65
# of observations	3,778	3,710	3,750	3,829	3,856	3,706
Panel B: Women's Responses						
Married, w/o 1st Cohabiting						
Complete Specialization	35.34	22.54	35.42	34.92	40.06	19.87
Some Specialization	48.91	47.33	44.90	40.70	42.15	64.07
Shared	15.75	30.13	19.68	24.39	17.79	16.06
# of observations	4,884	4,623	4,670	4,929	4,958	4,701
Married, 1st Cohabited						
Complete Specialization	27.50	17.00	29.69	33.06	41.06	17.26
Some Specialization	51.92	49.68	47.88	42.30	40.96	62.97
Shared	20.57	33.32	22.43	24.64	17.98	19.76
# of observations	7,257	6,876	6,945	7,333	7,360	7,049
Cohabiting						
Complete Specialization	23.28	17.12	23.40	24.54	28.70	16.40
Some Specialization	48.36	46.64	45.11	36.33	37.34	59.77
Shared	28.36	36.24	31.48	39.13	33.95	23.83
# of observations	4,080	3,984	4,012	4,099	4,097	3,860

averages by task and relationship status. The results for men are shown in Panel A, the results for women in Panel B. Clearly, there is substantial specialization – which is not possible in a single person household. The fraction reporting shared responsibility is lowest for Repairs, ranging from 9% to 24%, but never exceeds 50%. While twice as many cohabiters as compared to married persons report sharing responsibility for all six tasks, fewer than 3% of persons report such sharing. Couples do specialize.

As hypothesized, the degree of specialization is greater and statistically significantly different at the 1% level in every case for married as compared to cohabiting persons, with the exception of men's reporting of dishwashing which is significant only at the 3% level. As discussed above, there is little benefit to specialization in dish washing as a standalone activity. There is in addition evidence that married persons who cohabited together report specializing less in meal preparation and cleaning than married persons who did not first cohabit, but more than cohabiting persons. Married persons who cohabited together also report more specialization than cohabiting persons when it comes to shopping and bill paying.

While these statistics provide evidence that on average behavior is different for those in different types of relationships, they do not control for other household characteristics that might be related to specialization. Table 6 presents results from an ordered probit model that includes all the covariates included in the time use models. Only the coefficients identifying cohabiters and married couples who first cohabited are reported (complete results are available upon request). These coefficients identify differences in the degree of specialization as compared to

Table 6. Ordered Probit Models of Specialization.

	Meals	Dishes	Cleaning	Shopping	Bills	Repairs
Panel A: Men						
Married, 1st Cohabited	0.0858	0.0143	0.1096	0.0812	0.0060	0.0387
	(0.0360)	(0.0358)	(0.0358)	(0.0348)	(0.0340)	(0.0349)
Cohabiting	0.1365	0.0471	0.1931	0.1816	0.3030	0.1532
	(0.0463)	(0.0449)	(0.0445)	(0.0445)	(0.0435)	(0.0445)
p-value of Difference	0.1945	0.3849	0.0281	0.0086	0.0000	0.0029
Panel B: Women						
Married, 1st Cohabited	0.1093	0.0788	0.0671	0.0754	−0.0433	0.0774
	(0.0358)	(0.0363)	(0.0370)	(0.0354)	(0.0362)	(0.0341)
Cohabiting	0.1354	0.0864	0.1099	0.2041	0.2996	0.1384
	(0.0455)	(0.0440)	(0.0454)	(0.0450)	(0.0451)	(0.0432)
p-value of Difference	0.5003	0.8345	0.2556	0.0007	0.0000	0.0956

Notes: The dependent variable takes a value of 1 if 1 partner "always" performs the activity, 2 if 1 partner "usually" performs the activity, and 3 if the activity is shared. Thus, positive values indicate less specialization.

All the specifications include controls for state (7) and year (4), all the controls listed in Table 1, and a quadratic in age.

Robust standard errors in parentheses. The *p*-values indicate whether married couples who first cohabited specialize differently from cohabiting couples.

married couples who did not first cohabit. Positive coefficients indicate less specialization. Cohabiting couples report less specialization as compared to married couples who did not first cohabit in every activity, a difference that is statistically significant except in the case of men's reporting of dish washing activity. Married women who initially cohabited report significantly less specialization than married women who did not first cohabit in every task except bill paying. The magnitude of this effect is, however, less than that for cohabiting women which suggests that women transitioning from cohabitation to marriage might specialize more. Results are similar for married men who initially cohabited, except that the differences are not statistically significant for bills, repairs, or dishes. Thus, even when a substantial set of controls is incorporated, the evidence suggests that cohabiting couples specialize less than married couples and that cohabiting couples who marry may specialize more following marriage, but not as much as married couples who did not previously cohabit.

While these results control for a range of covariates, they reflect only correlations and do not reveal whether behavior changes as the type of relationship changes. It may be that those cohabiting couples who specialized more while cohabiting are subsequently more likely to marry. An analysis of how the transition between cohabitation and marriage influences the degree of specialization may reveal whether the differences observed between these persons is due to selection or due to a change in roles.

To evaluate this probability, a linear model of specialization is estimated with couple-specific fixed effects. The set of control variables includes all the covariates listed in Table 1 as well as the age, education, nativity, and disability status of the respondent's partner. The sample is limited to those observed at least twice. Many respondents are observed only married, but at least 673 couples are observed transitioning from cohabitation to marriage for each sample. The coefficient estimates for the dummy variable (Marrying) identifying those making this transition are presented in Table 7. Panel A presents the results for men, Panel B for women (full results are available upon request). Each column reflects a different task.

Every estimate is negative indicating that those transitioning from a cohabitation to a marriage on average, ceteris paribus, report specializing more. The magnitude and significance of this effect is largest for bill paying, indicating that even in Australia the act of marriage increases specialization in bill paying. Men report significantly more specialization in repair work as well as somewhat more in meals and dishes, women more in food shopping and dishes. These results provide some evidence that couples increase the degree of intrahousehold specialization when transitioning from a cohabitation to a marriage, perhaps because they feel more secure in a marriage. Adding controls for the length of each cohabitation and marriage to date does not significantly alter these results. The only time these measures are significant is in the case of food shopping. There is less specialization in food shopping the longer a couple is married.

Finally, in order to examine the gendered nature of these different activities and their interactions, a six-equation system of ordered probits is estimated separately by gender using the original categorical variables for which a code of 1 means the respondent always does the task and a code of 5 means the partner

Table 7. Changes in Reported Specialization for Those Transitioning From Cohabitation to Marriage.

	Controlling for Couple-Specific Effects					
Tasks:	Meals	Dishes	Cleaning	Shopping	Bills	Repairs
Panel A: Men						
Marrying	−0.0458	−0.0520	−0.0387	−0.0097	−0.1110	−0.0820
	(0.0276)	(0.0294)	(0.0279)	(0.0293)	(0.0302)	(0.0265)
# of Observations	12,720	12,024	12,240	12,962	13,113	12,721
# of Couples	4,018	3,887	3,933	4,078	4,099	3,992
# of Couples Transitioning	688	673	685	700	708	681
Panel B: Women						
Marrying	−0.0374	−0.0507	−0.0400	−0.0588	−0.1449	−0.0389
	(0.0271)	(0.0289)	(0.0287)	(0.0294)	(0.0297)	(0.0276)
# of Observations	13,716	12,958	13,102	13,877	13,932	13,168
# of Couples	4,280	4,149	4,157	4,320	4,323	4,150
# of Couples Transitioning	722	711	707	728	732	698

Notes: All the specifications include controls for state (7) and year (4). They also include a quadratic in age and all the controls listed in Table 1 except education and other time invariant personal characteristics.
Robust standard errors in parentheses.

always does the task. These results for the relationship measures are reported in Table 8. The base case is that of married persons who did not first cohabit. Panel A shows the results for men, Panel B for women. The set of control variables includes all the covariates listed in Table 1 as well as the age, education, nativity, and disability status of the respondent's partner (results available upon request) as well as state and year dummies. Negative coefficient values indicate that the respondent reported doing a greater share of the task. These estimates are distinctly more descriptive than causal in nature.

The results for men indicate that cohabiting men take on a significantly greater share of meal preparation, dishes, cleaning, food shopping, and bill paying and a lesser share of repair work than married men who did not first cohabit. Married men who previously cohabited take on a significantly greater share of meal preparation, dishes, cleaning, and food shopping as compared with married men who did not previously cohabit, but report performing a similar share of repair work and bill paying. The differences in reported shares between men who are cohabiting and men who are in marriages that were preceded by a cohabitation are all significant at the 10% level or better, with those currently married reporting a lesser share of all activities, except repair work which is generally male dominated but less so for cohabiting men.

The results for women are a close reflection of those for men. Cohabiting women and married women who first cohabited take on a significantly smaller share of meal preparation, dishes, cleaning, and food shopping and a significantly larger share of

Table 8. Results From a System of Ordered Probits.

	Meals	Dishes	Cleaning	Shopping	Bills	Repairs
Panel A: Men						
Married, 1st Cohabited	−0.1109	−0.1050	−0.0883	−0.0489	0.0111	0.0159
	(0.0236)	(0.0240)	(0.0245)	(0.0237)	(0.0234)	(0.0246)
Cohabiting	−0.1908	−0.1587	−0.1425	−0.1480	−0.0963	0.1113
	(0.0308)	(0.0315)	(0.0309)	(0.0304)	(0.0290)	(0.0325)
p value of Difference	0.0031	0.0510	0.0437	0.0002	0.0000	0.0009
Number of Observations	12,854	12,240	12,431	13,044	13,175	12,866
Panel B: Women						
Married, 1st Cohabited	0.1489	0.0896	0.0534	0.0457	−0.0353	−0.0517
	(0.0233)	(0.0237)	(0.0245)	(0.0238)	(0.0236)	(0.0241)
Cohabiting	0.1929	0.0928	0.0781	0.1548	0.0330	−0.1732
	(0.0307)	(0.0310)	(0.0313)	(0.0304)	(0.0291)	(0.0321)
p value of Difference	0.1028	0.9035	0.3586	0.0000	0.0061	0.0000
Number of Observations	13,315	12,681	12,803	13,437	13,492	12,897

Notes: The dependent variable takes a value of 1 if the respondent always performs the activity, 2 if the respondent usually performs the activity, 3 if the activity is shared, 4 if the partner usually performs the activity, and 5 if the partner always performs the activity. Thus, positive values indicate the respondent is less engaged in the activity.

All the specifications include controls for state (7) and year (4), all the controls listed in Table 1 (for each partner), and quadratics in age.

Robust standard errors in parentheses. The *p*-values indicate whether married couples who first cohabited report specializing differently from cohabiting couples.

repair work than married women who did not previously cohabit. Married women who previously cohabited report contributing a significantly larger share of shopping and bill paying as compared to cohabiting women, and a lower share of repair work.

Somewhat surprisingly, all the correlation terms (available upon request) are positive and statistically significant. This indicates that individuals who for unexplained reasons were more likely to report that they performed one task were also more likely to report that they performed each of the tasks. One might reasonably expect that if one partner performed more of one task, the other might compensate by performing more of another. At the least, given the gendered nature of many of these tasks, one might expect somewhat different correlations for repair work which is predominantly performed by men. The correlations between the unobservables associated with repair work and the other tasks were smaller, particularly for men, but still positive and statistically significant.

Technically in this specification both positive and negative coefficients could be indicative of increased specialization, with positive coefficients meaning the respondent specializes more and negative coefficients meaning their partner specializes more – as can be seen in the results for repair work as compared to the other activities. In addition, these coefficient estimates fail to convey information regarding the magnitude of the differences. To address these concerns, simulated marginal effects were calculated. These are reported in Table 9. Many of the

Table 9. Simulated Marginal Effects.

	From Married Did Not 1st Cohabit to …					
	Meals	Dishes	Cleaning	Shopping	Bills	Repairs
Panel A: Men						
Married, 1st Cohabited						
Always Me	**0.0064**	**0.0071**	**0.0023**	0.0027	−0.0025	−0.0053
	(0.0013)	(0.0016)	(0.0007)	(0.0013)	(0.0053)	(0.0082)
Usually Me	**0.0174**	**0.0224**	**0.0106**	0.0068	−0.0014	0.0019
	(0.0037)	(0.0051)	(0.0029)	(0.0033)	(0.0030)	(0.0030)
Shared Equally	0.0179	0.0090	**0.0203**	0.0092	−0.0002	0.0026
	(0.0039)	(0.0022)	(0.0057)	(0.0045)	(0.0005)	(0.0040)
Usually My Partner	−0.0184	−0.0254	−0.0179	−0.0088	0.0018	0.0006
	(0.0039)	(0.0058)	(0.0049)	(0.0042)	(0.0038)	(0.0010)
Always My Partner	**−0.0234**	**−0.0131**	**−0.0154**	−0.0099	0.0024	0.0002
	(0.0051)	(0.0031)	(0.0043)	(0.0048)	(0.0050)	(0.0004)
Cohabiting						
Always Me	**0.0119**	**0.0112**	**0.0040**	**0.0090**	**0.0231**	**−0.0362**
	(0.0020)	(0.0023)	(0.0009)	(0.0019)	(0.0070)	(0.0105)
Usually Me	**0.0308**	**0.0342**	**0.0176**	**0.0213**	0.0118	0.0110
	(0.0051)	(0.0068)	(0.0039)	(0.0044)	(0.0035)	(0.0031)
Shared Equally	**0.0297**	0.0122	**0.0322**	0.0262	0.0010	**0.0187**
	(0.0048)	(0.0024)	(0.0070)	(0.0053)	(0.0004)	(0.0055)
Usually My Partner	−0.0339	**−0.0385**	−0.0299	−0.0283	−0.0163	**0.0047**
	(0.0058)	(0.0077)	(0.0066)	(0.0059)	(0.0049)	(0.0014)
Always My Partner	**−0.0385**	**−0.0191**	**−0.0240**	**−0.0282**	**−0.0195**	**0.0018**
	(0.0061)	(0.0037)	(0.0052)	(0.0057)	(0.0059)	(0.0006)
Panel B: Women						
Married, 1st Cohabited						
Always Me	**−0.0489**	**−0.0222**	−0.0178	−0.0157	0.0116	0.0024
	(0.0077)	(0.0059)	(0.0082)	(0.0082)	(0.0077)	(0.0011)
Usually Me	−0.0001	−0.0118	0.0012	−0.0001	0.0018	0.0062
	(0.0006)	(0.0031)	(0.0006)	(0.0002)	(0.0012)	(0.0029)
Shared Equally	**0.0254**	0.0170	0.0125	0.0097	−0.0021	0.0087
	(0.0040)	(0.0046)	(0.0057)	(0.0051)	(0.0014)	(0.0041)
Usually My Partner	**0.0179**	**0.0143**	0.0035	0.0047	−0.0058	−0.0048
	(0.0028)	(0.0038)	(0.0016)	(0.0024)	(0.0039)	(0.0022)
Always My Partner	**0.0057**	**0.0027**	**0.0007**	**0.0014**	−0.0055	−0.0125
	(0.0009)	(0.0007)	(0.0003)	(0.0007)	(0.0037)	(0.0059)
Cohabiting						
Always Me	**−0.0626**	**−0.0229**	−0.0258	**−0.0517**	−0.0106	**0.0090**
	(0.0099)	(0.0076)	(0.0103)	(0.0101)	(0.0094)	(0.0018)
Usually Me	−0.0016	−0.0123	0.0014	−0.0029	−0.0019	**0.0220**
	(0.0011)	(0.0042)	(0.0006)	(0.0009)	(0.0017)	(0.0042)
Shared Equally	**0.0327**	0.0176	0.0182	**0.0325**	0.0018	**0.0287**
	(0.0052)	(0.0059)	(0.0074)	(0.0064)	(0.0016)	(0.0053)
Usually My Partner	**0.0238**	**0.0148**	**0.0052**	**0.0168**	0.0054	−0.0205
	(0.0039)	(0.0050)	(0.0021)	(0.0034)	(0.0048)	(0.0041)
Always My Partner	**0.0077**	**0.0028**	**0.0010**	**0.0054**	0.0053	**−0.0393**
	(0.0014)	(0.0010)	(0.0004)	(0.0011)	(0.0047)	(0.0072)

Notes: Robust standard errors in parentheses.

Bolded entries indicate marginal effects that constitute changes in excess of 10% from the observed distribution of responses for married persons who did not first cohabit.

differences are statistically significant and rather substantial in magnitude. However, even some of the smaller marginal effects represent substantial shifts in reported behavior. Bolded entries identify marginal effects that shift the average distribution reported by married persons who did not first cohabit by more than 10%.

Married men who first cohabited are substantially and significantly less likely to report that their partner "always" or "usually" prepares meals, washes dishes, or cleans as compared with married men who did not first cohabit, and more likely to report they always or usually performed the task. Many of these differences shift reported activity by more than 10%. While the marginal effects are statistically significant for shopping, they are not substantial. The marginal effects for repairs and bills are neither significant nor substantial. Differences between cohabiting men and married men who did not previously cohabit are even larger and extend to include repair and bill paying tasks. Again, most of the shifts are in the extreme values, though the fraction reporting shared responsibility does increase across the board and substantially for meal preparation, cleaning, and repair work.

For married women who first cohabited as compared to married women who did not first cohabit, the simulated marginal effects are significant for all tasks except bill paying, though only marginally so for shopping. The implied shifts are most substantial for meal preparation and dish washing, substantiating what men report, that married women who did first cohabit are less likely to always perform the activity and more likely to report that their partner performs the activity than married women who did not first cohabit. The simulated marginal effects for cohabiting women are generally larger and again focused more on the extreme values with some leeching into the shared category for meal preparation, shopping and repairs. Interestingly, while cohabiting men appear to report significant and substantial differences in bill paying responsibilities as compared to married men who did not first cohabit, cohabiting women do not.

Alternative specifications including indicators for recently formed relationships and measures of relationship duration generally find recently formed relationships do not have a statistically significant impact on sharing, but duration does. Controlling for respondent's age, longer lasting relationships are those that formed when the partners were younger. As younger persons face a longer time horizon, the benefits of specialization are greater and the cost of readjusting later is smaller, suggesting young persons should specialize more. Such appears to be the prediction as regards meal preparation, dish washing, and cleaning as the coefficients to duration in these equations when significant have a positive coefficient for men and a negative coefficient for women indicating that women are more likely to take responsibility for these tasks the longer lasting the relationship. The coefficients to relationship status, however, remain statistically significant indicating that the type of relationship is also significantly associated with specialization. Relationship status becomes less predictive of specialization for shopping, but more predictive for bill paying, with women who married without first cohabiting being significantly less likely and men who married without first cohabiting being significantly more likely to report responsibility. Results for repair work change little.

These results provide substantial support for the hypothesis that married couples specialize more than cohabiting couples, with women taking on more responsibility for the generally "female-typed" tasks of meal preparation, dishes, cleaning, and food shopping and men taking on more responsibility for repair work. There is also evidence that married couples who first cohabited on average share responsibility for the female-typed activities more than other married couples, but not as much as cohabiting couples – providing additional evidence that their behavior falls somewhere in the middle.

In sum, an analysis of who reports responsibility for the more narrowly defined tasks of meal preparation, dish washing, cleaning, food shopping, repair work, and bill paying provides substantial evidence of intrahousehold specialization and evidence in line with the proposed hypothesis that cohabiting couples specialize less than married couples. Fewer than 50% (and generally far less than 50%) of couple households report sharing responsibility for any given task and only about 3% report sharing responsibility for all six tasks, even though as singles they would have been solely responsible for them all. Using gender-neutral measures, married couples who did not first cohabit were found to report more specialization than currently cohabiting couples on almost all tasks, even after including a wide array of controls. Married couples who did first cohabit generally report more specialization than currently cohabiting couples, but less than married couples who did not first cohabit. Cohabiting couples are much less likely to specialize in bill paying as compared to married couples, not surprising as such couples are on average less confident about their relationship and so may be inclined to keep their finances separate. Specialization in dish washing, particularly as reported by men, is also less evident. This may be because dish washing is the task that is least likely to require skill and so can be shared at low cost. These results do not tell us whether the behavior is driven by the relationship status or by individual preferences that drive both task allocation and relationship status. However, estimates from a linear, couple-specific fixed effects model indicate that couples transitioning from cohabitation to marriage do report specializing more in all tasks following marriage, with differences in bill paying being particularly statistically significant. These results while not definitively indicative of a causal relation, are a step in that direction.

Joint modeling of reported responsibilities using an ordered probit that takes into account who performs the task reveals significant and substantial differences by relationship status. Women (men) who married without first cohabiting are much more (less) likely to report specializing in meal preparation, dish washing, and cleaning as compared to those who married after cohabiting or those who are cohabiting. The differences between those who are currently cohabiting and those who married without first cohabiting are similar in the case of food shopping. Men who are cohabiting report significantly and substantially less specialization in repair work as compared to men who married without previously cohabiting, a result mirrored by women. Cohabiting men were more likely to report responsibility for bill paying as compared to men who married without previously cohabiting, but the differences were not significantly nor substantially different for cohabiting women. Again, these results are not necessarily causal and there are too few observations per individual to allow estimation of an ordered model with fixed effects. Those who married without first cohabiting are on average about 10 years older than those currently cohabiting and may have grown up during a more socially conservative era when gendered behavioral norms were more customary.

8. CONCLUSION

The nature of couple households has changed considerably in the last 50 years with cohabitation rates rising and marriage rates falling. These changes have the potential to impact many outcomes, time use not the least of those. Couple households are able to pool their resources, take advantage of economies of scale and of intra-household specialization. The degree to which they do so likely differs from couple to couple, but may also differ by relationship type.

While a simple model predicts that persons entering into cohabiting relationships will specialize less than persons entering marriages if there are costs associated with changing activities, because on average the expected duration of cohabiting relationships is shorter than that for marriages, more complex bargaining models can yield similar predictions. Data from the 2001–2019 waves of the Australian HILDA survey are used to examine how time use changes as men and women transition into and out of relationships and also how reported specialization differs by relationship type.

Raw statistics indicate that on average, all partnered men report spending almost 1 hour less on housework as compared to unpartnered men (6.2 vs. 7.0). Partnered women average about 3.5 hours more than unpartnered women, with the differential higher for married (almost 6 hours) and lower for cohabiting women (less than 1 hour). Controlling for a wide array of control variables - including own education, household composition, and residential characteristics - nets similar differentials between partnered and unpartnered persons in an OLS specification. Of course, some of this differential may be attributable to selection.

To account for selection, the panel nature of the data is exploited to control for individual-specific, time invariant preferences and productivity that influence time use and may be associated with partnership formation. Doing so, we find that men entering relationships do not report spending significantly less time on housework and the effect observed for women is much smaller – a 1.2 hour increase for those entering cohabitations and a 3.7 hour increase for those entering directly into marriages. These results suggest that men who report less time on housework and women who report more time on housework select into relationships. Women transitioning into marriages from cohabitations report increasing their housework time by 0.9 hours, making up about one-third of the difference between these populations. How individuals would behave during this transition was not clearly predicted by theory but the results suggest some adjustment, a result consistent with the results from the task analysis. Extending the fixed effects analysis to consider jointly outdoor tasks, errands, and paid employment as well as housework provides some further though weak evidence of greater specialization in married couple households.

As these time uses each comprise a wide array of activities and different individuals may specialize in different activities, it is perhaps not surprising that evidence of intrahousehold specialization is difficult to observe clearly using time use data. To address this concern, we examine survey responses regarding who performs six much more narrowly defined household tasks: meal preparation, dish washing, cleaning, food shopping, bill paying, and repair work. With the possible exception of repair work, these are tasks that every household must complete. Singles have to do the tasks themselves (or hire outside help), while couples can specialize. There is substantial evidence from the raw data of intra-household specialization within couple households. Couples report sharing responsibility for all these tasks only about 3% of the time. Ordered probit analysis controlling for a wide array of variables reveals that specialization is greatest in married couples that did not first cohabit and least in cohabiting couples across all tasks. This difference is statistically significant in 19 of 24 cases (two genders, two relationship types, six tasks). To explore whether specialization changes as cohabiting couples marry, a simple linear model with couple-specific fixed effects is estimated. Results indicate that both men and women report increased specialization in all six tasks when transitioning to a marriage from a cohabitation, a differential that is statistically significant almost 60% of the time.

Joint estimation of ordered probits for all six tasks that take into account who does the activity not just the degree of specialization indicate that on average both men and women report that married women who did not first cohabit with their partner specialize more than other married women who specialize more than cohabiters in female-typed activities (meal preparation, dish washing, cleaning, and shopping). Both men and women on average report married men specialize more than cohabiting men in repair work. Bill paying is not as specialized an activity, particularly for cohabiting couples who, given the uncertainty of the relationship, are likely to keep their finances separate. That there is evidence of specialization in dish washing is a bit surprising as no particular skill is required for that task but bargaining theory suggests women entering marriages may feel more secure and so willing to take on that responsibility. Another unexpected finding is that the correlation terms suggest that when one partner reports specializing more for unobserved reasons on one activity, they are also more likely to report specializing in all six activities. One might expect some tradeoff between activities.

In sum, these share data provide substantial evidence that on average married couples specialize more than cohabiting couples, that couples transitioning from cohabitations to marriages do increase their specialization but may not specialize as much as other married couples, and that on average women bear the brunt of the specialization in meal preparation, dish washing, cleaning, and food shopping, while men on average bear the brunt of repair work. As shopping and bill paying are included in the "errands" time use measure, the fact that reports of specialization differ a bit between household members may obfuscate any pattern with respect to this activity in the time use analysis.

Given the shift away from marriage and toward cohabitation, it would be valuable to better understand both how and why time allocation differs between married and cohabiting couples. The assumption underlying this analysis is that cohabitors are less committed to their relationship and so less likely to accept a bargain that reduces the value of their alternative options. It would be useful to better understand the heterogenous motivations underlying the decision to cohabit rather than marry and use those motivations to model subsequent choices. Cohabiting couples who have children together may be more committed to their relationship. In addition, the birth of a child in general may result in revised household responsibilities. While the analysis here controls for the number of preschool age children, it does not directly examine changes around the time a child is born. These are avenues for future exploration.

The evolution of household time use and specialization influences and is influenced by market opportunities. This is true in the case of women who now face substantially better employment options, but is also true of such market-based alternatives to household services as childcare, ready cooked meals, and handy man operations. The evidence presented here suggests that persons in different types of relationships engage in different time use behavior. It would be of interest to know if they utilize market alternatives differently as well, as such behavior has the potential in turn to impact markets.

ACKNOWLEDGMENTS

This chapter uses unit record data from the Household, Income and Labor Dynamics in Australia (HILDA) Survey. The HILDA Project was initiated and is funded by the Australian Government Department of Social Services (DSS) and is managed by the Melbourne Institute of Applied Economic and Social Research (Melbourne Institute). The findings and views reported in this chapter, however, are those of the author and should not be attributed to either DSS or the Melbourne Institute. Research assistance from James Stratton is gratefully acknowledged. Thanks are due referees, including Shoshana Grossbard, who provided excellent suggestions.

NOTES

1. The sample is restricted to women less than age 45 in 2000 who were part of the original sample and in a relationship in January 2000.
2. 2020 data were not employed due to the expectation that COVID-19 likely changed behavior.
3. Less than 200 couples reporting peculiar, conflicting and/or overlapping relationships are dropped. Examples include couples reporting being married then cohabiting then married or married, divorced, and remarried or reporting dates that differ by more than three years.
4. Not all are included in each analysis as sample restrictions vary a bit and the availability of each dependent variable is not guaranteed.
5. Prior relationships are difficult to track. Unpartnered individuals who report they have never been married and individuals who were in a relationship when first observed are

included in the sample even if they had a previous cohabitation or marriage. No restriction is imposed on their partner's prior relationships.

6. Typical time is reported in hours in 2000, but in finer detail in subsequent years. All specifications include year dummies which should on average account for this differential measurement.

7. All the time measures are trimmed at approximately their 99th percentile (corresponding to cutoffs of 60 for housework, 30 for outdoor activities, 28 for errands, and 80 for paid employment). The sum of time spent on these four activities is also restricted to be no more than 110 hours per week.

8. Reported time is most variable for those entering a marriage not preceded by a cohabitation for which the sample size is the smallest by a factor of at least five.

9. That the change in time use in the year of a change is not generally as great as the change in subsequent years could be because, in the case of very recent partnerships, time allocations have not yet adjusted to reflect the new relationship. The empirical specification reported below will include a control for recent partnerships in order to account for such effects.

10. A dummy variable identifying cohabiters who were later observed married is never statistically significant, possibly because this outcome is only imperfectly observed, and not included in the results reported here.

11. A small number of respondents in households with two adults and no children over the age of four who replied the tasks were "Shared equally among household members" were recoded as "Shared equally between partner & self." Other responses were coded as missing.

REFERENCES

Altindag, D., Nunley, J., & Seals, A. (2017). Child-custody reform and the division of labor in the household. *Review of Economics of the Household, 15*, 833–856.

Barcus, J. (2019). My divorce cost me $17,695 — These were the most surprising expenses I faced. https://www.businessinsider.com/cost-of-divorce-unexpected-surprising-expenses-2019-8. Accessed on May 26, 2022.

Baxter, J., Hewitt, B., & Haynes, M. (2008, May). Life course transitions and housework: Marriage, parenthood, and time on housework. *Journal of Marriage and Family, 70*, 259–272.

Beaudry, P., & Lewis, E. (2014, April). Do male-female wage differentials reflect differences in the return to skill? Cross-city evidence from 1980–2000. *American Economic Journal: Applied Economics, 6*, 178–194.

Becker, G. (1965). A theory of the allocation of time. *The Economic Journal, 75*, 493–517.

Becker, G. (1981). *A treatise on the family*. Harvard University Press.

Bonke, J., Deding, M., Lausten, M., & Stratton, L. (2008). Intra-household specialization in housework in the United States and Denmark. *Social Science Quarterly, 89*, 1023–1043.

Borra, C., Browning, M., & Sevilla, A. (2021). Marriage and housework. *Oxford Economic Papers, 73*, 479–508.

Bumpass, L., & Sweet, J. (1989). National estimates of cohabitation. *Demography, 26*, 615–625.

Chiappori, P. (1992). Collective labor supply and welfare. *Journal of Political Economy, 100*, 437–467.

Chiappori, P., Iyigun, M., Lafortune, J., & Weiss, Y. (2017). Changing the rules midway: The impact of granting alimony rights on existing and newly formed partnerships. *The Economic Journal, 127*, 1874–1905.

Foster, G., & Stratton, L. (2018). Do significant labor market events change who does the chores? Paid work, housework, and power in mixed-gender Australian households. *Journal of Population Economics, 31*, 483–519.

Greenwood, J., & Guner, N. (2009). Marriage and divorce since World War II: Analyzing the role of technological progress on the formation of households. In D. Acemoglu, K. Rogoff, & M. Woodford (Eds.), *NBER Macroeconomics Annual 2008* (Vol. 23). University of Chicago Press.

Grossbard-Shechtman, A. (1984). A theory of allocation of time in markets for labour and marriage. *The Economic Journal, 94*, 863–882.

Grossbard, S., Gimenez-Nadal, J., & Molina, J. (2015). Household production and racial intermarriage. In S. Grossbard (Ed.), *The marriage motive: A price theory of marriage* (pp. 123–163). Springer.

Gupta, S. (1999). The effects of transitions in marital status on men's performance of housework. *Journal of Marriage and Family*, *61*, 700–711.

Horowitz, J., Graf, N., & Livingston, G. (2019, November). *Marriage and cohabitation in the U.S.* Pew Research Center.

Hurst, A. (2021). Average cost of a wedding: By state and feature. https://www.valuepenguin.com/average-cost-of-wedding. Accessed on May 26, 2022.

Juhn, C., & McCue, K. (2017). Specialization then and now: Marriage, children, and the gender earnings gap across cohorts. *The Journal of Economic Perspectives*, *31*, 183–204.

Juster, F., Ono, H., & Stafford, F. (2003). An assessment of alternative measures of time use. *Sociological Methodology*, *33*, 19–54.

Lafortune, J., & Low, C. (2017). Tying the double-knot: The role of assets in marriage commitment. *The American Economic Review: Papers & Proceedings*, *107*, 163–167.

Lamidi, E., Manning, W., & Brown, S. (2019). Change in the stability of first premarital cohabitation among women in the United States, 1983–2013. *Demography*, *56*, 427–450.

Lillard, L., Brien, M., & Waite, L. (1995). Premarital cohabitation and subsequent marital dissolution: A matter of self-selection. *Demography*, *32*, 437–457.

Lundberg, S., & Pollak, R. (1996, Autumn). Bargaining and distribution in marriage. *The Journal of Economic Perspectives*, *10*, 139–158.

Lundberg, S., Pollak, R., & Stearns, J. (2016, Spring). Family inequality: Diverging patterns in marriage, cohabitation and childbearing. *The Journal of Economic Perspectives*, *30*, 79–102.

Lundberg, S., Pollak, R., & Wales, T. (1997, Summer). Do husbands and wives pool their resources: Evidence from the United Kingdom child benefit. *Journal of Human Resources*, *32*, 463–480.

Manser, M., & Brown, M. (1980). Marriage and household decision making: A bargaining analysis. *International Economic Review*, *21*, 31–44.

McElroy, M., & Horney, M. (1981). Nash-bargained decisions: Toward a generalization of the theory of demand. *International Economic Review*, *22*, 333–349.

Nunley, J., & Seals, R. (2011). Child-custody reform, marital investment in children, and the labor supply of married mothers. *Labour Economics*, *18*, 14–24.

Polachek, S. (1975). Potential biases in measuring male-female discrimination. *Journal of Human Resources*, *10*, 205–229.

Pollak, R. (2013). *Allocating household time: When does efficiency imply specialization.* NBER Working Paper No. 19178.

Reinhold, S. (2010). Reassessing the link between premarital cohabitation and marital instability. *Demography*, *47*, 719–733.

Siminski, P., & Yetsenga, R. (2022). Specialization, comparative advantage, and the sexual division of labor. *Journal of Labor Economics*, *40*, 851–887.

South, S., & Spitze, G. (1994). Housework in marital and nonmarital households. *American Sociological Review*, *59*, 327–347.

Stevenson, B. (2007). The impact of divorce laws on marriage-specific capital. *Journal of Labor Economics*, *25*, 75–94.

Stevenson, B., & Wolfers, J. (2007). Marriage and divorce: Changes and their driving forces. *The Journal of Economic Perspectives*, *21*(Spring), 27–52.

Stratton, L. (2005). *The degree of intrahousehold specialization in housework and how specialization varies across couple households.* Presented at SOLE.

Watson, N., & Wooden, M. (2012). The HILDA survey: A case study in the design and development of a successful household panel study. *Longitudinal and Life Course Studies*, *3*, 369–381.

Wernli, B., & Henchoz, C. (2011). End of the conjugal relationship, gender and domestic tasks in Switzerland. *Population-E*, *66*, 637–662.

APPENDIX

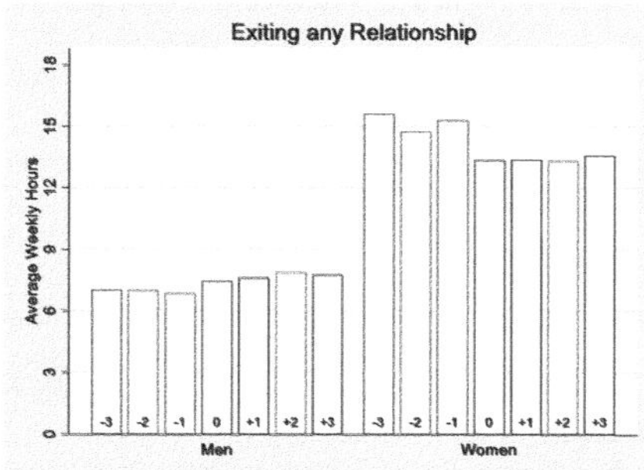

Responses from at least 1,035 men and 1,265 women.

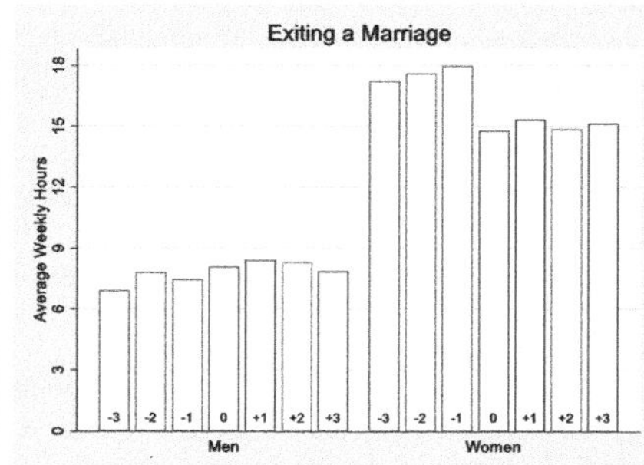

Responses from at least 137 men and 183 women.

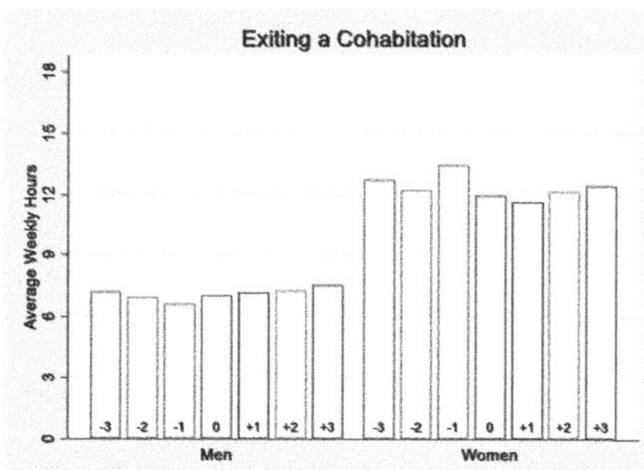

Responses from at least 567 men and 660 women.

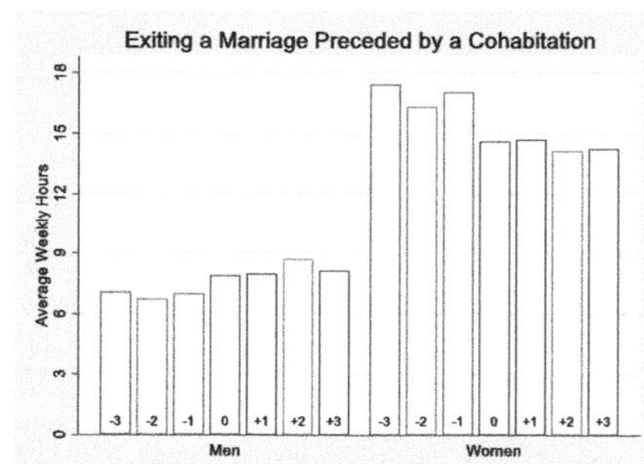

Responses from at least 331 men and 422 women.

Fig. A1. Time Spent on Housework as Individuals Exit Relationships.
Source: Data from the 2001–2019 waves of HILDA for persons responding at least once before and once after the end of a relationship. '0' reflects the transition year, -# the number of years before, and +# the number of years after.

CHANGE AND CONTINUITY IN AMERICANS' WORK DAY CHARACTERISTICS, 2019 TO 2021

Sarah M. Flood and Katie R. Genadek

ABSTRACT

The COVID-19 pandemic spurred major, and possibly enduring, changes in paid work. In this chapter, we explore the continuity and change in several work day dimensions, including where it is performed, the amount of time spent working, the length of the work day, and who people are with when they work, as well as variation across population subgroups. We use nationally representative data from the American Time Use Survey (ATUS) to analyze change across the 2019 to 2021 period. While the shift to working primarily at home in 2020 is dramatic and continuing into 2021, working primarily at the workplace remains the modal experience for Americans. We find differences by gender, education, parental status, and age in which workers perform their jobs at home, and we find much more continuity in how much people work and when they work.

Keywords: COVID-19; paid work; time use; inequality; remote work; work day characteristics

1. INTRODUCTION

The dramatic effects of the COVID-19 pandemic on the daily lives of Americans have received, and continue to receive, extensive scholarly attention.[1] In the United States, the coronavirus resulted in a public health crisis that led to stay-at-home orders and restrictions on who could leave their homes and upended the daily routines surrounding work, school, and leisure. For many Americans, the COVID-19 pandemic changed work, especially *where* work happened. However, there was unevenness regarding which workers could perform their jobs at home

Time Use in Economics
Research in Labor Economics, Volume 51, 219–245

ISSN: 0147-9121/doi:10.1108/S0147-912120230000051009

(Brynjolfsson et al., 2020), which parents could juggle work with distance learning and day care closures (Collins et al., 2021; Fabrizio et al., 2021), and which workers were most at risk of unemployment due to holding jobs in sectors most severely impacted by the pandemic (Dey et al., 2020).

The temporary changes in work following the onset of COVID-19 have led to discussions about the implications of the COVID-19 pandemic for the future of paid work (Alon et al., 2020; Ng et al., 2021) and reinvigorated scholarly interest in research on telework (Lyttelton et al., 2022; Pabilonia & Victoria, 2022). Much of the discussion prior to COVID-19 centered around flexibility, with telework being one of the features of flexibility, and detailed the characteristics of teleworkers, the reasons they teleworked, and the implications of telework for individuals and organizations (Allen et al., 2015; Bailey & Kurland, 2002; Noonan & Glass, 2012; Tavares, 2017). The literature informing our knowledge of COVID-19 impacts on work is often based on pre-COVID-19 data (Pabilonia & Victoria, 2022) or subpopulation analyses of workers (Fan & Moen, 2022; Teodorovicz et al., 2021b).

With telework seemingly a permanent fixture in the post-COVID-19 economy (Bloom, 2020), there is a need for broad population-level analyses comparing work prior to and during COVID-19. We fill the need by examining multiple dimensions of work, including where as well as the timing, duration, and in-person contact during work, and the extent to which the dramatic ways that the pandemic affected who worked and where they worked at COVID-19 onset persisted or whether there is a return to pre-pandemic work patterns. Building on existing descriptive evidence using the American Time Use Survey (ATUS) showing that the percent of workers working at home increased from just under one quarter in 2019 to 38.1% in 2021 (BLS, 2022b), this research serves as a foundation for the burgeoning literature on hybrid work schedules (Bloom et al., 2022), the prevalence of remote work (Hansen et al., 2023), productivity of at-home workers (Morikawa, 2023), and spillover impacts on housing and migration (Lee & Huang, 2022; Lei & Liu, 2022; Yörük, 2022).

More people were working from home during the COVID-19 period compared to the pre-COVID-19 period (Brynjolfsson et al., 2020; BLS, 2022b), but this was far from universal among workers (BLS, 2019, 2022a). In this chapter, we conduct the first detailed, population-level analysis of American work day characteristics in the COVID-19 era, including the location, timing, duration, and copresence of others during work. Our focus is on variation across work locations and population subgroups, and how these dimensions of work change over time, comparing COVID-19 onset data from May 2020 through December 2020 to the 2019 pre-pandemic period and to 2021. Understanding the aspects of work that are changing (and remaining stable) and heterogeneity in the population subgroups experiencing these changes are critical for individual health and well-being and employer responses to these changes. The importance of this endeavor is underscored by predictions that working from home will be a major part of the post-COVID-19 economy (Bloom, 2020).

We begin in Section 2 by situating the 2019 to 2021 period in context with an analysis of trends in where people worked from 2003 to 2021. Then we show heterogeneity in the 2019 to 2021 patterns by gender, education, parental status, and age. In Section 3, we examine more detailed characteristics of the work day from 2019 to 2021, and how work days vary by primary place of work over this period. We then analyze whether COVID-19 impacted working in multiple locations during a single work day in Section 4. Section 5 presents results from working at home versus the workplace by day of the week from 2019 to 2021. Finally, in Section 6 we further investigate working in the company of others, focusing on differences between parents and non-parents who work primarily at home.

2. PLACE OF WORK

The COVID-19 pandemic and the short-term restrictions placed on daily life to help mitigate the transmission of the coronavirus changed the world of work for many in the United States. Unemployment reached record highs in April 2020 as a result of restaurant and daycare closures, and major changes to industries, such as tourism and entertainment (Kong & Prinz, 2020). The COVID-19 pandemic affected workers unevenly with women, young workers, low-educated workers, and Hispanics disproportionately likely to experience job loss early in the pandemic (Dey et al., 2020). Employed individuals were encouraged to work from home when possible, and entire industries quickly adjusted to having fully remote workforces. When schools shifted to distance learning, many parents had to quickly devise strategies for managing distance learning as they were trying to work, both inside and outside of the home. Mothers of young children were the group that experienced the largest drop in employment in 2020 underscoring the impacts of distance learning as well as broader labor market changes for employment (Collins et al., 2021; Dunatchik et al., 2021; Fabrizio et al., 2021; Petts et al., 2021).

With this context in mind, we compare the daily work experiences of employed individuals over time. Our analysis is based on repeated cross-sections of data from the American Time Use Survey (ATUS) (Flood, Sayer et al., 2022).[2] ATUS data have been collected on an ongoing basis since 2003. However, due to the COVID-19 pandemic, data collection was paused starting March 17, 2020. Data collection resumed May 10, 2020. The gap in data collection means that full year time-use estimates for 2020 cannot be calculated, but it is possible to compare the pandemic period (May 10, 2020 to Dec 31, 2020) to surrounding years of data to understand the impact of COVID-19 on work-related behavior (Flood, Genadek, et al., 2022).[3] Using these nationally representative time diary data, we leverage rich detail on the activities individuals engaged in over the course of a 24-hour period as well as where, when, and who was with them.

We include individuals ages 18 and older in our analysis if they engaged in one or more minutes of paid work activities and activities related to paid work, such as socializing and eating.[4] The time diary also captures where people work for each distinct report of paid work on the diary day. While the data contain 15 distinct places (e.g., home, work, restaurant) and 11 distinct modes of transportation (e.g., car, bus, airplane) where work can be reported as being performed, several are very uncommon (e.g., working while bicycling). Across the 2019–2021 period, only 6.6% of activities reported were performed at a location besides home or work, limiting our ability to further disaggregate the other locations where work is performed. Thus, we differentiate working at home (home), at the workplace (work), and somewhere else (other), which includes working at any of the other 24 locations/modes of transportation on the survey day. We then classify respondents as working *primarily* in one of the three work location categories when more than half of the daily work time is spent at that location (Restrepo & Zeballos, 2022).[5] Our initial look at trends in where Americans worked using ATUS data from 2003 to 2021 is based on 81,093 diary days from Americans ages 18 and older.[6]

Fig. 1 shows the proportion of workers in each year between 2003 and 2021 working primarily at the workplace, at home, and somewhere else on the ATUS diary day.[7] While there was a small decrease in the proportion of workers working primarily at the workplace between 2003 and 2019 (from 83% in 2003 to 81% in 2019), and a corresponding small increase in the proportion working primarily at home (12% in 2003 to 13% in 2019), the sharp shift in where people worked occurred in 2020 as a result of the COVID-19 pandemic. In 2020, we estimate that 62.1% of workers worked primarily at the workplace and 33.9% worked primarily at home. And we observe a 5.5 percentage point increase in working primarily at the workplace in 2021 (67.6%) compared to 2020, which is

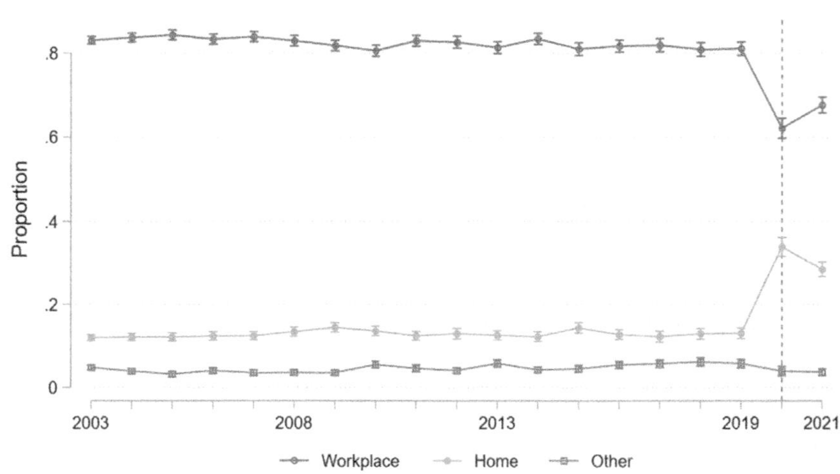

Fig. 1. Primary Work Location, 2003–2021.
Notes: Adjusted estimates based on models for years 2003 to 2021 that parallel models for 2019 to 2021 in Table A3. X-axis is survey year. Dashed vertical line indicates start of COVID-19 pandemic in 2020.

consistent with data from the Current Population Survey (BLS, 2022a). Despite the movement back to the workplace, the proportion of workers doing their jobs at the workplace on the ATUS diary day in 2021 remains substantially lower than pre-COVID-19 levels. Likewise, working primarily from home decreased by 5.5 percentage points between 2020 and 2021 to 28.4%. The proportion of respondents working somewhere other than at home or a workplace is incredibly consistent across the period. About 4% of respondents reported a primary work location other than home or the workplace on the diary day, and this reaches a high of 6.1% in 2018. This fell to 3.9% in 2020 (although this difference is not statistically significant) and remained at about that level in 2021. Thus, being physically at the workplace remains – even during 2020 – the modal experience for American workers.

A birds-eye view, however, masks heterogeneity in the kinds of jobs that can be performed at home and the characteristics of individuals who hold jobs that tend to require working on site versus those that can be done elsewhere. Given the relative stability of where people worked prior to the pandemic, we focus the rest of our analyses on the 2019 to 2021 period. We consider the 2019 estimates to be the pre-pandemic period, with the estimates from 2020 (May 10, 2020 to December 31, 2020) being the peak-pandemic period. While 2021 is still during the COVID-19 pandemic, this year also included the introduction of COVID-19 vaccines, the return to schooling for many children, and reductions in public policies limiting interaction, we consider this the precursor to the post-COVID-19 era.[8] Restricting our analysis to respondents who are aged 18 and older and who engaged in paid work on the ATUS diary day, our 2019–2021 sample includes 8,378 individuals.[9] We show the patterns of working at home stratified by gender, education, age, and parental status (see Fig. 2A–D).[10] Fig. 2A and C both show that while both men and women and parents and non-parents were more likely to work from home in 2020 compared to 2019, the increase was larger for women and for parents compared to men and non-parents, respectively. By 2021, the COVID-19-period gender gap returned to 2019 levels, and the parental gap that emerged during the pandemic was no longer evident in 2021. By contrast, prior to the pandemic, individuals with a college degree were slightly more likely to work at home than those in other education groups, but the education gap widened dramatically during the COVID-19 period (Fig. 2B). Working at home was an opportunity largely limited to workers with a college degree with more than half of college-educated workers performing their work primarily from home compared to less than 20% of workers with a high school degree in 2020. These gaps remain large in 2021 despite a larger reduction in the proportion of college-educated workers performing their jobs from home between 2020 and 2021 than for those without a college degree. Workers ages 18 to 30 are the least likely to work at home in each year (Fig. 2D). Pre-COVID-19 age gradients in the likelihood of working at home were much less pronounced in 2020 and 2021 compared to 2019.

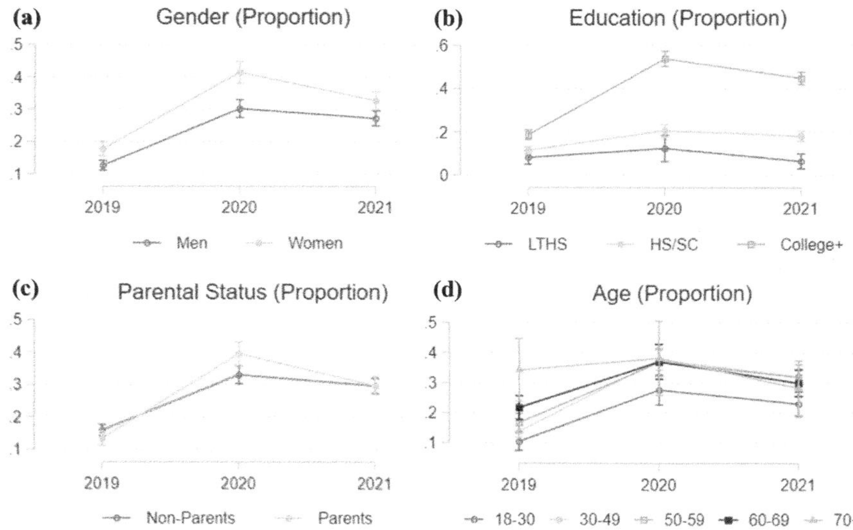

Fig. 2A–D. Gender, Education, Parental Status, and Age Differences in Working Primarily at Home by Year, 2019–2021.
Notes: Adjusted estimates based on models in Table A3. X-axis is survey year. LTHS=Less than High School Degree; HS/SC=High School Degree or Some College; College + = College Degree or Higher.

3. WORK DAY CHARACTERISTICS

Along with the work location changes for many Americans during and following the COVID-19 pandemic, it is likely that other aspects of the average work day changed as well. Thus, using the 2019 to 2021 ATUS data we analyze the amount of time per day spent working based on the time diary reports, and we also leverage unique aspects of time diaries to examine dimensions of work day length, work day timing, and copresence of others while working.[11] Given the dramatic changes in where people work, we investigate these work day characteristics by work location (see Table A4).[12]

Impacts of the pandemic on work time are mixed with workers in some industries, such as healthcare, working fewer hours (Hu & Dill, 2021; Kaushik, 2021; Wilensky, 2022) while employees in the service and entertainment industries working more due to limited staff availability after the initial shut downs (Huang et al., 2020). Despite the large shift toward working primarily at home as documented in the previous section, the amount of time that workers spend performing their jobs on the average day has remained stable. Our measure of time spent working comes from the time diary and is based on all the distinct reports of paid work reported on the diary day. The duration of each instance of paid work is summed across the day for each respondent and averaged across respondents who worked on the diary day to create a population average of work time for each year. Fig. 3A shows that the average amount of time worked per day was the same in 2019 and 2020 (7.6 hours) and increased slightly to 7.8 hours

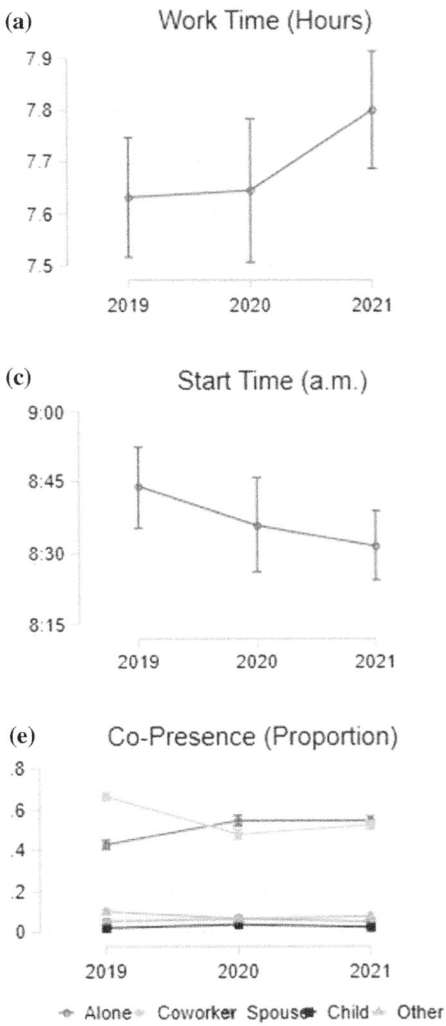

Fig. 3A–E. Work Day Characteristics by Year, 2019–2021.
Notes: Adjusted estimates based on models in Table A3. X-axis is survey year. Lines on Figure E indicate the proportion that respondents spent any time with types of people during paid work.

per day in 2021, though this difference was not statistically significant (see panel A of Table A3).

Previous evidence about how much one works based on where they work is mixed. Earlier work suggested that telework was often associated with longer work hours (Glass & Noonan, 2016; Noonan & Glass, 2012), though this was not the case during the pandemic for full-time white-collar workers (Teodorovicz et al., 2021a). Like Restrepo and Zeballos (2022), we find that the amount of time worked per day across years varied by where people worked (Fig. 4A and Panel A of Table A4). Work time was stable (just above 8 hours) between 2019 and 2021 for the workers who spent the majority of the work time at the workplace. And, prior to the pandemic, working at home was associated with substantially fewer minutes spent working than those working at the workplace (about 2.5 hours or 156 minutes per day). Total time spent working for those primarily working from home increased during the pandemic and again in 2021, but still did not reach levels of time spent working for those working primarily at their workplace. Time spent working from home was one and a half hours (92 minutes)

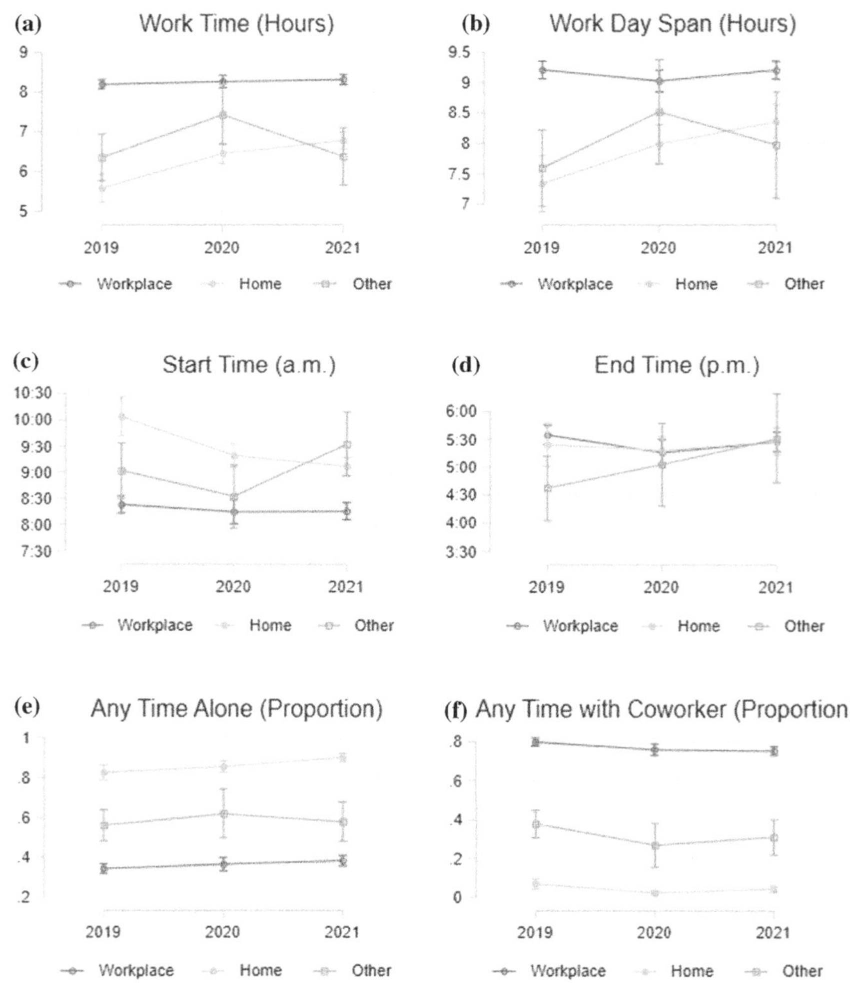

Fig. 4A–F. Work Day Characteristics by Primary Work Location and Year, 2019–2021.

Notes: Adjusted estimates based on models in Table A4. X-axis is survey year.

less on average per day than the average total minutes spent working by those working at the workplace in 2021.

The work day span (Teodorovicz et al., 2021b) indicates the length of time between the start of the first work activity in the day and the end of the last work activity of the day, making it distinct from the amount of time worked. There is some evidence that the work day span increased during the pandemic (DeFilippis et al., 2020; Teodorovicz et al., 2021a). We show a negligible decrease in the work day span between 2019 and 2020 followed by a slight increase in the work day span from 2020 to 2021 (Fig. 3B). The work day span patterns by where people work is similar to what we observed for work time – stability for individuals who work at their workplace and lengthening work day spans for individuals who work primarily at home between 2019 and 2021. Still, however, the work day span is shorter for those working at-home compared to those working at their workplace across all years.

We also examine the two components of the work day span – work start time and work end time – as distinct attributes of the work day. Fig. 3C and D plot work start time and work end time across the 2019 to 2021 period and Fig. 4C and D show these patterns by work location. Work start times were slightly earlier in 2020 and 2021 compared to 2019 (Fig. 3C). This was driven, though, by at-home workers whose average start time shifted from about 10:05 a.m. in 2019 to 9:20 a.m. in 2020 (see Fig. 4C and Panel C of Table A4). The average work start time of those at the workplace was about 8:20 a.m. across the 2019 to 2021 period. Work end times were 14 minutes earlier in 2020 compared to 2019, shifting from about 5:31 p.m. to 5:17 p.m. in 2020, but then returned in 2021 to similar levels as in 2019 (Fig. 3D). Fig. 4D shows convergence in the end of the work day by work location in 2021.

The final work day characteristic we examine is who else is present during paid work activities prior to the pandemic and during the pandemic. Prior to the COVID-19 pandemic, many employees in the United States likely had contact with others, especially coworkers or clients, depending on the industry and occupation. Patterns of social contact during work, however, shifted during the pandemic with the increase in remote work (Carlsten et al., 2021). Fig. 3E uses information from the time diary that indicates who else is in the room to describe the copresence of other types of people during paid work. The categories we show are overlapping; that is, they capture the proportion of respondents reporting on the day that they were ever alone or with a coworker, spouse, child, or someone else. The presence of a spouse, child, or a non-coworker during paid work activities was fairly uncommon between 2019 and 2021. We see decreases, though, in the proportion of workers with a coworker during work (0.67–0.48 between 2019 and 2020) and an increase in the share of workers who report being alone during paid work (43%–55% from 2019 to 2020). Working with a coworker increased slightly in 2021 but did not return to 2019 levels. Fig. 4E and F show dramatic differences, as would be expected, in workers who report being alone or with coworkers based on where they work. Those who work at home are more likely to report being alone and much less likely to report being with coworkers than those who work at the workplace.

As a robustness check, we conduct the same analyses just discussed for ATUS respondents who worked 4 hours or more on the ATUS diary day.[13] We find little variation in the amount of total time spent working per day across the 2019–2021 period or based on whether workers spend their day working primarily at the workplace or primarily at home. For those working at least 4 hours on the diary day, there is some evidence that the work day span is longer for those who work primarily at home compared to those working at the workplace or elsewhere. Longer work day spans among these at-home workers are driven by later work end times and presumably by workers interspersing more non-work activities in on the days they work primarily at home. Such activities might include laundry, running errands, or longer breaks filled by walks or phone calls. Overall, these results suggest that population-level differences between at-home and workplace workers (e.g., the shorter average duration of paid work at home and shorter work span) are partially explained by workers who are working shorter days, perhaps checking in with work on days they are not working or checking work email on weekends.

4. WORKING AT MULTIPLE LOCATIONS

How workers allocate their work time across locations was of increasing interest prior to the pandemic given technological advancements allowing many workers to perform their jobs using a computer with an internet connection from any location. Research focused on the 2003 to 2017 ATUS found that 72% of employed people performed all of their work at the workplace, though this declined by 19 minutes per day between 2003–2007 and 2013–2017 for individuals in professional jobs (Krantz-Kent, 2019). Using the same data source, the ATUS, we examine how a global pandemic coupled with technological capabilities transformed where people work.

Our previous analyses categorized the place of work based on where the *majority* of work time was spent differentiating between home, the workplace, and other locations. While simple to understand, this approach masks some of the complexity of where people do their work. For example, it oversimplifies the work days that begin at home and end at the workplace or vice versa and work days where a lunch meeting at a restaurant is sandwiched between working at the office. ATUS data allow us to describe the nuances of working in multiple locations on a single day. Accordingly, we examine combinations of work performed at home, at the workplace, and somewhere else on the diary day. Similar to the work of Krantz-Kent (2019), who used the same data source to examine the 2003 to 2017 period, we provide a snapshot of work location combinations focused on 2019 to 2021 to understand changes during the COVID-19 period.

Fig. 5 shows combinations of work performed at the workplace, at home, and in other locations across the 2019 to 2021 period.[14] Most workers in each year perform their jobs only at their workplace: 68% in 2019 to 53% in 2020 and back to 57% in 2021. While there was a big increase in working only at home in 2020, which coincided with the COVID-19 pandemic, this was the case for only 33% of

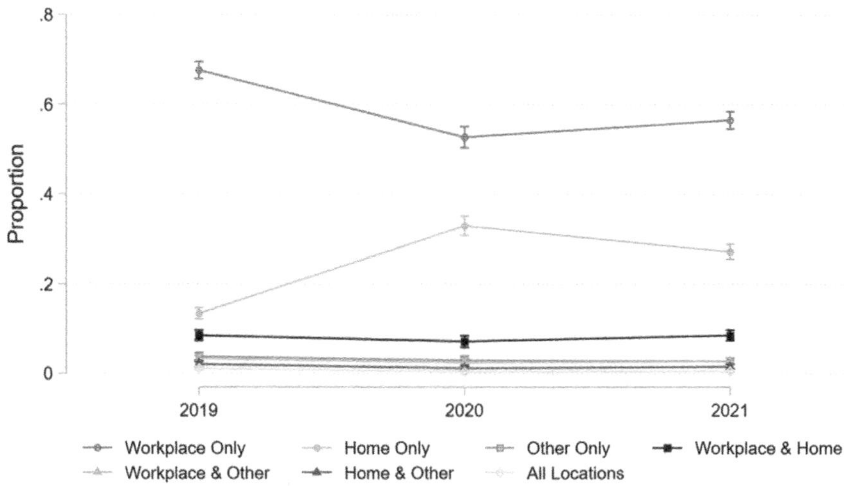

Fig. 5. Work Location Combinations by Year, 2019–2021.
Notes: Adjusted estimates based on models for years 2019 to 2021 that parallel those shown in Table A4. X-axis is survey year.

workers. Workers who spent time working at both the workplace and at home on the same day were the next largest group representing about 8% of workers across the three years. It is quite uncommon to only work somewhere other than the workplace or home and to combine other locations with the workplace or home and to work in all locations on a single day. The four least common work location combinations account for about 10% of respondents across each of the three periods.

5. PLACE OF WORK AND DAY OF THE WEEK

While there has been a dramatic increase in work being performed at home during the COVID-19 pandemic, it may also be the case that work at home tends to cluster on specific days of the week. Perhaps Friday or Monday are good days to work at home because they allow you to ease into or out of the work week. Or maybe Wednesday is ideal as a way to break up the week. The ATUS data are sufficiently large to make a comparison of the share of people primarily working at the workplace and at home across days of the week. We omit work in other locations because there are only a small number of observations on each day. Because most paid work tends to occur on weekdays as opposed to weekends, we limit our analysis to Monday through Friday.

Fig. 6A and B present the proportion of workers performing their work primarily at the workplace and at home, respectively, on the ATUS diary day.[15] In Fig. 6A, we again see the primacy of work primarily being performed at the workplace in 2019 followed by a decrease in 2020 and a slight

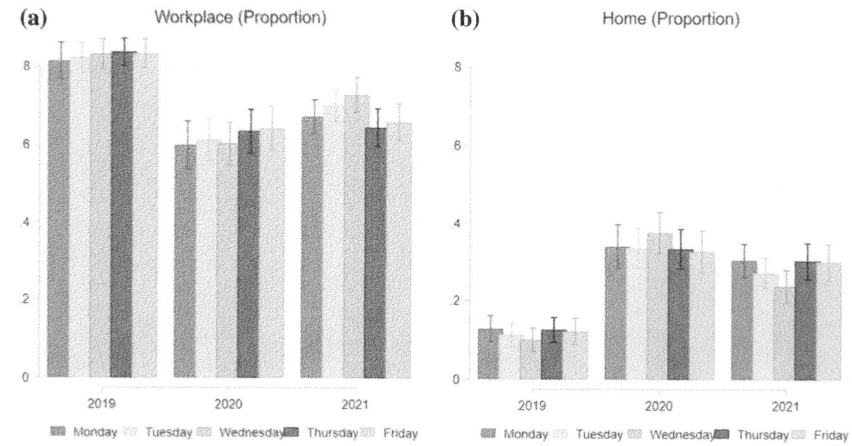

Fig. 6A–B. Workplace and Home as Primary Work Locations across Weekdays, 2019–2021.

Notes: Adjusted estimates based on models for years 2019 to 2021 that parallel those shown in Table A4 but include day-year interactions. X-axis is survey year.

uptick again in 2021. In 2019, there is striking similarity in the proportion of workers performing work at the workplace across days. In 2020, Thursday and Friday are slightly more likely to be days that people work at the workplace. The 2021 pattern is distinct, with Wednesday the day when most people work at the workplace and Monday, Thursday, and Friday the days that individuals are least likely to physically be at the workplace. Fig. 6B shows the patterns by year and day of the week in the proportion of workers working at home. While Wednesday was the least common work at home day in 2019 and 2021, it was the most common work at home day in 2020. In 2021, Monday, Thursday, and Friday are the days with the largest share of workers performing their work primarily at home. Despite the dramatic change across years, differences across days within year are much less pronounced. These patterns suggest that while some firms may be requiring in person work on certain days, there is a lot of heterogeneity in those days across firms such that a distinct pattern of working at home on certain days is suggested by the data, but the signal is weak.

6. PARENTS VS NON-PARENTS AND COPRESENCE FOR AT-HOME WORKERS

Childcare disruptions and school closures reduced parental labor supply as well as work hours during the COVID-19 pandemic, though workers who were able to telework were less affected (Amuedo-Dorantes et al., 2023; Garcia & Cowan, 2022). We showed earlier that parents were especially likely to shift to working at home during the COVID-19 pandemic. In light of this finding, we examine the copresence of others during work occurring at home, comparing parents and non-parents.[16] Copresence in the ATUS is based on who the respondent reports being in the room with them; respondents are able to report being alone or the presence of several different types of people. Prior to the COVID-19 pandemic, work was typically performed either alone or with coworkers.[17] Accordingly we differentiate between work alone or with coworkers and work done with anyone else in the room. We compare three measures of copresence for at-home workers: (1) the proportion of workers reporting any time working alone or with coworkers; (2) the minutes per day spent working alone or with coworkers; and (3) the share of daily work time spent alone or with coworkers.[18] If the respondent did not report being alone or with coworkers, someone else – a partner, children, another household member, or someone else – was reported as in the room during paid work.

Fig. 7A–C show that the majority of both parents and non-parents working primarily at home report time alone during work, very few report being with coworkers, and some report being with someone else while working at home.[19] Levels of working alone are higher for non-parents compared to parents (Fig. 7A) and working with someone in the room who is not a coworker – which includes any household or non-household members who are not coworkers – is higher for parents than non-parents (Fig. 7C). The prevalence of spending time working at home alone was higher in 2021 compared to 2019 and 2020, which may be explained by children being back in school and the return to the workplace for some partners and/or other household members or the creation of dedicated work spaces separate from shared spaces in the home. Fig. 7D-F show the average hours per day spent working alone, with a coworker, or with someone else across the 2019 to 2021 period. Differences in the amount of time that parents and non-parents spent working at home either alone, with coworkers, or with someone else were quite small in 2019. When work shifted from the workplace to home in 2020, non-parents spent 45 more minutes per day, on average, working alone than parents. This gap persisted into 2021. Fig. 7G-I show that the parental gap in the amount of time that workers spend alone was not a function of substantial differences in time spent working at home because we found no significant differences in the hours per day that parents and non-parents worked at home (see Table A4). Instead, the gap results from parents spending a significantly lower share of their time working alone and more time with someone besides a coworker. We observe a slight increase in the share of work performed with someone else in the room in 2020 for parents, as would be expected in light of childcare and school closures in 2020.

7. CONCLUSIONS

As a result of the COVID-19 public health crisis, many workers quickly shifted from performing their jobs at their physical workplaces to performing their jobs at home. Research and speculation on the how the pandemic affected

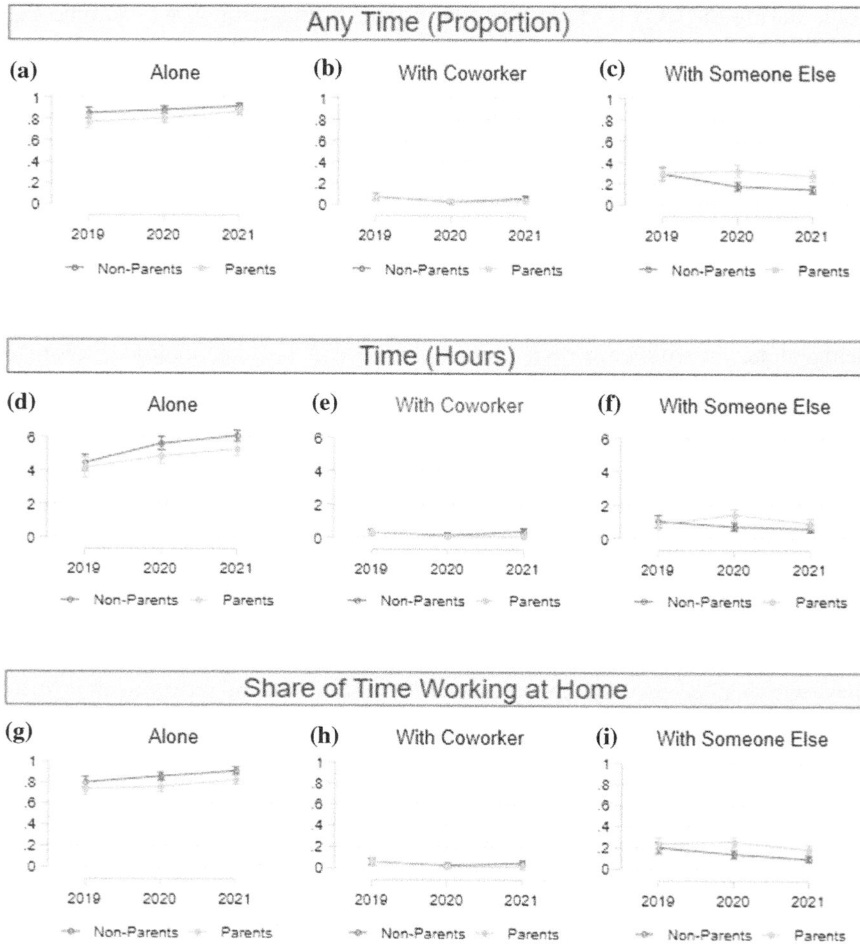

Fig. 7A–I. Working Alone, With Coworkers, or With Someone Else at Home by Parental Status, 2019–2021.

Notes: Adjusted estimates based on models for years 2019 to 2021 that parallel models in Table A4 for respondents who spend any time working at home. X-axis is survey year.

employment in certain sectors and subpopulations have exploded. There is a parallel interest in the long-term implications of COVID-19-induced changes in paid work. What we lack, however, is a population-level picture of how the pandemic influenced where, when, how much, and who workers are with when they do their jobs. Our work begins to fill this gap. Using repeated cross-sections of data from the ATUS, we provide a comprehensive view of how the COVID-19 pandemic changed paid work and for whom and provide a glimpse into the patterns that persist into 2021 following the initial shock of the pandemic.

The most striking impact of the COVID-19 pandemic for the employed population was where they performed their work. The proportion of workers who performed their work primarily at home more than doubled between 2019 and 2020. But still the majority of workers (62.1%) continued to perform their paid work primarily at the workplace. And while there were slight decreases in the proportion of workers who spent time working at multiple locations during the pandemic (11% vs. 15% in 2019 and 13% in 2021), most employed people spent their time working at a single location. Undoubtedly the rapid shift to at-home work for a sizeable segment of the population required adapting and learning how to work in a different way and the implications for individuals and firms require investigation. Parallel inquiries have and should continue to focus on the implications of the COVID-19 pandemic for the workers carrying out their jobs at the workplace.

Previous research has emphasized the heightened vulnerability during the COVID-19 pandemic of disadvantaged populations (Carlsten et al., 2021; Daly et al., 2020; Dey et al., 2020; Feldman & Bassett, 2021; Hawkins et al., 2020). Our findings are consistent with the mounting evidence regarding the differential impact of the COVID-19 pandemic on vulnerable populations. We show that the shift to at-home work occurred for most groups except the least educated and the most dramatic increases in working at home were experienced by the most educated workers. Differences in where workers perform their work by gender and parental status that grew in 2020 largely returned to their pre-pandemic sizes in 2021. The exception is with education differences. The most educated workers are the subgroup who continue to work at home even if at lower levels in 2021 compared to 2020. If working at home is considered a privilege, the least educated workers have lost ground in 2021 compared to 2019 while the most educated workers have gained ground; the work-at-home gap between the most and least educated workers has increased as a result of the COVID-19 pandemic.

In addition to where people work, other dimensions of paid work such as the length of work days, the timing of paid work during the day, and the copresence of other people during paid work have garnered some attention during the pandemic. Our investigation shows less change than might be expected in how much and when workers worked during the pandemic. The experiences of the employed population performing their work at the workplace is characterized by strikingly similar patterns between 2019 and 2021. And while we observe changes for workers who perform their jobs primarily at home, this is expected given the changing composition of the population working at home. And the increases in the amount of time employed people spend working primarily at home are no longer observed when considering only workers who put in a half day (4 hours) or longer, reflecting the shift in many full-time workers to performing their paid work at home. Our robustness checks for workers putting in more than 4 hours on the ATUS diary day show that at-home workers have longer work day spans, which may, on the positive side, indicate flexibility in when workers perform their work or, a longer work day span may reflect more interruptions, a negative consequence of working at home.

On work days, we find more differences in who workers are with. These entail both decreases in being physically with coworkers and increases in being alone or with family members while working, but these differences are much more subtle than the shift to at-home work. Given school closures and social isolation requirements during the COVID-19 pandemic, we also examined differences in who else is in the room while parents and non-parents are working at home. Our results suggest more interrupted at-home work experiences for parents and a lower share of focused work time (i.e., alone or with coworkers), but not to the extent that might have been expected. That said, many mothers simply left the labor force during the COVID-19 pandemic and subjective interpretations of the work experience may tell a different story about the impact of the COVID-19 pandemic on paid work experiences.

The COVID-19 pandemic has changed the landscape of paid work, especially for the privileged subset of workers who are able to perform their jobs away from their workplace. As such, hybrid work, where paid work is sometimes performed at the workplace and other times at some other location (typically home), is of high interest to workers and firms as well as the scholarly community. With the ATUS data, we are unable to examine work schedules and how they vary across days, which is how we typically think of hybrid work, but we were able to examine whether there are specific days where workers are more or less likely to work at the workplace versus at home. We found some suggestive evidence that the days employed people tend to spend physically at the workplace vary but the differences between specific days are not particularly large and there is not a distinct pattern across years. While hybrid work is of great interest to individuals and firms, ATUS data are not ideal for the study of work schedules, though they do suggest that the days individuals work primarily at home and at the workplace may be in flux and there may not be a "typical" day when workers are at the workplace or at home.

Despite the contributions of our work, there are some noteworthy limitations. First, the cross-sectional nature of these data does not allow us to examine how work arrangements changed for individual workers over time. Second, with the data we have, we do not know about the permanency of work at home arrangements. We know where people are working and how much they are working at different locations, but we do not know about the availability of policies for working at home, the frequency they work at home, the reasons people work at home, or the ways in which they perform work at different locations across the work week. Third, the ATUS copresence question asks who was in the room with you while you were doing the activity. This is a real limitation for examining copresence during remote work since virtual meetings and events can continue and workers are likely engaging with others even though they are not physically together. Finally, it is likely that the composition of the employed changed across our periods of study. We only examine the experiences of individuals working on the diary day, and with the abrupt change in employment directly following the onset of the COVID-19 pandemic, and the varied return to work across industries, the characteristics of those employed in each of our periods may vary (Dey et al., 2020; Kong & Prinz, 2020). This variation may be contributing to the differences we find.

Overall, our work shows the dramatic shift of paid work being done at the workplace to workers' homes between 2019 and 2020 as well as the slight retreat back to the workplace in 2021. While a sizable segment of the population works at home, our results also clearly show that working at the workplace continues to be the norm for the majority of workers in the United States. And there is surprising continuity in how much people work at home as well as the work spans of workers who perform their jobs at the workplace and those who work more than a half day at their homes. These findings underscore the strong influence of other social institutions and organizations like families, schools, and childcare centers on the rhythms of daily life.

ACKNOWLEDGMENTS

This work was supported by Minnesota Population Center grant P2CHD041023, University of Colorado Population Center grant P2CHD066613, and the Time Use Data for Health and Well-Being grant R01HD053654, all funded by the Eunice Kennedy Shriver National Institute for Child Health and Human Development.

NOTES

1. We are grateful to the anonymous reviewers, Solomon Polachek, and Daniel Hamermesh for useful comments on earlier versions of this chapter.
2. The ATUS is a time diary study of a nationally representative sample of Americans. ATUS sample members are invited to complete the survey two to five months after they exit the Current Population Survey (CPS). The CPS is a monthly household survey of the civilian, non-institutionalized population. One individual aged 15 or older per former CPS participating household was randomly selected to report their activities over one 24-hour period. ATUS data are collected using a computer assisted telephone interview, and the respondents report the activities they engaged in over a 24-hour period from 4:00 a.m. of a specified day until 4:00 a.m. of the following day, as well as where, when, and with whom activities were done. Data are collected all days of the week, and weekends are oversampled.
3. As a robustness check, we compared all of the analyses presented with analyses that limit 2019 and 2021 data to the May 10 to December 31 period for direct comparability with the COVID-period data collection in 2020. The results are qualitatively similar to restricting the 2019 and 2021 data to the May to December period. They are available upon request.
4. The specific activity codes that we classify as paid work are IPUMS ATUS activity codes 050101–050299 (see https://www.atusdata.org/atus-action/variables/activity#codes_section).
5. Time spent working on the ATUS diary day varies dramatically, ranging from one minute to nearly an entire day, though 95% of observations in the 2019 to 2021 period are between 40 minutes and 12 hours.
6. ATUS data collection was paused starting March 17, 2020 due to the COVID-19 pandemic. Data collection resumed May 10, 2020. The gap in data collection means that full year time-use estimates for 2020 cannot be calculated, but it is possible to compare the pandemic period (May 10, 2020 to Dec 31, 2020) to surrounding years of data to understand the impact of COVID-19 on work-related behavior (Flood, Genadek, et al., 2022).
7. Estimates are based on repeated cross sections of ATUS data from 2003 to 2021 (Flood, Sayer et al., 2022). We present predicted proportions based on Linear Probability

Models. We estimate the proportion of workers who work at each primary work location (home, workplace, other) adjusting for controls in Table A1. Full results are available upon request.

8. Currently ATUS data are only available through 2021. Future research should extend these analyses through 2023 and beyond to analyze the post-COVID-19 era.

9. Characteristics of the analytic sample by year, 2019 to 2021, are in Table A1.

10. Results are based on Ordinary Least Squares regression models with interactions between year (2019, 2020: May 10-December 31, 2020, and 2021) and demographic characteristics including gender (men and women); education (less than a high school degree, high school degree or some college, and college degree or more); parental status (coresident child under 18 – yes or no); and age (18–29, 30–49, 50–59, 60–69, 70+). Models include controls for race (white, black, and other races); household income (less than $25,000; $25,000–$49,999; $50,000–$74,999; $75,000–$149,999; $150,000+); Census region (South, West, Midwest, Northeast); diary day (weekend or weekday); holiday (yes or no). For ease of interpretation, we presented adjusted predicted values for each model graphically. Year-specific means for work day characteristics are in Table A1 and Table A2 contains means for all controls.

11. All descriptive statistics for work day characteristics by year, 2019 to 2021, are in Table A2. Regression results are in Table A3.

12. We estimate separate models for each primary work location; all models include controls from Table A1. We present year coefficients only to show significant differences across years in Table A4; full models are available upon request.

13. Full results available upon request. Models parallel those presented in Table A4 and include the full set of controls listed in Table A1.

14. We estimate the proportion of working in each location separately using Linear Probability Models and graph predicted proportions of working in that combination of places on the ATUS diary day. All models include controls in Table A1.

15. We do not present coefficients from models, but they are available upon request. All models include controls in Table A1.

16. Here we focus exclusively on copresence during work activities performed at home regardless of where the work time was primarily spent during the day.

17. When we refer to coworkers, this includes (1) boss or manager, (2) people the respondent supervises, (3) coworkers, and (4) customers.

18. We do not present coefficients from models, which include controls listed in Table A1, but they are available upon request. The share of time spent alone or with coworkers is the total number of minutes per day spent working either alone or with a coworker divided by the total amount of time spent working.

19. The proportion of workers performing their jobs primarily at home and reporting being with a coworker is expected to be low. This is because the ATUS asks who was with you in the room rather than who you were with more generally, which taps into physical presence. Workers could have been in meetings or working with their colleagues through Zoom or some other virtual meeting platform, but this should not be reported as time with coworkers if they were not physically present in the same room.

REFERENCES

Allen, T. D., Golden, T. D., & Shockley, K. M. (2015). How effective is telecommuting? Assessing the status of our scientific findings. *Psychological Science in the Public Interest*, *16*(2), 40–68.

Alon, T., Doepke, M., Olmstead-Rumsey, J., & Tertilt, M. (2020). *The impact of COVID-19 on gender equality*. https://www.nber.org/system/files/working_papers/w26947/w26947.pdf

Amuedo-Dorantes, C., Marcén, M., Morales, M., & Sevilla, A. (2023). Schooling and parental labor supply: Evidence from COVID-19 school closures in the United States. *ILR Review*, *76*(1), 56–85.

Bailey, D. E., & Kurland, N. B. (2002). A review of telework research: Findings, new directions, and lessons for the study of modern work. *Journal of Organizational Behavior*, *23*(4), 383–400. https://doi.org/10.1002/job.144

Bloom, N. (2020). How working from home works out. *Institute for Economic Policy Research (SIEPR). Policy Brief June*, 1–9.

Bloom, N., Han, R., & Liang, J. (2022). *How hybrid working from home works out*. [presented at "Labor Studies Program Meeting", November 18, 2022]. National Bureau of Economic Research Working Paper Series, No. 30292. https://doi.org/10.3386/w30292

Brynjolfsson, E., Horton, J. J., Ozimek, A., Rock, D., Sharma, G., & TuYe, H.-Y. (2020). *COVID-19 and remote work: An early look at US data*.

Bureau of Labor Statistics. (2019). *Job flexibilities and work schedules summary*. https://www.bls.gov/news.release/flex2.nr0.htm. Accessed on October 28, 2022.

Bureau of Labor Statistics. (2022a). *7.7 percent of workers teleworked due to COVID-19 in April 2022*. https://www.bls.gov/opub/ted/2022/7-7-percent-of-workers-teleworked-due-to-covid-19-in-april-2022.htm. Accessed on October 28, 2022.

Bureau of Labor Statistics. (2022b). *Percent participating on an avg day – Working at home, employed, on days worked*. T. A. (C). (Ed.). Bureau of Labor Statistics. https://data.bls.gov/cgi-bin/srgate

Carlsten, C., Gulati, M., Hines, S., Rose, C., Scott, K., Tarlo, S. M., Torén, K., Sood, A., & de la Hoz, R. E. (2021). COVID-19 as an occupational disease. *American Journal of Industrial Medicine*, *64*(4), 227–237. https://www.ncbi.nlm.nih.gov/pmc/articles/PMC8014565/pdf/AJIM-64-227.pdf

Collins, C., Ruppanner, L., Christin Landivar, L., & Scarborough, W. J. (2021). The gendered consequences of a weak infrastructure of care: School reopening plans and parents' employment during the COVID-19 pandemic. *Gender & Society*, *35*(2), 180–193. https://doi.org/10.1177/08912432211001300

Daly, M. C., Buckman, S. R., & Seitelman, L. M. (2020). The unequal impact of COVID-19: Why education matters. *FRBSF Economic Letter*, *17*(5), 1–5.

DeFilippis, E., Impink, S. M., Singell, M., Polzer, J. T., & Sadun, R. (2020). *Collaborating during coronavirus: The impact of COVID-19 on the nature of work*. https://www.nber.org/system/files/working_papers/w27612/w27612.pdf

Dey, M., Loewenstein, M. A., Piccone, D. S., & Polivka, A. E. (2020). Demographics, earnings, and family characteristics of workers in sectors initially affected by COVID-19 shutdowns. *Monthly Labor Review*, 1–29.

Dunatchik, A., Gerson, K., Glass, J., Jacobs, J. A., & Stritzel, H. (2021). Gender, parenting, and the rise of remote work during the pandemic: Implications for domestic inequality in the United States. *Gender & Society*, *35*(2), 194–205.

Fabrizio, S., Gomes, D. B., & Tavares, M. M. (2021). *Covid-19 she-cession: The employment penalty of taking care of young children*. International Monetary Fund.

Fan, W., & Moen, P. (2022). Working more, less or the same during COVID-19? A mixed method, intersectional analysis of remote workers. *Work and Occupations*, *49*(2), 143–186. https://doi.org/10.1177/07308884211047208

Feldman, J. M., & Bassett, M. T. (2021). Variation in COVID-19 mortality in the US by race and ethnicity and educational attainment. *JAMA Network Open*, *4*(11), e2135967.

Flood, S. M., Genadek, K. R., Sayer, L. C., & Drotning, K. (2022). *Navigating COVID-19 disruption in U.S. Time diary data*. IPUMS Working Paper Series.

Flood, S. M., Sayer, L. C., & Backman, D. (2022). *American time use survey data extract builder Version 3.1*. https://doi.org/10.18128/D060.V3.1

Garcia, K. S. D., & Cowan, B. W. (2022). *The impact of US school closures on labor market outcomes during the Covid-19 pandemic*. https://www.nber.org/system/files/working_papers/w29641/w29641.pdf

Glass, J. L., & Noonan, M. C. (2016). Telecommuting and earnings trajectories among American women and men 1989–2008. *Social Forces*, *95*(1), 217–250. https://doi.org/10.1093/sf/sow034

Hansen, S., Lambert, P. J., Bloom, N., Davis, S. J., Sadun, R., & Taska, B. (2023). *Remote work across jobs, companies, and space*. National Bureau of Economic Research Working Paper Series, No. 31007. https://doi.org/10.3386/w31007

Hawkins, R. B., Charles, E. J., & Mehaffey, J. H. (2020). Socio-economic status and COVID-19–related cases and fatalities. *Public Health*, *189*, 129–134. https://doi.org/10.1016/j.puhe.2020.09.016

Huang, A., Makridis, C., Baker, M., Medeiros, M., & Guo, Z. (2020). Understanding the impact of COVID-19 intervention policies on the hospitality labor market. *International Journal of Hospitality Management*, *91*, 102660. https://www.ncbi.nlm.nih.gov/pmc/articles/PMC7455155/pdf/main.pdf

Hu, X., & Dill, M. J. (2021). Changes in physician work hours and patterns during the COVID-19 pandemic. *JAMA Network Open*, *4*(6), e2114386. https://jamanetwork.com/journals/jamanetworkopen/articlepdf/2781284/hu_2021_ld_210110_1623443545.2938.pdf

Kaushik, D. (2021). COVID-19 and health care workers burnout: A call for global action. *EClinicalMedicine*, *35*.

Kong, E., & Prinz, D. (2020). Disentangling policy effects using proxy data: Which shutdown policies affected unemployment during the COVID-19 pandemic? *Journal of Public Economics*, *189*, 104257. https://doi.org/10.1016/j.jpubeco.2020.104257

Krantz-Kent, R. M. (2019). Where did workers perform their jobs in the early 21st century? *Monthly Labor Review*, 1–10.

Lee, J., & Huang, Y. (2022). Covid-19 impact on US housing markets: Evidence from spatial regression models. *Spatial Economic Analysis*, *17*(3), 395–415. https://doi.org/10.1080/17421772.2021.2018028

Lei, L., & Liu, X. (2022). The COVID-19 pandemic and residential mobility intentions in the United States: Evidence from Google Trends data. *Population, Space and Place*, *28*(6), e2581. https://doi.org/10.1002/psp.2581

Lyttelton, T., Zang, E., & Musick, K. (2022). Telecommuting and gender inequalities in parents' paid and unpaid work before and during the COVID-19 pandemic. *Journal of Marriage and Family*, *84*(1), 230–249. https://www.ncbi.nlm.nih.gov/pmc/articles/PMC8661776/pdf/JOMF-84-230.pdf

Morikawa, M. (2023). Productivity dynamics of remote work during the COVID-19 pandemic. *Industrial Relations: A Journal of Economy and Society*. https://doi.org/10.1111/irel.12327

Ng, M. A., Naranjo, A., Schlotzhauer, A. E., Shoss, M. K., Kartvelishvili, N., Bartek, M., Ingraham, K., Rodriguez, A., Schneider, S. K., & Silverlieb-Seltzer, L. (2021). Has the COVID-19 pandemic accelerated the future of work or changed its course? Implications for research and practice. *International Journal of Environmental Research and Public Health*, *18*(19), 10199. https://mdpi-res.com/d_attachment/ijerph/ijerph-18-10199/article_deploy/ijerph-18-10199-v2.pdf?version=1632882347

Noonan, M. C., & Glass, J. L. (2012). The hard truth about telecommuting. *Monthly Labor Review*, *135*, 38.

Pabilonia, S. W., & Victoria, V. (2022). Telework, wages, and time use in the United States. *Review of Economics of the Household*, *20*(3), 687–734. https://doi.org/10.1007/s11150-022-09601-1

Petts, R. J., Carlson, D. L., & Pepin, J. R. (2021). A gendered pandemic: Childcare, homeschooling, and parents' employment during COVID-19. *Gender, Work and Organization*, *28*(S2), 515–534. https://doi.org/10.1111/gwao.12614

Restrepo, B. J., & Zeballos, E. (2022). Work from home and daily time allocations: Evidence from the coronavirus pandemic. *Review of Economics of the Household*, *20*(3), 735–758. https://doi.org/10.1007/s11150-022-09614-w

Tavares, A. I. (2017). Telework and health effects review. *International Journal of Healthcare*, *3*(2), 30–36.

Teodorovicz, T., Sadun, R., Kun, A. L., & Shaer, O. (2021a). How does working from home during COVID-19 affect what managers do? Evidence from time-use studies. *Human-Computer Interaction*, 1–26.

Teodorovicz, T., Sadun, R., Kun, A. L., & Shaer, O. (2021b). *Working from home during COVID19: Evidence from time-use studies*. Harvard Business School.

Wilensky, G. R. (2022). The COVID-19 pandemic and the US health care workforce. *JAMA Health Forum*. https://doi.org/10.1001/jamahealthforum.2022.0001

Yörük, B. K. (2022). Early effects of COVID-19 pandemic-related state policies on housing market activity in the United States. *Journal of Housing Economics*, *57*, 101857. https://doi.org/10.1016/j.jhe.2022.101857

APPENDIX

Table A1. Individual Characteristics for Employed Respondents Who Worked on the ATUS Diary Day, 2019–2021.

	2019	2020 (May–Dec)	2021
Sample Size	3237	2079	3062
Gender			
Men	0.55	0.55	0.55
Women	0.45	0.45	0.45
Education			
Less than High School Degree	0.07	0.06	0.06
High School Degree or Some College	0.50	0.49	0.47
College Degree +	0.43	0.45	0.47
Parent (Has a Coresident Own Child Under 18)			
No	0.66	0.66	0.66
Yes	0.34	0.34	0.34
Age			
18–29	0.22	0.22	0.22
30–49	0.44	0.43	0.44
50–59	0.20	0.21	0.20
60–69	0.10	0.11	0.11
70+	0.03	0.03	0.03
Race			
White	0.80	0.80	0.79
Black	0.12	0.11	0.12
Other	0.07	0.08	0.09
Income			
Less than $25,000	0.10*	0.06	0.08*
$25,000–49,999	0.19	0.17	0.18
$50,000–74,999	0.19	0.19	0.20
$75,000–149,999	0.33	0.36	0.33*
$150,000 +	0.18*	0.21	0.21
Region			
Northeast	0.18	0.19	0.17
Midwest	0.24	0.22	0.23
South	0.37	0.38	0.37
West	0.21	0.21	0.22
Weekend			
No	0.86	0.87	0.87
Yes	0.14	0.13	0.13
Holiday			
No	0.99	0.99	0.99
Yes	0.01	0.01	0.01

Notes: $^{*}p < 0.05$ indicates a significant difference from May–December 2020 estimates.

Table A2. Work Day Characteristics for Employed Respondents Who Worked on the ATUS Diary Day, 2019–2021.

	2019	2020 (May–Dec)	2021
Sample Size	3237	2079	3062
Amount of Time Worked			
Hours worked on the diary day	7.63	7.67	7.79
Primary Work Location (Mutually Exclusive)			
Home			
%	0.14*	0.35	0.30*
Average hours per day	4.86*	6.69	6.96
Work			
%	0.80*	0.60	0.66*
Average hours per day	8.21	8.27	8.28
Other			
%	0.06*	0.04	0.04
Average hours per day	6.43*	7.47	6.23*
Combined Work Location			
Home only (%)	0.13*	0.33	0.28*
Work only (%)	0.69*	0.52	0.56*
Other only (%)	0.04	0.03	0.03
Multiple locations (%)	0.15*	0.11	0.14
Who People Are With			
Coworkers			
% any time reported	0.67*	0.48	0.52*
Average hours per day	5.12*	3.70	3.95
Spouse			
% any time reported	0.05*	0.07	0.05
Average hours per day	0.11*	0.23	0.15*
Children			
% any time reported	0.02*	0.04	0.03*
Average hours per day	0.04*	0.15	0.09*
Other			
% any time reported	0.10*	0.07	0.08
Average hours per day	0.50*	0.34	0.41
Alone			
% any time reported	0.42*	0.55	0.55
Average hours per day	2.09*	3.41	3.33
When People Work			
Work day span	8.76	8.72	8.93
Start time (hours since midnight)	8.74	8.58	8.53
End time (hours since midnight)	17.50	17.29	17.46

Notes: *$p < 0.05$ indicates a significant difference from May–December 2020 estimates.

Table A3. Ordinary Least Squares Regression of Work Day Characteristics 2019–2021.

	How Much	When			Copresence				
	Hours	Start Time (hours)	End Time (hours)	Work Day Span (hours)	Alone (Proportion)	Coworker (Proportion)	Spouse (Proportion)	Child (Proportion)	Other (Proportion)
	(1)	(2)	(3)	(4)	(5)	(6)	(7)	(8)	(9)
Panel A: Year Main Effects									
Year (ref = 2020 (May–Dec))									
2019	−0.01	0.13	0.23*	0.10	−0.12***	0.19***	−0.01	−0.02***	(0.03)***
	(0.09)	(0.11)	(0.12)	(0.11)	(0.02)	(0.02)	(0.01)	(0.00)	(0.01)
2021	−0.16	−0.07	0.17	0.24*	−0.00	0.04**	−0.02*	−0.01**	0.01
	(0.09)	(0.10)	(0.11)	(0.11)	(0.02)	(0.02)	(0.01)	(0.00)	(0.01)
Panel B: Year X Gender									
Year (ref = 2020 (May–Dec))									
2019	0.04	0.07	0.30*	0.23	−0.09***	0.17***	−0.00	−0.02***	0.01
	(0.12)	(0.15)	(0.15)	(0.14)	(0.02	(0.02)	(0.01)	(0.00)	(0.01)
2021	0.17	−0.04	0.32*	0.37*	0.02	0.02	−0.00	−0.01	0.00
	(0.12)	(0.14)	(0.15)	(0.14)	(0.02)	(0.02)	(0.01)	(0.01)	(0.01)
Gender (ref =Men)									
Women	−0.73***	0.50**	−0.02	−0.52**	0.02	−0.05*	0.01	0.03**	0.01
	(0.14)	(0.17)	(0.18)	(0.16)	(0.03)	(0.03)	(0.01)	(0.01)	(0.01)
Gender X Year									
Women X 2019	−0.12	0.15	−0.14	−0.29	−0.05	0.04	−0.02	−0.00	0.06**
	(0.19)	(0.22)	(0.23)	(0.22)	(0.03)	(0.03)	(0.01)	(0.01)	(0.02)
Women X 2021	−0.04	−0.06	−0.35	−0.29	−0.04	0.06	−0.03	−0.01	0.01
	(0.18)	(0.21)	(0.23)	(0.22)	(0.03)	(0.03)	(0.01)	(0.01)	(0.02)
Panel C: Year X Parent									
Year (ref = 2020 (May–Dec))									
2019	0.01	0.18	0.41**	0.24	−0.13***	0.17***	−0.00	−0.00	0.03*
	(0.12)	(0.15)	(0.15)	(0.14)	(0.02)	(0.02)	(0.01)	(0.00)	(0.01)

(Continued)

Table A3. *(Continued)*

	How Much	When			Copresence				
	Hours (1)	Start Time (hours) (2)	End Time (hours) (3)	Work Day Span (hours) (4)	Alone (Proportion) (5)	Coworker (Proportion) (6)	Spouse (Proportion) (7)	Child (Proportion) (8)	Other (Proportion) (9)
2021	0.18 (0.12)	−0.02 (0.14)	0.32* (0.15)	0.34* (0.14)	0.00 (0.02)	0.04 (0.02)	−0.01 (0.01)	−0.00 (0.00)	0.01 (0.01)
Parent (ref=No)									
Yes	−0.16 (0.15)	0.06 (0.17)	0.25 (0.18)	0.19 (0.17)	−0.03 (0.03)	−0.05 (0.03)	0.04** (0.01)	0.11*** (0.01)	−0.01 (0.01)
Parent X Year									
Parent X 2019	−0.06 (0.19)	−0.13 (0.22)	−0.53* (0.23)	−0.40 (0.22)	0.03 (0.03)	0.04 (0.03)	−0.03 (0.02)	−0.05*** (0.01)	0.01 (0.02)
Parent X 2021	−0.07 (0.19)	−0.15 (0.20)	−0.45* (0.22)	−0.30 (0.22)	−0.00 (0.03)	0.02 (0.03)	−0.01 (0.02)	−0.03 (0.01)	0.00 (0.02)
Panel D: Year X Education									
Year (Ref = 2020 (May–Dec))									
2019	−0.01 (0.13)	−0.06 (0.13)	0.05 (0.14)	0.11 (0.16)	−0.19*** (0.02)	0.30*** (0.02)	−0.03* (0.01)	−0.02** (0.01)	0.05*** (0.01)
2021	0.30* (0.13)	−0.07 (0.13)	0.41** (0.14)	0.48** (0.16)	−0.00 (0.02)	0.06** (0.02)	−0.02 (0.01)	−0.01 (0.01)	0.03* (0.01)
Education (ref=College +)									
Less than HS	0.48 (0.36)	−0.46 (0.51)	−0.45 (0.43)	0.01 (0.40)	−0.34*** (0.05)	0.31*** (0.06)	−0.06** (0.02)	−0.05*** (0.01)	0.06 (0.05)
HS & Some College	0.52*** (0.15)	−0.51** (0.17)	−0.24 (0.18)	0.27 (0.17)	−0.20*** (0.03)	0.26*** (0.03)	−0.04** (0.01)	−0.02* (0.01)	−0.01 (0.01)
Education X Year									
Less than HS X 2019	0.12 (0.47)	0.58 (0.62)	0.53 (0.56)	−0.05 (0.51)	0.24*** (0.07)	−0.26*** (0.07)	0.04 (0.03)	0.03* (0.01)	−0.07 (0.06)
Less than HS X 2021	−0.39 (0.45)	−0.19 (0.59)	−0.54 (0.57)	−0.35 (0.52)	0.09 (0.07)	0.01 (0.07)	0.01 (0.03)	0.00 (0.01)	−0.10 (0.05)
HS & Some College X 2019	−0.02 (0.19)	0.32 (0.22)	0.30 (0.23)	−0.02 (0.22)	0.12*** (0.03)	−0.20*** (0.03)	0.02 (0.02)	0.01 (0.01)	−0.03 (0.02)
HS & Some College 2021	−0.26 (0.19)	0.01 (0.21)	−0.46* (0.23)	−0.48* (0.22)	−0.01 (0.03)	−0.03 (0.03)	0.00 (0.02)	−0.01 (0.01)	−0.03 (0.02)

Panel E: Year X Age									
Year (ref = 2020(May–Dec))									
2019	−0.06	0.23	0.14	−0.09	−0.15***	0.11**	−0.00	−0.00	(0.04)
	(0.25)	(0.24)	(0.26)	(0.29)	(0.04)	(0.04)	(0.02)	(0.00)	(0.02)
2021	−0.00	0.28	0.41	0.13	−0.05	0.01	−0.00	−0.00	0.01
	(0.25)	(0.24)	(0.27)	(0.29)	(0.04)	(0.04)	(0.02)	(0.00)	(0.02)
Age (ref = 50=59)									
Less than 30	−0.01	1.00**	0.80*	−0.21	−0.23***	0.11*	−0.03	−0.00	0.04
	(0.26)	(0.32)	(0.32)	(0.30)	(0.05)	(0.05)	(0.02)	(0.01)	(0.03)
30–49	0.70**	0.28	0.95***	0.68**	−0.08*	0.01	−0.00	0.03**	0.00
	(0.23)	(0.21)	(0.24)	(0.26)	(0.04)	(0.04)	(0.02)	(0.01)	(0.02)
60–69	0.38	−0.03	0.24	0.27	−0.04	−0.01	−0.01	−0.00	−0.00
	(0.24)	(0.23)	(0.26)	(0.28)	(0.04)	(0.04)	(0.02)	(0.01)	(0.02)
70+	−0.72	0.16	−0.46	−0.62	−0.04	−0.04	0.09	−0.00	0.07
	(0.45)	(0.29)	(0.54)	(0.56)	(0.07)	(0.08)	(0.05)	(0.00)	(0.05)
Age X Year									
Less than 30 X 2019	0.41	−0.09	0.50	0.58	0.06	0.10	−0.00	0.01	−0.03
	(0.34)	(0.42)	(0.43)	(0.40)	(0.06)	(0.06)	(0.02)	(0.01)	(0.04)
Less than 30 X 2021	0.25	−0.40	−0.12	0.29	0.06	0.06	−0.01	0.00	−0.02
	(0.34)	(0.40)	(0.42)	(0.39)	(0.06)	(0.06)	(0.02)	(0.01)	(0.03)
30–49 X 2019	−0.09	−0.10	−0.13	−0.03	0.01	0.10*	−0.02	−0.03**	0.01
	(0.28)	(0.28)	(0.31)	(0.33)	(0.05)	(0.05)	(0.02)	(0.01)	(0.03)
30–49 X 2021	0.05	−0.43	−0.56	−0.13	0.05	0.03	−0.01	−0.03*	0.01
	(0.28)	(0.28)	(0.31)	(0.33)	(0.05)	(0.05)	(0.02)	(0.01)	(0.02)
60–69 X 2019	0.11	−0.22	0.20	0.42	0.07	0.03	−0.00	−0.01	0.01
	(0.32)	(0.32)	(0.35)	(0.36)	(0.06)	(0.06)	(0.03)	(0.01)	(0.03)
60–69 X 2021	0.40	−0.39	0.09	0.48	0.04	0.00	−0.01	−0.00	0.01
	(0.32)	(0.31)	(0.36)	(0.37)	(0.06)	(0.06)	(0.03)	(0.01)	(0.03)

(Continued)

Table A3. *(Continued)*

	How Much	When			Copresence				
	Hours (1)	Start Time (hours) (2)	End Time (hours) (3)	Work Day Span (hours) (4)	Alone (Proportion) (5)	Coworker (Proportion) (6)	Spouse (Proportion) (7)	Child (Proportion) (8)	Other (Proportion) (9)
70+ X 2019	−0.99	0.52	0.10	−0.42	0.06	−0.03	−0.05	−0.00	0.02
	(0.58)	(0.46)	(0.67)	(0.68)	(0.09)	(0.10)	(0.06)	(0.01)	(0.07)
70+ X 2021	−0.07	0.30	0.20	−0.10	0.02	0.03	−0.05	−0.00	−0.02
	(0.56)	(0.48)	(0.66)	(0.72)	(0.09)	(0.10)	(0.06)	(0.01)	(0.06)

Notes: Models include controls presented in Table A1.
Standard errors in parentheses
***$p < 0.001$, **$p < 0.01$, *$p < 0.05$

Table A4. Ordinary Least Squares Regression of Work Day Characteristics by Primary Work Location, 2019–2021.

	Work	Home	Other
Panel A: How Much (Hours)			
Year (ref = 2020 (May–Dec))			
2019	−0.06	−0.86***	−1.07*
	(0.10)	(0.22)	(0.49)
2021	0.05	0.32	−1.05
	(0.10)	(0.17)	(0.54)
Panel B: Work Day Span (Hours)			
Year (ref = 2020 (May–Dec))			
2019	0.18	−0.65*	−0.92
	(0.12)	(0.28)	(0.56)
2021	0.18	0.37	−0.55
	(0.12)	(0.21)	(0.63)
Panel C: Start Time (Hours)			
Year (ref = 2020 (May–Dec))			
2019	0.14	0.75***	0.49
	(0.15)	(0.22)	(0.42)
2021	0.01	−0.21	1.01*
	(0.15)	(0.14)	(0.46)
Panel D: End Time (Hours)			
Year (ref = 2020 (May–Dec))			
2019	0.32*	0.10	−0.43
	(0.15)	(0.24)	(0.50)
2021	0.19	0.16	0.46
	(0.15)	(0.18)	(0.56)
Panel E: Any Time Alone (Proportion)			
Year (ref = 2020 (May–Dec))			
2019	−0.02	−0.03	−0.06
	(0.02)	(0.02)	(0.07)
2021	0.02	0.05*	−0.04
	(0.02)	(0.02)	(0.08)
Panel F: Any Time With Coworkers (Proportion)			
Year (ref = 2020 (May–Dec))			
2019	0.04*	0.04**	0.11
	(0.02)	(0.01)	(0.07)
2021	−0.01	0.02*	0.04
	(0.02)	(0.01)	(0.07)
Panel G: Any Time With Someone Else (Proportion)			
Year (ref = 2020 (May–Dec))			
2019	0.02*	0.07*	0.03
	(0.01)	(0.03)	(0.08)
2021	0.01	−0.04	0.04
	(0.01)	(0.02)	(0.09)

Notes: Models include controls presented in Table A1. Standard errors in parentheses
$^{***}p < 0.001$, $^{**}p < 0.01$, $^{*}p < 0.05$

BLURRED BOUNDARIES: A DAY IN THE LIFE OF A TEACHER

Victoria Hunter Gibney, Kristine L. West and Seth Gershenson

ABSTRACT

The burnout, stress, and work-life balance challenges faced by teachers have received renewed interest due to the myriad disruptions and changes to K-12 schooling brought about by the COVID-19 pandemic. Even prior to the pandemic, relatively little was known about teachers' time use outside of the classroom, the blurring of work and home boundaries, and how teachers compare to similar professionals in these regards. We use daily time-diary data from the American Time Use Survey (ATUS) for 3,168 teachers and 1,886 professionals in similarly prosocial occupations from 2003 to 2019 to examine occupational differences in time use. Compared to observationally similar non-teachers, teachers spend significantly more time volunteering at their workplace and completing work outside the workplace during the school year. On average, teachers spend 19 more minutes working outside of the workplace on weekdays than observably similar non-teachers and 38 more minutes on weekends. The weekend disparity is particularly large among secondary school teachers. This suggests that before the widespread switch to online and hybrid learning necessitated by the COVID-19 pandemic, teachers were already navigating blurrier work-life boundaries than their counterparts in similar professions. This has important implications for teacher turnover and for the effectiveness and wellness of teachers who remain in the profession.

Keywords: Time allocation; teacher labor; occupational differences; work-life boundaries; job burnout; COVID-19

Time Use in Economics
Research in Labor Economics, Volume 51, 247–275

ISSN: 0147-9121/doi:10.1108/S0147-912120230000051010

1. INTRODUCTION

Teachers are the most important school-provided input (Gershenson, 2021; Hanushek & Rivkin, 2010). Accordingly, researchers have investigated teachers' work time and their use of classroom time and instructional strategies (e.g., Allen et al., 2021; Jones et al., 2022; Jones & Youngs, 2012; Krantz-Kent, 2008; Rowan, Camburn, et al., 2004; Rowan & Correnti, 2009; Rowan, Harrison, et al., 2004; West, 2014) including some preliminary evidence about how this was impacted by the disruptions of COVID-19 (Jones et al., 2022). Less is known, however, about when and where teachers complete their responsibilities and the potential impact on teachers' work-life balance.

Understanding teachers' time allocation – when and where they work and how they balance work and other activities – is critical to building realistic models of labor supply and to constructing policies that are responsive to the specifics of this market. Starting with a seminal call from Becker (1965), labor economists have included time constraints when describing household maximization problems and have shown that models that imply unconstrained choice in hours do not fit empirical data (Dickens & Lundberg, 1993). Whether and how teaching offers a different mix of hours and/or has different demands on time use can inform our understanding on both the extensive and intensive margins – that is who chooses and stays in the profession and as well as differences in work hours.

Time diary data like those used in this chapter are more accurate and provide more nuance than standard summary recall measures (Barrett & Hamermesh, 2019; West, 2014) and will better describe how teachers and similar workers navigate labor-home production tradeoffs. Specifically, one-off retrospective surveys that ask individuals about their time spent on specific tasks over the course of the past year or in a typical week, which constitute much of the extant evidence on teachers' time use, are fundamentally flawed in at least two ways (Harding, 1997; Juster & Stafford, 1991; te Braak, van Droogenbroeck, et al., 2022). First, relatively rare activities tend to be over-reported. Second, socially desirable activities tend to be overreported (and vice versa for stigmatized activities). Together, these measurement concerns raise doubt about accuracy of existing survey evidence regarding teachers' time use, particularly in activities like volunteering and working over the weekend.

An exception to this critique is Krantz-Kent (2008), who presented an early descriptive look at teachers' work patterns using ATUS time-diary data from 2003–2006 and found that compared to other employed professionals, teachers spent more time working on Sundays and more time working outside of their workplace. Another is Hamermesh (2018), who finds that in the higher education context, professors are more likely to work in the evenings and on weekends than other workers with a doctorate. We confirm and build significantly upon these findings with an expanded data set that includes 16 years of time use survey data, which offers greater power and allows for further disaggregation by teacher type and gender. We also develop and describe in detail a method using classifications from the US Department of Labor's online database O*NET (National Center for O*NET Development, 2022) to identify a more specific group of comparison occupations, which could be applied to other studies of occupational differences.

In addition to the standard utility maximization framework, we draw on theory from industrial psychology to frame our investigation of teacher time use. The work-family literature refers to the line between the spheres of work and home as a "border" with working individuals engaging in regular "border crossing" (Allen et al., 2014). In her foundational paper on work-family border theory, Clark (2000) describes borders between work and home as taking three main forms: physical, temporal, and psychological. A physical (or spatial) border delineates *where* work takes place, temporal borders indicate *when* work takes place, i.e., 9:00 a.m. to 5:00 p.m. or Monday through Friday, and psychological borders are rules or practices specific to an individual that separate their work-self from their home-self (Clark, 2000). Using time diary data, this article offers an initial exploration of the permeability of physical and temporal borders for teachers compared to those in similar professions.

A key concept in the work-family literature is the continuum of integration and segmentation, which describes the degree to which work and family roles are separated (Desrochers & Morgan, 2021). At one end of the spectrum is extreme segmentation, which involves low border permeability and low flexibility; these are workers who have rigid schedules and are barred from taking work home with them or handling home tasks while on the job. Extreme integration involves highly permeable and flexible borders; examples might be a freelancer who works from home and sets their own hours, or someone who runs a family business out of their home. Wepfer et al. (2018) found that workers with high work-to-life integration had less time to "recover" from work, were more exhausted, and had poor work-life balance.[1] Without sufficient recovery, sustained workload can lead to persistent or even irreversible negative effects, which can lower job performance and even cause physical or mental illness (Meijman et al., 1998).

Teachers' time use is important because the prevalence of work-life imbalance in the form of integration or reduced time spent in recovery activities has implications for teacher burnout, turnover, and student outcomes. Work schedules are relevant for the recruitment and retention of individuals to professions. Understanding how teachers spend nonwork time, the degree of permeability between work and home activities, and how teachers' nonwork time use compares to that of observationally similar non-teachers provides information on how teaching differs from alternative labor market options. One in four teachers reported that they were likely to leave their jobs by the end of the 2020–2021 school year in a nationally representative survey, up from one in six teachers pre-pandemic (Steiner & Woo, 2021). Carver-Thomas and Hammond (2017) found that 43% of teachers leaving the profession indicated family/personal reasons as an important factor in their decision.

Existing evidence about teacher time use primarily uses surveys of only teachers. That work has documented long working hours and a relationship between hours spent working and stress. In the UK context, Allen et al. (2021) find that the median teacher spends 50 hours per week at work. They also show that roughly 40% of teachers report working in the evenings and 10% report working during the weekend and that this has been relatively stable over the last 20 years, suggesting a consistent reality for the teaching profession. Additionally, Jerrim and Sims (2021) provide evidence from five English speaking countries and show that teachers that work longer hours are more stressed than teachers who work shorter hours. While they are unable to compare teaching to other professions, they find that tasks like grading that are often taken home for evenings and weekends are particularly likely to increase workload stress.

The current study uses time diaries from a nationally representative US survey to describe how teachers complete work-related activities during the week and across work and home spaces, how such allocations compare to professionals in similar occupations, and whether patterns in teachers' time use vary by teachers' demographic backgrounds. Our primary analyses focus on time spent in three work-related activities: working for pay in the respondent's main job, volunteering at the respondent's place of work, and working on main job duties while outside of the workplace. We also examine differences between weekday and weekend time use and between male and female respondents. Lastly, we consider occupational differences in time spent on recovery activities like sleeping, relaxation, recreation, and personal care, as well as paid and unpaid labor outside the respondent's main job like working a second job and providing childcare.

2. CONTEXT

Work-life balance is of particular concern for educators and has implications for student outcomes. In a survey of more than 8,000 Canadian elementary and secondary teachers (Froese-Germain, 2014), 54% indicated that they felt significantly torn between their teaching responsibilities and their responsibilities outside the workplace. A staggering 85% reported that work-life imbalance affected their ability to teach the way they would like to. A small qualitative study of public-school teachers in São Paulo, Brazil similarly found that "teachers endure conflict and imbalance between personal and work life, expressed as poor self-perceived leisure and recovery time" (Silva & Fischer, 2020). High job demands (on and off site) and lack of discretion predict a high need for recovery (Sonnentag & Zijlstra, 2006). Herman et al. (2018) found that 93% of teachers experienced high levels of stress in a study of 121 teachers from nine elementary schools in an urban Midwestern school district. The small share (about 3%) of teachers classified as high stress, low coping, and high burnout were associated with the poorest student outcomes.

In the survey of Canadian teachers, a majority (79%) reported that their stress related to work-life imbalance had increased in the last 5 years; only 4% said it had decreased over the same period (Froese-Germain, 2014). This may be related to the increased use of connecting technologies. In a study of 546 full-time public elementary school teachers recruited through two large teachers' unions in a Midwestern state, Park et al. (2020) found work intrusions at home, specifically being contacted after work hours via smartphones or email, can cause stress, negative rumination, negative affect, and insomnia. These incursions of the work sphere into the home sphere are indicative of what Clark (2000) refers to as border permeability.

It is also possible that public school teachers spend their time differently than private school teachers. For example, Green et al. (2008) found that public school teachers in the United Kingdom reported significantly more unpaid overtime hours per week than privately employed teachers. In the United States, differential application of labor laws may create occupational and sectoral differences in unpaid labor. The Fair Labor Standards Act (FLSA) prohibits employees from volunteering services to for-profit private sector employers; however, nonprofit private sector employees may volunteer with their employer (U.S. DOL, n.d.). The FLSA generally bars nonexempt public sector employers from allowing their employees to "volunteer" (without pay) additional time to complete the same work for which they are employed. However, under CFR Section 541.303, most teachers (public and private) are exempt from eligibility for overtime pay when they work greater than 40 hours per week, even if they earn less than the FLSA salary threshold for exempt workers or are paid by the hour (Schmitt et al., 2021).

Lastly, there is evidence of differences by gender and parenthood in work and home roles and time spent in recovery activities among educators. Froese-Germain (2014) found that female teachers were more likely than male teachers to report work-life imbalance. In a study of faculty at a research-intensive university, Misra et al. (2012) found that female faculty and mothers in particular carried higher loads of housework and care time but worked for no fewer hours than their male counterparts. Stengård et al. (2022) used a decade of data on a Swedish cohort of teachers to examine gender differences in time use and depressive symptoms. They found more depressive symptoms, emotional work demands, and unpaid work among female teachers, whereas male teachers spent more time on leisure activities.

3. DATA

Retrospective time diaries are the preferred way to accurately measure time use, as respondents are prone to overestimating time spent in rare and socially desirable activities when asked to recall a typical day (Juster & Stafford, 1991; West, 2014). As such, we use time diary data collected by the American Time Use Survey (ATUS) (Hamermesh et al., 2005; Hofferth et al., 2013).

The ATUS is nationally representative and has been consistently administered each year since 2003 by the US Census Bureau's Bureau of Labor Statistics. The ATUS collects a 24-hour retrospective time diary from one individual over age 15 per household from a subset of the Current Population Survey (CPS) sampling frame and links each time diary to demographic, employment, education, and income data from the CPS for all members of the diary respondent's household. Respondents are asked to sequentially report all activities from 4:00 a.m. the day prior to the interview through 4:00 a.m. on the day of the interview. Once all 24 hours of the diary day are accounted for, interviewers clarify which if any activities were completed as work or were otherwise income-generating and which if any were completed as a volunteer activity.

We use ATUS data from 2003–2019; using 16 years' worth of data allows for greater power and disaggregation compared to prior work in this topic (Krantz-Kent, 2008). Because weekends and certain demographic groups and months are oversampled by the ATUS, all subsequent analyses are weighted by person-day weights that account for unequal probabilities of sample selection across households, months, and days of the week. The weights also adjust for nonresponse based on observable characteristics.

We limit the analytic sample to respondents who completed the ATUS during the school year (i.e. September–May) because teachers' time use differs substantially during the summer months (Krantz-Kent, 2008; West, 2014).[2] The sample is further restricted to ATUS respondents who reported being employed full-time at the time of the survey, were between the ages of 22 and 62, and who hold either a four-year or master's degree. Finally, the sample is limited to those who indicated employment in either the public or private sectors; those who reported self-employment or for whom the sector variable was missing are excluded from analyses.

The sample of teachers includes the 3,168 respondents for whom inclusion criteria were met and reported a primary occupation of teacher. In the final sample of teachers, 7% (214) are pre-kindergarten or kindergarten teachers, 60% (1,916) are elementary or middle school teachers, 25% (786) are high school (secondary) teachers, and 8% (252) are special education teachers. We identify a comparison group employed full-time in similarly prosocial professions, such as therapists, registered nurses, and human resources specialists. Comparison occupations were identified using classifications from the US Department of Labor's online database O*NET (National Center for O*NET Development, 2022); the complete protocol for identifying comparison occupations is detailed in Appendix 1. There are 1,866 non-teachers in the study sample.

The primary dependent variables of interest are time spent working at the respondent's main job, working for the main job at a location other than their workplace, and volunteering at their workplace.[3] Secondary dependent variables of interest include other out-of-work time use categories, such as sleep, leisure, exercise, time spent working at a second job, and childcare.

We divide time spent on childcare into two types: primary and secondary childcare. Primary childcare is computed as the sum of time spent caring for and helping household children under the age of 18 and performing activities related to household children's education. At the end of the survey, respondents are asked about secondary childcare, which includes caring for a child under the age of 13 while simultaneously performing other tasks during the diary day.

Table 1 shows summary statistics for the teachers and non-teachers included in the analytic sample. For the time use variables, the first column reports the average number of minutes per day devoted to the activity[4] while the second column reports the average conditional on the respondent engaging in the activity during the diary day. The third column reports the percentage of respondents who engage in the activity (i.e., the extensive margin). For example,

Table 1. Descriptive Statistics, Teachers and Non-teachers, Representative Day in the ATUS 2003–2019 (Minutes/Day) for Non-summer Months.

	Teachers [N = 3,168]			Non-Teachers [N = 1,886]		
A: Activity (in Minutes)	(1) All	(2) If time >0	(3) 1{time = 1}	(4) All	(5) If time >0	(6) 1{time = 1}
Work for main job	328	444**	0.74	333	465	0.72
	(252)	(189)		(253)	(163)	
Work not at workplace	51***	148	0.35***	32	164	0.19
	(119)	(164)		(104)	(179)	
Volunteer at workplace	2**	85	0.02**	0	57	0.01
	(14)	(48)		(6)	(59)	
Socializing/relaxation/leisure	187	199	0.94	190	206	0.92
	(152)	(148)		(152)	(148)	
Sleep	490	490	1.00	491	492	1.00
	(109)	(108)		(117)	(115)	
Sports/recreation/exercise	13	71	0.19	13	65	0.20
	(38)	(59)		(35)	(55)	
Work for second job	13	201	0.07+	10	193	0.05
	(67)	(168)		(55)	(174)	
Primary childcare	36*	102	0.36***	32	107	0.30
	(74)	(92)		(72)	(97)	
Secondary childcare	122***	343*	0.36***	91	316	0.29
	(214)	(230)		(192)	(243)	
	B: Demographics					
Pre-K-Kindergarten	0.07			n/a		
Special Education	0.08			n/a		
Primary school	0.60			n/a		
Secondary school	0.25			n/a		
Hispanic	0.08			0.08		
White	0.89***			0.79		
Black	0.08***			0.15		
Asian	0.02**			0.04		
Female	0.77			0.75		
Age	40.7			40.3		
Masters	0.49***			0.38		
Public sector	0.82***			0.35		
Metro	0.84*			0.87		
Own child under 13	0.36***			0.30		
Number of own children in HH	0.80***			0.64		
Spouse/partner in HH	0.72***			0.64		
Spouse/partner (if present) employed	0.90***			0.84		
HH inc.< \$20k	0.02			0.02		
HH inc. \$20k to \$75k	0.41			0.43		
HH inc.> \$75k	0.53			0.50		

Notes: Standard deviation reported in parentheses. Means and standard deviations are weighted by sampling weights that adjust for unequal probability of selection across both days and households. HH = household.

$^{+}p < 0.10$, $^{*}p < 0.05$, $^{**}p < 0.01$, $^{***}p < 0.001$ indicate the statistical significance of the mean differences between teachers and non-teachers.

only 2% of teachers report any time volunteering at their workplace on the diary day, so the average time spent volunteering at work for all teachers is 2 minutes. However, for those who did report volunteering, the average time spent is 85 minutes.

These summary statistics suggest that teachers spend more time working outside their place of work, volunteering at their workplace, and engaging in childcare than non-teachers. They also indicate that 7% of teachers report working a second job on the diary day, compared to 5% of non-teachers, which is a statistically significant difference. Time spent on other nonwork activities such as sleep, leisure, and exercise does not appear to differ between teachers and non-teachers.

As seen in Panel B of Table 1, the comparison group closely matches the teacher group in age, household income, percent Hispanic, and percent female. Teachers, however, are more likely to be white, more likely to have a master's degree, much more likely to work in the public sector, and slightly less likely to live in a metropolitan area than non-teachers. Teachers are also more likely to have a spouse or partner in the household, more likely for that spouse or partner to be employed, more likely to have a child under 13 in the household, and on average have more total children in the home, compared to non-teachers. These latter differences especially may contribute to different time allocations. In the next section we describe regression analyses that adjust for these observable differences.

4. METHODOLOGY

We examine the predictors of time use (*T*) for teachers and non-teachers by estimating linear time-use regressions of the form:

$$T_i = \alpha + \delta \text{Type}_i + \beta X_i + u_i \quad (1)$$

where i indexes respondents, *Type* is a set of categorical indicators that describe the type of teacher (i.e., preschool, primary, secondary, special education, with non-teacher being the omitted reference group); X is a vector of respondent, household, and diary characteristics including day, month, year, and region indicators (fixed effects); and u is an idiosyncratic error term.[5] In addition to diary day controls, fully-specified models control for the respondent having at least one of their own children under the age of 13 at home, the total number of own children in the household, whether a spouse/partner was present and employed, present and unemployed, or not present, household income (low, medium, or high), race, Hispanic ethnicity, age, sex, whether the respondent lives in a metropolitan area, and whether they were publicly employed. Standard errors are clustered by state. We estimate Eq. (1) using the full sample of teacher and comparison group time diaries completed between September and May.

The linear model shown in Eq. (1) is estimated by ordinary least squares (OLS) with standard errors clustered at the state level to make statistical inference robust to arbitrary forms of heteroskedasticity and serial correlation within states over time (Gershenson, 2013; Kalenkoski & Pabilonia, 2014). OLS estimates of linear time-use regressions are preferred despite potential "pile-ups" at zero, as Stewart (2013) shows that OLS estimates are more robust than Tobit estimates when the nonparticipation is caused by measurement error attributable to the fact that time diary surveys sample days as opposed to longer time frames. For example, even if a respondent reports zero volunteer time on the diary day, it is possible that the respondent did volunteer on another day during the week or month of the time diary.

This raises an interesting and open question in time-use research: what is the appropriate or optimal length of a time diary survey? A 24-hour diary, like the ATUS, is ideal for daily activities like sleeping. In the aggregate, however, they may not be representative of longer time periods that include days with above and below average time spent on various activities. This amounts to an external validity question. Similarly, since time diaries typically sample days and not people, an individual diary may be misleading if it happens to catch someone on an "odd day" or performing a weekly or monthly activity such as doing laundry or waiting in an auto repair shop. The alternative would be a significantly more costly 7- or 14-day time diary, which would introduce its own set of survey response problems (te Braak, van Tienoven, et al., 2022). This debate is not particularly relevant to the current setting, however, where the focus is on group differences. Intuitively, because we are ultimately interested in teacher-days and non-teacher days, we have a de facto year-long diary for each group that averages out the "odd days" and the weekly and monthly activities.

5. RESULTS

Estimates of Eq. (1) for the main time-use variables are presented in Table 2 with diary day controls only (panel A) and with all control variables (panel B). Consistent with West (2014), Table 2 shows that secondary school teachers spend more time working in a given day than other teacher types. On average, secondary teachers work at their main job 29.6 minutes more per day (equivalent to 3.5 hours more per week) than the comparison group of non-teachers, which is a highly significant difference.

All four teacher types spend an average of 1–2 minutes more per diary day volunteering at their workplace than non-teachers, though the difference is only statistically significant for primary school teachers. Both primary and secondary teachers spend approximately 25 more minutes per day completing work at a location other than their workplace than comparable non-teachers. Pre-Kindergarten/kindergarten and special education teachers also spend more time working outside of school, but these differences are smaller and not statistically significant.

Table 2. Time Use Compared to Non-teachers.

A: Without Controls [N = 5,054]	(1)	(2)	(3)
Activity (in Minutes)	Work for Primary Job	Volunteer at Workplace	Work for Main Job, not at Workplace
All Teachers	2.1	1.4**	18.9***
	(6.9)	(0.5)	(4.6)
R^2	0.471	0.021	0.025
Pre K-Kindergarten	4.5	0.4	5.2
	(15.9)	(0.6)	(9.9)
Special Education	−17.7	1.1	9.6
	(14.6)	(0.8)	(9.3)
Primary (Elementary / Middle)	−4.8	1.3*	21.8***
	(8.0)	(0.6)	(5.1)
Secondary (High School)	24.2*	1.8+	18.6**
	(10.1)	(1.1)	(6.1)
R^2	0.472	0.021	0.026
B: With Controls [N = 4,783]	**(1)**	**(2)**	**(3)**
All Teachers	7.1	1.2***	23.5***
	(6.9)	(0.3)	(4.7)
R^2	0.482	0.032	0.032
Pre K-Kindergarten	5.4	0.8	9.0
	(16.5)	(0.7)	(9.9)
Special Education	−13.9	1.3	15.3
	(16.6)	(0.8)	(9.4)
Primary (Elementary / Middle)	0.3	1.3*	26.4***
	(7.8)	(0.6)	(5.3)
Secondary (High School)	29.6**	1.3	25.1***
	(10.3)	(0.8)	(5.9)
R^2	0.484	0.032	0.034

Notes: Standard errors in parentheses, all standard errors are clustered by state. Non-teacher is used as a reference category and is omitted from output. $^{+}p < 0.10$, $^{*}p < 0.05$, $^{**}p < 0.01$, $^{***}p < 0.001$.
A: Regressions condition on day of week, month, year, and holiday indicators.
B: Regressions condition on Panel A controls as well as region, demographic, and household indicators (see Appendix 3 for control variable details and coefficients).

Estimated coefficients for the control variables included in the models estimated in Table 2, Panel B are reported in Appendix 3. With the exception of medium and high household income predicting more time spent volunteering at work and Hispanic ethnicity predicting less time on work completed outside the workplace, the control variables generally do not significantly predict time spent in the activities of interest. For time spent volunteering at the workplace and working for the main job outside the workplace, we find that the full slate of control variables explains less than 5% of the variation in the data ($R^2 < 0.05$).

This is not uncommon in time use research, particularly for activities that are not done on a daily basis, as the single diary day format introduces substantial random measurement error (Kan & Pudney, 2008).

In Table 3 we present regression results for time spent on the three primary outcome variables separately for weekdays (Monday through Friday) and weekends (Saturday and Sunday). On an average weekday accounting for control variables, teachers spend nearly 1.6 more minutes volunteering at work, and 18.6 more minutes working not at their workplace than non-teachers. The two groups do not differ significantly in total time spent working on weekdays. When the

Table 3. Time Use Compared to Non-teachers, Weekdays Versus Weekends.

A: Without Controls	Weekday [N = 2,545]			Weekend [N = 2,509]		
	(1) Work for Primary Job	(2) Volunteer at Workplace	(3) Work for Main job, not at Workplace	(4) Work for Primary Job	(5) Volunteer at Workplace	(6) Work for Main Job, not at Workplace
All Teachers	−1.1	1.9**	12.2*	13.9*	−0.03	38.5***
	(9.6)	(0.7)	(5.4)	(6.1)	(0.2)	(4.8)
R^2	0.108	0.024	0.033	0.031	0.009	0.053
Pre K-Kindergarten	3.4	−0.4	−8.3	7.6	1.4	35.3**
	(22.2)	(0.6)	(12.0)	(11.5)	(1.5)	(10.1)
Special Education	−13.0	1.6	9.7	−18.9+	−0.2	16.3+
	(18.6)	(1.1)	(13.2)	(9.5)	(0.1)	(8.8)
Primary	−10.4	1.8*	16.9*	11.8+	−0.1	36.1***
	(11.3)	(0.8)	(6.3)	(6.1)	(0.1)	(5.2)
Secondary	24.0+	2.6+	6.4	31.2***	−0.2	51.9***
	(13.2)	(1.5)	(6.5)	(8.6)	(0.1)	(7.3)
R^2	0.112	0.026	0.035	0.037	0.014	0.058
B: With Controls	Weekday [N = 2,406]			Weekend [N = 2,377]		
All Teachers	3.1	1.6***	18.6**	23.3***	0.1	38.2***
	(9.1)	(0.4)	(5.9)	(5.4)	(0.3)	(5.5)
R^2	0.121	0.042	0.044	0.056	0.014	0.062
Pre K-Kindergarten	5.5	−0.03	−1.7	8.7	1.5	31.6**
	(23.6)	(0.6)	(12.3)	(11.7)	(1.5)	(10.5)
Special Education	−11.9	1.9	19.4	−7.9	−0.01	14.6
	(20.3)	(1.2)	(13.6)	(9.9)	(0.2)	(9.7)
Primary	−6.5	1.7*	23.2**	22.1***	−0.01	35.2***
	(10.5)	(0.8)	(6.7)	(5.9)	(0.2)	(6.2)
Secondary	28.7*	1.7	14.7*	42.9***	−0.1	56.0***
	(13.8)	(1.1)	(7.2)	(7.7)	(0.2)	(8.0)
R^2	0.124	0.042	0.046	0.061	0.018	0.069

Notes: Standard errors in parentheses, all standard errors are clustered by state. $^+p < 0.10$, $^*p < 0.05$, $^{**}p < 0.01$, $^{***}p < 0.001$.

A: Regressions condition on day of week, month, year, and holiday indicators.

B: Regressions condition on Panel A controls as well as region, demographic, and household indicators.

data is disaggregated by teacher type, we see that secondary teachers spend almost one-half hour longer working on weekdays than non-teachers.

Time use on weekend days is particularly relevant to understanding opportunities for recovery, as these are days when school is not in session and that theoretically serve as a break for teachers from work duties. The regression results indicate that weekends contain more work for teachers than for their non-teaching counterparts. Compared to non-teachers, all teachers on average spend 23 more minutes working overall and 38 more minutes working not at their workplace on an average weekend day. These differences are statistically significant for all teacher types except for special education teachers and range from 31.6 more minutes for Pre-K/kindergarten teachers to 56 more minutes for secondary teachers.

Tables 4 and 5 report the findings of Table 3, Panel B separately for women and men, respectively. There are very few male teachers in the Pre-K/K ($n = 7$) and special education ($n = 24$) categories, so these comparisons are limited to primary and secondary teachers. Female teachers spend more time working outside their workplace compared to female non-teachers on both weekdays and weekend days and more total time working on weekend days. Male secondary teachers work for approximately one hour more than male non-teachers on both weekdays and weekend days. The larger occupational difference for male secondary teachers compared to their female colleagues could be driven by male secondary teachers being more likely to serve in coaching roles for school athletic teams compared to female teachers (Knowles et al., 2020). Having a child under the age of 13 was a significant predictor of total time spent working for females but not males, suggesting a gendered difference in the impact of childcare responsibilities on time spent working.

In addition to including an indicator for public employment as a control in the main regression analyses, we estimate Eq. (1) separately for public employees and private employees to consider occupational differences within each sector; and estimate the effect of public employment in a sample restricted to teachers. The results of these analyses are presented in Appendix 4 and suggest that the differences we observe between teachers and non-teachers are largely driven by differences among public sector workers. We found modest differences between public and private sector teachers that suggest publicly employed teachers spend more time in all three of the time use categories of interest. Only the finding for total time spent working for the primary job (indicating that public teachers work 20.7 more minutes per day on average than private teachers) was statistically significant at a $p\text{-value} < 0.10$.

Table 6 presents the results of Eq. (1) for seven additional time use activities: sleep; socializing, relaxation and leisure; sports, exercise, and recreation; personal care; working a second job; providing primary childcare; and providing secondary childcare. The first four activities are types of recovery activities, activities one could due to reduce stress to a basal level to mitigate the negative impacts of sustained work-related stress. The latter three categories are types of paid and unpaid labor unrelated to the respondent's primary job.

Table 4. Time Use Compared to Non-teachers, Weekdays Versus Weekends, Females Only.

	Weekday [N = 1,654]			Weekend [N = 1,623]		
	(1) Work for Primary Job	(2) Volunteer at Workplace	(3) Work for Main Job, Not at Workplace	(4) Work for Primary Job	(5) Volunteer at Workplace	(6) Work for Main Job, Not at Workplace
Primary	1.3	1.4^{+}	31.1***	20.0**	−0.3	35.7***
	(13.4)	(0.7)	(7.4)	(6.9)	(0.2)	(6.8)
Secondary	13.9	0.4	23.3**	38.4***	−0.2	55.8***
	(15.7)	(0.8)	(8.3)	(11.0)	(0.2)	(11.2)
HH Characteristics						
Own child under 13	−50.3*	0.9^{+}	−5.1	−28.8*	0.7	−12.9
	(22.0)	(0.4)	(10.4)	(12.7)	(0.5)	(10.9)
Total number of own children in HH	9.7	−0.6^{+}	−1.4	9.3	−0.2	4.1
	(7.3)	(0.3)	(4.4)	(6.5)	(0.2)	(5.2)
Spouse/partner not employed	3.4	−0.2	13.3	21.0	−0.2	22.2
	(28.0)	(1.0)	(19.9)	(18.7)	(0.2)	(17.7)
Spouse/partner employed	7.4	−0.6	−2.8	−5.6	−0.1	−8.9
	(14.5)	(0.7)	(9.4)	(10.5)	(0.2)	(7.1)
Middle HH income	−35.3	−0.3	−12.7	−16.7	0.1	−9.1
	(57.4)	(0.8)	(23.1)	(33.3)	(0.1)	(26.3)
High HH income	−26.3	1.2	−10.9	−13.5	0.1	−5.8
	(57.0)	(0.8)	(20.3)	(33.4)	(0.1)	(26.2)
Demographics						
Black only	−9.8	−0.3	4.9	17.3	0.3	4.0
	(16.8)	(0.5)	(12.2)	(15.7)	(0.3)	(10.6)
American Indian, Alaska Native only	−33.8	−1.1	−41.6*	10.8	0.1	29.4
	(119.5)	(1.6)	(19.9)	(55.8)	(0.1)	(58.1)
Asian only	−28.0	−0.5	4.3	−16.7	−0.3	−21.4^{+}
	(55.9)	(0.8)	(24.8)	(15.9)	(0.3)	(11.0)
Hawaiian Pacific Islander only	49.7	−0.6	114.8^{+}	−52.2**	−0.3	−12.1
	(176.8)	(1.3)	(65.1)	(15.0)	(0.4)	(16.1)
More than one race	18.9	2.1	9.2	−10.4	−0.1	−18.0
	(45.6)	(2.2)	(24.8)	(29.9)	(0.2)	(11.6)
Hispanic	16.2	1.3	−3.0	−21.4*	−0.2	−16.1^{+}
	(26.8)	(1.3)	(7.1)	(10.4)	(0.1)	(8.8)
Age	0.5	0.0	−0.01	−0.03	0.0	0.3
	(0.7)	(0.0)	(0.3)	(0.5)	(0.0)	(0.4)
Metro area	−7.1	−0.5	−9.3	18.7^{+}	0.1	20.1*
	(13.4)	(1.1)	(10.7)	(10.1)	(0.1)	(8.0)
Public employee	−1.1	0.7*	−5.8	−11.7	0.1	7.8^{+}
	(15.9)	(0.3)	(8.3)	(7.8)	(0.2)	(4.2)
Constant	399.7***	−1.7	50.8*	93.4*	−0.6	21.6
	(69.8)	(1.8)	(24.7)	(41.4)	(0.5)	(35.5)
R^2	0.115	0.008	0.093	0.052	0.008	0.093

Notes: Standard errors in parentheses, all standard errors are clustered by state. HH = household. $^{+}p < 0.10$, $^{*}p < 0.05$, $^{**}p < 0.01$, $^{***}p < 0.001$. Regressions condition on region (northeast, Midwest, south, and west), day of week, month, year, and holiday indicators. Low HH income (omitted) < $20,000, middle HH income > = $20,000 and < $75,000, high HH income > = $75,000. Non-teachers, spouse/partner not present and white race are used as reference categories and are omitted from output.

Table 5. Time Use Compared to Non-teachers, Weekdays Versus Weekends, Males Only.

	Weekday [N = 557]			Weekend [N = 552]		
	(1) Work for Primary Job	(2) Volunteer at Workplace	(3) Work for Main Job, Not at Workplace	(4) Work for Primary Job	(5) Volunteer at Workplace	(6) Work for Main Job, Not at Workplace
Primary	−21.2 (17.2)	2.6 (2.1)	4.4 (10.7)	43.3^{+} (25.8)	0.6 (1.0)	39.5^{+} (19.9)
Secondary	54.5* (20.7)	3.9* (1.8)	10.7 (14.6)	62.8** (23.2)	0.2 (0.6)	68.7*** (17.3)
HH Characteristics						
Own child under 13	13.4 (40.2)	−2.5 (3.2)	11.5 (20.0)	4.3 (29.4)	0.5 (0.6)	−8.5 (18.8)
Total number of own children in HH	−1.8 (15.4)	0.4 (1.1)	2.4 (8.1)	−5.4 (10.3)	0.1 (0.1)	4.1 (7.9)
Spouse/partner not employed	−29.1 (38.4)	3.9 (4.4)	29.1 (27.7)	−19.9 (20.5)	−0.5 (0.3)	−8.7 (16.2)
Spouse/partner employed	−31.1 (22.7)	−1.2 (2.1)	12.3 (17.7)	−24.1 (19.4)	−0.6 (0.4)	−16.3 (17.0)
Middle HH income	−55.8 (60.3)	8.0 (5.3)	−37.5 (42.3)	−265.3^{+} (140.6)	0.0 (0.3)	−14.5 (47.2)
High HH income	−13.3 (58.5)	7.6 (4.9)	−44.7 (42.3)	−237.1^{+} (137.0)	0.4 (0.4)	3.6 (47.3)
Demographics						
Black only	−7.6 (33.2)	−3.8 (2.4)	12.9 (20.5)	14.0 (28.2)	−0.1 (0.1)	−8.3 (12.1)
American Indian, Alaska Native only	30.3 (54.6)	3.7 (3.4)	−22.0 (39.3)	−89.6^{+} (52.8)	−0.3 (0.7)	−81.6* (39.9)
Asian only	−74.6^{+} (42.7)	−0.2 (1.4)	−8.0 (28.1)	−17.6 (87.1)	−0.8 (0.7)	−21.8 (29.8)
Hawaiian Pacific Islander only	- -	- -	- -	−42.2 (45.4)	−0.8 (0.7)	20.4 (36.8)
More than one race	7.1 (44.2)	−1.3 (6.9)	−15.5 (27.6)	−15.9 (38.4)	−0.4 (0.3)	34.4 (22.3)
Hispanic	24.9 (28.4)	−3.3 (2.7)	−15.5 (12.6)	−24.1 (30.8)	0.8* (0.3)	−9.2 (22.0)
Age	0.3 (1.2)	−0.3* (0.1)	0.2 (0.7)	−1.1 (0.9)	0.0 (0.0)	0.1 (0.4)
Metro area	1.8 (20.1)	−3.7 (3.7)	−3.7 (15.1)	−28.3 (29.3)	0.4 (0.3)	−23.9 (22.4)
Public employee	−2.8 (23.3)	0.7 (1.3)	−38.1* (16.5)	−24.9 (24.8)	−0.5 (0.8)	−14.7 (21.3)
Constant	397.3*** (82.6)	9.3 (8.8)	95.1^{+} (50.1)	334.7* (152.9)	−0.9 (1.0)	56.1 (53.9)
R^2	0.239	0.167	0.098	0.204	0.032	0.103

Notes: Standard errors in parentheses, all standard errors are clustered by state. HH = household. $^{+}p < 0.10$, $^{*}p < 0.05$, $^{**}p < 0.01$, $^{***}p < 0.001$. Regressions condition on region (northeast, Midwest, south, and west), day of week, month, year, and holiday indicators. Low HH income (omitted) < $20,000, middle HH income >=$20,000 and < $75,000, high HH income >=$75,000. Non-teachers, spouse/partner not present and white race are used as reference categories and are omitted from output.

Table 6. Time Used in Recovery Activities (Columns 1–4) and Additional Labor (Columns 5–7) [N = 4,783].

Activities (In Minutes)	(1) Sleep	(2) Socializing, Relaxation and Leisure	(3) Sport, Exercise, Recreation	(4) Personal Care	(5) Working a Second Job	(6) Primary Childcare	(7) Secondary Childcare
Pre K-Kindergarten	−17.2⁺ (9.3)	4.7 (10.7)	−2.8 (2.4)	−0.05 (3.5)	1.2 (4.2)	6.4⁺ (3.7)	35.7** (11.7)
Special Education	7.4 (7.7)	−15.0 (13.0)	1.0 (4.5)	−1.8 (5.1)	8.5 (5.4)	4.2 (3.6)	10.9 (10.4)
Primary	1.9 (5.2)	2.8 (6.3)	1.0 (1.8)	−1.5 (1.9)	3.7 (5.5)	−1.5 (1.8)	15.2** (5.3)
Secondary	−10.1⁺ (5.6)	−16.0* (6.8)	2.6 (1.7)	−4.5⁺ (2.4)	11.7⁺ (5.9)	−7.7** (2.6)	4.5 (6.1)
			HH Characteristics				
Own child under 13	2.6 (5.4)	−21.1** (7.7)	−3.3 (2.6)	−4.4 (2.7)	−2.9 (2.9)	75.5*** (5.0)	306.9*** (11.4)
Total number of own children in HH	−9.6*** (2.1)	−12.0*** (3.4)	0.4 (1.4)	−1.7* (0.9)	−0.7 (1.2)	7.7** (2.3)	5.1 (5.0)
Spouse/partner not employed	−3.5 (5.5)	15.2 (10.2)	2.1 (2.3)	1.5 (3.3)	−1.3 (4.5)	5.0 (3.0)	11.6 (7.4)
Spouse/partner employed	3.9 (5.1)	−6.0 (7.8)	0.4 (1.4)	0.8 (2.9)	−4.7 (3.5)	8.3*** (1.5)	4.8 (3.2)
Middle HH income	20.5 (13.3)	30.1⁺ (15.0)	4.0 (3.0)	5.2 (4.0)	1.1 (7.4)	2.7 (4.3)	−3.7 (17.5)
High HH income	12.3 (13.3)	22.2 (15.5)	5.7⁺ (3.3)	5.0 (4.0)	0.7 (7.8)	2.3 (5.0)	−5.9 (17.8)
R^2	0.173	0.214	0.032	0.065	0.027	0.380	0.588

Notes: Standard errors in parentheses, standard errors clustered by state. ⁺$p < 0.10$, *$p < 0.05$, **$p < 0.01$, ***$p < 0.001$. Regressions condition on respondent demographics, region (northeast, Midwest, south, and west), day of week, month, year, and holiday indicators. HH = Household; low HH income (omitted) < $20,000, middle HH income > = $20,000 and < $75,000, high HH income > = $75,000. Non-teachers, and spouse/partner not present are used as reference categories and are omitted from output.

Results varied by teacher type. All teacher types were shown to spend more time on average working at a second job, though only secondary teachers to a statistically significant degree. Similarly, results indicated that all teachers spent more time providing secondary childcare, with those teaching grades Pre-K through 8th showing a statistically significant difference from non-teachers. Pre-K/kindergarten and secondary teachers both reported significantly fewer minutes of sleep compared to non-teachers. Secondary teachers also reported

Table 7. Time Use Compared to Non-teachers (Alternate Comparison Group).

With Controls [n = 9,967]	(1)	(2)	(3)
Activity (In Minutes)	Work for Primary Job	Volunteer at Workplace	Work for Main Job, Not at Workplace
All Teachers	13.4^{+}	1.3***	19.8***
	(8.0)	(0.3)	(3.5)
R^2	0.507	0.018	0.039
Pre K-Kindergarten	10.2	0.7	4.9
	(15.1)	(0.6)	(9.5)
Special Education	−5.6	1.2	11.4
	(18.1)	(0.8)	(8.6)
Primary	7.9	1.3*	23.3***
	(8.3)	(0.5)	(4.1)
Secondary	31.8*	1.6^{+}	19.4***
	(13.2)	(0.8)	(5.2)
R^2	0.507	0.018	0.040

Notes: Standard errors in parentheses, all standard errors are clustered by state. Non-teacher is used as a reference category and is omitted from output. $^{+}p < 0.10$, $^{*}p < 0.05$, $^{**}p < 0.01$, $^{***}p < 0.001$.

Regressions condition on day of week, month, year, and holiday, region, demographic, and household indicators.

significantly less time spent on personal care, which can include grooming, personal care for medical reasons, and connecting with a partner.

Finally, as a check of the robustness of our findings, we ran the regression shown in Table 2, Panel B using an alternately specified and much larger group of individuals in comparison occupations (n = 7,312), the details of which are provided in Appendix 1B.[6] The results of this analysis are presented in Table 7. The direction, magnitude, and significance of the fully specified regressions with the alternate comparison occupations were largely consistent with the main analysis. For work completed not at the workplace, estimated differences between teachers and non-teacher were slightly smaller as a whole and by teacher type for the alternate analysis compared to the main analysis group, but were still economically significant and within the confidence interval of the main results.

6. DISCUSSION

We present rich descriptive statistics about how teachers and observationally similar non-teachers spend time in three work-related activities and six activities outside of their primary jobs during the school year. The results described above have a variety of implications for education policy and research.

We find that teachers spend more time volunteering (completing unpaid labor) at work on weekdays and more time completing work for their main job overall and outside of work on weekend days than non-teachers. The latter indicates greater permeability of both temporal (when work takes place) and physical (where work takes place) boundaries for teachers compared to non-teachers. This type of work-life integration has been linked to reduced well-being and increased stress, which have implications for job satisfaction and turnover. Increased planning time during the school day could reduce the need to complete work on weekends. Supporting clear boundaries for both parents and colleagues as to when a teacher may be contacted regarding school-related issues outside of work may support less permeable borders, as suggested by Park et al. (2020). At the federal level, expanding overtime protection for teachers in the FLSA could impact an estimated 1.5 million teachers who would become newly eligible for overtime pay when they work more than 40 hours in the same week (Schmitt et al., 2021), which may reduce time spent on unpaid labor at the school where they work.

The most significant differences in time spent in recovery activities and other labor were seen between non-teachers and secondary teachers. Secondary teachers are spending more time working on both weekdays and weekend days, getting less sleep, less socialization, relaxation, and leisure time, and spending more time working a second job. These findings suggest that teachers' work demands may negatively impact their time for recovery activities. Insufficient recovery has serious implications for stress management and wellness, which in turn have implications for turnover. The heightened effect seen among secondary teachers may be of particular concern because secondary teachers often teach specialized subjects that require single-subject certification exams.[7] The U.S. Department of Education National Center for Education Statistics reported that from 1999–2012, public high schools consistently had a higher rate of vacant teaching positions considered "difficult-to-staff," compared to public elementary and middle schools (DOE NCES, 2015). More research is needed on the connection between recovery activities, teacher job satisfaction and well-being, and intent to leave the profession.

A final interesting, and policy relevant, finding is that teachers spend significantly more time engaged in secondary childcare than non-teachers. Additional investigation of time use data to tease out which primary activities are most associated with concurrent secondary childcare of household children could be helpful to understand the impact on teacher's work and recovery time and border-crossing practices. For instance, providing secondary childcare while completing work for their main job may suggest further work-life integration, or providing secondary childcare while engaging in activities typically deemed recovery activities may diminish the quality of recovery time.

Prior work using surveys of teachers helps to contextualize our finding that teachers work more during weekend days compared to non-teachers. For example, Jerrim and Sims (2021) provide evidence from teachers in five English speaking countries (including the United States) and find a strong relationship between longer working hours and higher level of stress. They also find that this is not a linear relationship and that the task composition matters for job satisfaction. Specifically, they show that tasks such as grading/marking papers are particularly likely to add to stress and that time with colleagues is less stressful. While we cannot observe what specific work-related tasks teachers are engaged in, we do see that they are more likely than non-teachers to work on the weekends, and it seems likely that these weekend activities are solitary activities like grading. Like Allen et al. (2021), we find evidence that teachers work substantial hours outside of the school day and we are able to add that they are more likely to engage in this border-crossing than non-teachers.

In sum, a nuanced understanding of how teachers spend their nonwork time, coupled with an analysis of work time, such as Krantz-Kent (2008) and West (2014), will lead to a better understanding of the pressures and commitments that teachers, the most important school-provided input, face on a daily basis and inform our understanding of teachers' extensive and intensive margin labor supply choices. Our findings affirm that teaching is not a job that one can "leave at the office" so bringing teachers' nonwork time use into the conversation is essential.

ACKNOWLEDGMENTS

The authors thank participants at the 2022 IATUR Conference, the editors, and two anonymous reviewers for providing helpful feedback and suggestions.

NOTES

1. Recovery is the temporary relief from an individual's workload and associated stress in order to replenish their physical and mental energy.

2. Descriptive statistics for key time use categories and demographics for the main analysis sample in the months of June, July, and August are presented in Appendix 2. Teachers work fewer minutes during summer months than they do during the school year, but greater than 50% work for their main job for more than zero minutes on an average summer day. West (2014) explored this phenomenon and provided three possible explanations for teachers having positive work hours in summer months even when they are "off": (1) teachers may be teaching summer school or work at a school that does not observe summer vacation, (2) the nine month school year often stretches into summer months, and/or (3) they may be attending teacher professional development trainings, workshops, or curriculum planning.

3. Volunteering is broadly defined by ATUS as "volunteer (unpaid) activities done by the respondent for individuals or institutions through formal organizations." For the purposes of this study, we created a custom time use category that captures minutes spent on Volunteer Activities (Time Use Code 150000) at Respondent's Workplace (Location Code 0102). ATUS provides hundreds of category activity examples for this activity, such as selling at concession stands, setting up for a walk-a-thon, selling raffle tickets, editing newsletters, organizing volunteer materials, etc. There is not an ATUS specification for unpaid labor performed for the respondent's employer. We use the location code as a proxy but this specification likely does not perfectly or exclusively capture unpaid labor performed by teachers, as school campuses can serve as community spaces for outside volunteer organizations.

4. All our analyses report time use in minutes per day, as this is how activities are captured in the ATUS and allows for finer comparisons. To further contextualize these descriptive statistics, however, consider this calculation of total time working in hours per week, which may be a more natural unit for comparing time use: On average and excluding holidays, teachers work an average of 36.6 hours during the week and 2.3 hours during the weekend. This compares to 36.8 hours during the week and 1.9 hours on weekends for non-teachers.

5. We also estimated versions of Eq. (1) that interact the teacher indicators with either a linear time trend or a full set of year indicators. These interactions are generally indistinguishable from zero, suggesting that there is no systematic change over the course of our sample in teachers' relative time use.

6. Importantly, the results are qualitatively similar when nurses are excluded from either of the comparison groups. This means that the results are not driven by nurses, who may be on systematically different schedules (e.g., working longer hours but fewer days per week, more likely to work holidays, etc.).

7. Teaching certification requirements vary by state; the most widely accepted credentialing system is PRAXIS administered by Educational Testing Service (ETS). Details on each state's requirements can be viewed at www.ets.org/praxis/site/test-takers/plan-your-test.html. Multi-subject credentials, sometimes called core academic skills or basic skills exam, are generally required to teach in self-contained classrooms typical of elementary schools. Single-subject credentials or subject matter exams certify knowledge in a specific subject, e.g., chemistry, computer science, French language, etc., which are more typical of high school and some middle school course offerings. Depending on the state, requirements for single-subject credentials may make secondary teachers less interchangeable for one another than teachers of lower grades.

REFERENCES

Allen, R., Benhenda, A., Jerrim, J., & Sims, S. (2021). New evidence on teachers' working hours in England: An empirical analysis of four datasets. *Research Papers in Education*, *36*(6), 657–681. https://doi.org/10.1080/02671522.2020.1736616

Allen, T. D., Cho, E., & Meier, L. L. (2014). Work–family boundary dynamics. *Annual Review of Organizational Psychology and Organizational Behavior*, *1*(1), 99–121.

Barrett, G. F., & Hamermesh, D. (2019). Labor supply elasticities, overcoming nonclassical measurement error using more accurate hours data. *Journal of Human Resources*, *54*(1), 255–265.

Becker, G. (1965). A theory of the allocation of time. *The Economic Journal*, *75*(299), 493–517.

Bureau of Labor Statistics and U.S. Census Bureau (BLS). (2022, June). *American Time Use Survey User's Guide: Understanding ATUS 2003–2021*. https://www.bls.gov/tus/atususersguide.pdf. Accessed on February 18, 2023.

Carver-Thomas, D., & Darling-Hammond, L. (2017). *Teacher turnover: Why it matters and what we can do about it*. Learning Policy Institute. https://doi.org/10.54300/454.278

Clark, S. C. (2000). Work/family border theory: A new theory of work/family balance. *Human Relations*, *53*(6), 747–770.

Desrochers, S., & Morgan, C. (2021). Boundary theory and work-family border theory research: A focus on boundary enactment. Work and Family Researchers Network, Work and Family Encyclopedia. https://wfrn.org/wp-content/uploads/2021/04/Boundary-Theory-and-Work-Family-Border-Theory-Research-Stephan-Cooper.pdf. Accessed on February 18, 2023.

Dickens, W., & Lundberg, S. (1993). Hours restrictions and labor supply. *International Economic Review*, *34*(1), 169–192.

Froese-Germain, B. (2014). *Work-life balance and the Canadian teaching profession*. Canadian Teachers' Federation. https://eric.ed.gov/?id=ED546884. Accessed on May 19, 2022.

Gershenson, S. (2013). Do summer time-use gaps vary by socioeconomic status? *American Educational Research Journal*, *50*(6), 1219–1248.

Gershenson, S. (2021). *Identifying and producing effective teachers*. Paper No. 14096. IZA Discussion.

Green, F., Machin, S., Murphy, R., & Zhu, Y. (2008).Competition for private and state school teachers. *Journal of Education and Work*, *21*(5), 383–404.

Hamermesh, D. S. (2018). Why are professors poorly paid? *Economics of Education Review*, *66*, 137–141.

Hamermesh, D. S., Frazis, H., & Stewart, J. (2005). Data watch: The American time use survey. *The Journal of Economic Perspectives*, *19*(1), 221–232.

Hanushek, E., & Rivkin, S. (2010). Generalizations about using value-added measures of teacher quality. *The American Economic Review*, *100*(2), 267–271.

Harding, D. J. (1997). *Measuring children's time use: A review of methodologies and findings*. Center for Research on Child Wellbeing. Working paper, 97-1.

Herman, K. C., Hickmon-Rosa, J., & Reinke, W. M. (2018). Empirically derived profiles of teacher stress, burnout, self-efficacy, and coping and associated student outcomes. *Journal of Positive Behavior Interventions*, *20*(2), 90–100.

Hofferth, S., Flood, S., Sobek, M., & Backman, D. (2013). *American Time Use Survey Data Extract System: Version 2.8* [dataset]. University of Maryland and Minneapolis, MN: IPUMS 2020. http://www.atusdata.org

Jerrim, J., & Sims, S. (2021). When is high workload bad for teacher wellbeing? Accounting for the non-linear contribution of specific teaching tasks. *Teaching and Teacher Education*, *105*, 103395. https://doi.org/10.1016/j.tate.2021.103395

Jones, N. D., Camburn, E. M., Kelcey, B., & Quintero, E. (2022). Teachers' time use and affect before and after COVID-19 school closures. *AERA Open*, *8*. https://doi.org/10.1177/23328584211068068

Jones, N., & Youngs, P. (2012). Attitudes and affect: Daily emotions and their association with the commitment and burnout of beginning teachers. *Teachers College Record*, *114*(2), 1–36.

Juster, F. T., & Stafford, F. P. (1991). The allocation of time: Empirical findings, behavioral models, and problems of measurement. *Journal of Economic Literature*, *29*(2), 471–522.

Kalenkoski, C. M., & Pabilonia, S. W. (2014). *Does high school homework increase academic achievement?* IZA Discussion Paper. No. 8142.

Kan, M. Y., & Pudney, S. (2008). Measurement error in stylized and diary data on time use. *Sociological Methodology*, *38*(1), 101–132.

Knowles, R., Hawkman, A., & Nielsen, S. (2020). The social studies teacher-coach: A quantitative analysis comparing coaches and non-coaches across how/what they teach. *Journal of Social Studies Research*, *44*. https://doi.org/10.1016/j.jssr.2019.04.001

Krantz-Kent, R. (2008). Teachers' work patterns: When, where, and how much do U.S. teachers work? *Monthly Labor Review*, *131*(March), 52–59.

Meijman, T. F., Mulder, G., Drenth, P., Thierry, H., & De Wolff, C. (1998). Handbook of work and organizational psychology. *Work Psychology*, *2*, 5–33.

Misra, J., Lundquist, J. H., & Templer, A. (2012). Gender, work time, and care responsibilities among faculty. *Sociological Forum*, *27*(2), 300–323.

National Center for O*NET Development. (2022). *O*NET OnLine*. https://www.onetonline.org/. Accessed on May 3, 2022.

Park, Y.A., Liu, Y., & Headrick, L. (2020). When work is wanted after hours: Testing weekly stress of information communication technology demands using boundary theory. *Journal of Organizational Behavior*, *41*(6), 518–534.

Rowan, B., Camburn, E., & Correnti, R. (2004). Using teacher logs to measure the enacted curriculum: A study of literacy teaching in third-grade classrooms. *The Elementary School Journal*, *105*(1), 75–101.

Rowan, B., & Correnti, R. (2009). Studying reading instruction with teacher logs: Lessons from the Study of Instructional Improvement. *Educational Researcher*, *38*(2), 120–131.

Rowan, B., Harrison, D. M., & Hayes, A. (2004). Using instructional logs to study mathematics curriculum and teaching in the early grades. *The Elementary School Journal*, *105*(1), 103–127.

Schmitt, J., Shierholz, H., & Kandra, J. (2021). *Expanding overtime protection for teachers under the Fair Labor Standards Act*. Economic Policy Institute. https://www.epi.org/publication/expanding-overtime-protection-for-teachers-under-the-fair-labor-standards-act/

Silva, J. P. D., & Fischer, F. M. (2020). Understudied school teachers' work/life balance and everyday life typologies. *Chronobiology International*, *37*(9–10), 1513–1515.

Sonnentag, S., & Zijlstra, F. (2006). Job characteristics and off-job activities as predictors of need for recovery and well-being. *Journal of Applied Psychology*, *91*, 330–350.

Steiner, E. D., & Woo, A. (2021). *Job-related stress threatens the teacher supply: Key findings from the 2021 State of the U.S. Teacher Survey*. RAND Corporation. https://doi.org/10.7249/RRA1108-1

Stengård, J., Mellner, C., Toivanen, S., & Nyberg, A. (2022). Gender differences in the work and home spheres for teachers, and longitudinal associations with depressive symptoms in a Swedish cohort. *Sex Roles*, *86*(3), 159–178.

Stewart, J. (2013). Tobit or not Tobit? *Journal of Economic and Social Measurement*, *38*(3), 263–290.

te Braak, P., van Droogenbroeck, F., Minnen, J., van Tienoven, T. P., & Glorieux, I. (2022). Teachers' working time from time-use data: Consequences of the invalidity of survey questions for teachers, researchers, and policy. *Teaching and Teacher Education*, *109*, 1–15.

te Braak, P. T., van Tienoven, T. P., Minnen, J., & Glorieux, I. (2022). Bias in estimated working hours in time diary research: The effect of cyclical work time patterns on postponing designated registration days. *Time & Society*, *31*(4), 508–534.

U.S. Department of Labor. *Employment Laws Assistance for Workers and Small Businesses, Fair Labor Standards Act Advisor: Volunteers at*. https://webapps.dol.gov/elaws/whd/flsa/docs/volunteers.asp. Accessed on February 21, 2023.

U.S. Department of Labor, Bureau of Labor Statistics. Occupational outlook handbook, field of degree. https://www.bls.gov/ooh/field-of-degree/home.htm. Accessed on January 20, 2022.

Wepfer, A. G., Allen, T. D., Brauchli, R., Jenny, G. J., & Bauer, G. F. (2018). Work-life boundaries and well-being: Does work-to-life integration impair well-being through lack of recovery? *Journal of Business and Psychology*, *33*(6), 727–740.

West, K. (2014). New measures of teachers' work hours and implications for wage comparisons. *Education Finance and Policy*, *9*(3), 231–263.

APPENDICES

APPENDIX 1. IDENTIFYING COMPARISON OCCUPATIONS TO TEACHERS

A1.1 Comparison Group for Main Analysis

O*NET OnLine is a database of over 900 occupations maintained the U.S. Department of Labor Employment and Training Administration. O*NET links each occupation to an ordered combination of three interests. The possible interests are:

- Realistic (R)
- Investigative (I)
- Artistic (A)
- Social (S)
- Enterprising (E)
- Conventional (C)

O*NET also assigns each occupation one of five Job Zones. A Job Zone is a group of occupations that are similar in how much education, related experience, and on-the-job training people need to do the work. https://www.onetonline.org/help/online/zones.

The five Job Zones are:

- Job Zone 1 – occupations that need little or no preparation
- Job Zone 2 – occupations that need some preparation
- Job Zone 3 – occupations that need medium preparation
- Job Zone 4 – occupations that need considerable preparation
- Job Zone 5 – occupations that need extensive preparation

Elementary, middle, secondary, and special education teaching occupations are all assigned to Job Zone 4 and have a primary interest of Social (S). Most occupations in Job Zone 4 require a 4-year bachelor's degree, but some do not. Social occupations frequently involve working with, communicating with, and teaching people. These occupations often involve helping or providing service to others.

There are 25 standard occupational classification codes (OCC) that correspond with non-teaching occupations also in Job Zone 4 with a primary interest of Social (S). Four of the 25 were excluded due to underspecification and/or substantive similarities to teachers, these are denoted by a *:

- *0230 – Education Administrators (excluded from analysis)
- 0420 – Social and Community Service Managers
  - 0425 – Emergency Management Directors (specified starting in 2010)
- 0560 – Compliance Officers, Except Agriculture, Construction, Health and Safety, and Transportation
  - 0565 - Compliance Officers (specified starting in 2010)
- 0620 - Human Resources, Training, and Labor Relations Specialists
  - 0650 - Training and Development Specialists (specified starting in 2010)
- 2000 – Counselors
  - 2005 – Rehabilitation Counselors (specified starting in 2018)
  - 2006 – Counselors, all other (specified starting in 2018)
- 2010 – Social Workers
  - *2011 – Child, Family, and school social workers (specified starting in 2018) (excluded from analysis)
  - 2014 – Social Workers, all other (specified starting in 2018)
- 2020 – Miscellaneous Community and Social Service Specialists
  - 2015 – Probation Officers and Correctional Treatment Specialists (specified starting in 2012)
  - 2016 – Social and Human Service Assistants (specified starting in 2012)
  - 2025 – Miscellaneous Community and Social Service Specialists, Including Health Educators and Community Health Workers (specified starting in 2012)

- 3240/3245 – Therapists, All Other/Other Therapists, Including Exercise Physiologists (Occupation name and code changed in 2010)
- 3130 - Registered Nurses
- 3210 - Recreational Therapists
- *2720 - Athletes, Coaches, Umpires, and Related Workers (excluded from analysis)
  - *2722 – Coaches and Scouts (specified starting in 2018) (excluded from analysis)
- 4620 – Recreation and Fitness Workers
  - 4622 - Recreation Workers (specified starting in 2018)

A1.2 Alternative Comparison Group for Robustness Check

Teachers come from a variety of educational backgrounds. The typical entry-level degree for K-12 teachers is a bachelor's degree.

The Bureau of Labor Statistics (BLS) identifies 37 distinct fields of degree and the top 10 employing occupations for workers with each degree. Using these data, we identified 24 fields of degree for which either elementary, middle, or secondary teacher is among the top 10 occupations of degree-holders. Within these fields of degree, we identified 34 non-teacher occupations that were among the top 10 for degree holders in these 24 fields *and* that BLS identifies as having a bachelor's degree as the typical entry-level degree.

Fields of degree in which either elementary, middle, or secondary teacher is among the top 10 occupations for graduates:

- Biology
- Communications
- Culture and Gender Studies
- Education
- English
- Family and Consumer Sciences
- Fine and Performing Arts
- Foreign Language
- History
- Interdisciplinary Studies
- Law and Legal Studies
- Liberal Arts
- Library Science
- Mathematics
- Military
- Natural Resources
- Philosophy and Religion
- Physical Science
- Psychology
- Public Policy and Social Services
- Recreation and Fitness

- Security and Protective Service
- Social Science
- Theology

We identified 36 occupations with similar degree requirements to teachers (typical entry-level education is bachelor's according to BLS) that were also among the top 10 occupations for holders of the above degrees. Art Director does not have a specific OCC code and is therefore excluded as a comparison occupation, Coaches and Scouts were excluded for underspecification and potential substantive similarities to teachers, bringing the number of comparison occupations to 34.

- Registered nurses
- Personal service managers, all other; entertainment and recreation managers, except gambling; and managers, all other
- Physical scientists, all other
- Market research analysts and marketing specialists
- Marketing managers
- Human resource specialists
- Chief executives
- Management analysts
- Social workers, all other
- Writers and authors
- Editors
- *Art directors (excluded from analysis)
- Graphic designers
- Designers, all other
- Interpreters and Translators
- Software developers and software quality assurance analysts and testers
- Dietitians and nutritionists
- Financial managers
- Computer programmers
- Data scientists and mathematical science occupations, all other
- Computer and information systems managers
- Computer systems analysts
- Airline pilots, copilots, and flight engineers
- Environmental scientists and specialists, including health
- Conservation scientists
- Biological scientists, all other
- Clergy
- Chemists
- Geoscientists, except hydrologists and geographers
- Medical and health services managers
- Social and community service managers
- Therapists, all other

- Probation officers and correctional treatment specialists
- Accountants and auditors
- Directors, religious activities and education
- *Coaches and Scouts (excluded from analysis)

APPENDIX 2. TIME USE FOR TEACHERS AND NON-TEACHERS IN SUMMER MONTHS

Table A2.1. Descriptive Statistics, Teachers and Non-teachers, Representative Day in the ATUS 2003–2019 (Minutes/Day) for Summer Months (June, July, August).

	Teachers [N = 924]			Non-teachers [N = 616]		
A: Activity (in Minutes)	(1) All	(2) If Time > 0	(3) 1{Time = 1}	(4) All	(5) If Time > 0	(6) 1{Time = 1}
Work for main job	188*** (233)	354*** (214)	0.53***	309 (264)	459 (173)	0.67
Work not at workplace	45 (108)	145 (158)	0.31+	41 (117)	167 (176)	0.25
Volunteer at workplace	2 (23)	156 (112)	0.02+	0 (4)	71 (169)	0.00
Socializing/relaxation/leisure	225+ (163)	246** (156)	0.92*	208 (155)	216 (150)	0.96
Sleep	505** (106)	505** (106)	1.00	479 (132)	479 (132)	1.00
Sports/recreation/exercise	28* (62)	88 (85)	0.31*	20 (50)	82 (69)	0.25
Work for second job	16 (78)	285 (177)	0.06	11 (62)	223 (185)	0.05
Primary childcare	40*** (86)	123* (113)	0.33**	24 (69)	99 (109)	0.24
Secondary childcare	159*** (258)	460*** (246)	0.35***	90 (206)	363 (255)	0.25
B: Demographics						
Pre-K-Kindergarten	0.08			n/a		
Special Education	0.08			n/a		
Primary school	0.60			n/a		
Secondary school	0.25			n/a		
Hispanic	0.06			0.07		
White	0.90***			0.77		
Black	0.07***			0.18		
Asian	0.01***			0.05		

Table A2.1. *(Continued)*

	Teachers [N = 924]			Non-teachers [N = 616]		
A: Activity (in Minutes)	(1) All	(2) If Time > 0	(3) 1{Time = 1}	(4) All	(5) If Time > 0	(6) 1{Time = 1}
Female	0.75			0.74		
Age	40.3			41.4		
Masters	0.49***			0.37		
Public sector	0.79***			0.36		
Metro	0.81**			0.89		
Own child under 13	0.36***			0.26		
Number of own children in HH	0.78***			0.56		
Spouse/partner in HH	0.71+			0.65		
Spouse/partner (if present) employed	0.88			0.87		
HH inc.< $20k	0.03			0.03		
HH inc. $20k to $75k	0.38			0.43		
HH inc.> $75k	0.56+			0.50		

Notes: Standard deviation reported in parentheses. Means and standard deviations are weighted by sampling weights that adjust for unequal probability of selection across both days and households. HH = household.

$^{+}p < 0.10$, $^{*}p < 0.05$, $^{**}p < 0.01$, $^{***}p < 0.001$ indicate the statistical significance of the mean differences between teachers and non-teachers.

APPENDIX 3. CONTROL VARIABLE COEFFICIENTS FOR MAIN ANALYSIS

Table A3.1. Reproduction of Table 2, Panel B - Teacher Type With Control Variable Coefficients [n = 4,783].

Activity (in Minutes)	(1) Work for Primary Job	(2) Volunteer at Workplace	(3) Work for Main Job, not at Workplace
Pre K-Kindergarten	5.4	0.8	9.0
	(16.5)	(0.7)	(9.9)
Special Education	−13.9	1.3	15.3
	(16.6)	(0.8)	(9.4)
Primary	0.3	1.3*	26.4***
	(7.8)	(0.6)	(5.3)
Secondary	29.6**	1.3	25.1***
	(10.3)	(0.8)	(5.9)

Table A3.1. *(Continued)*

Activity (in Minutes)	(1) Work for Primary Job	(2) Volunteer at Workplace	(3) Work for Main Job, not at Workplace
	HH Characteristics		
Own child under 13	−26.4⁺ (13.6)	0.3 (0.6)	−2.3 (8.1)
Total number of own children in HH	3.6 (4.4)	−0.3 (0.3)	0.4 (3.2)
Spouse/partner not employed	0.8 (15.9)	0.1(1.1)	18.9 (12.9)
Spouse/partner employed	−1.3 (7.8)	−0.8 (0.7)	0.8 (5.4)
Middle HH income	−52.9⁺ (27.8)	1.2* (0.6)	−20.8 (13.8)
High HH income	−43.2 (28.1)	1.8** (0.6)	−20.0 (12.9)
	Demographics		
Black only	−0.7 (9.8)	−0.6 (0.5)	1.8 (7.3)
American Indian, Alaska Native only	−1.0 (43.6)	−0.6 (0.7)	−11.7 (16.4)
Asian only	−19.3 (26.9)	−0.4 (0.5)	−1.2 (8.7)
Hawaiian Pacific Islander only	4.7 (110.2)	0.1 (1.4)	46.3 (55.3)
More than one race	3.7 (30.2)	1.1 (1.4)	−0.1 (16.6)
Hispanic	0.4 (19.0)	0.2 (0.8)	−11.9* (5.0)
Female	−4.1 (9.2)	−1.2 (0.7)	−0.01 (5.0)
Age	0.4 (0.4)	−0.04 (0.0)	0.3 (0.2)
Metro area	−6.0 (8.4)	−1.0 (0.9)	−1.3 (7.1)
Public employee	−2.5 (8.2)	0.6⁺ (0.3)	−8.3 (5.3)
Constant	90.27* (38.5)	1.331 (1.9)	48.82** (17.8)
R^2	0.484	0.032	0.034

Notes: Standard errors in parentheses, all standard errors are clustered by state. $^{+}p < 0.10$, $^{*}p < 0.05$, $^{**}p < 0.01$, $^{***}p < 0.001$. Regressions condition on region (northeast, Midwest, south, and west), day of week, month, year, and holiday indicators. Low HH income (omitted) < $20,000, middle HH income > = $20,000 and < $75,000, high HH income > = $75,000. Non-teacher, spouse/partner not present and white race are used as reference categories and omitted from output.

APPENDIX 4. ANALYSIS OF SECTORAL DIFFERENCES IN TIME USE

Table A4.1. Time Use Compared to Non-teachers, Publicly Employed Versus Privately Employed.

A: Without Controls	Public [N = 3,335]			Private [N = 1,719]		
	(1) Work for Primary Job	(2) Volunteer at Workplace	(3) Work for Main Job, not at Workplace	(4) Work for Primary Job	(5) Volunteer at Workplace	(6) Work for Main Job, not at Workplace
All Teachers	25.2**	1.6**	33.1***	−20.3+	0.3	10.9
	(8.6)	(0.5)	(4.6)	(11.4)	(0.3)	(8.0)
R^2	0.501	0.030	0.035	0.444	0.031	0.052
Pre K-Kindergarten	25.7	0.3	22.8+	−3.4	0.7	−7.8
	(20.8)	(0.6)	(13.1)	(21.9)	(1.2)	(12.1)
Special Education	7.8	1.1	26.3*	−63.8	2.1	−13.0
	(15.0)	(0.8)	(10.3)	(56.4)	(2.6)	(13.2)
Primary	19.5*	1.6*	35.5***	−34.2+	−0.3	15.8+
	(9.2)	(0.6)	(5.0)	(17.5)	(0.3)	(8.9)
Secondary	44.4***	2.0	31.3***	11.2	0.6	19.5
	(11.7)	(1.3)	(6.3)	(18.1)	(0.8)	(11.7)
R^2	0.503	0.030	0.036	0.446	0.034	0.055
B: With Controls	Public [N = 3,158]			Private [N = 1,625]		
All Teachers	28.6**	1.4**	33.9***	−17.6	0.5	12.4
	(8.6)	(0.5)	(4.9)	(11.2)	(0.3)	(7.7)
R^2	0.513	0.044	0.041	0.465	0.033	0.084
Pre K-Kindergarten	26.7	0.7	21.5	1.9	1.0	−0.8
	(21.3)	(0.7)	(13.1)	(24.6)	(1.2)	(10.7)
Special Education	8.3	1.4	26.9*	−54.5	2.4	0.9
	(14.8)	(1.0)	(11.0)	(43.9)	(2.6)	(13.5)
Primary	24.3*	1.6*	35.2***	−36.7*	−0.01	16.0+
	(9.1)	(0.7)	(5.3)	(16.6)	(0.2)	(9.2)
Secondary	46.5***	1.2	35.5***	20.4	0.8	16.8
	(11.6)	(1.1)	(6.7)	(18.6)	(0.8)	(12.8)
R^2	0.514	0.044	0.042	0.468	0.039	0.086

Notes: Standard errors in parentheses, all standard errors are clustered by state. $^+p < 0.10$, $^*p < 0.05$, $^{**}p < 0.01$, $^{***}p < 0.001$.

A: Regressions condition on day of week, month, year, and holiday indicators.

B: Regressions condition on region, diary day, demographic, and household indicators.

Table A4.2. Time Use of Public Teachers Compared to Private Teachers.

	Teachers Only, Public Vs. Private		
With All Controls	(1) Work for Primary Job	(2) Volunteer at Workplace	(3) Work for Main Job, Not at Workplace
Public	20.7^{+}	1.0	3.8
	(11.7)	(0.6)	(7.9)
N	3002	3002	3002
R^2	0.496	0.043	0.038

Notes: Standard errors in parentheses, all standard errors are clustered by state. Regressions condition on region, diary day, demographic, and household indicators. $^{+}p < 0.10$, $^{*}p < 0.05$, $^{**}p < 0.01$, $^{***}p < 0.001$.

Printed and bound by CPI Group (UK) Ltd, Croydon, CR0 4YY

16/12/2025

14793774-0003